The Greatness of Oliver Cromwell

The Greatness of
OLIVER CROMWELL

MAURICE ASHLEY

COLLIER BOOKS, NEW YORK

COLLIER-MACMILLAN LTD., LONDON

First Collier Books Edition 1962

Second Printing 1966

The Greatness of Oliver Cromwell was published in a hardcover edition by The Macmillan Company. The Macmillan Company, New York. Collier-Macmillan Canada Ltd., Toronto, Ontario. Printed in the United States of America.

Foreword

THE ZEN BUDDHISTS believe that it is impossible for one human being to know another, however intimate they may be, and that is confirmed by common experience. How much more difficult therefore it is to understand a statesman who has been dead for three hundred years and about whom the historical evidence is far from complete. In a recent book another great statesman, Sir Winston Churchill, referred to Oliver Cromwell as a "smoky soul." But aren't we all?

I have been reading, writing, and lecturing about Oliver Cromwell now for more than a quarter of a century, and I certainly would not pretend to be able to describe the precise workings of his mind. The most I try to do in this book is to measure his place in history, as I see it after years of study. I would venture to affirm that he is not a figure who lends himself to an immediate judgment, any more, say, than the first Duke of Marlborough. With all deference to Sir Winston Churchill, to whom I personally owe much, I feel strongly, for example, that in condemning Cromwell, as he does, for his military conduct in Ireland, he is merely reasserting a popular historical opinion, which needs to be critically re-examined and not repeated every generation. I have attempted to do that in Chapter 15. But the main question that I have asked myself in writing my new biography is that suggested by its title: in what did Oliver Cromwell's historical greatness really consist?

I am indebted to Mr. A. H. Woolrych of Leeds University for reading the book in manuscript, to Mr. C. K. Adams, C.B.E., Director of the National Portrait Gallery, and Mr. Oliver Millar, M.V.O., Deputy Surveyor of the Queen's Pictures, for their advice about illustrations, and to my colleague, Miss Patricia Entract for invaluable assistance.

MAURICE ASHLEY

London, April 1957

I have corrected a number of slips for this edition. I am grateful to Professor Paul Hardacre and Mr. R. T. Clark for pointing out some of them.—M.A.

Contents

Foreword   5

1. When Envy is Laid Asleep by Time   13

2. Cromwell's Place in Society   27

3. Cromwell's Religion   41

4. Cromwell and the Long Parliament   58

5. Cromwell and the Coming of Civil War   77

6. England Prepares for Civil War   93

7. Cromwell as Soldier: The First Campaigns   107

8. Cromwell as Soldier: The Battle of Marston
   Moor   124

9. Cromwell the Statesman: The Self-denying
   Ordinance   140

10. Cromwell and the New Model Army: The
    Battle of Naseby   154

11. Cromwell the Politician: The Fight for Liberty
    of Conscience   169

12. Cromwell the Conciliator: "We would have
    Healed Babylon, but She would not"   184

13. Cromwell the Avenger; the Second Civil War
    and the Execution of King Charles I   197

14. Cromwell and England in 1649   216

15. Cromwell in Ireland   228

16. Cromwell in Scotland: Dunbar and Worcester   241

17. The Foundation of the Protectorate   260

18. The First Months of the Protectorate   276

19. Cromwell and the First Protectorate Parliament   291

20. The High-water Mark of the Protectorate   307

21. Cromwell and the Second Protectorate
     Parliament   323

22. Cromwell and the Golden Scepter   339

23. The Death of Oliver Cromwell   350

24. The Greatness of Oliver Cromwell   359

    Select Bibliography   371

    Index   377

Maps and Plans

1. England and Wales: Campaigns of 1642 and 1643   114

2. The Yorkshire Campaign of 1644   128

3. Battle of Marston Moor, 1644   131

4. The Naseby Campaign of 1645   161

5. The Campaign of 1648   201

6. The Irish Campaign of 1649-50   229

7. Scottish Campaigns of 1650-51   248

8. The Worcester Campaign of 1651   256

The Greatness of Oliver Cromwell

Chapter 1

When Envy is Laid Asleep by Time

ON THE LAST day but one of August 1658, tempests broke over England and gales continued for several days. On the afternoon of September 3, in the calm that succeeded the storms,[1] Oliver Cromwell died in Whitehall Palace beside the river along which London's traffic moved, whence his friends had planned to take him in a last despairing effort to save his life. Seven weeks later "the most noble and puissant Oliver, Lord Protector of the Commonwealth of England, Scotland, and Ireland, and the dominions and territories thereunto belonging" was given a state funeral and his coffin was interred in Westminster Abbey.

The funeral procession was led by the Knight Marshal on horseback, with his black truncheon tipped at both ends with gold. In the middle of the long line of mourners walked Sir John Ireton, Lord Mayor of London, a younger brother of Cromwell's most devoted friend, mentor, and son-in-law, who had been dead for seven years. After him came four drums with escutcheons of the banner of England. Towards the end, behind the wooden and waxen effigy, drawn in an open chariot covered with velvet, followed the chief mourner, Cromwell's eldest son-in-law, Lieutenant-General Lord Fleetwood. But the Lord Protector's successor, as was the custom of kings, was not there at all. A Fellow of All Souls, Oxford, who noted such details of the funeral,[2] wrote that less could not have been performed "to the memory of him to whom posterity will pay (when Envy is laid asleep by Time) more honor than I am able to express." "But, alas!" he continued, "how true are the words of the wise King, 'Vanity of vanities, all is vanity,' seeing that, after all this funeral pomp and grandeur, his dead body was lastly . . . taken out of his grave and hanged for a traitor."

On May 29, 1660, King Charles II, so long exiled by Cromwell's victories, arrived at Whitehall Palace, where his enemy had expired. That day the effigy of the Lord Protector was removed from the Abbey, and after torches had been lighted, was made fuel for one of the many bonfires burned to celebrate the restoration of the royal Stuart line. Eight months later, on January 30, 1661, precisely twelve years after King Charles I had been executed, the coffin containing the reputed carcass of Cromwell was carried from Westminster to the Red Lion Inn in Holborn, and put on a sledge which drew it to Tyburn. The embalmed remains were taken out of the coffin and hanged from ten in the morning until sunset, and then buried in a pit beneath the gallows, except for the skull. The head had been cut off with an ax, and was mounted upon a pole on the top of Westminster Hall by the Common Hangman, to be execrated by a jeering mob.[3] History scarcely affords a more tragic contrast than that between the pomp of the funeral of 1658 and the ribald and revolting spectacle at the Tyburn gallows in 1661. But the Royalists and their scribes never ceased to malign the memory of the dead Puritan ruler. For Cromwell had killed their King, while they, after all, had only been able to hang Cromwell's bones.

*　　　*　　　*

Opinions about Cromwell's character and attainments have varied unceasingly with the passage of three hundred years. About few other statesmen in history have so many conflicting judgments been expressed. It has been said that historians are accustomed, when they declare their moral convictions, to act as avengers who lift up the fallen and beat down the proud, and certainly on no figure in modern times has the historian exercised that prerogative more industriously than upon Oliver Cromwell. The impulse was first given by the fury of the returned Royalists, and for close on two hundred years little of worth was written in his defense.

So universal was the agreement on Cromwell's actions and motives in the eighteenth century that Dr. Samuel Johnson could declare that "everything worth saying about him had already been said." Except for a couple of books,[4] the popular historians of the century followed the Royalist party line, whether the fabrications of James Heath's *Flagellum* (1663) or the rolling periods of the first Earl of Clarendon's *History of the Rebellion* (1702). The conception that then prevailed was excellently summarized by the novelist Tobias Smollett, who in 1758 described Cromwell's character as "an amazing conjunction of enthusiasm, hypocrisy, and ambition, courage and resolution, penetration and dissimulation, the strangest compound of virtue and villainy, baseness and magnanimity, absurdity and good sense we find in the annals of mankind."

Smollett's *History* was, in fact, a hasty compilation—he is said to have covered a century a month—intended to rival a similar money-spinning enterprise of David Hume, the Scottish philosopher. Hume himself, while also uncritically accepting the stories of Royalist biographers, tried to be impartial. He admitted that Cromwell was "an eminent personage . . . in many respects and even a superior genius," but, like Smollett, he detected a "mixture of so much absurdity"—beloved word in the eighteenth century—"with so much penetration," and affirmed that it was "by fraud and violence" that he had "rendered himself first in the state." Although many of the official papers of John Thurloe, Cromwell's Secretary of State, had been published in 1742 and contained material for a fair appraisal of the Protector at work, these views were even followed by Mark Noble, the clerical antiquarian, whose book, *Memoirs of the Protectoral House of Cromwell* (1784), was virtually the first attempt to assemble all the facts about Cromwell's career and ancestry without bias. As late as 1839 John Forster, later the biographer of Charles Dickens, held it to be "indisputably true" that Cromwell had "lived a hypocrite and died a traitor."

While Cromwell lived he had enemies both on his right and on his left. To the Royalists he was, in the words of the Earl of Clarendon, "a brave, bad man"; to the republican stalwarts he was equally a betrayer who had "sacrificed the public cause to the idol of his ambition." Only an author of genius could hope to disturb so broadly based and tirelessly repeated a verdict. Early in 1840 the Scottish mystic, Thomas Carlyle, who had contemplated writing about Cromwell for nearly twenty years, told Emerson: "I have got within this last twelve months actually as it were to see that Cromwell was one of the greatest souls ever born of English kin," and in a lecture given in May he declared that whereas "few Puritans of note but find their apologists somewhere . . . one Puritan, and almost he alone, our poor Cromwell, seems to hang yet on the gibbet and find no hearty apologist anywhere. Him neither saint nor sinner will acquit of great wickedness."[5]

It was not until the autumn of 1845, however, that Carlyle published his book entitled *The Letters and Speeches of Oliver Cromwell. With Elucidations*. This piercing work, decorated with rhetoric, converted many contemporaries in an age when serious reading was a popular hobby. Forster, formerly the purveyor of traditional opinions, confessed after reading it that "Cromwell was as far removed on the one hand from fanaticism, as on the other from hypocrisy." Carlyle's epic exerted its impact not only on general readers but also on university historians. David Masson's *Life of Milton* (1859) reflected the influence of Carlyle's persuasiveness. The scholarly Samuel Rawson Gardiner, who devoted most of his life to original researches into seventeenth-century history (the first volume of his *History of England* appeared in 1863) concluded that Cromwell "in the world of action was what Shakespeare was in the world of art, the greatest and most powerful Englishman of all time." This more commendatory judgment held sway throughout the last quarter of the nineteenth century. Gardiner was naturally receptive, for he himself had a Puritan upbringing and claimed descent from the Cromwells. But John Morley, a Liberal statesman without such predilections, who published a biography of Cromwell in 1900, also saw Cromwell as a "rare and noble type of leader" who strove to reconcile liberty and order and sought a moral base for political power. Another fine scholar, Sir Charles Firth, presented Cromwell as a "great man" with "magnitude of mind" whose deeds survived him to transform British history.

In the twentieth century the pendulum has still been swinging, though less violently than in the Victorian age. To some authors—Roman Catholics and High Anglicans in particular —he has remained, in spite of Carlyle, Gardiner, Morley, and Firth, little more than Clarendon's "brave, bad man." Yet among popular authors he still commanded admirers: John Drinkwater, who wrote a play about Cromwell, thought that "vexed in soul as he often was, he continued always to care above all for the well-being of England, which for him meant the individual liberty and enlightenment of the English people."

But in the nineteen-thirties a spate of books appeared both in Britain and abroad infused by the spirit of the Age of Guilt or of Fascism. It is true that as late as 1931 a book entitled *Oliver Cromwell. the Champion of Liberty,* was published in London, but later biographers rewrote his life with the prancings of Mussolini and Hitler before them. Passages in the contemporary reports of the French, Dutch, Scandinavian, and Venetian envoys in Cromwell's England appeared to fortify the idea that the Lord Protector, however worthy his aims, was by nature a despot and enemy of liberty. For example, the Venetian special envoy, Sagredo, had written that Cromwell was "a man of firm and solid judgment who knows the nature of the English people as a riding master his horse, and therefore, with a single movement of his cane, he makes them whirl about on every side."[6]

Did not that recall the saying that Napoleon had loved the French as a cavalry officer loved his horse? Thus in 1937 came biographies called *Cromwell, the Conservative Dictator,* and *Cromwell: A Dictator's Tragedy.*[7] One authority, who completed in 1947 a new edition of his letters and speeches in four volumes, reached this conclusion: "He led Puritanism to military victory and glory, overthrew Anglicanism if only for a time—broke through the divinity that hedged in a King, and set up a brief personal dictatorship."[8]

More sympathetic biographers have been conscious, in a world where psychoanalysis has become the fashion, of the manifold paradoxes in Cromwell's career. John Buchan, however, rekindled in 1934 the ardor of his fellow Scot, Thomas Carlyle. To him Cromwell was another Caesar who belonged "to a small circle of great kings, though he never sat on a throne." Yet this "iron man of action" . . . "left nothing that endured." Dr. C. V. Wedgwood has confessed that she finds him a perplexed Atlas, and has observed that Cromwell "achieved nothing either through Parliament or in the constitutional sphere"; while Dr. G. M. Trevelyan, in his mature conclusions about the statesman "whom no other land could have produced," agrees with Dr. Wedgwood that he was the embodiment of negative virtues, not the father of new institutions, but the savior of his country "first from absolute monarchy, then from Presbyterian tyranny, and finally from chaos and dismemberment."[9] We live now indeed in a mysterious universe, as far from the unchallenged Christian convictions of the mid-seventeenth century as from the scientific optimism of our grandfathers, and thus our judgments about the heroes of the past are at their best cautious, at their worst skeptical. We may speak cagily of Cromwell's "intense *narrow* patriotism" or of his *"delusions* of Providential grandeur." But no intelligent modern historian will deny to him the essentials of greatness in its noblest sense.

* * *

What of foreign verdicts? Interpretations of Cromwell's character and record by European historians have both a more limited and a broader approach than those of his biographers at home: more limited in that few of them have grasped the character of English Puritanism, and have therefore supposed that an upstart general's appeals to the Almighty were insincere; broader because they have, on the whole, been more capable of estimating Cromwell's deeds in an international framework. To begin with, a completely false picture prevailed in Europe, because a life of Cromwell by Gregorio Leti, an Italian Catholic turned Calvinist, published in 1691, "determined the Continental conception of him for over a century." Leti offered his readers a cunning and bloodthirsty tyrant devoid of taste, scruples, or even amusing vices. Thus while the *Flagellum* of James Heath, the Royalist propagandist, molded English ideas of Cromwell long after it had been written, Leti's nonsensical embroideries have equally misled foreigners. Indeed, it was not until after the publication of Carlyle's book in the middle of the nineteenth century that a reasoned appreciation of Cromwell came from a European author.

François-Pierre-Guillaume Guizot, the Liberal Prime Minister of the French "bourgeois King" Louis-Philippe, was dropped by that monarch as the hurricane arose that swept away the French monarchy forever, and after his retirement from politics this able man devoted himself to historical writing. His book on *The History of Oliver Cromwell and the English Commonwealth* (1854) had three merits: first, it was reflective, intelligent, and reasonably impersonal; secondly, it was largely based upon the dispatches of the French ambassador in the England of Cromwell's days; lastly, it was written by a man who himself had been at the heart of European affairs. Guizot concluded that Cromwell "is, perhaps, the only example which history affords of one man having governed the most opposite events, and proved sufficient for the most various destinies." In the last sentence of his book might be detected Guizot's wistful resignation over his own experiences as a statesman: "God does not grant to these great men, who have laid the foundations of their greatness amidst disorder and revolution, the power of regulating at their pleasure, and for succeeding ages, the government of nations."

Guizot could understand the magnitude of Cromwell's work in encompassing a revolution and at the same time making Britain a Great Power in Europe. So could the German historian, Leopold von Ranke, whose *Englische Geschichte* began to apear five years later, in 1859. Von Ranke also discarded the portrait of Cromwell as a hypocritical adventurer who became a tyrant. "The supreme authority," he wrote, "was not his aim. It was to aid him in realizing those ideas of religious liberty, as understood by Protestants, and of civil order and national independence, which filled his whole soul." Von Ranke admired, too, the energetic foreign policy of the Puritan ruler who "carried the key of the Continent in his girdle" and the rectitude of the champion of civil law and private property.

Both Guizot and von Ranke seized upon the paradoxes— or contrasts—in Cromwell's behavior: his slowness and his impatience; his destructiveness and his conservatism; his instinct for liberty and his love of order. They both recognized, just as later British historians were to recognize, that Cromwell fashioned no new institutions—such as the Emperor Napoleon had left behind him to embody his genius and honor his name. But they did not take that too tragically for, after all, they themselves had witnessed the Continental revolutions of 1848 and realized the incredible difficulties of carrying through a revolution and preserving a nation's strength while at the same time initiating permanent and constructive reforms.

More recent Continental historians have lacked the penetration and good sense to be found in these two vigorous nineteenth-century works; later German authors were chiefly concerned with Cromwell either simply as a soldier or as a prototype of this own National Socialist dictator. Praise was then the order of the day. Was not Hitler, too, an inspired Puritan? One German, writing in 1932, emphasized that Cromwell knew that he was a born leader and that the English people knew it too; another in 1933 extolled "a great hero"; a third in 1935 depicted him as a patriotic soldier, who first organized victory at home and then devoted himself to giving his country a novel and successful foreign policy, a policy of ideas rather than aggression. In 1937 Dr. Ernest Barker was able to titillate an audience in Hamburg with an illuminating, if slightly far-fetched, comparison between Cromwell and Hitler. In Mussolini's Italy also much admiration was shown for Cromwell, although an Italian biographer, writing in 1932, thought that none of his ideas were realized, that he did more harm than good to his country, and that he had died in an atmosphere of hatred and ruin.

American historians, on the whole, have been unfriendly to Cromwell, since all their instincts have induced them to sympathize with his republican opponents and critics. Yet an American President, Theodore Roosevelt, wrote the most fulsome biography of Cromwell to be published in the United States. Roosevelt, it is true, recoiled from the twilight hero-worship practiced by Carlyle, who had spoken of the end of the Protectorate as being "the last glimpse of the God-like vanishing from England," and insisted instead that Cromwell, "the greatest Englishman of the Seventeenth century," had in fact "headed a movement that produced the English-speaking world as we at present know it." Cromwell could not have hoped, Roosevelt argued, to set up a form of government founded on large social and religious principles, but he did win a struggle by his sword that ultimately left the English-speaking peoples free and masters of their own destinies. It is to be observed that Roosevelt, like Guizot a practicing statesman, laid less store than bookish historians by Cromwell's failure to create permanent political institutions. Other American authors have ranged between the sentimental and the cynical, and have drawn Cromwell either as a monster or a victim of tragedy. To one American historian, the late Professor Wilbur Cortez Abbott, we owe not only a bibliography of Cromwell[10] but also a full edition of, and a commentary upon, his writings and speeches. Professor Abbott was an enthusiast who reckoned Cromwell among the immortals. But, as Europe became menaced by the dictatorships of our own times and the Japanese struck at Pearl Harbor, Professor Abbott's portrait became overcast. In the end the unconstructive nature of Cromwell's achievement is reiterated, a hint of unscrupulousness is discovered in his methods, and some of the stories of his enemies are taken almost at their face value. A pristine admiration for the Puritan hero is tempered by the buoyancy of American individualism.

*   *   *

In seeking to understand how Cromwell has appeared to the historians of the past, it is necessary to distinguish what they thought about his character from the way in which they assessed his deeds. To the authors of the Restoration period, as to some contemporaries, he was a proven dissembler. He had risen by promising to be loyal to the ideals of an egalitarian or platonic commonwealth, but had then gathered the supreme power into his own hands. If to the Royalist and republican writers he had assumed the part of the savior of his nation from the autocracy of Charles I in order first to kill the King and then to destroy Parliament, the eighteenth-century historians regarded him as a rogue who had deliberately or mistakenly adopted a religious cant as a means to satisfy his own ambitions. He was, wrote David Hume, "at bottom as frantic an enthusiast as the worst of them, and in order to obtain their confidence, needed but to display those vulgar and ridiculous habits which he had early acquired, and on which he set so high a value."

Thomas Carlyle denied all that. He dilated upon the sincerity of Cromwell, and believed it was because a later generation was incapable of understanding his religious enthusiasm that he was in fact misunderstood completely:

> We have wandered far away from the ideas that guided us in that century [Carlyle wrote] . . . and we must endeavour to return, and connect ourselves therewith again. . . . The Christian doctrines, which then dwelt in every heart, have now in a manner died out of all hearts—very mournful to behold; and are not the guidance of the world any more. . . .

Since Carlyle few historians have thought Cromwell either hypocritical or ridiculous. Lord Morley pictured him as being of melancholic temperament relieved by flashes of high exaltation. Sir Charles Firth considered him to be a man of integrity, large-mindedness, and profound religion whose faith tended to make him a fatalist and an opportunist. Later scholars, influenced, though sometimes unconsciously, by the Marxist approach, have drawn attention to Cromwell's conservatism as an heir of the Reformation settlement. Psychologically minded authors have argued that he was the constant subject of deep-rooted mental conflicts.

Such have been some of the changing opinions of his character. But few of his early critics, even including his personal enemies, withheld admiration for what he did. Royalist historians were wont to admit reluctantly that in comparison with the tergiversations of King Charles II or King James II, the foreign policy of the Lord Protector caused Britain to be respected and feared in the world of his time. The realists of the eighteenth century could not fail to praise his courage in bringing about the end of the civil wars or resisting the anarchic programs of social revolutionaries. Then the picture altered again. The nineteenth century found in him the fibers of a reformer and quoted with approval his condemnation of the legal system of his day and his early defense of his poorer neighbors threatened with the loss of their ancient rights. He ceased to be the mere destroyer of the monarchy. The general faded into the ruler. In 1827 Henry Hallam noted in his *Constitutional History* that Cromwell "would neither reign with parliaments nor without them . . . and never meditated a naked and avowed despotism." His bust has long graced the hall of the London Reform Club, and his statue with Bible and sword in hand still guards the Houses of Parliament. Indeed, the historians of the later Victorian age recognized him as more nearly akin to Hampden and Pym than to Frederick the Great or Napoleon.

In our own times the emphasis has shifted to the negative character of his statesmanship. Nothing constructive, we are assured, was done between 1642 when King Charles I left his capital and 1660 when his son returned to it. The argument is further pressed that because Cromwell left confusion behind him, was unable to provide adequately for his succession, and offended many earnest leaders of the Puritan community, he personally ensured the Royalist return and reaction. Indeed, it has been suggested that Cromwell's attempt to translate into practice his ideal of a Chosen People was in itself fatal to the permanence of the Commonwealth. While, broadly, present-day authors—so often perplexed in their own lives—have shown a more sympathetic understanding of the complications of Cromwell's mind than their predecessors, they have finally dismissed him as an historical failure—for he solved no political problem and bequeathed no constitutional or social heritage.

*   *   *

The historiography of Oliver Cromwell is of importance because it discloses why popular judgments have often been perverted or poisoned at the source. In the seventeenth and eighteenth ceturies the method of writing history as chronicle still largely prevailed, and these chronicles were regarded as records of events that had actually happned. In fact, Royalist propaganda swept the board. In the so-called Age of Enlightenment it became the fashion to write "philosophical" history, often based on these chronicles, in which grand generalizations and moral reflections took precedence over mastery of the facts. In David Hume's *History of England* there is hardly a statement about Oliver Cromwell's character or policy which is not false, the reason being that Hume was content to follow the accounts of Cromwell's enemies; in consequence the conclusions of that distinguished philosopher about Cromwell are of little value. Another thing may be said about the eighteenth-century historians: they most of them regarded the manifestations of the Puritan spirit in politics as simply ludicrous. Whatever we may believe now, we hardly believe that. The nineteenth century was at once more romantic and more serious. Lord Byron praised Cromwell's bravery, and Thomas Carlyle's vindication was in a way the last fling of a romantic age, though it also inspired a more just handling of the evidence.

The year 1850 roughly marks the watershed between the romantic and the scientific approaches. For in the eighteen-fifties both Guizot and von Ranke used the reports of foreign envoys in London to illuminate the history of the Protectorate, some years before Gardiner published his pioneer investigations derived from every source then at his disposal. Lord Acton said: "The secret of Ranke's art was to rescue the public man from the cheap judgment seat, the short shrift" and "to rescue universal history from the hands of the philosopher." By 1900, the *annus mirabilis* of Cromwellian literature, the victory of the scientist was almost complete. Indeed, remarkably few Cromwellian documents of first-class significance have appeared during the past fifty years. Academic historians have concentrated rather on the technical aspects of the Cromwellian age, its financial, social, and economic arrangements, changes in constitutional theories, colonial ideas, and military tactics. It is in the light of such information that it is now possible to offer a fresh portrait of Oliver Cromwell and his times and reassess his place in history.

Moreover, we are now no longer obsessed with the urge to rewrite the seventeenth century as avengers of a dictator's victims or of an anointed sovereign's blood. Nor perhaps is one's instinct so compelling today to worry over the value of institutions in measuring what a statesman has done in the past. In the first half of the present century, thinking men and women were brought up to believe that the right political and economic institutions could bring mankind happiness and uplift and transform the very character of human beings. We are no longer so confident about this. The art of government, many are inclined to suspect, turns on a wise understanding of men as they are, upon moderation and tolerance, courage in meeting each crisis and the gift of conciliation when tempers cool. It is surely proper that we should recognize where we stand in the stream of time. For the political historian, however hard he tries to be impartial, is never a self-effacing storyteller. It is now known that the very fathers of the "scientific history" of the seventeenth century, scholars like von Ranke and Gardiner, were deeply affected in their writings by the political atmosphere of their own lifetimes. Can we really claim to be "all scientists now"? In choosing what he wants to tell, the historian selects, consciously or unconsciously, the approach fitted to his own temperament and the spirit of his own age. If he salutes the ghosts of his predecessors, he sets himself to destroy both their fables and their fancies: yet he has his own. A great man can only be convincingly re-created in terms of his own age interpreted by ours.

It is the aim of this book to show, in the light of modern knowledge and from the standpoint of our own times, three hundred years after Oliver Cromwell died, the character of his greatness.

Notes

1. Clarendon, *History of the Rebellion and Civil Wars in England* (ed. W. D. Macray) (1888), VI, 91, speaks of the storm "some hours before and after his death." Leopold von Ranke, *A History of England* (English trans., 1875), 211, says that the storms had ceased the night before Cromwell died. Professor Abbott, myself, and others have fallen into the popular Royalist trap that "Cromwell died, as he lived, in a storm."

2. Sir John Prestwich, *Respublica* (1787), 172 seq., quoting his ancestor, the Rev. John Prestwich.

3. F. J. Varley, *Oliver Cromwell's Latter End* (1939), and Karl Pearson and G. M. Morant, *The Portraiture of Oliver Cromwell with Special Reference to the Wilkinson Head* (1936), both go into detail about the burial, exhumation, and hanging of Cromwell's remains, quoting the relevant authorities. I do not accept Varley's conclusion that Cromwell's body was never buried in Westminster Abbey, which depends too much on George Bate, *Elenchus Motuum nuperorum in Anglia,* etc. (1662). Bate was

one of Cromwell's doctors, but his narrative, written at the time of the Restoration, is quite untrustworthy.

4. Isaac Kimber, *The Life of Oliver Cromwell*, etc. (1725); John Banks, *A Short Critical Review of the Political Life of Oliver Cromwell* (1739).

5. Quoted in C. H. Firth, introduction to *The Letters and Speeches of Oliver Cromwell* (ed. S. C. Lomas, 1904).

6. Quoted in E. Momigliano, *Oliver Cromwell* (1932), 311.

7. *Oliver Cromwell: A Dictator's Tragedy* was by Mary Taylor Blauvelt. I was the author of *Oliver Cromwell, The Conservative Dictator*. This book, which I began to write soon after I left Oxford, was profoundly influenced by the rise of Mussolini, Hitler, and Stalin, and by many years of Conservative government in Britain. The Spanish translation, published in Buenos Aires in 1948, contains corrections of fact. I know more about Cromwell (and recent dictators) than I did then, and the emphasis of the present book is different. In Sir Winston Churchill, *History of the English-Speaking Peoples,* II (1956), of which the chapters on Cromwell were written in 1938–39, he is also treated more or less as a twentieth-century dictator.

8. W. C. Abbott, *Writings and Speeches of Oliver Cromwell,* four vols. (1937–47). This is an indispensable work. All the *verbatim* quotations in the present book for which sources are not indicated will be found in Abbott.

9. G. M. Trevelyan, *An Autobiography and Other Essays* (1949), 173.

10. W. C. Abbott, *A Bibliography of Oliver Cromwell* (1929); see also *Writings and Speeches,* IV, and the select bibliography at the end of this book. All the biographies mentioned in this chapter will be found in these bibliographies.

Chapter 2

Cromwell's Place in Society

OLIVER CROMWELL WAS born on April 25, 1599, in Huntingdon, a royal borough and a pleasant little market town through which the river Ouse gently flows. Its population was under two thousand, but it contained four churches. At one of them, that of St. John the Baptist, Oliver was christened four days after his birth. In those times everyone went to church, but two generations later few in Huntingdon did, for by then most of the inhabitants were Nonconformists—a change that crystallized the revolution through which Cromwell was going to live.[1]

When Oliver was a child the Cromwells were the most important people in the town. His uncle, the head of the family, occupied the lovely Elizabethan manor house of Hinchingbrooke which had been built by his grandfather just the other side of the river from the High Street; thence it held sway over the neighborhood like a little palace.

Huntingdonshire was a rural county with modest pretensions to prosperity; it was agreeable enough in summer, but hard going for travelers when the rains came. Much of the county was a swamp, forming part of the fenland of 700,000 acres that composed a huge watery wasteland in eastern England: Huntingdon and Cambridge were western frontier towns of the Fenland, which was bounded on the east by the coasts of Lincolnshire and Norfolk. Amid the silt and mud a rough class of men and women scraped a precarious livelihood. The antiquarian William Camden wrote, eleven years after Cromwell was born, that the fenlanders were "a kind of people according to the nature of the place where they dwell, rude, uncivil, and envious to all others whom they call upland men, who stalking on stilts apply their minds to grazing, fishing, and fowling. The whole region itself, which in winter seasons and sometimes most of the year, is overflowed by the spreading water of the rivers, Ouse, Granta, Nene, Welland, and Witham, having not leads and sewers large enough to void away." These rivers, the Ouse in particular, followed tortuous courses, and spilled over their banks because the outfalls were inadequate to carry their contents away into the

27

Wash. Engineers differed over whether the right solution was to cut straight channels or to deepen the beds. But in any case little or nothing had been done to reclaim these interminable bogs at the beginning of the seventeenth century, though a general draining act to recover "drowned and surrounded lands" had finally reached the statute book in 1600. It was the duty of gentlemen living in the outposts of the fenlands to do what they could, especially in times of flood, and Oliver's father and uncle served on the Commission for Sewers. The Commission had both judicial and executive functions and often met in Huntingdon, but had no right to undertake reclamation. Nevertheless, the two Cromwells were among those who pressed on the Privy Council of King James I the feasibility of draining the fens, which was only started in earnest, however, in 1630, and then not as a State but as a private enterprise. Meanwhile the black marshlands debased the welfare of the county, though they gave its primitive and insular inhabitants a sense of independence and resourcefulness.

Up to the Reformation much of the best land in Huntingdonshire had belonged to the Church. The Benedictine Abbey of Ramsey, for example, owned twenty-four manors in the county. There had also been a Benedictine priory at St. Neots, the Cistercian Abbey of Sawtrey, a nunnery occupying the site of the Manor of Hinchingbrooke, and properties of the Austin Friars in Huntingdon itself. These monks and nuns do not appear to have been either remarkably good or bad landlords, but the complaint had been laid that they were in no sense improvers; during the Middle Ages the Abbot of Ramsey obstructed the Ouse with mill pools and exacted dues for the use of the riverway, and in so far as any concern had been expressed about reclaiming the fens, it had been by the Crown and not by the Church. Some land outside the fens had been enclosed as pasture by its owners before the reign of King James I, with serious consequences for former arable cultivators.

Only six years before Cromwell was born, a man, his wife, and daughter were executed in Huntingdon for the crime of witchcraft. In general, the county was poor and backward, a somewhat austere and flat relic of the Middle Ages. It boasted few or no titled or ancient families. The monks and nuns had long since disappeared, having been ousted or pensioned off; in their places reigned the Cromwells of Hinchingbrooke, with their relatives and friends scattered throughout the county, some of them extremely wealthy, others, including Oliver's own parents, of more tenuous means, all of them acting as leaders in local affairs and quite a few of them representing their neighbors in the House of Commons whenever it met and even being on friendly terms with the Court.

The Cromwells had, in fact, stepped into the shoes of the old Church in Huntingdonshire as owners of land, directors of public opinion, and dispensers of charity. Their fortunes had been created at the Reformation. Oliver's great-great-great grandfather on the paternal side is said to have come from Wales with King Henry VII and to have belonged to a respectable Glamorganshire family. He settled in Putney as Steward of the Manor of Wimbledon. In fact, the story of the Cromwells begins (and was later to continue) in what is now the London suburb of Putney but was then a flourishing little port, for at Putney passengers from the City would disembark from the Thames and take to the road. It also had a thriving fishery and breweries, and there Oliver's great-great-grandfather Morgan Williams, besides holding a post at Court, sold beer on a large scale. This Morgan Williams married Katherine, a daughter of another and less reputable brewer named Walter Cromwell, a vigorous character of Norfolk stock, whose son Thomas rose to be the Minister of King Henry VIII responsible for the dissolution of the monasteries. Richard, son of Morgan Williams and Katherine Cromwell, was virtually adopted by his meteorically successful uncle and took his name. He helped Thomas Cromwell to dispose of the monasteries, was knighted, and won the approval of the King by conducting himself handsomely when jousting. At Westminster in 1540, attired in white velvet with stockings cut in the Burgundian fashion, he overthrew all challengers to earn from his monarch his knighthood and a diamond ring. Thus the son of Morgan Williams, the Putney brewer, was transmuted, by the fickle wand of royal favor, into Sir Richard Cromwell, a courtier of substance and standing, a gallant if not entirely perfect knight.

Sir Richard acquired by ground-floor purchase the bulk of the possessions of the rich Abbey of Ramsey (then worth over £1,700 a year), and most of the monkish properties in Huntingdonshire as well as other land outside the county. He served as a captain of cavalry or, as others say, a general of infantry, in Flanders, and died in an odor of honor and affluence in 1546, his uncle and patron having sensationally perished for treason on a scaffold at Tower Hill six years earlier.

Sir Richard's eldest son, Henry, sunning himself in his inherited opulence, built himself mansions both at Hinchingbrooke and Ramsey and entertained in the lavish manner expected of the *nouveaux riches*. He was Sheriff of Huntingdonshire and Bedfordshire, and Queen Elizabeth I was his guest at Hinchingbrooke. Apart from that, his most notable undertaking was to raise forces to protect Huntingdonshire if the Spaniards by some mischance should have penetrated into the fenlands after landing from their armada in the fifteen-eighties. No such disaster occurred, however, and Sir Henry Cromwell was able piously to observe: "Our good God confounded their devices . . . and with His mighty and stretched out arm did most miraculously deliver us." Sir Henry, having acquired for himself the nickname of "the Golden Knight," passed on in 1603, and was succeeded in the family estates by his eldest son, Oliver, who followed his precedent of elegant entertainment. King James I was his guest for the first time when he traveled from his Scottish capital to pick up his new crown. The King is then reported to have said to him: "Morry, mon, thou hast treated me better than anyone since I left Edinburgh." As a reward, he knighted his host and used Hinchingbrooke as a frequent port of call for hunting and shooting. The Scots King adored hunting, though he was a poor sportsman and frequently fell off his horse.[2] But entertaining kings is an expensive amusement, as Sir Oliver Cromwell soon discovered. The King came to treat Hinchingbrooke as if it were his own home: in October 1623, for example, he wrote to Sir Oliver ordering him to kill as many pheasants as possible in his outwoods but none in his park until the royal party arrived. When the King was there, open house was kept: "whoever entered the house," noted a contemporary, "which to no man was denied, tasted what they had a mind to, and after a taste found fullness, no man like a man being denied what he would call for. As this bounty was held back to none within the house, so for such poor people as would not press in, there were open beer-houses erected wherein there was no want of bread and beer, for the comfort of the poorest creatures." Thus the beer, once brewed at Putney to sustain the Cromwell income, flowed freely and copiously upon the lawns of the Palace of Hinchingbrooke, while the King shot his pheasants or hunted foxes. But debts accumulated and the magnificence of two generations had to be requited by borrowing from the London moneylenders and selling a large portion of the family properties. Sir Oliver thought it might be an excellent idea if his King liked Hinchingbrooke enough to buy it from him at a reasonable price "penny for penny"; after all, King James had acquired Theobalds from Sir Robert Cecil, but before he could decide upon this new proposition the King was dead. Two years later, in 1627, Sir Oliver disposed of the estate elsewhere, and retired to his other house at Ramsay, where he spent his days more reticently but with unabated loyalty to the Stuarts until the good age of ninety-three. If this is now a half-forgotten tale of clogs to clogs in three generations, it is because the main Cromwell story was to be another, bigger and more tragical, to be projected onto the national stage by Sir Oliver's nephew and namesake, who lived half a mile from Hinchingbrooke down the High Street at Huntingdon, and by the date the great house changed hands had become the master in his own home.

The Cromwells were fecund, though the offspring of their fertile marriages did not always survive the hazards of early childhood. Oliver himself had many uncles and aunts; he had seven sisters and two brothers, and he was to be the father of nine children. As the family proliferated, its fortunes spread thin. Oliver's father, Robert Cromwell, was the second son of Sir Henry and inherited landed property worth £300 a year in the money of those days. His mother is said to have had a settlement on her marriage of £60 a year. Robert Cromwell farmed land in and around Huntingdon, and owned a malthouse and a dovecote. He had been educated cursorily at Queen's College, Cambridge, and the Inns of Court. Besides serving as Commissioner for Sewers and Justice of the Peace, he was at one time sheriff of the county, and he had represented Huntingdon in the Parliament of 1593, a year or two after his marriage. Cromwell's mother came from a Norfolk family named Styward or Steward. Her elder brother, Sir Thomas, was a gentleman of means who lived in Ely. She was a widow when she married Robert Cromwell, her first husband and their only child having been buried in Ely Cathedral in 1589. Not much is known about Oliver's parents. Robert was a self-effacing country gentleman of careful and charitable frame of mind. His "most loving and kind wife," Elizabeth, earned a reputation for prudence and wisdom. Robert died in middle age, but his wife survived until she was eighty-nine. If one may judge from what are believed to be their authentic portraits, they were quiet, religious, self-respecting people, with none of the flamboyance of the extravagant uncle at Hinchingbrooke.[3]

Something of the social and religious atmosphere of the Cromwell family has come down to us in letters written when Oliver was a young man. Here is a letter written by his uncle Henry to his aunt Joan about the death of his uncle Phillip:

> I received your letter at Ramsey church door as I was coming from performing my last duty to your brother Phillip who was buried this present day at Ramsey. He departed this life on Sunday last about one of the clock in the afternoon. He led a religious life, died most religiously, so as we may assure ourselves that he is in the place of joy. God grant us that live hearts truly to imitate the good examples of good people gone before us, that living in the fear of God, we may die in His favor. He has left behind him many children with small means: a hundred pounds apiece will be the uttermost that can be wrought for them out of his estate. One daughter he has left here which I could wish you would be pleased to take to you at least wise till she may be provided for: for otherwise she will be in great danger to be lost for education. . . .

In a later letter by the same writer about his convalescence after an illness he says:

> I praise God I am now somewhat recovered both in health and strength and I assuredly hope in some sort I am, by God's gentle hand of visitation, fitted and prepared for a better life, nothing doubting but God will perfect his work begun in me by the operation of his holy spirit.

In general, these letters are impregnated with an intimate Christian feeling. One of Aunt Joan's correspondents reminded her that "we are exhorted to do good while we have time," and urged her "to a fresh assault on the Covenant of Grace." Others kept her informed of the news of Protestant victories in the Thirty Years' War then raging in Germany. Her brother-in-law touched on the oddities of the daughters of Eve: "Women are cruel this year," he observed in 1631. "Saturn reigns with strong influence: another wife has given her husband a poison of melted lead but it was because he came home drunk."[4]

Not only were the Cromwells a rootedly Protestant family, living as they did on the sites of the destroyed monasteries, priories, and nunneries, but the eastern counties as a whole were from the earliest times subject to the persuasions of the Continental reformers. In the reign of Queen Elizabeth I many refugees from Roman Catholic Europe had settled in different parts of East Anglia, notably in the weaving town of Norwich. The University of Cambridge, where the professor of divinity, Thomas Cartwright, had first expounded the Presbyterian gospel, contained before the Civil Wars broke out seven or eight colleges where the heads were enthusiastic Calvinists; and Robert Cromwell's friend, Dr. Thomas Beard (a witness to his will), who was the schoolmaster of Huntingdon, was a forthright Puritan publicist. Robert sent his son when he was seventeen to Sidney Sussex College, Cambridge. Sidney was then a hotbed of Puritanism, one of the few Cambridge colleges which had an unconsecrated chapel without an altar, and whose Master was a man of morbidly introspective character, ascetic habits, and the sworn foe of all ritualism.[5] It is a reasonable deduction that Cromwell's parents deliberately raised him in a Puritan environment and as the scion of a family all of whose members were highly conscious day in and day out of their duty to God and their dependence upon His mercies.

Oliver Cromwell therefore was born and brought up in a markedly Protestant district in a county where the economic outlook was poor, at least until the fens should be drained, but where his own family was rich and influential but of declining fortunes. When his father died in 1617, he left two thirds of his estate in trust for twenty-one years to provide for his widow and her daughters. They can scarcely have had even the £100 each left to the children of his brother Phillip. Cromwell's brothers had died as children, and he himself thus became at the age of eighteen head of his family with a meager inheritance and dubious prospects. It is true that as soon as he was twenty-one he married the daughter of a prosperous London merchant, but what marriage portion she brought him is not known. He had to mortgage his own small possessions to find a settlement for her. After farming in Huntingdon for eleven years, he sold up his lands for £1,800, and moved down the social ladder to become a tenant farmer in St. Ives, where he settled in 1631 as a cattle grazier. After another five years he succeeded to the bulk of the estate of his maternal uncle, Sir Thomas Steward, who had no other heirs, "a handsome if somewhat complicated inheritance," and once more he became a landlord, this time in the town of Ely. By the time the Long Parliament met in 1640, when Oliver was forty-one, he had an income of about £500 a year, that is to say, he was somewhat better off than his father had been. This was still hardly more than modest for a country gentleman with a large family to support. It has been calculated that at least two thirds of the members of the House of Commons at that time were in the category of rich men, while 90 per cent of them were fairly well-to-do. Thus Cromwell brought up the rear.

Yet, though his fortunes may have oscillated, Oliver Cromwell belonged to the English ruling classes. After all, the families, ranging from "esquires" or "gentlemen" with incomes of £500 or £600 a year upwards to an aristocracy with a rent roll as high as £20,000, constituted only a fraction of the whole population—but they were the people who counted. Whatever his exact place in the social scale, it is scarcely an exaggeration to say that through his sisters and cousins and aunts Oliver Cromwell was related to almost every family of importance in the country. He is known to have had at least twenty relatives in the Long Parliament. The Mashams, the Barringtons, the Hampdens, the Dunches, the St. Johns, the Trevors, and the Lukes, and dozens of other flourishing families, were connected with him. When he was M.P. for Cambridge, a brother-in-law was the senior member for Huntingdonshire, another brother-in-law sat for Merionethshire, a cousin for Wendover, another cousin for Newtown in the Isle of Wight, and a second-cousin for one of the Hampshire boroughs. Indeed, recent analysts of the Long Parliament did not even attempt "to explore the great network of Oliver's relations in the House," though they emphasized that the most striking feature of the parliamentary representation in the eastern countries was the large number of members who were related to one another.[6]

Above all, the Cromwells were a parliamentary family. Not only had Oliver's great-grandfather, grandfather, and father all been M.P.'s, but his uncle, Sir Oliver, was four times an M.P., his uncle Henry sat in Parliament from 1604 to 1611, and his uncle Richard was a member for Huntingdon in the reign of Queen Elizabeth I. Although Sir Oliver had sold many of his properties in Huntingdonshire by 1627 and gave up his seat as senior knight for the county, Oliver himself was elected as one of the members for the borough of Huntingdon in the following spring. The parliamentary world of the early seventeenth century scarcely allowed for the existence of carpetbaggers, and a family like the Cromwells, which had virtually ruled Huntingdonshire for three generations and had far-flung connections through the eastern counties, even though their estate was small compared with what it had once been, enjoyed, as it were, a prescriptive or almost dynastic right to go to Westminster to air their grievances and speak for their neighbors. The Protestant pattern of this group of eastern counties and the close interrelationship among the parliamentary families in them meant that when in 1642 the Long Parliament began to be divided between supporters and opponents of the King, only a minority of the M.P.'s there were Royalists. Once again Cromwell was fairly typical of his time and place in society.

But in Oliver Cromwell, too, the compulsions of heredity were profound. First was the Welsh strain in his character. A fellow Member of Parliament, who was no admirer of his, noted his fervent eloquence when he was still hardly known in the House. The reports of his speeches that have come down to us are neither complete nor satisfactory, but the indications are that he had at least a few of the gifts of the great Welsh orators. He was a lover of music, both instrumental and vocal, as most Welshmen are, and his simple humor was of a Welsh kind. Secondly, he had the makings of a cavalry officer. No doubt he was invited to hunt with his uncle at Hinchingbrooke, and he was a god sportsman and lover of horses. Though it is unlikely that he went abroad in foreign service before the wars, as a number of Englishmen did, he had at least as much experience as most of the cavalry officers who fought for King Charles I, and by temperament plenty of martial spirit. As to religion, for all their indulgences at the table or in the field, the Cromwells were a pious family accustomed to attribute health and happiness to the workings of a Providence that was always imminent in their everyday lives.

Did Oliver Cromwell belong to the rising or declining gentry of his times?[7] During the hundred years that covered the period from the dissolution of the monasteries to the outbreak of the civil wars, an energetic and thriving middle class was establishing itself in England, as it was also doing in contemporary France. In some cases it made money by buying land cheaply and developing it in a businesslike manner or by enclosing it so that farming became more profitable than it had been under medieval methods. Others did well out of offices granted to them by the Crown and exploited by them for personal gain. Many began in the reign of Queen Elizabeth I to venture into commerce on a widening scale, to invest successfully in trading companies or in mining, or even to take shares in ships engaged in buccaneering or smuggling. The magnates of the City of London were becoming immensely rich, and in the first fifty years of the seventeenth century every government had to go to them to borrow at any moment of crisis. Finally a professional class was emerging. Not only were lawyers obtaining an excellent living, for seldom were men more litigious than they were then, but doctors were beginning to earn good money, being transmuted from superior apothecaries into smart physicians. In the Long Parliament were many men with incomes of over £1,500 a year, and the boast that had been heard in an earlier House of Commons that they could buy the House of Lords three times over seems to have epitomized a genuine change in the relative position of peers and middle classes in contrast with earlier times. In sum, the middle classes were expanding rapidly, and, unlike the French, they were extremely politically minded; and the demand which was pressed by John Pym and other leaders in the Commons, when Oliver Cromwell was a young man, for a more generous share in the government was founded upon their consciousness of economic power.

But the small landlord or gentleman farmer did not always or necessarily share in the prosperity of the new middle classes. For while prices were rising, rents did not rise with them. One knight, Sir John Oglander, complained in 1632: "It is impossible for a mere country gentlemen ever to grow rich or raise his issue. . . . By only following the plow he may keep his word and be upright, but he will never increase his fortune." This was especially the case if he had to maintain appearances, providing higher education for his sons, marriage portions for his daughters, and hospitality for his neighbors. He might of course marry advantageously; at that date it has been said "of the many branches of the land market the marriage market was the most important." In the history of the Cromwells marriage loomed large as an economic asset. By marriage the Cromwells mingled with the trading class. The beginning of the family had been the marriage of Morgan Williams to the sister of the highly successful merchant Thomas Cromwell. In the next generation Sir Henry had wedded the daughter of a Lord Mayor of London. Then Sir Oliver Cromwell had taken as his second wife the widow of Sir Horatio Pallavicino, an astute Genoese moneylender, and his cousin Henry had married Lady Pallavicino's daughter.[8] The younger Oliver himself had married the daughter of a flourishing fur dealer, while his maternal grandfather was a man of means. In fact, the family fortunes were kept afloat by judicious marriages.

On the other hand, the abundant landed wealth that had been amassed by the Cromwells of Hinchingbrooke had been dissipated. Left an orphan in adolescence, Oliver had witnessed the resounding crash of his rich uncle, the sale of many of his properties, moneylenders foreclosing on the debts he had owed to them, and himself had suffered the setback of being unable to make farming pay on his patrimony at Huntingdon. It is true that country gentlemen did not have to pay regular taxes (apart from tithe due to the Church), but they were subject to exactions from two extravagant kings, whose own incomes were in a state of decline and who profited from their right to impose outworn medieval demands for contributions, and to call upon their subjects for aid in times of war or threatened war by the exercise of their royal prerogatives. Oliver himself only just escaped being made a royal ward after his father died—and that right of wardship (by which the Crown obtained money from orphans) was one of the most widely felt grievances of the gentry. It is also likely that Oliver had to pay his share both of the forced loans and the ship money levied by King Charles I.[9] All these were undoubted irritations in hard times. Still, Oliver had not been brought up to any active expectations of wealth; he was the son of a second son who had always lived in a modest way. If his father had managed on an income of £300, together with whatever he had obtained from his wife, Oliver himself had by the age of thirty-seven at least £500 a year, together with what his own wife had brought him. He had inherited not only from his uncle Thomas but also from his uncle Richard. Though he was of the lesser gentry, in terms of income he was now upon a rise and not upon a decline. A man who could afford, as he was able to do, to invest £500 in Irish lands in 1641 and two months later to contribute a further £500 towards the cost of the defense of Parliament, was by no means in desperate circumstances, and many of his friends and relations were well-to-do.

The consciousness of grievances felt by the middle classes in seventeenth-century England, as with the French *bourgeoisie* on the eve of the revolution of 1789, was in any case sharpened not by poverty but by a sense of frustration. They thought they had the right to rule their country because they were an increasingly valuable element in it. Many of them heartily disliked the policies of the Court, the bungled war against Spain, the ineffective assistance given to the French Protestants, the ritualistic program of the archbishops, the inept campaigns conducted by the King against his own subjects, the Scots. In his own county Cromwell saw—or thought he saw—the draining of the fens being mismanaged and church services inadequately provided. Above all, he was convinced that the religious organization of the country was thoroughly bad. He heard the call, that young men hear, to put the world right.

Such glimpses of Cromwell as we have in these days are of a natural leader of men whose strong temper sometimes took complete control of his being even to the extent of affecting his health.[10] In his character was a striking mixture of the introvert and the extrovert: on the one side were the inner communings that preceded his conversion, the doubts, the prayers, the self-reproaches, and, on the other, an indignation that grew into social protest so that what he thought was wrong became injustice and what he believed to be right was God's will. Later as a figure upon the national stage he learned to keep his temper in check, except when under provocation it burst out beyond denial. But when first he entered politics he possessed very little self-control, and it was, above all, what he regarded as religious wrongs that incited him to denunciations in the fiercest terms of King and Government.

As soon as he took his seat in the House of Commons at the age of twenty-nine, he attacked the rulers of the Church angrily, and continued to do so persistently during the early months of the Long Parliament. His awareness of religious and constitutional injustices was determined to only a limited extent by his material circumstances. His place in society simply ensured him opportunity to protest, just as his youthful freedom from the rule of father or brothers gave him the habit of leadership. For he had been born into the parliamentary middle class which had already savored its strength and been encouraged to assert itself more forcibly by the failure of the Stuart kings to keep it in order as Queen Elizabeth I had done. But his impulse towards revolutionary activity was primarily religious and not, in any direct sense, economic. His early letters and speeches are not those of an aggrieved farmer, but of a Christian gentlemen who, burning with an injured faith, was eager to serve in a crusade to purify the English Church.

Notes

1. Cf. *The Victoria County History of Huntingdonshire*, I and II (1926 and 1932).

2. D. Harris Willson, *King James VI and I* (1956); Godfrey Davies, "The Character of James VI and I," *Huntington Library Quarterly*, V (1942).

3. Portraits of Cromwell's parents are reputedly at Chequers. I was refused permission to see them by the Chequers Trust. The portraits hitherto believed to have been of them at Hinchingbrooke and reproduced in S. R. Gardiner, *Oliver Cromwell* (1899), are now thought to be portraits of members of the Montagu family. I am obliged to the Earl of Sandwich for this information.

4. Egerton MS. 2654, ff. 138, 243; *Historical Manuscripts Commission Report*, VII (1879), 548; *Transactions of the Essex Archaeological Society*, New Series, I (1878) and II (1884).

5. G. M. Edwards, *Sidney Sussex College* (1899); C. W. Scott-Giles, *Sidney Sussex College: A Short History* (1951). The Master of Sidney Sussex kindly allowed me to examine the College register.

6. Detailed discussions of the membership of the Long Parliament are in D. Brunton and D. H. Pennington, *Members of the Long Parliament* (1954), especially Chapter V for the Eastern Association. Mary Frear Keeler, *The Long Parliament, 1640–1641*, contains biographies of the original members, and among other things analyzes the incomes of the members. I am less convinced than some reviewers of the first book that it has proved that there was no 'class' element in the civil wars.

7. H. R. Treavor-Roper, *The Gentry, 1540–1640* (1953), criticizes an article on "The Rise of the Gentry," by R. H. Tawney, published in 1941. Professor Tawney replied in *Economic History Review*, Series II, Vol. VII. Other historians, including Mr. Lawrence Stone and Mr. D. H. Pennington, do not accept Mr. Trevor-Roper's views. But many of his arguments are powerful and persuasive, and I am greatly indebted to his stimulating work. David Mathew, *The Social Structure of Caroline England* (1948), describes the rise of a professional class. Sir John Oglander's *Commonplace Book* was published in 1936, edited by Francis Bamford. Mr. Godfrey Davies is of the opinion that Sir John's views on farming may not have been typical.

8. For the Pallavicinis or Palavicinos, see Lawrence Stone, *An Elizabethan, Sir Horatio Palavicino* (1956).

9. Abbott, *op. cit.*, I, 71, reproduces evidence that Cromwell was fined for refusing to accept knighthood, but I suspect the entry may be a forgery as his name was added after the list was completed. Forgeries about Cromwell's early life are numerous.

10. J. L. Sanford, *Studies and Illustrations of the Great Rebellion* (1858), collects the stories of Cromwell's early life and his alleged hypochondria.

Chapter 3

Cromwell's Religion

PURITANISM REACHED its zenith in the middle of the seventeenth century, and when the dissenters were expelled from the Church of England in the reign of King Charles II, Nonconformity became part of the British way of life, indelible and unforgettable. Because Oliver Cromwell was so eminent a figure and a champion of the Puritan cause, it is easy to imagine that he was the creator rather than the creation of that extraordinary force in British history. But when Cromwell died in 1658, the Puritan movement was already over a hundred years old—for the Reformation itself had been the mother of dissent.

At first the Puritans were little concerned either with theology or politics.[1] The early English Protestants in the reign of King Henry VIII, while they insisted upon the value of the Bible, translated into English, as the ultimate moral authority, and upheld the doctrine of a Christian's justification by his faith rather than his behavior, were loyal to the Crown and repudiated any revolutionary ideas. However, after Roman Catholicism had been restored for a time in the reign of Queen Mary I, a transformation came over English religious opinion. For when Queen Elizabeth I succeeded her sister upon the throne and decided again to renounce the authority of the pope, she was obliged to rely upon the services of a number of English churchmen, who had taken refuge overseas during the reign of Queen Mary, had sat at the feet of the Continental Protestant reformers, and imbibed radical notions about the relations of church and state. Some of the returned exiles then fancied introducing into England the Presbyterian scheme of church government that was being practiced in Geneva under the direction of the French theologian John Calvin, but the majority aimed simply at continuing, if at a faster speed, the purification of the Church which had been begun under the first Tudors. Most of these Protestant enthusiasts sought to refashion the English Church after the model framed in the reign of King Edward VI rather than to translate the discipline of the Swiss Church to a less rarefied climate. All of them were determined to destroy every remnant

of "foul idolatry," to ban all vestments—even the humble surplice—images, symbols, or "popish" ceremonies, and to place
upon the Holy Communion no miraculous interpretation.
They wanted, as they put it, not merely to unhorse the pope,
but also to take away his stirrups so that he should never be
in the saddle again. Secondly, they lifted the reading of the
Bible, now translated into English by Protestant zealots (indeed, William Tyndale, the first English translator, has also
been described as the first English Puritan), to the forefront
of their religious exercise. Lastly they regarding preaching as
the linchpin of the public services. For them the Bible came
before the Prayer Book and the preacher before any public
act of worship. Exhortation in the pulpit and prayer in the
home: such was the handy and unadorned machinery of their
eager faith.

The Calvinist doctrine of predestination was accepted by
nearly all English Christian leaders, thinkers, and teachers in
the reign of Queen Elizabeth I. It was not in any way a speci-
fically Puritan doctrine. The belief that God choose of His
own inscrutable volition to "save" some and to condemn
others to perdition, that men are "justified" by their faith and
only show forth their salvation by their lives, was no party
creed. Articles drawn up at Lambeth in 1595 (four years before Cromwell was born), under the presidency of the Archbishop of Canterbury, asserted that God had from everlasting
predestined some people to life and had reprobated others to
death, and that it was not in the power of any man to be
saved by his own efforts. The Elizabethan archbishops and
bishops, virtually without exception, were Calvinists in theology, and Calvin's *Institutes* were recognized textbooks in the
universities. When, in December 1604, the Archbishop of
York acknowledged the receipt of instructions from King
James I to proceed against the Puritans, he expressed dislike
for their "fanatical zeal," but pointed out that they agreed
with the Church "in the *substance* of religion." The doctrine
of predestination could be read in the Book of Common
Prayer and descried in the Thirty-nine Articles of the Church
of England.

During the reign of Queen Elizabeth I, therefore, what the
Puritans were urging was not any change in doctrine but
simpler services and more preaching. They complained, in
John Milton's words, that "the hungry sheep look up and are
not fed." Most of the clergy were not educated men and did
not preach, but read homilies out of prescribed books. This

was largely for economic reasons. In theory the Church was entitled to receive "tithe," a tenth of the produce of the land, but in fact the parish clergy were in general badly paid. Most livings were quite inadequate to maintain a learned man. The property rights of lay patrons stood in the way of improvement. Vicars were allowed only the "small tithes" that were hard to collect plus the beggarly stipends paid by lay rectors who had come to own the "great tithes." Thus many clergy were little better off than agricultural laborers, and were frequently compelled to supplement their incomes in other ways —by cultivating the soil or even keep an inn.[2] To fill the gap created by such "blind mouths," lecturers would be hired by Puritan laymen to preach and expound the Bible. And in parishes where the clergy themselves were Puritan-minded (being appointed by Puritan patrons), they would meet the laity and discuss portions of the Scripture with them on weekdays. Thus Puritanism spread, to the dismay of the Queen. She was equally opposed to the provision of lectures and to the weekly meetings or "prophesyings," as both seemed to her to be subversive of order in Church and State. She incited her archbishops to suppress prophesyings and discourage excessive preaching. By 1585 these Puritan activities had been checked but not eradicated.

It had not been until towards the middle of the Queen's reign that two new manifestations of the Puritan spirit were disclosed. One was a movement directed against the bishops and the other a trend towards asceticism. The attack on the bishops was launched by a Cambridge university professor, Thomas Cartwright, an able theologian, popular preacher, and facile writer, who was deprived of his professorship for his views in 1570 and afterwards expelled from his Fellowship. He asserted that the episcopacy as a disciplinary body had no basis in Scripture and ought to be cut away root and branch. Archbishops, who came—indirectly—from the bottomless pit of Hell, should be abolished altogether; bishops should be confined to preaching and teaching; and the clergy ought to be elected by their congregations, while presbyters or elders were the proper persons to enforce discipline in the Church. By the 1580's, though their advocate was cast into prison, these theories had taken a grip upon many English Protestants.[3] Secret synods known as "classes" met in many parts of the country, including Cambridge itself, with the object of adapting the Anglican services to the Presbyterian pattern. It was urged by the critics of the episcopacy that the bishops were for the most part "pluralists"—that is to say, they held a larger number of offices than they could possibly fill honestly —and that many of them exploited their properties, for example by alienating their land or letting it cheaply to relatives and friends. In fact, the Elizabethan bishops were far from being either lazy or corrupt.[4] But the Queen battened upon their incomes, and they were often driven to doubtful devices to maintain their positions and meet their expenses. Their characters were by no means bad—they were not habitually absentees from their sees, and they were frequently aware of the need of Church reform. Yet among the middle classes there was much jealousy of their powers and possessions and of the enforcement of discipline by their courts. The right of the bishops' and archdeacons' courts to punish sexual offenses and to interfere with testamentary dispositions was far from popular.

As to asceticism, it would be wrong to regard it in the years of Cromwell's youth as exclusively typical of the Puritans. Asceticism, after all, was common enough in the medieval Church, and was practiced by monks and friars up to the eve of the Reformation. Indeed, logically those who believed most ardently that they were predestined by special election to eternal life need not have been overanxious about their personal behavior. No system of penances or indulgences was prescribed for them. Their militant belief in their calling to serve the Lord had little in common with the contemplative frame of mind cultivated in the monastic cell. Yet in fact the character of the Puritans as seen in their surviving letters and diaries was built out of a close concentration on the ethical life, upon a search after altruistic standards, and upon the avoidance of all suspicion of sins. The motive force for their self-denial was "the desire to experience the immediate feeling of satisfaction which came from approaching an ideal state of mind."[5] They did not regard the living of a good life as a sign or proof of their election, but, being conscious of their vocation, they delighted to follow the pattern of God's will as they saw it. They had not been forbidden the pleasures of food or drink or music or the married life by their master, John Calvin, or his disciple, Thomas Cartwright. But their very certainty of salvation drove them to undertake the sternest duties and the most minute self-examinations, and induced them to set a shining example to the reprobate.

*　　　　*　　　　*

Oliver Cromwell's parents, as we have seen, were quiet Protestant gentry who unquestionably acquiesced in the prevailing doctrine that all Christians are elected by grace to salvation, that men could not earn their passage to Heaven but only take it once it was booked. Oliver attended the Free School in Huntingdon, of which the master was a friend of his father, the very strict predestinarian, Dr. Thomas Beard. There was also an assistant master who may have done much of the actual teaching. At any rate, the curriculum consisted of spelling, reading, and arithmetic, and of a great deal of Scripture, including the study of the Psalms and Biblical history. The Authorized Version of the Bible had been completed in 1611 when Oliver was twelve, and was read by him both at school and at home. How thoroughly he knew the Authorized Version and the Psalms is attested by all his later speeches. He seems to have read a book written by Dr. Beard called *The Theatre of God's Judgment Displayed,* first published in 1587 and several times reprinted; and he was impressed by Sir Walter Ralegh's *History of the World,* which appeared in 1614 and was based upon almost the same argument as Dr. Beard's book. The argument, illustrated in each case with incredible ingenuity, was that the system of rewards and punishments administered by the Almighty in the hereafter also applied "even in this life." The rulers, princes, and great ones of the earth were far from exempt from God's judgment; indeed, being more hardened to sin than most, in the end they received the direst punishments. Dr. Beard is said to have sought "to teach morality by fear." Oliver feared God, but not man. What moved him both in Beard's teaching and Ralegh's *History* were the numerous examples of eminent persons who neglected to search their consciences and ensure that they rightly understood God's will. When he came to govern himself, he would make no such mistake. "He that ruleth over men," he told the Nominated Parliament of 1653, quoting the Book of Samuel, "must be just, ruling in the fear of God."

He met a splendid example of this Protestant hyperconscientiousness during the short year he was in residence at Cambridge. Oliver was admitted into Sidney Sussex on April 23, 1616, as a Fellow Commoner. In those days there were three kinds of students—scholars (the poorest but the nursery of dons), pensioners, and a privileged and well-to-do minority, the Fellow Commoners. Only three other Fellow Commoners were admitted in the same year as Cromwell. They had to pay fees and other dues, to present the College with a piece of silver plate upon their arrival; they had the right to eat with the Fellows at the High Table, and undertook in return not to corrupt either the Fellows or the scholars. In order that he might be instructed in religion and God's truths, Cromwell slept in the same room as his tutor, Dr. Richard Howlett, who had been elected a Fellow in 1610 and later became a Dean in Ireland. The Master of the College, Dr. Samuel Ward, was a distinctive figure in the world of theology and churchmanship. A learned Calvinist, he held fast by the virtues of restraint and was rigid about standards of behavior. On the other hand, he was a notorious "pluralist," so much so that his friends remonstrated with him about the number of offices he had collected and made little jokes about it behind his back. Pluralism did not worry Dr. Ward, but everything else did. When he was a stuttering young don he confided to a diary his perplexities over his carnal musings and dreams, his "wicked and adulterous thoughts" when he went to the fair, his gluttony at the table, his laziness about getting up in the morning, his drinking late at night, his neglect of his prayers, and in general his "overmuch delight" in the transitory pleasures of this world. All that was natural enough in a Cambridge divine in his early twenties. But the habit of detailed self-examination continued throughout his life. When, after Cromwell had left Sidney, Dr. Ward took it into his head to venture into the seas of matrimony in middle age, he carefully listed in his diary the pros and cons in regard to his prospective bride. To console himself lest his suit should fail, he noted that "the party was worldly minded" and might "not be forward in religion"; and he regretted that she had shown "a want of discretion, or love, or both, in not signifying before our coming that she could not condescend to the mayor"; while he found it "a great private check not to be respected in my first love." Still he took the plunge and married a widow. Dr. Ward brooded as much over the "sins of this land" as over his own love life, over its profaneness and irreligion, the excesses in apparel and drinking, the "disobedience and contempt for authority among the younger sort" and "the toleration of notorious offenders." But perhaps he forgot, as a respectable middle-aged clergyman might easily forget, the days when he himself had gone "to the tavern with such lewd fellows, albeit I knew them not." He would have found the entry in his diary.

Two years after Cromwell left Cambridge, Dr. Ward was invited by King James I to be one of the English delegates at the Synod of Dort, a conference on religion between English and Dutch theologians. At the Synod, Ward was careful to see that "nothing should be defined which might gainsay the Confession of the Church of England." On their return, after a solemn feast, he and his fellow delegates were received graciously by the King at Greenwich, and Ward aspired to a bishopric for his trouble (though he did not obtain it). But when King Charles I, who, unlike his father, had not been brought up in the Calvinist theology, came to the throne, Dr. Ward was much afraid that "popery would increase" through the influence of Charles's Roman Catholic Queen, and he resented the fact that after he himself had been Vice-Chancellor, that unpopular royal favorite, the first Duke of Buckingham, was foisted upon the university as its Chancellor by order of the King. Ward picked out as an occasion for mourning that day when the Archbishop of Canterbury first urged that the surplice should be worn in his old College of Emmanuel: "God grant," he prayed, "that worse things do not follow the so strict urging of this indifferent ceremony. Alas, we little expected that King James would have been the first who permitted of it to be brought into our College. . . ." Later he expressed his distaste for Archbishop Laud's "innovations," though he did not hesitate to write to him to ask his permission to continue to be a pluralist. He also protested against Laud's claim to exert his authority over the university at all. When another Cambridge divine (John Nevile of Pembroke Hall) had the boldness to preach justification by works instead of by faith and to argue that the outward act of baptism took away sin, Ward rebuked him for "gross heresies." He consistently controverted "the error of free will." He maintained that the Thirty-nine Articles plainly averred "a gratuitous predestination of some and not of all." He bewailed the signs of weakening in the full-blooded Calvinist beliefs in the 1630s. To him mankind had plainly been divided by Christ into "those wholly of the Church Militant and those that are not." If he did not demand the reformation of Church discipline or organization, he dosed himself unremittingly with the unadulterated waters of theological Calvinism.[6]

The character and position of Dr. Samuel Ward are important in the story of Cromwell's life for two reasons: first, because Oliver Cromwell knew him at a critical period in his adolescence, when he first left home and on the eve of his father's death. One of Dr. Ward's admirers wrote that "he was so good a man that he was Tutor as well as Master to the whole College."[7] A privileged Fellow Commoner must have enjoyed the benefits of his teaching, serious conversation, and example. Nothing would be more likely to have impressed a youngster of seventeen than the advice and instruction that were given to him by a scholar with a first-class mind in the congenial atmosphere of the ancient university. Secondly, Ward is in himself a fine instance of the complexities of early seventeenth-century religion. In his theology and his morals he could be, and has been, described as a typical Puritan. He had no love for the Duke of Buckingham, Archbishop Laud, or Queen Henrietta Maria. Yet he was the friend of bishops, an outrageous pluralist, and a loyal supporter of the Crown both before and during the Civil War. But, like his pupil Cromwell and most of Cromwell's friends in the Parliaments of 1628-29 and 1640-41, Dr. Ward was assured that the ecclesiastical program of King Charles I and Archbishop Laud was a revolutionary one, aimed at imposing novelties both in ritual and doctrine upon the Protestant Church of England. Though in matters of constitutional thought Cromwell and his friends were themselves in the end to put forward revolutionary claims to power far wider than the Commons of England had ever enjoyed before, one of the chief reasons for their campaign against King Charles I was a conservative one: they were convinced, as Dr. Ward was convinced, that in the 1630s the very structure of Protestant Christianity was being undermined. But Cromwell thought that the villains of the piece were the same men who were responsible for the leadership in the Church, namely the bishops. Hence his animosity against them. It was to be a dominating impulse in his early career.

*   *   *

Although his heredity and environment were emphatically, and at times aggressively, Protestant, Oliver Cromwell did not undergo spiritual conversion until he was about twenty-eight, when he had been married for eight years and was the father of five children. He suffered the throes of mental, physical, and spiritual agony before he realized that he was indeed one of God's Chosen. Then the light broke through, and for ever afterwards he was grateful for the mercy of God who gave "springs in a dry and barren wilderness where no water is":

Truly [he afterwards told a cousin] no poor creature hath more cause to put forth himself in the cause of God than I. I have had plentiful wages beforehand, and I am

sure I shall never earn the least mite. The Lord accept me in
His Son, and give me to walk in the light, and give us to
walk in the light, as He is the light. . . . One beam in a dark
place hath exceeding much refreshment in it. Blessed be His
name for shining on so dark a heart as mine! You know
what my manner of life hath been. Oh, I lived in and loved
darkness, and hated the light. I was a chief, the chief of
sinners. This is true; I hated godliness, yet God had mercy
on me. Oh the riches of His mercy! Praise Him for me,
pray for me, that who hath begun a good work would perfect it to the day of Christ.

This act of conversion was a common experience among the
early Puritans and was always painfully realized. For only
God could elect or reject. Men could no more convert than
baptize themselves. Professor Knappen writes:[8]

To find the wicket gate one must renounce and report
every known sin. . . . Not only the present mode of life
but all the past must be dragged into the white light on conscience, dissected and examined with a determination to
overlook no slightest failing or secret desire. When the depth
of iniquity became apparent it was contrasted with the
height of God's standard. . . . Thus the penitent reached a
state of "holy desperation" . . . and cast himself wholly on
the mercy of God. Then came the peace that passeth all
understanding . . . assurance of salvation as the Holy Spirit
convinced him that by justifying faith he was numbered
among the elect.

The hatred of past and present sins which came with conversion, and the love of God which was felt in thankfulness
for His mercy, were in themselves a sufficient proof of election. But the good works that followed it were not; they were
imposed upon men merely as an obligation by the Covenant
of Grace; they showed only that one's faith was real. Finally,
the very conviction of everlasting salvation, that writing of the
convert's name in the Book of Life, incited him "to put forth
himself in the cause of God," to be, like another Puritan of
Cromwell's time, Archibald Johnston, God's instrument for
the "welfare of His Church, Satan's overthrow, Antichrist's
ruin and comfort of the Godly."

Thus God chose Oliver Cromwell as His servant and mis-
sionary, and lit in him the faith that gave assurance of salva-

tion. Now he became conscious, as Dr. Samuel Ward was conscious, that Providence was concerned with every single detail of his daily life. No longer was he one of the multitude who "loved darkness rather than light, because their deeds were evil." Now he would perfect the good work that God had begun in him. In future he would look always to His Providences, for they would indicate or confirm what was right.

Whether in the turmoil of political crisis or at the moment for decision upon the field of battle, Cromwell would go on his knees and seek to interpret God's will. It was not always easy to determine—in his future career there were to be many agonizing hesitations—yet in the end through reflection and waiting he thought he perceived how events were shaping to disclose the guidance of Heaven. "If thou wilt seek to know the mind of God in all that chain of Providence," he once told a correspondent, "laying aside thy fleshly reason, seek of the Lord to teach thee what that is; and He will do it." "Is it an arm of flesh that doth these things?" he asked after his Irish campaign. "It is the Lord only. God will curse that man and his house that dares think otherwise. Sir, you see the work is done by divine leading." Oliver Cromwell shared with William Gladstone an ideal of personal conduct in the subjection of the human will to God by two parallel processes:[9]

> The first that of checking, repressing, quelling, the inclination of the will to act with reference to the self as centre: that is, to mortify it. The second, to cherish, exercise, and expand its new and heavenly power of acting according to the will of God. . . .

That is what Gladstone wrote to his wife when he was thirty-five, echoing, in the language of Eton and Oxford, the conviction which the teachings of Huntingdon Free Grammar School and Sidney Sussex College, Cambridge, had brought to Cromwell when he, too, was in his thirties.

But how could one always be sure that one interpreted God's will correctly? Cromwell was aware that one might "make too much of outward dispensations" or be misled by "fleshly reasonings." Yet it was seldom that he, or indeed any of his contemporaries, recognized that Providence was "a two-edged sword that might be used either way." On the contrary, he was to find in the success of the causes to which he dedicated himself "remarkable providences and appearances of the Lord." He believed in his star as much as Napoleon was to do.

So he was always to fight and pray in an unsullied faith, sometimes in a passionate exuberance, more often in a calm certainty. He was God's chosen vessel and believed he was directed by Him upon the way of wisdom.

Thus Cromwell came to interpret the will of God for himself. He liked to read the Bible and provide his own glosses upon it. Though he listened to others preaching, he willingly preached himself. He did not want priest, ritual, or ceremony to intervene between him and his Maker. That was why he had come to detest the bishops, because he regarded them not as spiritual or nursing fathers but as mere administrators and disciplinarians who were trying to impose "flat popery" again upon the English people. He said as much in his maiden speech in the Commons (made soon after his conversion, in February 1629). Self-discipline he accepted, but as to government he preferred to take his own part in it, to help determine his own mode of worship, and above all select his own kind of preacher. It is likely that soon after the Parliament of 1628-29 was dissolved by the King, he began to sympathize not with the expanding Presbyterian movement that had had its advocates in Cambridge and elsewhere since the turn of the century, but with the much smaller group of Puritans who were known as Separatists, Independents, or Congregationalists.

This movement originated at the beginning of the century with Robert Browne, who had been a minister in Cambridge and Norwich. But it received its first impetus from the setting up of a number of congregations under the patronage of English merchants residing in Holland and later by colonists in New England. Among the ministers who served the congregation in Holland was Hugh Peter, who was later to be one of Cromwell's army chaplains. The essence of Congregationalism or Independency was that each congregation should be treated as a Christian unit on its own, voluntarily constituted and relatively free from interference by any hierarchy. "Believers," wrote one of the founders of the movement,[10] "do not make a particular Church, although peradventure many may meet and live together in the same place, unless they be joined by a special bond among themselves." The Independents, on the whole, adhered to the current Calvinist theology, were opposed to ritualism, reveled in preaching, and saluted the Bible as the mainspring of moral authority; it was only over the question of Church organization that they differed fundamentally from Cartwright and the Presbyterians, who wanted to capture the

Church intact and substitute their own hierarchy for the existing one directed by the bishops.

Cromwell supported the provision of lecturers to make good the deficiencies of the parish clergy by delivering sermons from the pulpits or even the market crosses in country towns. He wrote one of his earliest letters that have come down to posterity about a local lecturer. In 1633, soon after he had been promoted Archbishop of Canterbury, William Laud had ordered that a lecturer at Cromwell's native town of Huntingdon should be suppressed because he had been appointed by laymen. (King Charles I had already imposed severe restrictions on lecturers four years earlier and it was in this same year 1633 that a large-scale Puritan attempt to use economic means to reorient the Church was defeated by the Government.) In his letter Cromwell urged that funds should be raised to continue such a lecture—whether the one in Huntingdon itself or elsewhere in the country is not certain —saying

> it were a piteous thing to see a lecture fall, in the hands of so many able and godly men as I am persuaded the founders of this are, in these times wherein we see they are suppressed by the enemies of God His truth. . . .

The payment of a preaching minister by an independent group of laymen was the kernel of Congregationalism. At the time he wrote this letter (from St. Ives in January 1635) Cromwell was of course still an ordinary member of the Church of England who attended his parish church in the usual way. But he wanted his clergy to be men to his own taste; and it may be supposed that Laud's success in destroying Puritan schemes to transform the Church by patronage paved the way in enthusiastic converts like Cromwell to a more revolutionary frame of mind.

From the moment that he became Archbishop of Canterbury (in August 1633), Laud directed with single-minded enthusiasm an energetic if not entirely effective campaign against the Puritan movement aimed at sustaining order and uniformity throughout the Church of England.[11] His friend Richard Neile had become Archbishop of York, and another friend, Matthew Wren, Bishop of Norwich and afterwards Bishop of Ely. Wren's searching inquiries into the beliefs of the clergy and laity in East Anglia had made him especially obnoxious among the Puritans of Cromwell's acquaintance. Laud himself gave orders that everywhere in his province altars should be placed at the east end of the churches and railed in, that additional preachers or lecturers should be allowed only if approved by the church authorities, and that discipline should be enforced against all clergy who gave their services a Puritan twist by omission or commission, and he even demanded that Protestant refugee communities in Ipswich and Canterbury should be harried into conformity. Laud himself was not much interested in dogmatic controversy. His preoccupation was above all with peace, order, and the beauty of holiness, and he hit the Puritans hard. To him and his disciples it seemed only right that "God's services shall no longer put on pure sluttishness for pure religion." "God the Holy Ghost," said his friend Bishop Wren, "breathes not but in His Holy Church." But contemporaneously with Laud's spring cleaning of the Church were also to be seen the beginnings of an antipredestinarian movement in high places. In a letter to his friend Archbishop Ussher of Armagh, in 1634, Dr. Samuel Ward grumbled that "novelties were too much favoured nowadays," and among novelties or "new opinions" he included the heresy of believing in free will.[12] Launcelot Andrewes, the saintly Bishop of Winchester, had started a quiet rebellion against the prevailing Calvinist theology in Cambridge a long time before that, and this had found its parallel in Oxford when Laud was elected Chancellor of the University in 1630. Dr. Ward's friend and biographer, Thomas Fuller, asserted that in the late thirties "the name altar began to oust that of Lord's Board or Communion Table." High Churchmen were talking about the Real Presence of Christ in the Sacraments, and Dr. Ward himself complained in a letter that he had never known the University in a worse condition than it was since he first became a member forty-six years earlier. In another letter Ward congratulated Ussher on boldly preaching a sermon before the King dealing with the repression of the "Arminian faction"; that is to say, those who, like Andrewes and Nevile and a small group of bishops favored by the new King, obstinately believed in free will and justification by good works. For to Ward and his friends "the point of free will" was anathema, the central ground of all other errors in the theology of their time, the "novelty" most surely designed to dim the radiance of the Gospel and subject the Grace of God to the mere desires of man.

We do not know how far, after he left Cambridge, Cromwell had kept in touch with Dr. Samuel Ward and his orthodoxies. But Oliver's election later as M.P. for the town of Cambridge while he himself was living in Ely suggests that he had been maintaining a close interest in the affairs of the town and university. And he had, for example, asked a Cambridge Fellow to stand godfather to his son Richard. It is reasonable to suppose that Cromwell acquired his violent views about the leaders of the Church of England in the 1630s, not only through his resentment against the iron rule of Archbishop Laud and Bishop Wren as it impinged upon Puritanism in the eastern counties, but also through his sympathy with the Puritan criticisms of the High Church "novelties" expressed by Dr. Ward and his fellow Calvinists at the High Tables in Cambridge.

*   *   *

Long before he became a member for Cambridge, Cromwell had expounded in the House of Commons his attitude of mind on the subject of religion. Indeed, the only surviving record of his part in the Parliament of 1628-29 is the speech which he delivered in the Committee on Religion on February 11, 1629. Before the second session of that Parliament had opened, William Laud had received his first important appointment as Bishop of London, and the King had, upon Laud's advice, published a declaration in which as Defender of the Faith and Supreme Governor of the Church he gave the order that no "unnecessary disputations" should be suffered which might "nourish faction in Church or Commonwealth"—a blow for uniformity and against the Puritan sects. The Committee on Religion, over which John Pym presided, being sympathetic towards the Puritan point of view, had refused to be silenced, and had retorted by condemning all "innovations" in religion, drawing attention to the growth of "popery" under the shadow of the Queen, and censuring all who introduced "popery or Arminianism" as "capital enemies" of the state. Oliver Cromwell in his unique surviving speech complained that High Churchmen and near-papists were being promoted to rich preferments in the Church, while honest clergy who attacked popish doctrines were being deliberately muzzled by unsympathetic bishops.

Cromwell was then nearly thirty years old. Another eleven years were to pass before he was again elected to Parliament. That was when he was forty, when all his nine children had been born and he was established as a landowner and farmer in Ely; he had become a man of substance, taking an active part in the affairs of the town, was a master of Biblical phraseology, and a recognized spokesman for the Puritans in the eastern counties. His election to the "Short Parliament" took place in March 1640; and there he listened with approval to John Pym's protests against "the new ceremonies and observances which had put upon the churches a shape and face of popery." In the "Long Parliament," to which he was again elected as a member for Cambridge in October 1640, Cromwell became one of those who directed the offensive now directly set in motion against the religious policy of King Charles I and Archbishop Laud. He vehemently defended John Lilburne, a young London apprentice who had distributed unlicensed Puritan pamphlets; he was nominated to a subcommittee of the Grand Committee on Religion which concerned itself with the scarcity of preaching ministers, and he was appointed to another committee to investigate the complaints against Bishop Wren of Ely. His first speech in this Parliament (on February 9, 1641) was in support of nine articles of impeachment drawn up against Matthew Wren, who was thereupon voted unfit to hold office in church or state. In that same February, Cromwell was named a member of yet another committee to consider an act to end superstition and idolatry; in May he moved "to turn the papists out of Dublin," and advocated a bill to abolish the bishops "root and branch" from the English Church; in September he delivered an attack upon the Common Prayer Book and brought forward a motion in favor of the afternoon lecturers forbidden by King Charles I, and in October (after the recess) he demanded, "root and branch" having so far failed, the exclusion of the bishops from the House of Lords.[13]

This list does not contain all that Oliver Cromwell did in the early days of the Long Parliament, but it includes much of it, and it shows how to him the religious question was then paramount. In two of his early letters we read also of the anxiety that he felt over his religion. In February 1641, he wrote to a London merchant who had business in Scotland asking him to send him "the reasons why the Scots desire to enforce uniformity in religion between the two kingdoms," and in May he forwarded to the mayor and aldermen of Cambridge a copy of the "protestation" just passed by Parliament whereby all its members swore to defend with their life, power, and estate the "true Protestant religion" against "all popery and popish innovations." During the second session of the Long Parliament, after King Charles I left London, it was Oliver Cromwell who continued to urge the total abolition of bishops from the Church of England.

At forty, Oliver Cromwell was a man of firm religious convictions, of sanguine temper, and high conscientiousness. Brought up as a Protestant in one of the most profoundly Protestant areas of the country, he had steeped himself in the Bible, he had learned from his schoolmasters and from his friends at Cambridge University the essential structure of the predestinarian faith, he had undergone spiritual conversion as a young married man, he had acquired the independent character of the fenlanders, and he had resented the strict uniformity which Archbishop Laud and his local bishop, Matthew Wren, had been imposing upon the Church. Cromwell had felt, too, as his mentor Dr. Samuel Ward had believed, that the advocacy in influential quarters—including the Court—of the doctrines of free will and justification by works presaged a reversion towards the popish faith that had been enforced before the reign of Queen Elizabeth I. He therefore devoted the bulk of his time and effort in the three Parliaments wherein he was a representative of the eastern counties to the service of religion, to the battle against "novelties," to the campaign to oust the bishops, and to the struggle to destroy ritual and promote preaching. In all that he did not see himself as a revolutionary. On the contrary, he was convinced that he was defending the "true Protestant faith" that he had learned at his mother's knees. He was purging the Church of impurities and excrescences, and reaffirming the omnipotence of God against those who would have put it second to the free will of mere man. Providence, he believed, had called upon him in his life's summer, as a member of the classes pertinaciously climbing to power in the land, to put right the balance in church and state by a process not of reformation but of healing restoration. He was no radical or man of the people; he saw himself merely as a humble instrument of God, warmed to anger by what he conceived to be spiritual wrongs. Through that he rose to some sort of political leadership. But above all it was his rough independence of spirit that at first distinguished him in the group of friends and relations, led by Pym, who met at Westminster in fighting mood at the moment of revolution in English history.

Notes

1. Of numerous books on Puritanism two of the best and most recent are W. Haller, *The Rise of Puritanism* (1938) and M. M. Knappen, *Tudor Puritanism* (1939). John Stoughton, *Ecclesiastical History of England* (1881), stresses the Calvinist creed of the Elizabethan Church.

2. For a detailed development of the arguments about patronage, titles, and the rise of Puritanism, see Christopher Hill's brilliant book, *Economic Problems of the Church from Archbishop Whitgift to the Long Parliament* (1956). Mr. Hill's discussion of the suppression of the Puritan attempt to establish lecturers by buying up impropriations and advowsons is supplemented by Isobel M. Calder, *Activities of the Puritan Faction of the Church of England, 1625–33* (1957).

3. Cf. A. F. Scott Pearson, *Thomas Cartwright and Elizabethan Puritanism* (1925).

4. A. L. Rowse, *The England of Elizabeth* (1950), puts up a spirited defense of the Elizabethan bishops.

5. M. M. Knappen, *Two Elizabethan Puritan Diaries* (1933), 9.

6. Samuel Ward's diary belongs to Sidney Sussex College, Cambridge, where I was allowed to read it, together with other memorabilia of Dr. Ward. The diary has been edited and published by Professor M. M. Knappen. For Dr. Ward I have also consulted correspondence in Add. MSS. 5821, 32093, Sloane MS. 1325, Harleian MS. 3783, Tanner MSS. 72 and 73, Richard Parr, *The Life of James Usher* (1686), and Thomas Fuller's *The History of the Worthies* and *The Church History of England;* J. E. Bailey, *Thomas Fuller* (1874).

7. David Lloyd, *Memoirs of those Persons who suffered for the Protestant Religion* (1668).

8. M. M. Knappen, *Tudor Puritanism*, 393.

9. Quoted in Sir Philip Magnus, *William Gladstone* (1955).

10. William Ames, *The Marrow of Sacred Divinity* (1643).

11. Cf. H. R. Trevor-Roper, *Archbishop Laud* (1940).

12. Parr, *op. cit.*, 470.

13. For Oliver Cromwell's speeches and activities in the Long Parliament, see W. H. Coate, *The Journal of Sir Symonds D'Ewes* (1942), published since Abbott's first volume appeared.

Chapter 4

Cromwell and the Long Parliament

THE IDEA of "sovereignty" or the absolute state, under which men in a more democratic age chose to live, was scarcely known to poltical thinkers of the early seventeenth century. The conception of sovereignty arose with the Civil War—it did not cause it. What men believed in then was described by them as a "balanced polity," each organ of government having limited authority. That was the theory on which Oliver Cromwell was brought up and from which he was never to depart.

The meaning of a "balanced polity" was this[1]: the king's powers were limited by the so-called "law of nature," by the terms of his coronation oath, by the common law, as administered in the courts, which protected property rights, and by the rights of Parliament. To these limitations Puritans, like Cromwell's schoolmaster, Dr. Beard, added the subordination of the king to the will of God. Even Sir Francis Bacon, a pillar of monarchy in the reign of King James I, admitted that the king's act and grants were limited by the law. Sir John Hayward, also writing in King James's reign, quoted Seneca with approval: "The king has empire, every man his particular property in all things." In his *Institutes* the much respected lawyer, Sir Edward Coke, remarked: "The Common law hath so admeasured the prerogative of the king, as he cannot take nor prejudice the inheritance of any." "The king," observed another lawyer, Sir Henry Finch, "hath a prerogative in all things that are not injurious to the subject." In other words, the accepted view in the early seventeenth century was that while the king was the head of the Commonwealth, his powers were not absolute, but were circumscribed by the property rights of his subjects, which were firmly protected by law.

If at the beginning of the century educated Englishmen did not think of their king as an absolute sovereign, they certainly urged no such claim for Parliament. The most that was ever argued was that the power of the king in Parliament was greater than his powers out of Parliament. But the deduction was not drawn (although it was to be drawn later) that

Parliament was therefore superior to the King. On the contrary, Parliament was regarded as the great council of the realm, summoned by the king from time to time to vote taxes, enact laws, and express grievances. But Queen Elizabeth I had insisted that it had no right to concern itself with religion, foreign affairs, or "mysteries of state." Even John Pym and Sir John Eliot, severe critics of the monarchy, confessed that Parliament could not trespass on the king's rights or the rights of the Church, while statute laws, like the royal prerogatives, were subject to considerations both of precedent and property. Bills thought to be against the "fundamental law" of the kingdom were rejected, and judges questioned and sometimes even set aside statutes if they violated the laws of God or nature or the rights of property.

Such was the constitutional outlook at the outset of the century. Nevertheless, both king and Parliament attempted to widen their own powers. King James I insisted that he held his authority directly from God, that he himself was the supreme, indeed the sole, lawgiver, that Parliament was merely an advisory body summoned by him when he felt inclined and then only because it was the custom of the land. But towards the end of the reign he had yielded concessions to Parliament, allowing the House of Commons, for example, to discuss foreign affairs. And in 1629 King Charles I complained that the House "hath of late years endeavoured to expand their privileges by setting up general committees for religion, for courts of justice, trade, and the like." It was, in fact, in the Parliament of 1628–29, the first in which Oliver Cromwell sat, that broader constitutional claims were foreshadowed. How did this come about?

The primary impulse was undoubtedly the unpopularity of the first Duke of Buckingham, "one of the handsomest men in the world," the brightly lit favorite alike of King James I and King Charles I, and his abject failure as a statesman and general. "I think," observed Sir Edward Coke, "the Duke of Buckingham is the cause of all our miseries. . . . That man is the grievance of grievances." Because they distrusted Buckingham's policies and extravagances, the Commons had limited the grant of customs duties or tonnage and poundage to King Charles to one year only. The King had then responded by demanding "forced loans" from his subjects, and had imprisoned over seventy persons who refused to pay. When the Parliament of 1628–29 met, it at once protested against such "arbitrary taxation and arbitrary imprisonment" as being contrary to the "ancient fundamental liberties of the kingdom." It obliged the King to accept a "Petition of Right" by which he admitted that he had, in fact, broken these "fundamental laws." Subsequently Buckingham was assassinated, an event that the Puritans regarded as a judgment of the Almighty. "Europe never had a greater or more potent subject," noted Sir John Oglander, who was no Puritan, when he heard of the murder, "and as his death was sudden and strange, so must all those look for the like that maintain their greatness merely on the favour of the prince, without any merits of their own or the approbation of the commonwealth."

After Buckingham died and the Petition of Right had been reluctantly granted, the King continued to levy tonnage and poundage without parliamentary consent and refused to allow his officers to be questioned in the Commons for doing so. Cromwell and his friends, in the second session of the Parliament of 1628–29, also turned to their initial assault on the bishops, and the King, irritated beyond measure and shattered by his favorite's assassination, dissolved the Parliament, but not before the Commons had voted three resolutions condemning "innovations" in religion, attacking the levying of tonnage and poundage without its consent, and declaring that any merchant who paid it was a betrayer of the liberties of England. King Charles I, remarking that Parliaments "are in the nature of cats that ever grow cursed with age," determined to take a holiday from them and govern personally. For eleven years he succeeded in ruling without a Parliament.

In the Petition of Right all that the Parliamentarians had asserted was that the King had broken the "fundamental laws" and must promise in future to respect them, just as in their original criticism of his religious policy what they urged was that "innovations" were being introduced contrary to the true Protestant faith. In their attitude there was as yet no revolutionary overtone. But their leaders were beginning to stake higher claims. They were already saying that they had the right "in the name of the nation" to discuss matters of religion and foreign policy, topics which had been denied to them by Queen Elizabeth I. In her reign very few had thought that Parliament was an institution representative of the nation as a whole and responsible to it. Once, however, quarrels had developed over spheres of influence—on the one side over the king's right to collect taxes without the consent of Parliament, on the other over the right of Parliament to lay down the law about religion or foreign policy—the doctrine of a "balanced polity" whereby "the prerogative of the king and the liberty of the people have a reciprocal relation and respect" was in the process of being undermined. But it needed the passage of time and the impact of events before the climate of opinion could be changed and the views of thinking men adjusted to a fresh approach to political realities.

*   *   *

Cromwell, it seems, took a modest, not to say retiring, part in the Parliament of 1628–29. Like most men who do not like simply to hear the sound of their own voices, he spoke only about what he knew—in his case it was about religion. But it may be supposed that he learned much, that he digested the lessons of the debates on the Petition of Right, and that he acquired sufficient experience to enable him to become a valuable working member of Parliament when he was called to serve there again. But it was eleven years before he returned to Westminster.

*   *   *

By dispensing with the services of Parliament for a period of eleven years, King Charles I unbalanced the national "polity" and provoked the Puritans. For Parliament, ever since the early days of Queen Elizabeth's reign, was the heart of Protestant England. In governing without Parliament the King's intentions were of the noblest. His was no despotism or police state. He was an idealist, conscious of his duty both to God and to his people. In a speech delivered to the judges before they left London on the summer assizes in 1635, Lord Coventry, the Lord Keeper, expounded the principles of King Charles's system of government.[2] They were, he told the judges, to do equal justice between rich and poor, to guard against the corruption of officials, to prevent "men of countenance and power" from exploiting their positions, and to put a stop to the "high oppression" of land enclosures. Meanwhile the peace of the kingdom would be ensured by the fine navy that the King was building to uphold the sovereignty of the seas: "the wooden walls are the best walls of this kingdom." The ordinary courts of justice were supplemented by the prerogative courts established under the Tudors—the Star Chamber, the High Commission, the Council of the North at York, and by the Privy Council itself. These courts aimed at keeping the overweening subject in check and had the right to inflict torture to procure evidence. The poor law was generously administered, and efforts were exerted to reduce distress by the provision of work for the unemployed. Abroad, though the King engaged in elaborate and ill-considered intrigues to reinstate his sister's husband on the throne he had lost in Germany, he managed to avoid becoming entangled in foreign war, and because England was at peace while the rest of the world was at war trade flowed into the kingdom. So during these years when Parliament was not sitting prosperity prevailed in the land and the King thought himself the happiest in Christendom.

The King was serious in his intentions but lazy in his habits. Like his father, he spent many hours hunting; like his son, King Charles II, he applied himself only spasmodically to business. He was irresolute (his friends knew that) and easily swayed. After the Duke of Buckingham had been assassinated, his affections were centered upon his French Roman Catholic Queen, with whom he had slowly but completely fallen in love. She was wedded as much to her religion as to her husband, and the favors conferred upon her circle and upon the Roman Catholic ambassadors in London strengthened the Puritan suspicion that a Catholicizing conspiracy was being hatched at Court. King Charles I—like Cromwell—loved music and horses, and he also devoted time and money to his collection of paintings. He himself had "singular skill in limning and pictures, was a good mathematician, not unskilful in history, well read in divinity, and no less in the laws and statutes of this nation, would write his mind singularly well and in good language and style, only he loved long parenthesis."[3] He was always gracious and charming, but not a practical man. Like King Louis XVI of France and Tsar Nicholas II, he was "weak" not "bad," the predestined victim of the revolutionary block. Indolence at Court eddied out into mismanagement in the provinces. Most of his councillors were smaller minded than the King was himself; they were not "evil," but they were self-seeking. Only two of them were single-minded: the stalwart Yorkshireman, Thomas Viscount Wentworth, later Earl of Strafford, and

Archbishop William Laud, who had neither wife, children, nor interests outside his work.

*   *   *

In the early 1630s, while the Puritan-minded George Abbot was still Archbishop of Canterbury, it seemed just possible that a way of living within the Church might be found between men like Oliver Cromwell, who loved their lectures and their Bibles, their simple services and their introspective approach to worship, and the High Church minority who stressed the value of ritual in the churches and the inspiration of the sacraments. But when in 1633 Abbot was succeeded by Laud, a pugnacious cleric who thrust forward his diocesan visitations in pursuit of a strict policy of uniformity, that hope faded. In the same year Wentworth (who earlier had been imprisoned for his refusal to pay the forced loan), having completed a useful spell of office as President of the North, arrived in Dublin to rule over Ireland as Lord Deputy. In Ireland Wentworth gradually built up the royal finances and created a small but effective army. He established law and order, suppressed piracy, and saw to the administration of justice and the elimination of corruption. But at the same time he carried on the traditional English policy of upholding an alien Protestant Church and settling an alien Protestant minority, who stole much of the land from the Irish people. And just as Laud's policy led to a pent-up resentment against the discipline of the Church authorities—which Oliver Cromwell was to describe as "the tyranny of the bishops"—so Wentworth's conduct in Ireland sowed the seeds for Irish revolt.

To pay for ruling without a Parliament, since the expenses of administration could not be met out of the customary royal revenues even in this time of profound peace, the King's Treasury Commissioners were driven to a number of unpopular expedients. Tonnage and poundage was exacted in defiance of the House of Commons, and indeed was increased by a new book of rates; the medieval forest laws were invoked for the benefit of the Crown and mulcted many a wealthy landowner; gentlemen with incomes above £40 a year were fined if they refused to take a knighthood; monopolies, as for the making of an indifferent soap, were sold to private corporations; and finally "ship money" was demanded, not only from all the seaports but also from inland towns.

The first ship-money writ was issued in October 1634, when King Charles I was contemplating a scheme for an Anglo-Spanish alliance against the Dutch. Then the ports (apart from London) were asked to provide sums of money instead of building ships. In July 1635 ship money was demanded from inland towns, and the demand was not even accompanied with any stirring appeal to those who were unexpectedly required to contribute. It caused much complaint. The sheriff of Dorset, for example, reported that the money was paid "like drops of blood, and some sell their only cow which should feed their children, and some come to the parish." No war was then being envisaged, and though pirates swarmed in the Channel and off the Irish coast, that did not appear to justify so elaborate a departure from precedent. Still, the King asked the judges to confirm that the levy was legal, and they did so. One of the justices explained, when a test case was brought before the Court of King's Bench "there was a rule of law and a rule of government, and that many things which might not be done by the rule of law might be done by the rule of government." This dictum, which was in effect the argument employed in defense of most of the King's actions during the eleven years, was startling to country gentlemen who, like Cromwell, had received their smattering of law in the Inns of Court. What now had become of the "natural law" and the "fundamental rights" of property? Yet Wentworth and all the King's advisers and apologists insisted on the King's "double power"—ordinary and absolute; the absolute prerogative power being one that he might always invoke whenever he himself judged a crisis to exist. An American scholar has recently written:

> By extending the emergency and discretionary power of the King and enlarging his trust, the royalists so exalted the absolute power that little room was left for the subjects' rights and property, and they so tipped the scales in favor of the prerogative that the old balanced constitution no longer existed.[4]

Thus to the grievances aroused against the bishops was added the dislike of "illegal taxation" which was brought to a head in another test case, this time argued in the Court of Exchequer by Cromwell's cousin, John Hampden; and when

Parliament met again these two themes fused and exploded into civil war.

*   *   *

Oliver Cromwell (like his future son-in-law, Henry Ireton) always had an "eye for property." Yet it never weighed upon him in the same sense that his religion did. Speaking of the causes of the Civil War in 1655 he said:

> Religion was not the thing at first contested for, but God brought it to that issue at last, and gave it unto us by way of redundancy; and at last it proved that which was most dear to us. And wherein consisted this more than in obtaining that liberty from the tyranny of the bishops to all species of Protestants to worship God according to their own light and consciences, for want of which many of our brethren forsook their native countries to seek their bread from strangers, and to live in howling wildernesses; and for want of which also many that remained here were imprisoned and otherwise abused, and made the scorn of the nation?

In his other speeches and letters only a very few significant references to the rights of property are to be found. One is when he criticized the extreme views of the Levelers; another when in discussing the case for manhood suffrage he said that it would tend to anarchy if no other "bound or limit" were set to the franchise than "the interest of breathing." It has been argued that Cromwell and his fellow "country-house radicals" among the "declining gentry" were resentful of the fact that they did not share in the offices and perquisites enjoyed by the courtiers and their friends.[5] It is possible that such resentment existed, but in Cromwell's case no definite evidence has yet been found for such an assumption.

What we do know, however, and indeed the incidents are virtually all that remain to us from these "lost years" in Oliver Cromwell's life, is that in two cases he expressed indignant concern over the property rights of the impecunious fenlanders. These had little or nothing to do with the recent royal exactions. In one case he came to the conclusion that a new oligarchical form of government that had been set up in Huntingdon before he left the town in 1631, and in which he himself had been allotted a place, was working against the interests of the poorer inhabitants. He told the Lord Privy Seal that the mayor and aldermen had been given the right to alter the distribution of the townsmen's cattle in the common fields of the town and had been permitted to impose excessive fines. The new charter was then revised to meet Cromwell's objections to it, and the cattle were allowed to roam the commons as they had done before. Secondly, when he thought many of the fenlanders were being unfairly treated in the matter of reclamation (this was after he came to live in Ely), he offered "they paying him a groat for every cow they had upon the common, to hold the drainers in suit for five years" so that "in the meantime they should enjoy every foot of their commons."[6] In other words, Cromwell's attitude to property was determined by a "distributionist" conception of justice—that of "the three acres and a cow"—and not by any personal form of greed for wealth or office. Like other men of modest means and ancient principles in his time, he no doubt objected to the imposition of taxes, under the excuse of questionable emergencies, to which Parliament had not given its consent; but, so far as is known, he paid his ship money and knighthood fine without demur. When his anger was expressed—and it was a terrible anger—it was against injustices to the poor and, above all, the "tyranny of the bishops."

*　　　*　　　*

In the summer of 1637 the King's Government appeared never to have been firmer nor the country more prosperous. To the poet Thomas Carew these seemed to be "halcyon days." Peace had been maintained in a world at war; the royal finances had been balanced; the holiday from Parliament had caused few or no protests; Thomas Wentworth was ruling powerfully in Ireland; Laud's policy for the Church was disturbed only by the occasional outbursts of a few fanatics. Yet this very year was to be the turning point in what was afterwards called "the eleven years' tyranny." In June three brave and defiant Puritans, condemned by the Court of Star Chamber for libels against the bishops, were brutally punished in London, and their sufferings and sermons from the pillory aroused sympathy from the mob. The judgments in the Exchequer Court in the Hampden case on ship money, given over a period of months, showed a lack of unanimity for the King's case. Hampden's counsel, Oliver St. John, another friend of Cromwell, had invoked a number of impressive precedents that had shaken the equanimity of the judges, however agreeably disposed towards the prerogative; indeed, three of the twelve judges had actually found in favor of Hampden on the main question. Afterwards the collection of ship money had been dangerously affected and indeed undermined. Thus at the moment when the King's two principal aims—the financial independence of the Crown and the imposition of uniformity on the Church—appeared to be nearing the point of realization, they met with a grave check. Within three years resistance to the collection of ship money became almost nationwide. Lord Finch, the Lord Chancellor, complained: "I know not how it comes about that there is not alacrity and cheerfulness given to the obedience of His Majesty's writs for ship money." In spite of the Laudian visitations Puritanism remained unabashed, and was particularly vehement in the area where Cromwell lived. The vicar of St. Ives, his former parish, reported, for example, that his entire congregation had refused to take the sacraments at the altar rails. Finally King Charles's openly pro-Spanish policy received much criticism. For men recalled the good old days of Queen Elizabeth I when Spain had been the great national enemy. Cromwell always recalled them himself.

While the King's authority was being increasingly defied in England, a more concentrated and dangerous opposition was forming in Scotland. Since the Stuarts had obtained their acceptable heritage in England, they had tended to neglect their Scottish realm. But King James I, by playing off the nobility against the clergy, had managed to maintain his position there and had in fact reinstated a limited form of episcopacy. King Charles I, however, had provoked the nobility by attempting confiscations, and true to his policy of uniformity had tried to fasten a version of the English Book of Common Prayer on the Scottish Kirk. This had created instant antagonism, especially in Edinburgh, Glasgow, and the Lowlands. Towards the end of July 1637, a tumult in St. Gile's Church in Edinburgh was the signal for revolt. "The Mass," it was asserted, "is entered among us!" The following February enthusiastic Scottish Calvinists flocked to subscribe to a National Covenant in defense of "the true reformed religion" and (ironically) "the King's honour." Only a few wealthy landowners stood aloof. Broadly the Scottish nation accepted the Covenant, and demanded that the obnoxious service book should be withdrawn. But the King would not give way. "I will rather die than yield to these impertinent and damnable demands," he exclaimed. Though warned of the low state of his finances, adequate for times of peace but insufficient to sustain war of any kind, he determined to punish the recalcitrant Scots. But even his Lord High Admiral despaired. "The King's magazines," he wrote, "are totally unfurnished of arms and all sorts of ammunition, and commanders we have none either for advice or execution; the people through all England are generally so discontented by reason of the multitude of projects daily imposed upon them, as I think there is reason to fear that a great part of them will be readier to join with the Scots than to draw their swords in the King's service." In November 1638, an Assembly of the Scottish Kirk, meeting in Glasgow, abolished the episcopacy, thus setting an example to the English Puritans. The King took up the challenge of the Covenanters and the Kirk. But he marched upon a hopeless mission. After an almost farcical affray at Whitsun 1639, a pacification was patched up in Berwick, the King being obliged to agree to call the Scottish Parliament and another meeting of the Kirk Assembly to settle the future and meanwhile to grant an act of pardon and oblivion. The Pacification of Berwick only papered over the cracks, and a second Bishops' War was to follow. In preparation for this second war the King sent for his ablest adviser, Thomas Wentworth, now Earl of Strafford, from Dublin. Under his chairmanship a Council of War met three times a week in the English capital to concert plans. The Lord Deputy, himself an old House of Commons man, urged the King to summon a meeting of Parliament and invite it to give him its moral and material support in fighting the rebellious Scots. Thus it was that, after an absence of eleven years, Oliver Cromwell found himself in April 1640 again a member of Parliament.[7]

* * *

The choice of Cromwell as member for Cambridge was logical. He was a former M.P. for the neighboring county town, he was a man of standing in nearby Ely, and he had made himself prominent in local affairs, especially as the champion of the men of the fenlands. Moreover, it may be supposed that since Matthew Wren had become Bishop of

Ely in 1638, Cromwell had been a spokesman of the Puritans against the High Church tendencies of the new bishop; this may be deduced from the part he afterwards took in attacking Wren in the House of Commons. Finally he was known as the cousin of John Hampden, the hero of the ship-money case. Only one obstacle stood in the way of his election: he had to be a freeman of Cambridge. The difficulty was overcome by his taking lodgings in the town and being sworn in as a freeman on the payment of a penny to the poor. But the burgesses played for safety. As their other member they elected Thomas Meautys, Clerk of the Privy Council, who had been recommended to their favor by the Lord Keeper. The two members for the University were both later to support the Parliamentary side in the Civil War, but one of them had served on the High Commission and the other had been nominated by the Chancellor of the University. Thus though Cambridgeshire can be described as a Puritan county, which had actively resisted the payment of ship money, no rough-and-ready classification of its representatives was possible. When they went up to Westminster to attend Parliament in April 1640, they were all still going there to serve in the King's Great Council, to express the grievances accumulated over eleven years, and to vote such laws and taxes as they considered to be necessary.

In fact, this Parliament was a fiasco. The King, who stuttered slightly, left it to the Lord Keeper to put his case. John Pym, the fat little bearded businessman who had already constituted himself a leader in the House during the last Parliament, retorted with a long speech outlining the grievances felt both over religion and taxation. He has been described as the architect of a middle party. But the truth is that as yet no parties existed in the House, at any rate in the modern sense of the word. Pym's speech, though moderate in tone, had revolutionary implications, for he claimed that "the powers of Parliament are to the body politic as the rational facilities of the soul to a man." Undoubtedly he spoke the sense of the House as a whole. When King Charles offered to give up ship money in return for taxes voted in support of the war, the Commons resolved to do nothing "till the liberties of the House and the kingdom are cleared." Within three weeks the King dissolved the Parliament, and Cromwell returned home after the brief, disappointing, and fruitless session.

Thus the King had to wage the second Bishops' War

against the Scots without the backing of Parliament. His advisers became pessimistic. "I think, as you do," wrote Archbishop Laud to Wentworth, "Scotland is the veriest devil that is out of Hell."[8] Once again the scratch royal army was hopelessly beaten. Among the humiliating terms of the treaty concluded at Ripon was a clause that the King should again call a Parliament in London. So, before the year was out, Cromwell was back at Westminster as member for Cambridge, this time with a prosperous chandler as his Puritan colleague.

*   *   *

The structure of the Parliament which met in November 1640 and was to be known as the Long Parliament, has lately been subjected to exhaustive analysis, and the social origins of those who later fought for and against the King have been traced in detail. Yet again one must beware of anachronisms. When Parliament met, no simple divisions existed. The King had to call Parliament because he had promised to pay the victorious Scottish army, encamped on English soil, large sums of money, and only a vote from Parliament could procure them. The members arrived at Westminster determined to right the wrongs that had been left unsettled at the time of the Short Parliament. The King's ministers and friends attempted, as they had always done in the past, to secure the representation of a number of courtiers in the House, and, in fact, a few constituencies that normally accepted a royal recommendation on this occasion refused to do so. For example, the Recorder of London, whom King Charles had intended to appoint Speaker of the House of Commons, was rejected by the City. And in general the grip of the local gentry is said to have tightened as a result of the general election. But no "party struggle" had occurred in the constituencies, nor was any notable difference to be detected between the kind of men who were elected to represent the counties and those who were elected for the boroughs, which had narrower franchises and might therefore have been thought to be more subject to influences of one kind or another. In three quarters of the constituencies there were probably no contests at all. And little evidence has been found to show that Pym, Hampden, and his friends—who included Cromwell—did much organized electioneering or personal canvassing. An American historian has written:

"Although there were election strategies to which both sides resorted, it would be erroneous to conclude that the results were determined in the majority of cases by the 'organization' of either faction."[9]

But is not even the word "faction" an anachronism? When the Long Parliament first assembled, it consisted neither of parties nor of factions. The King had a handful of spokesmen in the House, but when it came to the crux it was seen that those who were prepared to support the royal policies without any qualification were a small minority. Men like Edward Hyde, Viscount Falkland, and Sir John Culpepper, who later became Royalist leaders, agreed on almost every question with their fellow members in the early months of this Parliament. Except over ecclesiastic questions, no divisions were taken on important issues. And even after the first recess a clergyman was sent to the Tower of London for a fortnight for "reporting we had sides and parties in the House which was but one body so to set a division amongst us."[10]

The temper of the entire House was extremely critical of the King's policies, of the incompetencies that had brought about the two Scottish wars, and was Puritan in tone. Almost without exception, members favored reducing the civil powers of the clergy and bringing to justice the "evil counsellors" of the King. John Pym himself was neither an extreme Puritan nor an overt revolutionary. "His position," wrote Dr. Gardiner, "was purely conservative. . . . To him Parliament was the most conservative force in existence. It was the guardian of the old religion and of the old law against the new-fangled nostrums of Strafford and Laud." Moreover, he was far from being a republican. Even during the assault directed by him against the "evil counsellors" of the King, Pym said that "The King and his people are obliged to one another in the nearest relations. . . . He is the husband of the commonwealth." At the same time, little organization or leadership prevailed in the House. Committees were set up almost haphazardly to consider grievances in England and in Ireland. Debates oscillated between matters of national importance and purely local affairs. Cromwell, for example, interested himself in "innovations" practiced in Cambridge— the ten-year-old grievance of Dr. Samuel Ward. After the long intermission of Parliaments, almost every member had some particular injury to complain about or some remedy to demand. The presence of the Scots on English soil put the Commons in a position of unique strength. They were resolved to continue sitting until every woe had been righted and every wrongdoer punished.

Cromwell, with his deep Puritan convictions, his anger against Dr. Wren and the other bishops, and his vehement style of speaking, steadily rose to the fore in the first months of the Long Parliament. We have only the testimony of men who afterwards became his enemies about the impression he exerted upon the House of Commons. Hyde, for example, wrote later: "When he appeared first in Parliament he seemed to have a person in no degree gracious, no ornament of discourse, none of those talents which used to recruit the affections of standers-by." . . . In other words, he was almost the exact opposite of King Charles I. But, Hyde continued: "As he grew into place and authority his parts seemed to be renewed as if he had concealed faculties till he had occasion to use them."

He sat on many committees and spoke in a number of debates. It is true and possibly significant that, so far as our knowledge goes, he did not take part in the impeachment of the Earl of Strafford, his fellow member in an earlier Parliament, for Cromwell, as we shall see, was never a vengeful man. But on December 30, 1640, after a brief Christmas recess, he moved the second reading of the bill for holding annual Parliaments. This was later converted into a bill for triennial Parliaments, was passed by both Houses, and was accepted by the King on February 16, 1641.

Cromwell's concern over the "root-and-branch" bill to abolish the bishops has already been mentioned. This was a far-reaching measure intended not only to abolish archbishops and bishops but also their chancellors, deans and chapters, and archdeacons, in fact, to destroy the whole hierarchy of the Church of England as it existed then and still exists today. It appears to have been drafted by Oliver St. John, the lawyer who had represented Hampden in the ship-money case and was later to be appointed Solicitor General by the King. But Cromwell, with another friend of his, Sir Henry Vane, with whom he was on terms of intimacy and whom he nicknamed "Brother Herne," also had a hand in it, and so did another M.P., Sir Arthur Haselrigg. Its presentation to the House was actually entrusted—and this is a curiosity exemplifying the "non-party" character of the Parliament—to a member who did not himself believe in it, Sir Edward

Dering. Dering apparently hoped that the introduction of the bill would force the House of Lords to agree to expel the bishops from their chamber, and thereby reduce them to the spiritual functions which, he believed, they had exercised in the primitive church. But the Commons showed itself to be divided sharply over the merits of the bill, and though it received a second reading by a small majority, Parliament as a whole was not yet in the mood for so drastic a measure. Even the less contentious proposal, also warmly advocated by Cromwell, to exclude the bishops from the House of Lords, was confronted by the difficulty that the Upper House was unwilling to change its constitution at the behest of the House of Commons. In fact, over "root and branch" Cromwell was an extremist. Even his cousin Hampden told Falkland, one of the defenders of episcopacy, that he would be content with the more moderate policy of depriving the bishops and clergy of their secular offices.

In spite of all Cromwell's personal efforts, the religious question took a secondary place during the first year of the Long Parliament. The House's outstandingly successful achievement was its all-round attack on the King's ministers. Cromwell's part is unknown or negligible. An Act of Attainder was passed against the Earl of Strafford and forced upon the King, who let his faithful servant be martyred by law; Archbishop Laud, now old and feeble, was impeached, and both were eventually executed. Other royal ministers prudently fled the country. And the King, after his complete failure to protect any of them, gave way on all sides, even assenting to a bill whereby the Parliament could not be dissolved without its own consent and agreeing to bills declaring ship money and other royal exactions to be illegal, abolishing nearly all the prerogative courts, and in general depriving the Crown of all the extraordinary powers it had possessed and exercised since the days of the Tudors. But the King and Queen, though fully realizing their predicament, were by no means prepared to acquiesce in any severe or final diminution of the Crown's prerogative. They were not prepared to adapt themselves, as in more modern times an emperor of Japan and a shah of Persia have done, to a new constitutional position. At first King Charles had hoped to regain his place in the sun by a policy of concession and moderation and by taking some of the principal parliamentarians, including John Pym, who was offered the post of Chancellor of the Exchequer, into his service. That plan might conceivably have worked. But in his heart the King felt certain that his authority was a sacred thing and must be restored, if necessary by force. He still had at his disposal the army fashioned by the dead Earl of Strafford in Ireland, which was manned largely by Roman Catholics. He had some faint hopes of aid from the Dutch, since the only son of Prince William of Orange had just married his daughter. Finally, after a peace treaty had been agreed with the Scottish Covenanters, he fancied he might be able to unite the Scottish forces with the remains of his own English army. The Scots had a number of reasons to be discontented with the English Parliament, over questions both of commerce and religion. The King imagined he might be able to enlist their nationalist ardors in his own cause. At the time Pym took these daydreams seriously, and sent after him a parliamentary commission which included John Hampden when, on August 10, 1641, the King left London for Scotland. Cromwell and his fellow members, who had labored through a heavy and destructive session of ten months, soon granted themselves a brief holiday.

Just before the House of Commons adjourned themselves they again debated the Book of Common Prayer. Cromwell and the more Puritan-minded members were ruffled because little or nothing had yet been done about religion. They had of course been busy on other things. But were other things more important than religion? The root-and-branch bill, though it received its first two readings and was debated in committee, had by now been shelved. Sir John Culpepper, Cromwell's chief opponent over "root and branch," resisted equally those who "did vilify and contemn the Common Prayer Book." Cromwell vainly retorted that "there were many passages in it which divers learned and wise divines could not submit unto and practise." The most to which he could persuade the House to agree was that sermons should be given in all the parishes of England in the afternoons "at the charge of the inhabitants of those parishes where there were no sermons in the afternoon." An instruction was also published about the position of the communion table in the churches, reversing the orders of the late Archbishop Laud, but the House of Lords obstructed all violent changes. Next day the House dispersed.

To sum up Cromwell's career in the first session of the Long Parliament: like Pym and all the other leading parliamentarians who had received the finishing touches to their educations in the Inns of Court, Cromwell believed in the idea of a "balanced polity" with the Crown's rights limited by the property rights of his subjects. But his conduct in the House of Commons showed that what moved him most to wrath against the King and the King's ministers of state was not the invasion of property rights but the "innovations" in the Church promoted by Laud, Wren, and the other High Church bishops. He was outspoken about the need to abolish the bishops altogether, to reform the Prayer Book, to spread preaching thickly, and to restrict the Church services to the Protestant simplicities. He was passionate in attacking the accredited leaders of the Church, and in defending the Puritan martyrs who had criticized them earlier. Cromwell, like Pym and Hampden, was in no sense a conscious revolutionary. And in so far as he advocated sweeping changes in the religious organization of the country, he was largely defeated in this first session. Nevertheless, he had distinguished himself as a man of weight and a fearless Puritan. But it was not until the Long Parliament resumed its work in October 1641 that he revealed himself as more than an excitable country squire of intense faith and a modest worldly position, and proved himself, what he was always to be, not a constitutional reformer or a political thinker, but a man of action, capable of becoming the ruler of his country.

Notes

1. The constitutional history of the early seventeenth century has recently been subjected to intensive study, chiefly by American scholars on whose work the argument of the first part of the chapter is based: W. H. Coates, "Some Observations on the Grand Remonstrance," *Journal of Modern History,* IV, No. 1 (1932); F. Wormuth, *Royal Prerogative, 1603–1649* (1939); W. K. Jordan, *Men of Substance* (1942), who adopts the opposite position to that of Mr. Trevor-Roper; J. H. Hexter, *The Reign of King Pym* (1942); Harold P. Cooke, *Charles I and his Early Parliaments* (1942); C. H. McIlwain, "The English Common Law Barrier against Absolutism" in *American Historical Review,* XLIX (1943); Margaret A. Judson, *The Crisis of the Constitution* (1949); George L. Mosse, *The Struggle for Sovereignty in England* (1950). Striking British contributions are B. H. G. Wormald, *Clarendon, Politics, History and Religion, 1640–1660* (1951), and J. W. Gough, *Fundamental Law in English History* (1955).

2. Quoted in S. R. Gardiner, *History of England,* VIII, 78.

3. Quoted in W. Lilly, *True History of King James the First and King Charles the First* (1715).

4. Margaret Judson, *op. cit.,* 153.

5. *See* H. R. Trevor-Roper, "Country-house Radicals, 1590–1660" in *History Today* (1953), II, 461, based on his book, *The Gentry, 1540–1640* (Economic History Review Supplement, No. 1, 1953).

6. Add. MSS. 25302, ff. 48–50; *Calendar of State Papers (Domestic), 1631–1633,* 501, obviously wrongly placed.

7. I am deeply indebted to C. V. Wedgwood, *The King's Peace* (1955) for this section.

8. Cit. H. R. Trevor-Roper, *Archbishop Laud,* 363.

9. Mary Keeler, *op. cit.,* 11.

10. See W. H. Coates's edition of D'Ewes and introduction.

Chapter 5

Cromwell and the Coming of Civil War

WHEN THE SECOND SESSION of the Long Parliament opened in the autumn of 1641, Oliver Cromwell was forty-two and a half, in the prime of life. He is virtually the Cromwell of the portraits which Robert Walker painted before the Civil Wars ended. The long brown hair flowing down the back of his neck, the piercing blue-gray eyes, the aquiline nose, and the strength of the face are common to most of his portraits. But in the pictures by Walker he wears, too, a slightly puzzled and visionary air. The chin is pointed and the plain white collar lends a Puritan aspect to the martial figure in armor. If these portraits are contrasted with the later miniatures by Samuel Cooper, one can say that this is a man still moving forward into the unknown. He is the Seeker. With Cooper the chin has become squarer and perhaps a little flabby, but the face is calmer, more humane; it is still strong, but the touch of fanaticism has disappeared. In Cooper's portraits can be seen a man in authority who has mellowed.

By this time Cromwell's family life had become stabilized; all his children had been born—indeed, his eldest son, Robert, had already died at the age of eighteen in May 1639, "a promising youth who feared God beyond most men." Oliver had received his inheritances and was happily settled in Ely. But his work in the opening months of the Parliament had been his first complete experience of the nation's affairs. He had met and consulted with the principal figures in the House of Commons; he had mastered the essence of public business; he had served on important committees; and "he had called attention to himself by his uncompromising hostility to the Church, by his ill-regulated and undisciplined but dangerous qualities as an antagonist."

These last qualities he had shown in particular during one of the debates on the abolition of the bishops, when he was reproved for his unparliamentary language and threatened with being called to the Bar of the House to apologize to his opponent; on another occasion when he was speaking about the punishment of an apprentice for distributing libels against the Queen, his fervor impressed one of his audience sufficiently for him to recall it years afterwards in his memoirs. But the most striking feature of his conduct in the House had been his attacks on the Church. Convinced that he himself had found salvation and that only the individual Christian, by studying his heart and conning his Bible, could interpret the will of God, he was opposed to any rigid discipline and in favor of the right of each congregation to choose its own ministers. Whereas his friends John Pym and John Hampden would have accepted a compromise over Church matters and perhaps come to terms with men like Edward Hyde and John Culpepper, who were afterwards called into the King's counsels, Cromwell himself was the irrepressible advocate of "root and branch," determined that all should be allowed to worship God not according to rod and book but by their own light and consciences.

In terms of the reformation settlement of King Henry VIII, Cromwell's wish to put an end to the bishops was clearly a revolutionary demand. For it was the paradox of the Long Parliament that all its early criticisms of the King's administration and remedial legislation had been put forward in the name of conservatism, of the defense of old institutions. The whole House was agreed that the King's exercise of his prerogatives, both in the levying of extraordinary taxation and through the dispensation of justice in his prerogative courts, had been contrary to the common law or the "fundamental laws" of the kingdom. Archbishop Laud and the Earl of Strafford were held to have committed treason by the improper stretching of their powers; Strafford was condemned because he was alleged to have advised the King to bring over the Irish army to attack his own subjects. It is true that in order to protect their position the Commons had compelled the King not only to promise to call Parliament at least once every three years, but also not to dissolve the existing Parliament without its own consent. That indeed was the first revolutionary blow. But it had been struck not so much because members of Parliament, like Cromwell, had been intent on setting out new claims as because a chasm had opened between the monarch and many of his subjects. Queen Elizabeth I had done her best to understand and to soothe, and at times had given way to the middle classes who attended her Parliaments. King James I, whatever his shortcomings, had been reared in a Calvinist environment and, sensing something of the feelings of the new classes in his southern kingdom, was wise enough not to provoke them too far. But King Charles I lived in a narrower world where pride and affection blinded him to realities. Like Louis XIV, soon to become King of France, he did not altogether trust his subjects, and they did not all trust him.

The atmosphere of suspicion that hung between Parliament and the King was marked by three decisions taken in the late summer of 1641. First, the two Houses published an "ordinance" promulgated without the authority of the King, a startling extension of their authority (though naturally a medieval precedent was exhumed to sustain it); secondly, the parliamentary commission that had followed the King to Scotland, nominally to help him to conclude the treaty of peace, was engaged upon spying into his movements; lastly, during the short adjournment of the Parliament each House set up a committee to watch over events and correspond with the joint committee that had been sent to Scotland. Thus Parliament never loosened its grip upon the nation's affairs.

*　　　*　　　*

When the Commons reassembled on October 20, 1641, the political skies were overcast. A desultory plot on the King's behalf engineered by a group of drunken professional soldiers in the neighborhood of Edinburgh had been magnified into the story that the young and attractive Earl of Montrose had offered to kill the Covenanting chiefs, lay hold of Edinburgh, and take up arms for Charles I. Far more dangerous than imaginary plots in Scotland was the outbreak of a rebellion in Ireland begun by the Catholics in Ulster, who hoped, now Strafford had gone, that they might be able to extort from the Government in London the same concessions that the Covenanters had won for their Kirk in Scotland. This rebellion, with its accompanying murders of Protestants, was not, however, known to the House of Commons until a few days after its first meeting.

For a few days matters continued along their customary ways. With unabated ardor Oliver Cromwell resumed his campaign against the bishops. Before the recess thirteen bishops had been impeached for allowing Convocation to continue sitting after the dissolution of the Short Parliament. Cromwell now moved that these bishops should be suspended from voting in the House of Lords while the Bishops Exclusion Bill was under discussion. When King Charles was in Scotland he had appointed five new bishops (most of them moderate men) to fill the vacancies in the episcopate. On October 29 Cromwell moved that the investiture of these new bishops should be suspended. He spoke with particular bitterness against one of them, Dr. Houldsworth, the Master of Emmanuel and Archdeacon of Huntingdon. Here the opinion of the Member for Cambridge and former Member for Huntingdon was no doubt heard with respect, though Dr. Houldsworth appears to have been harmless.

But the Commons had more urgent questions to settle even than the future of bishops. John Pym was engaged in pressing forward two proposals intended further to pare the powers of the monarchy. In the first place it was urged not merely that the "evil" counsellors of the King should be removed, but that Parliament should henceforward have a right of veto on the appointment of all officers of state. Edward Hyde resisted this proposal on the ground that the choice of great officers was a "hereditary flower of the Crown." He had also opposed the Bishops Exclusion Bill, and thought in general that public affairs were in a good condition if they could be preserved as they were. Thus for a moment the proposal hung fire. Pym's other idea was that Parliament should draw up and publish a "grand remonstrance" to the King, that could be published as an appeal to the nation recalling every wrong he had done during his reign.

When the news of the Irish rebellion reached London at the beginning of November, striking terror into all Protestant hearts, it gave a fresh impetus to John Pym's determination to wrest more of the King's authority away from him. It was clear that the insurrection must be suppressed. But the Commons were agreed that the King could not be trusted with a relief army to put down these popish rebels. Was he not himself, as his support of Laud had shown, "popishly inclined"? Was not the Queen the focus of papal propaganda in the kingdom? In any case, supposing the royal army were victorious, might the King not turn it, as Strafford (so they believed) had advised him to turn it, against his obstreperous English subjects? This distrust of the King, which made Parliament afraid to give him control over another army, led, more than any other single cause, to the first Civil War.[1] On November 6 Oliver Cromwell moved to desire the House of Lords to join with them in passing an ordinance to give the Puritan-minded Robert Devereux, Earl of Essex, the power "to assemble at all times the trained bands of the kingdom on this side Trent for the defence thereof till further order be taken by Parliament." Essex had already been put in command of the trained bands by King Charles himself, but the intention of Cromwell's motion was to acquire the control of military appointments for Parliament.

Three days later the Grand Remonstrance was read for the first time; among the complaints listed in its 206 clauses was one relating to the draining of the Fens, and Cromwell was called upon to explain what had happened there. But more significant than the long list of grievances was the petition to the King that preceded them. This petition insisted that the King's Council still included men who favored and promoted "pressures and corruptions" and demanded that "for the future Your Majesty will vouchsafe to employ such persons in your great and public affairs, and to take such to be near you in places of trust, as your Parliament may have cause to confide in." It also again required that the bishops should be deprived of their places in the House of Lords.

Over these revolutionary constitutional changes, which were proposed by Oliver Cromwell and his friends, the House of Commons was at last split asunder. The nucleus of an opposition had been provided by some of those who had resisted "root and branch" and partly by men, like Edward Hyde, who thought that the punishment of the King for his "eleven years' tyranny" had now gone far enough and henceforward King and Parliament ought to work together for the good of the country. Hyde and his group neither wished to pluck the flower of prerogative from King Charles I nor to provoke him further by publishing his errors. They asked for time to consider the charges set out in the Remonstrance. Cromwell himself could not understand why there was need to postpone the discussion. To him the issues were plain. He thought that the outcome of the debate was certain and that few would dare to oppose the Remonstrance. In that he was completely mistaken. The final debate was unique in the history of the century; it began at midday on November 22 and continued till one the next morning. Hyde, Falkland, and Culpepper resisted the Remonstrance with all their skill in argument as being ill-timed, grossly insulting in tone, and unconstitutional in character. A few modifications were introduced in deference to their criticisms, but John Pym, brandishing the overriding argument of "necessity," triumphed in the end. The Grand Remonstrance was carried by 159 votes to 148. The final scene after the vote was one of unparalleled excitement, with swords banged and rattled and the large minority asking to record their protest. "During the small hours of November 23," observes a recent historian,[2] "the Parliamentarians as a party which fought the civil war was born." But for Hyde and his friends, who were later to become Royalists, it was near to a moral victory. According to Hyde himself, writing some years afterwards, Cromwell told Falkland after the debate that "if the Grand Remonstrance had been rejected, he would have sold all he had the next morning, and never seen England any more."

Thus at last the House of Commons had ceased to be either a part of the King's Great Council or a harmonious institution laboring in a common and traditional faith; it had become divided into parties in deadly opposition to one another; the veneer of conservatism had vanished, and Oliver Cromwell himself, the root-and-branch man of the first session, had taken his place as one of John Pym's first lieutenants in the last stage of the battle with the monarchy for power. The plea of "necessity," which Pym had invoked on behalf of the Grand Remonstrance, was to drive Cromwell along uncharted paths. No man rises so high as he who knows not where he is going.

*　　*　　*

Two days after the Grand Remonstrance had been passed King Charles I returned to London. In Scotland he had completely failed to enlist a Royalist party; on the contrary, he had been compelled to do in Edinburgh what Pym was demanding from him at Westminster, namely to appoint his ministers in accordance with the wishes of his Parliament. The Earl of Argyll, the acknowledged leader of the Covenanters, had been created a marquis and his power seemed to rest "on those very classes, the representatives of the counties and boroughs, who made up the House of Commons at Westminster." Ireland was ablaze. Pym was increasing his demands for constitutional concessions. Nevertheless, the King was unfailingly optimistic and uncommonly gracious. In reply to the Grand Remonstrance he temporized, promising to meet his subjects' wishes "in a parliamentary way," and even thanked Parliament for its qualified promises to aid him in supressing the Irish rebellion. Though he refused to give up the right to appoint his own ministers, he again invited Pym to become Chancellor of the Exchequer and actually appointed Culpepper and Falkland to posts in his Council. Fnally, after his absence he tried all he knew to invoke the traditional loyalty of London to the throne. The lord mayor and aldermen were keen Royalists and received him enthusiastically. Cromwell was not too pleased about this.

> Mr. Cromwell [noted a parliamentary diarist] brought in a testimonial of one James Best dwelling in Paternoster Row by which he witnessed that one (whom he named not lest he should withdraw himself) had said: that this House was offended that the City of London gave the King such great entertainment and that the said House did send to the said City not to entertain him.

Best was required to testify to these indiscreet but no doubt well-founded observations.

Meanwhile the pressure against the bishops, still damned with the stigma of the Laudian era, was undiminished. The rising in Ireland had appeared to illuminate the perils of popery returning to England. The temper of the Commons had already been revealed when one of its members had ventured to suggest that a Latin psalter might be restored to a Roman Catholic gentlewoman from whom it had been taken. To restore it to her, the House had decided, would be to make her "guilty of idolatry and superstition." Three days after this odd incident the Commons had voted, by a majority of 124 to 99, that the bishops had in fact themselves already introduced "idolatry and popery" into the Church of England. Thus the King, who, whatever he might have yielded to the Scots, was still inflexibly resolved to uphold the Church of England, was confronted by men diametrically opposed to his own way of thinking. He insisted that he would maintain the Protestant religion as established in the time of Queen Elizabeth at the hazard of his life and all that was dear to him; but the feelings of Protestant London were indicated by the appearance of demonstrators crying out "no bishops" in Palace Yard.

The majority of the Commons, including Cromwell, remained unshaken in their suspicions of the King. "The same men who had brought in the root-and-branch bill to regulate the Church, now brought in a root-and-branch bill to regulate the army."[3] They would neither allow King Charles to control the militia nor entrust him with the dispatch of an expeditionary force to fight the Irish. While arguments on these questions flashed to and fro between the two Houses of Parliament and the King continued to withstand the extreme demands accompanying the Grand Remonstrance, the London mob demonstrated unceasingly. The House of Lords resented the menaces of the apprentices; the Commons, who had no guard to protect them from intimidation by the Crown, did not. Oliver Cromwell was asking that the King should remove the Earl of Bristol from his counsels at the very time when Bristol's son was asserting that, in view of the menaces of the rabble, Parliament was no longer free.

In this highly charged atmosphere the King and the majority of the Commons feared the worst of each other. The King believed that the leaders of the Commons had deliberately incited the London mob with the object of overthrowing the monarchy. The leaders of the Commons thought that the withdrawal of their own guard placed them in danger of violence. And they were not so wrong. Without consulting his new counsellors, the King retorted to rumors that the Queen was to be impeached by coming to the House himself with a big armed retinue intending to arrest five of its members and indict them for treason. But they were forewarned and found protection among their friends in the City. Frustrated in his desperate and belated *coup d'etat,* King Charles withdrew from London, and the shadows of the coming civil war lengthened over the land.

Queen Henrietta Maria, who inspired the coup (though some such action had earlier been suggested by Strafford), was ready to fight with help from abroad, if it could be obtained. She threatened to enter a nunnery if her husband did not show himself to be a man, and for a time he seems to have contemplated seizing the strong places in his kingdom and fighting it out with the Commons. Before the end of February 1642, Henrietta Maria herself had sailed to Holland to pawn the Crown jewels in order to raise money for war. Meanwhile, though his wisest advisers besought him to go back to London, the King stayed out of the city, and engaged in long-distance negotiations. The leaders of the Commons wanted the control of the militia and the appointment of the officers in command of all the forts and garrisons. They sent one of their own members, Sir John Hotham, to secure Hull, which was an arsenal as well as a port, and they compelled the King to change the Lieutenant of the Tower of London.

But as yet neither party was anxious to push matters to extremities. During February the King adopted a more conciliatory policy. Though he would not give up complete control of the militia, he offered some concessions, and he accepted the Bishops Exclusion Bill, hoping thereby to preserve the bishops in their spiritual functions. He also called Edward Hyde into consultation in framing soft answers to some of Parliament's more outrageous demands. Indeed, Hyde and Pym still had one thing in common up to the spring of 1642: both hoped that negotiations with the King might yield peace with security, though to achieve that the King would unquestionably have been compelled to give up many of his established constitutional rights.

*   *   *

Oliver Cromwell was not one of the five members whom the King had vainly tried to arrest: William Strode, who introduced the bill for annual Parliaments (Cromwell had moved the second reading), was among them, and so was his cousin Hampden. A slightly more extensive list might easily have included his name. At any rate, during the first half of the new year he was proving himself to be the "practical, willing, and industrious lieutenant of his leader, Pym." On January 14 he asked for the appointment of a committee to consider means to "put the kingdom in a posture of defence." On February 1 he lent £300 for the succor of Dublin. Earlier he drew the attention of the House to an accusation leveled against a justice of the peace in Huntingdon, who was reported to have said "if King and Parliament should differ, the most of the gentry would be for the King, and that he had 1,000 men ready to assist."

But even in those hectic days Cromwell did not forget his old love, "root and branch." Sir Edward Dering, who first introduced the bill to abolish the bishops and deans at the request of Cromwell and Vane, had since published his own arguments in favor of what he called a "primitive episcopacy." His was one of a number of plans put forward as a compromise over the future government of the English Church. Cromwell was against any kind of compromise. Angrily he demanded that Dering's book should be burnt; that an M.P. should be selected to confute its obnoxious doctrines; and the unlucky knight was sent to the Tower for a week. Cromwell himself was appointed to a committee to draw up yet another bill for disabling the bishops.

The middle of March was the turning point in the negotiations with the King. After King Charles had finally refused to give way on the question, the two Houses on March 5 passed an ordinance taking upon themselves the control of the militia. The King absolutely refused to accept this, and on March 16 sent a message from Cromwell's native town of Huntingdon saying that no ordinance passed without his consent could have the force of law. On March 17 Cromwell was appointed, along with Pym, Hampden, and others, to examine the King's message and to find out "who were the advisers thereof." In fact one of the advisers was Cromwell's and Pym's old colleague in the House, Edward Hyde. By now the King had decided to go north and rally his supporters and resources there. The battles lines were being drawn and Cromwell himself was in the front of them.

*　　　　*　　　　*

Meanwhile the problem of Ireland had become bedeviled by English politics. The Lords Justices, who ruled the country after the execution of Strafford, had at their disposal only some 3,000 soldiers scattered all over the country. The original rising in Ulster had degenerated into a *jacquerie* of inflamed peasants, and the Ulster rebels were soon reinforced by the Irish Catholic Lords. But the English Parliament moved in a leisurely way. First it dwelt on the question of how to keep the control of the relief army out of the hands of the King; secondly on whether it was advisable to send a Scottish as well an an English force to the rescue. An Impressment Bill to raise men in England hung fire and was a source of squabbling between the two Houses. A few troops had found their way to Ireland by February, and well-officered and trained men proved more than a match for a horde of unarmed peasants. But after four months the rebellion was too widespread to be put down except by a large army. Parliament at length decided to find money to pay for restoring order in Ireland by means of a wholesale confiscation of Irish land. It was declared that 10,000,000 acres, a third of the entire country, had become liable to confiscation, and that a quarter of it should be assigned to subscribers to a war loan. King Charles I assented to a bill for that purpose on March 19, 1642, virtually the last act of agreement ever reached between him and his Parliament. Cromwell busied himself over the matter. He was on a commission "for speeding and despatching the business of Ireland," and later on another to administer the defense of Ireland; and he was among the first to subscribe £500 for a thousand acres in

Leinster. Furthermore, he reported to the House "that the strength of the papists was so great about the town of Monmouth as they feared if some speedy course were not taken it would be in as great danger shortly as Ireland." That report, however, proved exaggerated. He also concerned himself over seditious pamphlets and tumults against the activities of Parliament; over the defense of Hull, to which the King was denied admission; and he carried a report to the House of Lords about a Royalist demonstration on Blackheath.

On May 20 the House of Commons declared that the King was preparing to attack Parliament, and from this moment the planning of civil war was intensified. Cromwell took an increasing interest in the strategic situation. The King, it was obvious, needed to keep open communications with the Continent, from which he hoped for assistance organized by his Queen. As he had established his headquarters at York, after vainly attempting to gain control of Hull, Parliament was anxious to obtain hold of all the ports and fortresses in the northeast. On May 23 Cromwell was appointed to a committee whose business it was to prevent forces being raised for the King in Yorkshire, and to secure the obedience of that county to Parliament. On June 1 Cromwell informed a committee, which was considering reports of a fleet being gathered in Norway and Denmark to assist the Royalists, that ships had been stationed to guard Tynemouth and Newcastle in order to prevent the landing of arms for the King. On the following day he was named one of the members to whom the carrying out of a parliamentary ordinance for raising new military and naval forces was committed.

As summer came the drums were beating everywhere in the country. They were beating for volunteers for service in Ireland. In the counties new Lords Lieutenant and Deputies named by the parliamentary majority were trying to organize the militia, while the King retorted by issuing his own Commissions of Array. On June 17 the Earl of Newcastle succeeded in seizing Newcastle upon Tyne for the King—Cromwell was on a committee of nineteen to inquire into how that had happened. Twelve days earlier he had produced another £500 as his personal contribution to the defense of Parliament. At the beginning of July he was asking the remnant of the House of Lords (many of whose members had by now joined the King in York) to agree to Cambridgeshire and other counties executing Parliament's militia ordinance, and on July 15 he moved that the town of Cambridge should be invited to raise two companies of volunteers. That was in pursuit of the decision taken by Parliament three days before to create an army "for the safety of the King's person and the defence of both kingdoms," with the Earl of Essex as its commander. Cromwell's name appears in almost every aspect of Parliament's military activities during the tense and unhappy months of June and July 1642.

While Cromwell and his colleagues were absorbed in their preparations for war, they were far too busy to stop and think how and why the war was coming. After Hyde and the members who had been opposed to the destruction of the episcopacy and to Parliament seizing the power of the sword had left Westminster to join the King in York, the revolutionary group in London had proclaimed their final demands on the monarchy in "Nineteen Propositions' sent to the King on June 2. These formed an ultimatum asking the King completely to surrender his executive authority and military power and to abandon the Church of England to the rule of the Puritans. It had come to that at last. The King realized that to assent to such an ultimatum would be to give up all but his formal functions, and he refused to do it. Yet Parliament still talked glibly about defending the King and the Church. Such was the paradox. What was the reality?

Even today historians differ violently about the causes of the civil wars.[4] How deep were the social causes? It cannot be denied that from the early days of Queen Elizabeth I the classes represented in the House of Commons, consisting chiefly of gentry, had become increasingly influential, vocal, and demanding. By the time the Long Parliament was elected they had been reinforced by lawyers, merchants, and financiers with a rich sense of their claims to power. During 1641 the Long Parliament, its members acting together almost as one man and given their opportunity by King Charles's failure in his Scottish wars, succeeded in destroying many of the royal prerogatives. But Oliver Cromwell and his friends were unwilling to let matters rest there, for two reasons: first, because while the King had given way over the prerogative courts, the irregular taxes, and the new monopolies, and had admitted the right of Parliament to meet frequently, he had not yielded to the full Puritan demands for the reform of the Church; secondly, after the King's vain intrigues in Scotland, his attempt to arrest the five members, and the Queen's voyage to Holland in search of money and help, they did not trust their unstable and uxorious ruler to keep the bargains that he had concluded with them. They had exerted their strength and made good their claims, but they were not at all sure that they could maintain their position.

As late as February 1642, the differences between men like Pym and Hyde might have been bridged except that the former did not trust the King and the latter did. Now, by way of reaction against the "arbitrariness" of one half of the House of Commons, those who either desired the Church to remain much as it was or who felt they must be loyal to their King, right or wrong, were ready to fight for him; while those who, like Cromwell, regarded the bishops as tyrants or worse and feared and suspected the real designs of the Court and its "popish" entourage, were convinced that for the sake of their own salvation and, ultimately even of the King's immortal soul, they must be ready to do battle. The English Civil War was not the product of petty passions, of intrigues, jealousies, or spite. Each side had its faith and principles. But at the crux, as in most wars, the trigger was pulled not by malice but mistrust.

*   *   *

It was natural that in making ready for war each member of Parliament should assume responsibility for the measures in his own constituency. The University of Cambridge was far from being enthusiastically Royalist. It had genuinely mourned the death of King James I, but Charles's reserved manner was contrasted unfavorably with his father's loquacity. Moreover, the University had resented the way in which the late Duke of Buckingham had been thrust upon it as its Chancellor. Nor were the Colleges uninfluenced by the spirit of Puritanism, stemming from Professor Cartwright and the prevailing atmosphere in the eastern counties. The heads of nearly half the Colleges were vigorous Calvinists, though that did not necessarily prevent them, as in the case of Dr. Ward of Sidney Sussex, from being Royalists. If the University was only lukewarm in its attitude towards the King (who had paid it a flying visit on his way north), the town, as it had already shown by its choice of representatives for the Long Parliament, was definitely Puritan. Cromwell was therefore in a position to call upon it for support. During July not only did he persaude the two Houses of Parliament to agree to the county putting the parliamentary militia ordinance into execution and to the town enlisting companies of volunteers, but he advanced out of his own pocket £100 for the purchase of arms by the High Constable of the county.

The King, assuming that both his Universities would be loyal, had on June 29 invited the Colleges to lend him money at interest of eight per cent. Cambridge proved less generous than Oxford, although Sidney Sussex, still under the Mastership of Dr. Samuel Ward, contributed £100 (four times the amount of Ward's own annual salary) and set aside plate of equivalent value until it had been repaid. (The piece of plate that Cromwell had given the College when he was a Fellow Commoner was not available for the purpose, as it had already been sold to buy land for the College.[5]) Not content with this, the King had on July 24 sent another letter to the University suggesting that as the Parliamentarians might sequester the College plate, it should all be committed to his own custody. The Colleges did not take kindly to this ingenious proposal, but some of them agreed to dispatch a few pieces to the royal treasury. Did that plate ever in fact leave the town of Cambridge? The story that is usually told is that the Cambridge Royalists managed to smuggle a good deal of plate to King Charles I in Nottingham, even though Cromwell did his best to prevent it. This story rests mainly on three sources, all of which are derived from St. John's College, the center of the local Royalist movement. A detailed account appears in a life of John Barwick, a Fellow of St. John's, which was written by his brother and published eighty years after the events. A shorter and less specific reference is in a pamphlet entitled *Querela Cantabrigiensis*, which simply says that the designs of one "Master Cromwell" were frustrated and "his opinion as of an active subtile man thereby somewhat shaken and endangered." This pamphlet was in fact compiled in Oxford from materials supplied by Dr. Barwick in London. Yet why should one trust as serious evidence of Cromwell's deeds in Cambridge a Royalist pamphlet published in Oxford?

The facts about the dispatch of the plate appear to be these. It was not until August 8 that St. John's College decided to send some of its plate to the King. Two days later a certain captain of the Cambridgeshire trained bands, on orders from the Sheriff of Cambridgeshire, arrived in Cambridge to convoy the plate and barricaded himself against Cromwell in the Court of King's College. Cromwell himself had made his last appearance in the House of Commons on August 1 before leaving for Cambridge. He had then been instructed to prepare a scheme to send more volunteers to Ireland and, with three others from Cambridge, to carry out plans to buy plate and horses, and obtain money. We do not know exactly when he arrived in Cambridge. But the captain of the trained bands was arrested by him on August 10, and five days later it was reported to the House of Commons that "Mr. Cromwell in Cambridgeshire has seized the Magazine of the Castle at Cambridge and hath hindered the carrying of the plate from that University, which some report was to the value of £20,000 or thereabouts." It is perfectly true that other plate from Cambridge may earlier have been smuggled out to the King. Queens' College, for example, had agreed to send him plate on August 3. But it is also known for certain that Cromwell and his friend and brother-in-law, Valentine Walton, who was an M.P. for Huntingdonshire, were taking active military steps at least as early as August 4 or 5 to intercept the plate. The Royalist tale that Cromwell was over-reached and that a large quantity of plate was received by the King in Nottingham is unlikely, and is tainted at its source.[6]

The point is of importance because Oliver Cromwell's arrest of the captain of the Cambridgeshire trained bands, his impounding of the plate assigned to the King, and his seizure of the castle were among the very earliest actions of the Civil War. It is certain that the House of Commons was pleased with what he had done; for he received indemnity for "stopping the plate that was going to York"; he was given orders to care for the safety and peace of Cambridge, exercise its trained bands and volunteers, and disarm Roman Catholics, and was commanded to block bridges and ferries between Cambridge and King's Lynn to prevent arms or horses from reaching the King in the north. On August 22 King Charles set up his standard in Nottingham and a week later Cromwell himself began to enlist his own troop of horse at his old home town of Huntingdon, with John Desborough, another brother-in-law, as its quartermaster. During the summer months he had been one of the most eager and tireless of all the members of Parliament who were preparing to fight the King as well as supervising the war in Ireland. Cromwell now moved from his desk to his saddle, with faith in his cause and determination in his heart. He was never to lose a battle or to fail in a campaign. There is no real reason to suppose that his very first action, the securing of Cambridge for his own side, was other than faultlessly executed.

Notes

1. I find this argument of Dr. C. V. Wedgwood convincing.

2. B. H. G. Wormald, *op. cit.,* 28.

3. S. R. Gardiner, *History of England* (1884), X, 95.

4. Four distinguished historians, Dr. C. V. Wedgwood, Mr. H. R. Trevor-Roper, Mr. D. H. Pennington and Mr. Christopher Hill, took part in a discussion broadcast on the B.B.C. Third Programme on March 23 and 27, 1955, on "The Causes of the English Civil War." The most striking thing about the discussion was how deeply they disagreed.

5. My attention was drawn to this by the Master of Sidney Sussex College.

6. Both W. C. Abbott and Alfred Kingston, *East Anglia and the Great Civil War* (1896), suggested that the Royalists bamboozled Cromwell, but it seems to me that they relied too much on the evidence of Dr. John Barwick. The other side of the case is well put by F. J. Varley, *Cambridge during the Civil War* (1935).

Chapter 6

England Prepares for Civil War

"THOU WOULDST THINK it strange," wrote Sir John Oglander, the Isle of Wight Royalist, who had an income just a little above Cromwell's own, in observations left for the benefit of his posterity, "if I should tell thee there was a time in England when brothers killed brothers, cousins cousins, and friends their friends. . . . When thou wentst to bed at night, thou knewst not whether thou shouldst be murdered afore day. . . . Sacrilege was a virtue, and to rail against sovereignty esteemed a high piece of piety." This shock and fear were widely felt among the gentlemen of England who found themselves or their families, much against their wills, engulfed in the Civil War.

It is easy to understand why they were mystified by the play of events. The older generation was accustomed to the idea of the monarchy and the Parliament as harmonious bodies, each with its own recognized place in the scheme of society. Queen Elizabeth I and her Parliaments had experienced their differences, but in the end the old Queen and her faithful Commons had discovered a means of living and working together, and even King James I had envisaged the possibility of holding a "parliament of love." In 1642 men and women who were not normally much concerned with politics searched their minds and wondered what it was all about.[1] Both sides were thought not to be free from blame for the pass to which affairs had come. Some who lived in the country spoke of their disappointment in the work of the Long Parliament, complained of the new burdens imposed upon them, and thought that promises had been broken at Westminster; others went on their knees to King Charles I as he perambulated the Midlands and the north, and begged him to go back to Whitehall and make it up with the representatives of his subjects. Could not King and Parliament even now mend their quarrel somehow? Such was the heartfelt cry heard throughout the land in the summer of 1642.

Even after King Charles I had set up his standard at Nottingham with much ceremony, he submitted to pressures to exert one last effort to conciliate Parliament. He did so only to receive a more than dusty answer. For on September 6 not only was his peace offer spurned, but Parliament insisted on the punishment of all men who had already committed themselves to his side. That was to inflame the wounds of war before it had begun. The lords and gentlemen who had ridden away from their homes to join their King in the north or who had sent him money and plate now knew that they must stick to him to the very end—or betray him utterly.

Two generalizations have often been published about England at the opening of the Civil War: the first is that, on the whole, the peers and better-off gentry were for the King, while the lesser gentry, the yeomen, and the mercantile and industrial classes were against him; the second is that geographically the country could be divided by a line running southwest from Scarborough to Plymouth, the area above the line being Royalist and that below the line being Parliamentarian. Modern investigations, at any rate those concerned with the structure of the Long Parliament, have induced some skepticism about the class character of the two sides that fought in the Civil War,[2] and, as to the geographical division, it can safely be said, in the light of our knowledge of local history, that few counties in England could be given a political label in 1642. In some counties the majority of the boroughs were clearly for Parliament, while the big landlords and their relatives were for the King. In other counties sympathizers from each side came together to work out schemes whereby the war that they saw was coming, or which, if skirmishes and blood-letting meant anything, had already come, could be thrust away from their own borders. Such schemes were discussed in Cheshire, Lancashire, Yorkshire, Nottinghamshire, Somerset, Dorset, Devon, and Cornwall. But by the autumn plans for local neutralization were impracticable; neither Parliament nor the King would assent to them.

Indeed, ever since the Militia Ordinance had been promulgated by Parliament in March and the King had retorted with his own Commissions of Array, both sides had their agents everywhere at work looking for support from men of influence and means, trying to obtain control over such arms and horses as were available, and laboring to arouse the enthusiasm of the "trained bands." The usual procedure on the Parliamentary side was for the House of Commons to send down the local M.P. into his own constituency and instruct him to join with the Lord Lieutenant and Deputy Lords Lieutenant of the county approved by them, or with the mayor and aldermen in the case of boroughs, to impound stocks of ammunition and weapons, and to frustrate the Kings' Commissioners of Array. On the King's side it was usually expected that the local magnates, from the royal Lord Lieutenant downwards, would at their own expense raise soldiers and forward arms and plate to his headquarters.

But the truth was that outside London very little in the way of trained man power was to be had. In peace time the militia met only one day a month during the summer for perfunctory training, and much of the time was spent in carousing rather than on drill. The god that presided at the monthly exercises of the trained bands, observed a contemporary, was Bacchus and not Mars. In Devonshire it was said that half of the trained bands in the county did not even know how to handle their weapons. Sir John Oglander related how when in the summer of 1639 the Earl of Portland, the commander of the Isle of Wight, paid a visit of inspection he "killed deer, spent wine, and made good cheer, but never called a muster or consulted about the affairs of the county." Afterwards he went across to Portsmouth to meet the Governor, Colonel Goring (who surrendered the town in the early days of the war). They drank more wine and shot more game. "I may truly say," remarked the diarist, "that in the space of six days there never was so much powder fired, except against an enemy." In fact, in the halcyon days before the clouds broke over Scotland and Ireland few Englishmen took their soldiering seriously. The bulk of the militia, who formed the bone of contention between Parliament and the King after he left London, were no more trained for war than the special constabulary of later times.

The King did have the advantage that a number of the officers who had fought on the Protestant side in the Thirty Years War or for the Dutch against the Spaniards were ready to serve him (though others, like Sir Thomas Fairfax and Phillip Skippon, enlisted on the side of Parliament). Moreover, the hunting and shooting squires were to make pretty good cavalry officers under the inspired leadership of the King's young nephew, Prince Rupert of the Rhine. If one were to judge from some of the contemporary evidence that has survived, one would assume that a large reservoir of Royalist officers existed—especially if the terms officer and gentlemen are considered synonymous. "The King's side were almost all gentlemen," wrote Oglander, "and of the Parliament's few."

"There were very few gentlemen or men of quality," wrote Hyde, speaking of Yorkshire, "who were actively or factiously opposed to His Majesty." "All the nobility and gentry and their dependents," noted Mrs. Hutchinson in her memoir of her husband, "were generally for the King"—she was speaking of Nottinghamshire where she lived. But apart from the fact that officers alone do not constitute an army, even these generalizations were not valid. In Yorkshire the Fairfaxes, men of influence and standing, rallied to the Parliamentary side. In the Isle of Wight Oglander himself was said to be "the only delinquent," that is to say, the only active Royalist, and after his remark about "almost all gentlemen" being on the King's side, he admitted that his own brother George was "a most violent man for the Parliament's cause." As to Nottinghamshire, where the royal standard was set up, the King himself disarmed the trained bands in the neighborhood, preferring their weapons to their company, and while southern Nottinghamshire, on the whole, was Royalist, the north was much inclined to Puritanism.

Let us look a little more closely at the English counties, and see the kind of pattern that existed when the Civil War broke out.[3] In Lancashire, for example, the great man was James Stanley, Lord Strange, son and heir to the sixth Earl of Derby. He was the King's Lord Lieutenant not only in Lancashire but also in Cheshire. Like all the Stanleys in modern times, he wielded immense influence and wealth. Other local magnates were King's men. Warrington, Bury, Rochdale, Preston, Lancaster, and Wigan were all Royalist in sympathy. Warrington was so keenly Royalist that Lord Strange had begged the King to raise his standard there instead of at Nottingham. But Manchester, a town with a population of some 5,000, which was beginning to prosper by weaving, was Parliamentarian; so were Salford, Blackburn, and Bolton, and much of the southeast. And when as early as July 15 Strange tried to gain control of the magazine in Manchester, he was rebuffed and had voluntarily to withdraw from the town, and during the early stages of the war the men of Manchester sallied forth and captured Royalist Preston. On September 27 King Charles I invited the Roman Catholics of Lancashire to arm in his defense, and they did all they could for him. Young William Blundell of Crosby, for example, raised a hundred dragoons and ventured everything he had for his King. But he was crippled for life at the siege of Lancaster in 1643, and this so-called Royalist and Roman Catholic county played only a minor part on the King's side. Though it had the reputation of being the most Catholic county in England and was always a center of Royalist hopes, it was in fact a crisscross of divided loyalties.

Cross the Pennines into Yorkshire. Yorkshire was by no means uniformly Royalist. The resentment over the enlistment for the first hapless Bishops' War had bitten wide and deep. In July 1640 the gentry of York had protested against the billeting of soldiers (an inevitability since there were no barracks) as being contrary to the promises given by the King in the Petition of Right. In September of that same year many of the gentlemen of Yorkshire had petitioned for the summoning of Parliament to remedy their grievances. During meetings held in and around York in the summer of 1642 contradictory feelings were expressed. Not only were many of the small towns, later to become famous as centers of the woolen textile industry, both Puritan and anti-Royalist, but even in Hull a strong Puritan element existed, since much of the town's trade was with Holland and many of its inhabitants were the descendants of Dutch merchants. On the whole, the West Riding was for Parliament, and the North and East Ridings were Royalist. Many influential gentry were devoted to the King, and were ready to sacrifice their lives and properties for him:

> We do not suffer here alone;
> Though we are beggar'd, so's the King.
> 'Tis sin t'have wealth when he has none;
> Tush, poverty's a royal thing!

Just as royal exactions alienated tough Yorkshire yeomen, so Parliament's demands when it assumed full powers angered the well-to-do. "I hope the parliament will laye no more taxes on the cuntrye," wrote a Yorkshire lady from Malton in May 1642, " for rents are paid noe where"; and a fortnight later: "I wish all ware well ended, for things stand in soe ill a condition here as we can make no money of our Colpits. If rents faill and those faill to, we shall be A hard case." None of those Yorkshire people wanted war in the least; they hoped for some compromise or, failing that, local neutrality. They certainly did not desire to fight their own friends. The Fairfaxes, who became the first leaders of the Yorkshire Parliamentarians, were on terms of intimate friendship with those who became heroic Royalists. The

Hothams, who had occupied and held Hull for Parliament, were far from being political fanatics. Indeed, a letter written by young Hotham to the Earl of Newcastle (a Royalist) typified the attitude of the people who counted in Yorkshire; in his letter he said that he hoped neither side would conquer in the war—"for it will then be as it was between Caesar and Pompey: whosoever had the better, the Roman liberty was sure to have the worse."

The King had set up his standard in Nottingham because it appeared to him as if in the group of counties lying to the south of Yorkshire he had found a strong group of adherents. If he could assemble and concentrate his forces in this area, he might occupy inner lines, and if his Queen could bring succor through one of the northern ports and Colonel Goring retained his hold on Portsmouth, the rebels in London, that "sink of iniquity," might in time be overwhelmed. Yet the loyalties of the Midlands were mixed. In Nottinghamshire itself public opinion was not altogether Royalist. "Though the gentlemen of ancient families and estates in that county were for the most part well affected to the King," wrote Edward Hyde, "yet there were people of inferior charges who by good husbandry, clothing, and other thriving had gotten very great fortunes and by degrees getting themselves into gentlemen's estates were angry they found not themselves in the same esteem and reputations with those whose estates they had." All the peers and most of the gentry who lived around the small towns of Nottingham and Newark were for the King, but they did not rush eagerly to serve his cause, while an energetic minority, including young Henry Ireton of Attenborough and his friends, were from the beginning supporters of the Parliamentary side, and so was the Mayor of Nottingham.

The neighboring counties were equally mixed in their sympathies. Northern Lincolnshire tended to be Royalist, but the south was on the whole Parliamentarian. The little county of Rutland, which had two Royalist M.P.s in the Long Parliament and had accepted ship money more amiably than most counties, was nevertheless violently anti-"papist." While the oldest son of Viscount Campden, the doyen of the county Royalists, was among the first to raise a regiment of horse for King Charles, Sir Edward Harington, the leading Parliamentarian, managed to secure the magazine at Oakham for his own side. Still Lord Grey of Groby, who was later put in command of the Midland Association of counties by Parliament, testified that if he had not entered Rutland in the nick of time, "I am confident in one week the whole county would have been drawn into a body against the Parliament."

Neighboring Leicestershire was a cockpit parceled out between the families of Hastings and Grey. The northern and western parts were Royalist, the southern and eastern parts Parliamentarian. In this county it was the Royalists who ultimately succeeded in laying their hands on the county magazine. But the town of Leicester itself was Puritan, and Prince Rupert provoked it by brusquely demanding £2,000 from its coffers; he obtained only £500 after the King had intervened. In Bedfordshire again the county magnates were at loggerheads: the Earls of Cleveland and Peterborough were for Parliament; the fifth Earl of Bedford showed impartiality or perhaps schizophrenia by first supporting Parliament and later changing sides. In Warwickshire, as in Bedfordshire, there was a nice balance among the great men: the Earl of Warwick and Lord Brooke (owner of Warwick Castle) were for Parliament, while the haughty and wealthy Earl of Northampton led the Royalists. Brooke and Northampton were the two rival Lords Lieutenant, but the former defeated the latter in an early skirmish and the county soon fell under Parliamentary control. Farther south much of Berkshire and Hertfordshire were Royalists, but the towns— Watford, for example— were often for Parliament. Thus while in the Midlands many gentry were disposed to be loyal to Church and King, frequently the more active and uninhibited members of the ruling classes were Parliamentarians.

In Oxford and Cambridge the townsfolk were for Parliament and the Universities were for the King. In both Universities undergraduates volunteered to drill and to fight for him. But in the Fenlands behind Cambridge the eastern corner of England was more wholeheartedly for Parliament than any part of the north or Midlands was for the King. Pockets of Royalism were to be found in Cambridgeshire and in Norfolk, but few Royalists were to be discovered either in Essex or Suffolk. And even in Norfolk the enormous balance of feeling both in Norwich and in the county as a whole was with Parliament. Cromwell's original instructions had not been limited merely to gaining military control of the town of Cambridge but extended to the county as well, and his influence in and knowledge of Huntingdonshire were invaluable to his side. Soon his opportunities and activities stretched out from the Fenlands to the sea. Thus it was not long before this entire group of counties fell under the control of Westminster.

South of London, where much of the prosperity of the country lay and where it might have been thought that the influence of Westminster would be decisive, there was still no obvious uniformity of sympathies. If Surrey tended to be Parliamentarian, Kent was divided and Hampshire was largely Royalist. In Sussex the Earl of Arundel was Royalist (but he stayed out of the war), while the Earl of Northumberland was a Parliamentarian. The gentry were equally divided; some of them indeed were Roman Catholics. The burgesses and yeomanry, on the other hand, were usually supporters of Parliament, and in the east and southeast were often keenly Puritan, but west Sussex contained a fair number of Royalists.

To the southwest it seems again as if class divisions were more accentuated than in other parts of the country. In Dorset the trading and manufacturing classes, who had been extremely resentful over the levying of ship money, were hostile to the Crown; the little ports were vehemently anti-Royalist. The mayors of Dorchester and Poole were staunch Parliamentarians, and Weymouth was described as "very malignant." Yet Corfe Castle was a Royalist stronghold, and Sherborne was the last fortress in the south of England to hold out for the King in 1642. Similarly, in neighboring Somerset, the landowners and country gentlemen were for the most part King's men and the traders and clothiers Parliamentarians; as in Dorset, most of the towns favored Parliament.

The outlying communities in the west tended to be for the King. Cornwall, a poor county, had painful memories of the incompetence of the first Duke of Buckingham and, like Dorset, had opposed the levying of ship money to sustain King Charles I's fatuous foreign policy. Nor had it at all liked being called upon to provide pressed men for the far-away second Bishops War. Here, too, was a clash of rival families and interest and an independent spirit fermenting in the boroughs. But little or no Puritanism had yet manifested itself in an area later to become a stronghold of Nonconformity. Ancient loyalties to the Crown—for Cornwall was a Royal Duchy—and zeal for the Church rather than any enthusiasm for the King's conduct or policy enlisted the help of the gentlemen of Cornwall as of neighboring Devon. But the opposition was sincere and soundly organized. Men who had been justices of the peace believed that the King's rule before the Long Parliament met had been unconstitutional and a danger to the liberty of his subjects. In fact, the gentlemen of Cornwall were fairly evenly divided and the port of Plymouth was Parliamentarian. Cornwall, like distant Yorkshire, would infinitely have preferred to stay neutral.

Other western counties—Herefordshire and Worcestershire, for example—had predominant Royalist sympathies, and so had the whole of Wales except Pembroke. Into these meagerly populated districts Puritanism had penetrated little. But the contribution they were to afford to the King's cause was not large. Speaking of parts of Worcestershire, the Reverend Richard Baxter said unkindly that "all the drunkards went into the King's army and were quickly killed," a reflection that found its parallel in Sir John Oglander's remarks about the Royalists of Hampshire and the Isle of Wight. "The civil war in Wales," it had been observed, "was very largely a settling of private scores rather than an assertion of principle, and the Welsh gentlemen were even more reluctant than most to leave their own battlefields and fight where they were needed." And in the border counties abutting on Wales, reaching from Cheshire to Shropshire and Monmouthshire, it was also true that the Royalist gentry were unwilling to do much more than keep the fighting away from their own homes. The grand strategical plan that was advocated in royal circles towards the end of 1642 for crushing the enemy by converging movements from Yorkshire and Cornwall was vitiated by the fact that local rivalries and local exclusiveness invariably outweighed any complete and unselfish dedication to the King's service.

It is in the light of such a brief survey of England on the eve of the Civil War that Oliver Cromwell's part can best be appreciated. Everywhere the Royalists hesitated, for though the King had no army they regarded it as incredible that he should not come to terms with Parliament. They could not believe that men of standing would have the impiety to take up arms against a lawful King or that God would fail to protect him. They were moved by loyalty and faith rather than by political reasoning; even the King's Knight Marshal or Standard Bearer felt himself "bound in honour to fight for a cause with which he could not sympathize." Doubts existed on the Parliamentary side also. But the challenge had been flung down, and John Pym and his supporters were ready and willing to battle for what they believed to be just and Christian aims. And when it came to practicalities, their thoughts were closely fixed upon essentials. When Cromwell frustrated the dispatch of the plate from Cambridge to the King, took hold of the town's arsenal, and blocked and set guards upon the main routes through the county to prevent help being sent to the Royalist headquarters, he did what was most necessary to secure the area for his own side. Though he had orders to exercise the Cambridge militia, he seems to have recognized that the so-called trained bands were of negligible value. Men of spirit and high morale would volunteer. What was first needed was to secure arms, money, and horses, and to stop them from reaching the King. When he started to enlist his own troopers he raised them mainly from men in Huntingdonshire (rather than in Cambridge) whom he knew and trusted and whom he could train himself. In less than a month he accomplished much; by the end of August his first duties in the eastern counties had been completed. A week after he had secured the whole of Cambridgeshire for Parliament and mustered his first cavalry troop, he was back at Westminster serving on a committee of eight to discuss with representatives of the House of Lords and the Common Council of the City of London how to collect money and plate. On the same day he was instructed to go to the Isle of Ely, where his home was. Thus from the very outset of the war he was concerned not with mere paper schemes or propaganda but with the realities of war.

In terms of tangible things from the beginning, nearly all the advantages rested with his side. London dominated the country to a far greater extent than it does today, and after a minor *coup d'état* in the City in August 1642 the Royalists were ousted from control of the local government, and the wealth of the capital was at the disposal of Parliament. That was a matter of the first necessity, since although Parliament was able to raise taxes by assessment on many of the counties and to levy customs duties at the ports, it was always necessary to borrow from merchants and financiers (whether under the guise of commissioners or tax farmers or simply as moneylenders) to find pay for soldiers and to buy supplies. Besides London, the Parliamentary side ruled almost all the ports in the kingdom; and towns like Portsmouth and Hull were not only strategical assets but also armories and arsenals. Finally Parliament—ironically enough—had command of the ship-money fleet which King Charles I had built up at the price of almost universal national unpopularity.

At first what was most urgent was weapons and not men. The enterprise of men like Cromwell at Cambridge, Harington at Oakham, or Captain Thomas Holcroft in Manchester had enabled their side to lay hands on the contents of many a useful magazine. Parliamentary control over the home counties gave access to the busy forges of Kent and Sussex. The arms laboriously collected by the King for the Bishops' Wars, which had been carefully stored in Hull, were convoyed by sea to a safe refuge in the Tower of London. King Charles, for his part, had to obtain his heavier weapons by importing them from abroad across the stormy North Sea commanded by a hostile navy to one or two small ports, like Bridlington, that were held by his supporters. Throughout the early days of the fighting, weapons were scarce in both camps. Armories were found to contain obsolete weapons like longbows and battle-axes, and men had sometimes to be equipped merely with cudgels and staves. The King's side had only one notable advantage: they were at first better off for horses.

In man power there was little to choose between the two sides. Most Englishmen were well fed and physically fit, and if they were willing to fight could be transformed into good soldiers, capable of carrying and working the cumbrous weapons of the time. But few or none of them were trained. The prolonged period of peace under King James I and the the incompetencies of the Buckingham regime had killed the old military traditions. The two Bishops' Wars had disclosed how feeble was the discipline of the pressed men from the English shires as compared with the high morale and professional conduct of the Scots. If Parliament possessed, in the militia regiments of the City of London, consisting of some eight thousand men who had undergone serious training during the years before the war, the nucleus of an army— provided they could be induced to fight beyond the City boundaries—the King could call upon a cavalry force of value recruited from the outdoor staffs of the wealthy peers who answered the call of his drums. As in the southern states during the American Civil War, the King's army was overrun with colonels but usually they commanded no more than a troop of horse since they had to raise their cavalry at their own expense. On Parliament's side, on the other hand, an immediate financial grant was given to any captain who could enlist his own troop.

The cavalry was to be the decisive arm almost throughout

the entire course of war.[4] In the earlier battles it represented over half of all the men in the field. The cavalrymen were the cream of both sides. Except for a famous regiment of "lobsters" under Sir Arthur Haselrigg of Leicestershire, the mounted soldiers were usually lightly armored. For weapons they carried short swords and pistols, while the lance had practically disappeared. There were also a limited number of dragoons, who were simply mounted infantry. At the beginning of the war the role of the cavalry was not clear. It was not yet accepted as a shock force. The cavalry might trot forward on one side and the other then advance slowly and both halt before firing their pistols. Prince Rupert, the young officer in command of the King's cavalry, and Cromwell himself, soon put an end to such stultifying tactics; the pistol fell into disuse, and the cavalry became an agressive assault force attacking hand to hand with the sword.

The infantry were divided into pikemen and musketeers. The pikemen carried a long pole, generally of ash wood, with a spearhead of iron or steel; they also wore short swords, and were armored at the breast and back. Their pikes might be eighteen feet long, but they were often chopped down as being unmanageable. The musketeers had little defensive armor: they wore leather doublets and an iron-pot headpiece. Their weapon was the extremely clumsy matchlock: the match with which the weapon was fired consisted of cord boiled in vinegar. The heavy bullets were carried in a belt or bandolier. The regimental powder was transported in barrels, and the actual muskets were so heavy that they had usually to be fired from wooden rests stuck in the ground. Nevertheless, the musketeers were effective defensive soldiers in wooded or broken terrain, and could there wreak havoc among the cavalry. But in the open they had no means of resisting a charge by horse unless they were adequately protected by the pikemen. The musketeers formed in rows, six or more, each row retiring, after it had fired, to the rear. Pikemen in the center and musketeers on the flanks was the original formation of the infantry in the Civil Wars. The proportion of musketeers to pikemen was as two to one. The infantrymen were paid at the rate of 8d. a day, the cavalry troopers three times as much.

The cannon of the time, like the muskets, were unwieldy weapons, hard to transport and difficult to maneuver. But both sides thought it worth while to have artillery; it was essential for sieges and was by no means without value in battle. The artillery ranged from the culverins which fired a ball weighing up to twenty pounds to drakes with a ball of under three pounds. But even the lighter cannon could be discharged only fifteen times an hour.

Thus, broadly, when the two contestants, trying to throw off local patriotisms and would-be neutralities, set about improvising national armies at the outset of the Civil War, military traditions, tactics, and weapons were crude and elementary in the extreme: the pikemen with their poles too long for them to handle; the musketeers who had to go through twenty or more drill motions before they could contrive to fire their weapons, and who were then as likely to kill their comrades as their enemies; the cavalry, enthusiastic but ill-disciplined; and the cannon whose bark was worse than its bite and which needed oxen or a team of horses to be dragged across the ill-made roads—all these had to be welded into a fighting army. Plenty of officers had seen some sort of service abroad, but how could they wage war without men? The so-called trained bands were untrained, and the men most easily pressed into service were habitually the scum of the land.

Outside London drill and discipline were hardly known. The men who had been called to fight the Scots had been a mere mob. Marching and weapon training had scarcely been practiced except spasmodically. Problems of commissariat and administration had seldom been tackled, or if they had been tackled, as during Buckingham's expeditionary campaigns and the Bishops' Wars, only with disastrous results. In fact, a unique opportunity presented itself for a man to master the whole subject of the military art, as it were, upon a clean slate, free from professional cautiousness or humdrum ideas. Other great soldiers in modern history could scarcely have arisen in such circumstances because they were nearly all born in countries accustomed to military traditions with a recent background of war. George Washington, for example, had fought in the English army against the Indians before he rose to the highest command in the War of Independence. Lee and Grant were regular officers before they proved their genius in the American Civil War. Napoleon Bonaparte was already an artillery officer when the French revolution began. But in Cromwell's England were no regular officers, no recent wars worthy of the name, except those waged upon the high seas, no barracks or garrison towns, hardly even a military manual other than those published on the Continent. Possessed of a flaming temper, an uncomplicated faith, a gift for action, first exemplified in Cambridgeshire, and an experience of administration acquired in the committees of the House of Commons, Oliver Cromwell was to prove himself the man of the hour when England reluctantly and confusedly went to war with herself.

Notes

1. Cf. F. P. Verney, *Memoirs of the Verney Family during the Civil Wars* (1892), II, chap. 2.

2. See especially Brunton and Pennington, *op. cit.*

3. This chapter is based on a thorough examination of the relevant volumes of the *Victoria County History* (variable in quality), the many local histories of the Civil War (which also vary in quality), and other sources too numerous to list.

4. C. H. Firth, *Cromwell's Army* (1921) is the standard book. A visit to an exhibition held in London in 1956 to commemorate the three-hundredth anniversary of the Grenadier Guards reminded me of how exceedingly difficult it must have been to fight with an eighteen-foot pike.

Chapter 7

Cromwell as Soldier: The First Campaigns

ON SEPTEMBER 13, 1642, the day when King Charles I left his headquarters at Nottingham, Captain Oliver Cromwell received orders to muster his troop of cavalry and join the army commanded by the Earl of Essex. Essex, a melancholy, conservative, pipe-smoking general, had set out from London on September 9. Both the King's army and the Parliamentary army marched westwards. Each numbered about 14,000 mem, the bulk of them without any experience of war, lacking training and discipline, and incompletely armed. The men under Essex were more adequately equipped with weapons and money than were the King's—a few of his infantry carried nothing except cudgels—but the Royalists had some goodish cavalry. The King had originally named the Earl of Lindsey as his commander in chief, but later gave Prince Rupert exclusive control of the cavalry. The Earl of Lindsey thereupon resigned, to die gallantly in the first big battle of the war. The Earl of Essex, for his part, was refused the far-reaching powers that he sought from Parliament. A proud man, he resented this. Thus neither commanders nor men were happy as the two armies felt for each in the west of England.

The Royalist army moved from Nottingham to Shrewsbury, and a force was pushed forward to take Worcester. The Parliamentarians, after occupying Oxford, advanced upon Worcester and Hereford, and it was at the picturesque stone bridge of Powick, outside Worcester, that the first clash of the Civil Wars, as also the last in 1651, took place. Here Prince Rupert put the Parliamentarians to flight, but then withdrew and let them enter Worcester. After that, the intelligence on both sides being indifferent, the armies lost each other. But suddenly, in the second week of October, Essex learned the startling news that the King's army, by-passing the towns of the Midlands, was marching south upon London itself. The Earl bestirred himself and began a forced march eastwards, leaving his cannon behind him and many of his troops scattered. The armies met at Edgehill near Warwick, on the edge of the Cotswolds. The battle was obscure and bloody. The King's army charged along its whole front. The Parliamentary left wing was beaten back on its base. The Parliamentary right was overrun, but two of its best cavalry regiments there fought on, and though checked by Royalist pikemen, saved their side from disgrace. Colonel John Hampden, who reached the battlefield late in the day, was able to stanch with his brigade the pursuit of the beaten right wing, and next morning urged the Earl of Essex to resume the battle. But Essex had had enough. Though Puritan valor retrieved the day, the King was allowed to occupy Oxford in triumph. Judged in terms of morale and strategic consequences, Edgehill was a victory for the Cavaliers.

The battle of Edgehill was fought on October 23.[1] Within three weeks, after a rest and refit, the King prepared to conquer London. On November 12 Prince Rupert overwhelmed two Parliamentary regiments at Brentford, bursting out of the mist and thrusting his enemies into the river. As at the battle of the Marne, nearly three centuries later, when Paris was in peril, every military effort was exerted to save the capital. Bridges had hastily been constructed across the Thames. The trained bands came streaming along the western road all through the night. The whole of the next day the King's commanders contemplated the grim hosts of Londoners lining the neighborhood of Turnham Green. The experts on both sides, with professional caution, advised against fighting. The Royal army slowly withdrew to Oxford, where it took up its winter quarters. The first phase of the Civil War was at an end.

What part did Cromwell's troop play in all this? No one knows for certain. But it seems likely that when the Earl of Essex hurried to Edgehill, Cromwell's was among the troops left scattered, and that it came up and joined Hampden's brigade in stemming the pursuit by Prince Rupert. Again it is probable enough that Cromwell withdrew with the remains of Essex's army on London. He was, after all, an M.P. and Parliament was in session. Moreover, as his actions next year were to show, he always wanted to be in the thick of the battle. So he may have stood behind the palisades at Turnham Green before leading his troop back into the eastern counties to train and recruit before the next campaign.

By the middle of December 1642, Cromwell's troop was eighty strong. Its losses at Edgehill had not merely been replaced but its establishment had been increased. Parliament decided at this time to form an Association of the Eastern Counties for military purposes: Cambridgeshire was included in it but not Huntingdonshire, which became part of a Midland Association formed at about the same time. The commander of the Eastern Association was Lord Grey of Wark, that of the Midland Association Lord Grey of Groby; both were major generals under the Earl of Essex. Captain Cromwell was appointed a member of the large committee that was responsible for organizing both these associations. The associations of counties were probably copied from a similar arrangement made by the King's side in the north, and were not, as events proved, satisfactorily grouped. Big committees are not the best means for running wars. And the two Lord Greys were chosen for their local influences rather than their prowess as soldiers. Thus an amateurish air still pervaded the Parliamentary methods after Edgehill. Cromwell was quickly to appreciate that.

At the beginning of January 1643, Cromwell was in his place in the House of Commons acting as a teller for a motion depriving the King's supporters of any prospect of indemnity. But he was soon back in Cambridge with his troop. Evidently the ruling powers in London considered that his services were of most value in defending his constituency. On February 6 Lord Grey of Wark raised him to the rank of colonel. His troop of horse was already being converted into a regiment, and later he was to command a double regiment of fourteen troops.[2] The training of such a regiment admirably suited the needs of his temperament. For he saw that it was now the right way to win the war.

Soon after the battle of Edgehill, Cromwell had in fact told his cousin Colonel Hampden that new regiments were what were most wanted, and that he believed he himself might be of service in forming them. He said that he thought the reason why the Parliamentary troops had been beaten "on every hand" was that they were wanting in spirit. "You must get men of a spirit," he told him, "a spirit that is likely to go on as far as gentlemen will go, or else I am sure you will be beaten still." That was the first principle he followed in raising his own "Ironside" regiment. He believed wholeheartedly that he was engaged upon a religious war. Had not the King told his army that they were going to fight Baptists, atheists, and the like, and did not the Parliamentary leaders speak of the "fury and cruelty of the popish army"?[3] Thus he took "special care to get religious men into his troop." "Pray raise honest, godly men," he wrote to some wellwishers, "and I will have them of my regiment." When his regiment was nearly formed, he wrote: "Truly mine are honest men such as fear God." "Most of them," wrote a later observer, were "freeholders and freeholders' sons, and who upon a matter of conscience engaged in this quarrel, and under Cromwell." It was later urged against him by his critics that his choice of officers and men for his regiment was from "mean and common men." That was merely the other side of the medal. "He would give them the title of godly precious men . . . if you look upon his own regiment of horse, see what a swarm there is of those that call themselves godly." So wrote the Earl of Manchester, who was for a time Cromwell's superior officer.

Cromwell would not tolerate for one moment any reflections on the characters of the officers who served under him simply because they were on a lower social rung than the peers and gentlemen of large estate who officered the royal armies. The captain of one of his troops, a certain Ralph Margery, came in for such criticism because he was thought to be no gentleman, or at least one of very small estate. Margery and his troop came from Suffolk, and Cromwell wrote to the Suffolk Committee: "If these men be accounted troublesome to the county, I shall be glad you would send them all to me. I'll bid them welcome. And when they have fought for you, and endured some other difficulties of war which your honester men will hardly bear, I pray you then let them go for honest men. . . . Better plain men than none, but best to have patient of wants, faithful and conscientious in the employment, and such, I hope, these will approve themselves to be." Speaking in another letter in defense of Captain Margery, he warned the Suffolk Committee: "I beseech you to be careful what captains of horse you choose . . . a few honest men are better than numbers. . . . If you choose honest men to be captains of horse, honest men will follow them, and they will be careful to mount such." His policy was vindicated. "As far as I could learn," wrote the Reverend Richard Baxter, who was on intimate terms with one of Cromwell's captains, "they never once ran away before an enemy." "They would as one man stand firmly," wrote Bulstrode Whitelocke later, "and charge desperately."

The careful manner in which Cromwell recruited his troopers largely explains the quality of his regiment. But he also exercised strict discipline. Attempted desertion was punished by a public whipping. When in the summer of 1643 he had two thousand men under his command, a Parliamentarian newspaper held them up as a model to others:

> No man swears but he pays his twelvepence; if he be drunk, he is set in the stocks or worse; if one calls the other Roundhead he is cashiered, in so much that the counties where they come leap for joy of them and come in and join with them. How happy were it if all the forces were thus disciplined.

As has ever been the tradition in the modern British army, if the commanding officer imposes a discipline unknown in civilian life his first solicitude is for the well-being of his men. In October 1643, Cromwell wrote as follows to his cousin Sir Thomas Barrington, Deputy Lord Lieutenant of Essex, in the Eastern Association:

> It is against my will to be troublesome to my friends. I had rather suffer under some extremities, were it my particular, but that which I have to offer concerns those honest men under my command, who have been, who are, in straits if want of clothes, boots, money to fix their arms, to shoe their horses be considerable, such are theirs not in an easy degree, truly above what is fit for the state to suffer. Sir, many may complain they are many weeks behind of pay, many who can plunder and pillage; they suffer no want. But truly mine(though some have stigmatized them with the name of Anabaptists) are honest men, such as fear God, I am confident the freest from unjust practices of any in England, seek the soldiers where you can. . . . I hear such mists are cast to darken their services. . . . Take no care for me . . . but for my poor men, help them what you can, for they are faithful.

He had constantly to press the counties for the soldiers' pay. "I have little money of my own to help my soldiers," he reminded his friend and cousin, Oliver St. John, "my estate is little." "I think it is not expected," he wrote on another occasion to the Essex authorities, "that I should pay your soldiers out of my own purse"; but, as he informed the Cambridge commissioners, "if we have not more money speedily," all his troops, who were but half clothed, would be "exceedingly discouraged." Choice of spirited volunteers, sternness of discipline, care of personal needs, and punctuality of pay, these were the making of Cromwell's Ironsides.

From the beginning of the war Cromwell recognized the part in it that was going to be taken by the cavalry. When some young people in Norwich offered to raise funds to provide the Eastern Association with a foot company, he sent his thanks but advised them that their foot company should be turned into a troop of horse "which indeed will (by God's blessing) far more advantage the cause than two or three foot companies." He had observed what Prince Rupert's horsemen had done at Edgehill; and his experiences there were confirmed by the battles in which he distinguished himself during 1643. To him speed was the essence of success in war, whether in its preparation, in advance, or attack. In nearly every letter he wrote while his Ironsides were forming could be read the doctrine of speed. "If you can contribute to our aid, let us speedily participate thereof," he wrote. "At least do what you may with all possible expedition." "I beseech you hasten supplies." "It exceedingly imports the kingdom that he hasten to us." "It's no longer disputing; out instantly all you can." "Let your return be speedy to Norwich." Such are a few typical passages on different subjects.

All this did not represent mere impatience or anxiety, but it did show the zeal of the volunteer soldier to come to grips with the enemy. In Cromwell was none of that temporizing maneuvering for position or weighing of the odds that characterized most of the professional officers with their memories of siege warfare in the Low Countries. "We have here," he wrote from Huntingdon in April 1643, "about six or seven troops of horse, such, I hope, as will fight. It's happy to resist such beginnings betimes." When it came to actual battle, he looked for the earliest opportunity to charge the enemy. Finally, unlike many of the county commanders throughout the land, he rarely worried about purely parochial dangers. When in May 1643 a number of his fellow officers refused to join with him in an attack on the Royalists in Lincolnshire because they were afraid that Leicester and other towns in the Eastern Association would then be exposed to assult, he observed: "It were better in my poor opinion that Leicester were not than there should not be an immediate taking of the field by your forces to accomplish the common end."

A clear picture of a vigorous, uninhibited Christian soldier can be obtained from the letters that Oliver Cromwell wrote after he took up arms and formed his own regiment. Here was no armchair critic, but a field commander instinct with a simple but profound tactical and strategic insight. It has often been said that the art of generalship consists above all in the ability to collect and maintain supplies more than in the gift of maneuver. Cromwell's organization of his double cavalry regiment in 1643 constituted his apprenticeship. Administrative obstacles were there to be overcome, discouragements to be ignored, circumspection to be avoided. He believed that his cause was just; he knew that the morale of his men was high. Once they were provided with the equipment they wanted and instilled with the need for speed and aggression, he was certain that they would be victorious.

*   *   *

It is by no means easy to simplify the strategy of the Civil War. At first sight it appears as a welter of local struggles and confused shiftings of forces. John Pym, for all his energy as an administrator, was no strategist and left the direction of military affairs to the Earl of Essex, and there was, in fact, no unified command or general plan of campaign. And on the Royalist side, though it has been said that King Charles was better than Essex at strategy, he had little genius for war and trusted no one completely; indeed, his vacillations were to lose him all. Prince Rupert was his most accomplished general and Queen Henrietta Maria his most daring adviser, but he divided and ruled.

At the beginning of 1643 the Earl of Essex had his headquarters in Windsor while the King with the bulk of his army faced him in Oxford. In Yorkshire the Earl of Newcastle with another army based on York outnumbered his opponents.[4] William Cavendish, the first Earl of Newcastle, was an immensely wealthy man, "amorous in poetry and music, to which he indulged the greatest part of his time; and nothing would have tempted him out of these paths of pleasure, which he enjoyed in full and ample fortune, but honour and ambition to serve the King when he saw him in distress." After he had defeated Lord Fairfax of Cameron at Tadcaster in December 1642, Newcastle had established himself as far west as Pontefract and had pushed a cavalry force as far south as Newark in Nottinghamshire. But Hull remained

THE CAMPAIGNS OF 1642 & 1643

Area under Royalist control in Autumn 1643

Sites of Battles are underlined

10 0 10 20 30 40 50
Miles

a thorn in his side. In the west of England Sir Ralph Hopton, with an army largely manned by Cornishmen, won a series of victories for the King, but Prince Rupert failed to take Bristol, and a capable Parliamentarian general, Sir William Waller, secured Bristol, Malmesbury, and Hereford. At the opening of the spring campaign the Earl of Essex laid siege to Reading, which had been one of the royal outposts of Oxford, and it was evacuated. But the key to the situation was the expected arrival of the Queen with arms and money from the Netherlands. In spite of the Parliamentary command of the sea, she reached Yorkshire safely in March with a convoy. Could she now join the King at Oxford and fortify and invigorate him for a decisive action?

Between York and Oxford lay an area of divided loyalties. Derbyshire, Nottinghamshire, and Leicestershire were now mainly controlled by Parliament, and the Eastern Association, where Cromwell was active, was a threat on the flank of the Queen's line of advance. Soon after her arrival in Yorkshire the Royalist forces occupied a number of important places in the Midlands. In April Prince Rupert undertook a campaign to clear the way for the Queen; he took Lichfield in Staffordshire, which had changed hands before, and by the middle of May reinforcements of arms and ammunition had arrived at Oxford from the Queen.

Looked at from Cromwell's point of view and that of the forces of which his regiment formed a part, the strategic center was the little market town of Newark, which constituted a salient or dagger pointing at the heart of the Parliamentarian territory; it commanded the lowest bridge over the river Trent and the main road south from Yorkshire. If Newark were wrenched from the Royalists, the Earl of Newcastle could be locked in on three sides and the King's army in Oxford severed from his partisans in the north. During March Cromwell had completed the fortifications of Cambridge and had strengthened the hold of his side on the eastern counties by occupying Lowestoft and King's Lynn, taking prisoners in both these places. While his superior, Lord Grey of Wark, went to assist in the siege of Reading, Cromwell moved as far north as Peterborough and seized Crowland on the frontier between the two parties. He now urgently pressed for an attack on Newark. Had this succeeded, the Queen's convoy might have been intercepted and the war shortened. Hopeful rumors filled the Parliamentarian press. Cromwell was reported to have ten troops of horse (600 to 800 men) and 2,000 foot under his command, and to be expected to attack the Cavaliers in Newark, who were plundering and pillaging near the walls of Lincoln itself. A plan was formulated for Cromwell's force to link up with the men of Lincolnshire, Nottinghamshire, and Leicestershire, take Newark and push across the Trent into Yorkshire. The combined army would have amounted to as many as 8,000 men, and if they could have reached the Fairfaxes they might have loosened the Royalist hold on the north of England. But the plan fell through because of delay and muddle. On May 13 Cromwell ran into the enemy near Grantham, and in his first independent fight won a victory over a slightly larger force. "After we had stood a little above musket shot," he reported afterwards, "the one body from the other, and the dragooners having fired on both sides for the space of half an hour or more, they not advancing towards us, we agreed to charge them and, advancing the body after many shots on both sides, came on with our troops at a pretty round trot, they standing firm to receive us; and our men charging fiercely upon them, by God's providence they were immediately routed, and ran all away, and we had the execution of them two or three miles." A hundred were killed, forty-five prisoners and four or five colors taken before the victors marched away to Lincoln. There was a somewhat disproportionate air of self-congratulation about his report—as in George Washington's disptach after his first victory over the Indians—natural enough in a hitherto untried commander. For after a reconnaissance he found himself still too weak to attack Newark, and had to withdraw to Nottingham.

The skirmish at Grantham is of significance only as being the initial blooding of the Ironsides and as containing the first cavalry charge headed by Oliver Cromwell. Its deeper meaning in Cromwell's military career is different. Some historians have spoken as if before Grantham Cromwell had already been reinforced by other troops from the Eastern Association. But that was not the case. After the event what the newspapers said was this:[5]

Colonel Cromwell, whose fidelity none question, is up and down in Lincolnshire; it were to be wished that he and the Lord Grey [of Wark] and Sir John Gell [the Parliamentary commander in Derbyshire] had joined together to have withstood the convoy that came from Newark with the ammunition.

In fact his military perception was vindicated but thwarted. Nine days after Cromwell's success at Grantham Sir Thomas Fairfax won a bigger victory at Wakefield, where he took 1,500 prisoners including the Royalist General Goring. But he was outnumbered by two to one and appealed to Cromwell for help. Cromwell was anxious to respond, though he was now short of supplies and money, and his foot and dragoons were ready to mutiny. He had now been joined at Nottingham by the forces from Derbyshire and Leicestershire. The commander in chief, the Earl of Essex, had himself ordered the rendezvous, and the general hope or expectation was that the united army would now at last attack Newark, advance to the aid of Fairfax in Yorkshire, and prevent the Queen from reaching the King. But they sat still waiting to see which way the Earl of Newcastle would move, justifying their inaction on the ground that their mere presence had weakened the Royalist concentration in Yorkshire. Lord Fairfax was disappointed and brushed aside their excuses. Cromwell was not of course in command of the combined forces but was one of five colonels, and he soon realized that there was a traitor in the camp: this was young Colonel Hotham, son of the Parliamentary commander in Hull, who had been seduced from his allegiance by the Queen. Fierce quarrels broke out between him, Cromwell, and Lord Grey of Wark, and on a complaint from Cromwell being laid before the Committee of Safety Hotham's arrest was ordered, and Sir John Meldrum, a Scottish professional soldier, was sent down to take over the command from the ineffectual Lord Grey. Hotham fled to his father, and together they attempted to betray Hull. The port was saved, but on June 30 the Fairfaxes were overwhelmed at the battle of Adwalton Moor, outside Bradford. They themselves escaped in safety to Hull, where Lord Fairfax was appointed Governor in place of the elder Hotham. But almost the whole of Yorkshire had fallen into Royalist hands. A fortnight later the Queen joined the King in the Midlands, after passing through Newark on the way. At the end of July Prince Rupert, at his second attempt, took Bristol, the second largest port in the kingdom.

The month of July 1643, therefore, marked the lowest point in the fortunes of the Parliamentarians. Sir William

Waller was defeated by Sir Ralph Hopton in Gloucestershire.
In the same month John Hampden was mortally wounded in
an obscure skirmish. Pym refused an offer of resignation
from the Earl of Essex, but he appointed the Earl of Manchester as commander of a new army in the Eastern Association. Cromwell's progress as a soldier was recognized by
his being made Manchester's deputy.

*　　　　*　　　　*

The successes of the Royalists elsewhere understandably
encouraged their friends in the north and east of England.
Lincolnshire became the scene of intense military activity,
for this was the frontier land between the armies of the Earls
of Newcastle and Manchester.

In the third week of July a Royalist force from Newark
advanced on Peterborough and called upon it to surrender.
But meanwhile Lord Willoughby of Parham, the Parliamentarian leader in the county, had moved from Lincoln and
surprised Gainsborough by a night assault. Gainsborough
was a place of strategic value, for not only did it guard a
bridgehead over the Trent but its occupation by the Parliamentarians cut off Newark from the Earl of Newcastle's
army in Yorkshire. A cavalry force, commanded by Lord
Charles Cavendish, Newcastle's cousin, set out to recapture
Gainsborough, and Lord Willoughby appealed to Cromwell
for aid. Cromwell took incisive action. Calling for reinforcements from Cambridgeshire and Suffolk, he drove the Cavaliers from the neighborhood of Peterborough and then laid
siege to them in Burghley House near Stamford. When they
refused to surrender he first brought up his cannon and next
drew up the musketeers attached to his cavalry. Thereupon
the garrison marched out, laid down their arms, and were
dispatched as prisoners to Cambridge.

Cromwell immediately rode north, and met cavalry and
dragoons from Nottingham and Lincolnshire, making up a
force of 1,700 men, at a point ten miles from Gainsborough.
A cavalry skirmish followed. Cavendish had deployed four
regiments upon a sandy tableland a mile south of Gainsborough. Both sides boldly advanced to the charge; the Parliamentarians had to ride uphill, picking their way through
rabbit holes. Sir John Meldrum, who was in command, was
in the van and Cromwell in the rear. The Parliamentarian
horse re-formed from column into line, Cromwell being on

the right. "We came up horse to horse," he wrote, "where we disputed it with our swords and pistols a pretty time, all keeping close order, so that one could not break the other." Eventually the Royalists were thrust back and pursued for five or six miles. But Cavendish's own regiment, which was held in reserve, "a very full regiment," remained unbroken. Cromwell foresaw this danger. He gathered together three troops of his own regiment and four Lincolnshire troops to meet it. When Cavendish charged the Lincolnshire men, Cromwell fell upon his rear and routed him. Two men who were to become loyal servants to Cromwell in the future took part in the action. Major Edward Whalley, the second in command of Cromwell's regiment, recalled from the pursuit, was to the fore in the victorious charge; Captain-Lieutenant James Berry, who commanded Cromwell's own troop in his regiment, slew General Cavendish with a sword thrust through his ribs as his beaten men were driven back into a quagmire.

But all was not over. Though the purpose of the operation was attained when powder and muntions were delivered to Lord Willoughby in Gainsborough, news was soon received that a fresh force of the enemy was arriving north of the town. After contact had been established it was realized that the bulk of Newcastle's army had come to the rescue. There was nothing to be done but to retire. Newcastle's cannon struck terror into many hearts. Willoughby's foot, who had been moved out to protect the town, were driven off, and Cromwell's tired cavalry had to be thrown into the battle to cover the retreat. The officers rallied their troopers. Meldrum commended Cromwell for his "discretion and valour," and he himself noted that "Major Whalley did in this carry himself with all gallantry becoming a gentleman and a Christian." Though Cromwell, in three letters, made the best he could of God's blessings and encouragements at Gainsborough, the fact remained that two days after the fight the Royalists reoccupied the town and Willoughby withdrew to Boston. Almost the whole of Lincolnshire was thus lost to Parliament.

The Gainsborough fight had, however, its place in Cromwell's development as a soldier. First it is a tribute to the strength of his personality that although Sir John Meldrum and Lord Willoughby were both his superior officers, while other colonels were at least his equals, not only at the siege of Burghley House but also in the skirmish with Cavendish,

Cromwell himself appears to have taken control. His regiment, now completed, was fully blooded. And he himself had mastered two aspects of the military art: he had reformed his men in face of an unbeaten foe at the crisis of the fight, and he had carried out a withdrawal almost without casualties before a stronger enemy.

His abilities were recognized at Westminster. On the day of the fight at Gainsborough he was appointed Governor of the Isle of Ely in addition to his new command under the Earl of Manchester. On August 4 the Speaker wrote to him that the House of Commons "do exceedingly approve of your faithful endeavours for God and the Kingdom," and to assure him that " no power they have shall be wanting to improve the good affections of these Associated counties."

None of the other commanders in this theater of the war except Sir Thomas Fairfax had Cromwell's courage, resourcefulness, or single-mindedness. Willoughby wrote to tell him that "since the business of Gainsborough the hearts of our men have been so deaded as we have lost most of them by running away."[6] Meldrum attributed the retreat from Gainsborough to the cowardice of the dragoons. Good officers do not blame their men. Frightened of the Earl of Newcastle's advance, troops now refused to leave their home counties. But Newcastle had his own local cares. After advancing as far as Nottingham, he found that his Yorkshire soldiers were restive so long as Hull remained a menace to their flank and rear. Ignoring repeated orders from King Charles I to march south, he returned north in the third week of August and laid siege to that port.

*   *   *

That month John Pym, who had less than six months to live, and the other members of the Parliamentary Committee of Safety who directed the war, were feverishly trying to recover the initiative. A deputation from the two Houses went to Edinburgh to seek the alliance of the Scots, and the terms of a military and political agreement embodying another "Solemn League and Covenant" were accepted in London on September 25. Three armies were in the process of reconstruction, the army of the center under the Earl of Essex, that of the east under the Earl of Manchester, and that of the west under Sir William Waller. Weekly assessments were levied on the fifteen counties still in the control of

Parliament, and a new tax, the excise, was imposed both on imports and on domestic produce. The King, as Cromwell noted, was "exceedingly strong in the west," but elsewhere the Parliamentary armies went over to the offensive. The Earl of Essex marched to the relief of Gloucester, which was being besieged by Prince Rupert. After the Earl had entered Gloucester, King Charles attempted to block his way back to London. A drawn battle was fought at Newbury in Berkshire, and both armies retired to lick their wounds.

Meanwhile the Earl of Manchester received orders to resume the offensive in Lincolnshire. It was first necessary to clear his rear by suppressing a Royalist revival at King's Lynn. The Earl of Manchester undertook the siege, while Cromwell covered it. But on September 11 Cromwell announced that he was ready to march to the relief of Hull. For a month the Fairfaxes had kept the Earl of Newcastle's army at bay. It was the measure of Sir Thomas Fairfax's courage and judgment that since he had no use for cavalry in the besieged city, he had dispatched sixteen troops to join Cromwell in Boston, shipping them by sea down the Humber. Fairfax was indeed an officer of a different caliber from the others with whom Cromwell had had to deal. Thirteen years the younger, this gaunt, dark Yorkshireman, known as Black Tom or "the Rider of the White Horse," had none of the ultracautiousness of the other officers who had learned their trade on the Continent. A man of culture who grew roses and translated the Psalms, he was a gentle and clement Puritan, much loved by his soliders. But he was no weakling. His courage was superb and his sense of duty unassailable. Like Cromwell he was a first-class administrator as well as a fighting commander.

The two men met for the first time when Cromwell repaid Fairfax's generosity by himself carrying a supply of powder and muskets into Hull. Here he took part in a day of fasting and humiliation. Four days later, on September 26, Fairfax returned the visit by meeting Cromwell and Lord Willoughby of Parham at their Lincolnshire base of Boston. Fairfax brought with him twenty-one troops of horse and dragoons. Meanwhile the Earl of Manchester had taken King's Lynn, and on October 2 dispatched part of his infantry to reinforce the troops at Boston. The Parliamentarians then moved north. In their line of advance was a Royalist stronghold, the castle of Bolingbroke. The Earl of Manchester besieged the castle, and Sir John Henderson, the Royalist Governor of Newark, came to the rescue. Battle was joined near the hamlet of Winceby; Fairfax was in command, while Cromwell led the van. Here therefore amid the hillocks of eastern Lincolnshire the two finest Roundhead commanders of the Civil War fought side by side for the first time. The two armies were evenly matched, but all was over in half an hour. The Puritan troopers charged downhill singing psalms. Cromwell's horse was killed under him at the first charge, but Fairfax coming up in a second wave routed the enemy. Six hundred Royalist soldiers were killed, and many were drowned in the waters of the fens. The discipline of Cromwell's Ironsides and Fairfax's Yorkshiremen was conclusively demonstrated. The battle of Winceby took place on October 11. Next day the Earl of Newcastle raised the siege of Hull, and soon afterwards Lincoln surrendered to the Parliamentarians. Indomitable Newark was subjected to a blockade. It refused to yield. And the Earl of Manchester, a mild general who was no Napoleon, retired into winter quarters, while Oliver Cromwell went home to Ely.

In the campaign of 1643 Cromwell had rapidly served his apprenticeship in the art of war. He had directed no important battle or siege, yet he proved his mettle not merely to his fellow Puritans but to himself. There is no introspection in his surviving letters; indeed, as far as they carry us, in war he was the complete extrovert. He said what he thought in unrestrained terms about his fellow commanders and their soldiers. He thought poorly of officers like Meldrum and Willoughby with whom he had to serve, but in Thomas Fairfax he recognized and saluted an equal. Moreover, he had gathered round him a group of officers who were with him until the end, men like his cousin Edward Whalley, Henry Ireton (who, like Whalley, came from Nottinghamshire and whose troop was embodied in Cromwell's regiment), and James Berry, who had started life in an iron foundry in the Midlands; all these men were unbending Puritans and magnificent fighting soldiers. But Cromwell himself possessed the indefinable quality of leadership: they looked to him and obeyed him. They perceived in him that gift of pugnacity, which attributed success to the Almighty and failure to the incompetence of others, that would assuredly win the war for their side.

Notes

1. For the battle of Edgehill, see *inter alia* Godfrey Davies's article in *The English Historical Review* (1921) and A. H. Burne, *The Battlefields of England* (1950), 191 seq. I examined the part in the battle played by Oliver Cromwell in my *Conservative Dictator,* 81–82, 334; the best account is in C. H. Firth, "Raising of the Ironsides," *Transactions of the Royal Historical Society,* XIII (1899).

2. For the raising of the Ironsides, see Firth, as above; James Caulfield, *Cromwelliana* (1810).

3. Egerton MSS. 2647, f. 93; *Perfect Diurnall,* October 9, 1643; Clarendon, *History of the Rebellion,* etc.

4. For Newcastle, C. H. Firth's edition of *The Life of William Cavendish, Duke of Newcastle* (1907).

5. *Special Passages,* May 9–16, 1643.

6. Egerton MSS. 2647, f. 120.

Chapter 8

Cromwell as Soldier: The Battle of Marston Moor

IN ACCORDANCE WITH the terms of a treaty signed in the previous November, a formidable army of over 20,000 Scotsmen, under the command of the "old little crooked soldier" Alexander Leslie, Earl of Leven, marched into England on January 18, 1644, to assist the Parliamentary armies in their struggle against the King.[1] The price of the alliance had been a down payment of £100,000 and the acceptance of the Solemn League and Covenant. But the English Puritans had not thereby undertaken to align their religion precisely with that held and practiced by the Presbyterian Kirk of Scotland. The younger Sir Henry Vane, the friend of Cromwell, a man of wit and resource and by no means an orthodox Puritan, had been one of the commissioners appointed to negotiate the treaty, and he had been advised by the Reverend Philip Nye, who had acquired Separatist or Independent sympathies during a period of ministry in the Netherlands. When in July 1643 Parliament had set up as assembly of divines and laymen at Westminster to determine the future religious organization of the country after the abolition of the bishops, Oliver Cromwell and Henry Vane had insisted upon Independent representation in it. The terms of the Solemn League and Covenant, which provided for "the reformation of religion in the kingdoms of England and Ireland . . . according to the Word of God and the example of the best reformed Churches," were finally so framed that they did not commit the English Parliament to a hard-and-fast Presbyterian hierarchy. On the very day that the Westminster Assembly was called upon to swear allegiance to the Covenant, Nye gave an address reminding his hearers that they were not bound by it to "a servile imitation of their northern brethren." Thereupon the members of the Assembly and 112 members of the House of Commons swore to the Covenant.

But Oliver Cromwell, who, as his later conduct showed, had doubts both about the wisdom of the religious settlement and the necessity for the Scottish military alliance, did not himself take the Covenant until February of the following year. On that date an ordinance enforcing the signature of the Covenant on all Englishmen over the age of eighteen was enacted. It has been suggested that Cromwell then accepted it partly because Parliament had promised that in the reformation of the Church of England existing congregations should be left untouched, and partly because he could only continue to exercise a command in the army by doing so. In any case, he was a reluctant Covenanter.[2]

He had by that time been promoted to the rank of lieutenant general under the Earl of Manchester. During the few months since the Earl had become commander in chief of the Eastern Association Cromwell had proved himself to be the most capable of the senior officers under him, and the definitive appointment as second in command was logical. Cromwell was never a major general, but the relation between the two ranks differed from what it is today. A lieutenant general, in fact, was sometimes junior in rank to a major general.[3] But Cromwell was not, as were some lieutenant generals, merely the commander of the cavalry or of the artillery: his appointment, which carried the pay of £5 a day, was as lieutenant general "of horse and foot."

The third in command of the Earl of Manchester's army was Major General Laurence Crawford, a Scottish professional soldier from Renfrewshire of the sternest Presbyterian persuasions. At first the Earl of Manchester and General Cromwell worked amicably enough together. In January Cromwell had asked in a speech in the Commons that the Earl of Manchester's command should be extended to Lincolnshire because of the incompetence of Lord Willoughby of Parham, who also had "very loose and profane commanders under him." That was agreed, and later in the year a Scots observer in London noted that the Earl of Manchester depended greatly on General Cromwell, whom he described as "a very wise and active head, universally well beloved as religious and stout" though "a known Independent or favourer of sects."[4]

But between Cromwell and Crawford no love was lost. Crawford may easily have looked askance at the farmer from Ely as an amateur soldier pushed to the top by his political friends. In the spring Crawford arrested Lieutenant William Packer, an officer in Cromwell's own regiment, for refusing to take the Covenant. Cromwell at once remonstrated with Crawford for "checking such a man . . . he being a godly man." Packer was a Baptist; so was Lieutenant Colonel Henry Warner in Crawford's own regiment. Crawford also laid a complaint against Warner because he had failed to take the Covenant. Cromwell wrote firmly, to Crawford upon the matter. Suppose Warner were a Baptist, he asked, "shall that render him incapable to serve the public?"

> Sir, the state, in choosing men to serve them, takes no notice of their opinions, if they be willing faithfully to serve them, that satisfies. I advised you formerly to bear with men of different minds from yourself; if you had done it when I advised you to it, I think you would not have had so many stumbling-blocks in your way. It may be you judge otherwise, but I tell you my mind.

Here a fundamental difference of outlook was sharply defined. The Earl of Manchester was a Presbyterian and a member of the Westminster Assembly. Crawford was a keen Scottish Presbyterian. Parliament had insisted that everyone must take the Covenant, for it was a condition of the Scottish alliance. But Cromwell did not look at things in that way. To his mind the Civil War was a religious war to secure the right of the individual Christian to worship in accordance with his own conscience. Anyone who was an honest Christian soldier could serve in that cause. But the Presbyterians wanted a single unified Church, without bishops, upon the Calvinist pattern: they had no interest in toleration, and they thought they might compel the King to accede to their demands. Cromwell, Vane, and the Independents were convinced that the Holy Spirit could manifest itself in the local congregations—even in an army troop, even in an individual believer. They had small hope that anything less than complete and decisive victory over the King would secure for them their ideal of a free Christian community.

In Ely, where Cromwell lived and where he was now Governor of the island, a center of the Independent movement was being established, making it "a place for God to dwell in." Cromwell personally enforced there the ordinances of Parliament and of the Westminster Assembly against the use of the surplice and the Book of Common Prayer. But exaggerated stories were circulated both then and later about his iconoclasm. He realized that it was far better for the clergy themselves to obey the new order than to allow the Puritan soldiery to break up the services in the cathedral and elsewhere. He reminded an offending clergyman that he was a man under authority, but spoke as his loving friend. To see

Cromwell as an intolerant image-smasher and desecrator of churches is to misunderstand his character as it was forming under the stress of war.

*   *   *

The Earl of Manchester's army, with Cromwell as its effective head, was but one of five operating on behalf of Parliament in 1644. The Earl of Essex, still nominally the commander in chief, was no longer completely trusted at Westminster. He had become apathetic and defeatist. "There is but a step between us and death," he said, "and what is worse slavery." Many regarded him both as lethargic and pacific. Moreover, he was now subject to orders to an extent that he had not been while Pym was alive. Pym had died early in December, and a Committee of Both Kingdoms had been set up to direct the war. Essex, Manchester, Leven, Sir William Waller, the Earl of Warwick (the Lord High Admiral), and Cromwell himself were all members of it, though their military duties prevented them from attending regularly. Sir Henry Vane was the guiding spirit in this Committee and Vane was no idler or defeatist.[5] Essex complained that the new authorities favored the Earl of Manchester's army at the expense of his own, making it stronger than his and granting it more money. Waller's army was becoming virtually independent of the commander in chief, as were also those under Manchester and Fairfax, while the Scottish army, though subject to the orders of the Committee of Both Kingdoms, obviously had a special status.

In spite of the forebodings of the Earl of Essex the cause of the Parliamentarians was beginning to prosper. As soon as the Scots entered England, Newcastle's hitherto commanding position in the north had been undermined. Newcastle had been created a Marquis by King Charles I for his services in the previous year. The loyal Marquis, who had passed the winter not unagreeably in Welbeck, one of his large country houses, rallied to his duty and marched to try to stop the Scots as they moved south upon Northumberland and Durham. Their advance relieved all pressure on the Fairfaxes, and Sir Thomas Fairfax marched across the country into Cheshire, where at the battle of Nantwich he defeated reinforcements sent to King Charles I from Ireland. The Marquis of Newcastle, menaced with being caught between three enemy armies, those of the Scots, the Fairfaxes,

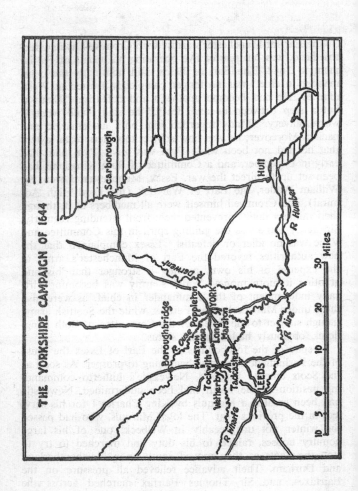

THE YORKSHIRE CAMPAIGN OF 1644

Scarborough

Hull

R. Humber

R. Derwent

Boroughbridge

R. Ouse

Poppleton

Long Marston

YORK

MARSTON MOOR

Tockwith

Wetherby

Tadcaster

LEEDS

R. Aire

R. Wharfe

Miles

30   20   10   0   5   10

and the Earl of Manchester, appealed desperately to his King in Oxford for help. The King hesitated. His policy was now of an empirical kind. He himself remained in the Midlands while permitting Prince Rupert to make lightning dashes to relieve threatened points and hoping for further triumphs from Hopton's army in the southwest. In April the Marquis of Newcastle, pressed back by the Scots, shut himself up in York. Meanwhile Prince Rupert had led a brilliant expedition to the relief of Newark and later into Lancashire, but Hopton, fighting as the subordinate of the Earl of Forth, who was sick with gout, had been defeated at the battle of Cheriton in Hampshire. The armies of the King and the Earl of Manchester sparred at each other between the university towns of Oxford and Cambridge. At one point General Cromwell had carried out a raiding expedition beneath the very walls of Oxford itself; at another he had destroyed a Royalist outpost which lay between Newport Pagnell and Oxford. Such joy as he may have felt in these minor successes was marred by the death of his second son, who, like himself two years before, bore the name of Captain Oliver Cromwell and was stamped by his devotion to "God's cause" in his father's image. We do not know where that boy of twenty-one lies buried or whether his father attended his funeral. All we have is a note signed by Cromwell and Manchester appointing a certain Captain Browne to fill his place as commander of the fourth troop in the Ironside regiment. Then the war went on.

*   *   *

The Marquis of Newcastle had been obliged to retire into York, after he had boldly confronted the Scots in Durham, because of another victory won by his old foes, the Fairfaxes. Sir Thomas Fairfax, recalled to Yorkshire from his campaign in Cheshire, met his father near Goole in the first week of April 1644. Lord Bellasis, the Royalist Governor of York, had thought to prevent the Fairfaxes from going to the help of the Scots by occupying Selby, a strategic town lying between Leeds and Hull and south of York itself. Bellasis, who was a cousin of the Fairfaxes, was completely outmaneuvered by them, and after a forced march the Scots joined the victorious army under Lord Fairfax at Tadcaster on April 19. York was then considered to be the second town in England, a walled and turreted city, bestriding the Ouse and crowned by its slender Minster. Sir Thomas Fairfax was dispatched in a deputation to the Earl of Manchester to invite him to share with his Yorkshiremen and the Scots in the honor of besieging this famous and ancient city.

The Earl of Manchester had just successfully stormed Lincoln, while Cromwell had covered the assault. Manchester at once accepted the invitation to take part in the siege of York, and sent Cromwell ahead with the cavalry. On June 2 the three commanding generals, the Earl of Manchester, Lord Fairfax, and the Earl of Leven, conferred before York, and Manchester's army was assigned the northern sector stretching from the Ouse to the river Fosse, just above where the northern angle of the wall protected the Minster. Major General Crawford did not endear himself to his colleagues when, without informing them, he prematurely exploded a mine on Trinity Sunday (June 16) "ambitious to have the honour alone," as Sir Thomas Fairfax mildly phrased it, but the scaling party failed to carry the breach thus created in the walls. All that happened was that St. Mary's Tower, a repository of historic documents, was laid in ruins. Fortunately Fairfax, who himself lived in the neighborhood, had already paid to have the documents copied. Twelve days later the besieging army abandoned all attempts to effect another breach, for the news was received that Prince Rupert, who had been harrying Lancashire, had crossed the Pennines and was on his way to raise the siege. Deciding to try to intercept him, the Parliamentarians marched west, but Prince Rupert evaded them by crossing to the north side of the Ouse. On July 1 the Marquis of Newcastle, who for a month had held out in York against an army three times the size of his own, sent greetings to his rescuer, "the most gallant and heroic Prince Rupert," in his camp outside the city.

* * *

At first the leaders of both armies were divided about the wisdom of fighting. The Marquis of Newcastle when he met Prince Rupert asked him "not to attempt anything as yet upon the enemy,"

for he had intelligence that there was some discontent between them, and that they were resolved to divide themselves, and so to raise the siege [of York] without fighting;

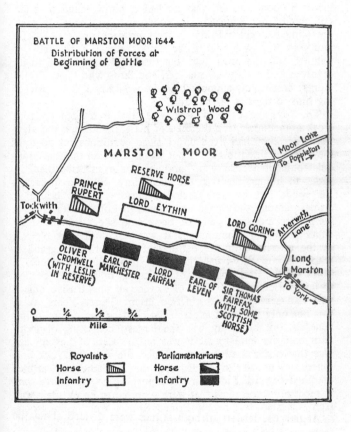

BATTLE OF MARSTON MOOR 1644
Distribution of Forces at
Beginning of Battle

Wilstrop Wood

MARSTON MOOR

Moor Lane
To Poppleton →

RESERVE HORSE

PRINCE
RUPERT

LORD EYTHIN

Tockwith

LORD GORING

Atterwith Lane

OLIVER
CROMWELL
(WITH LESLIE
IN RESERVE)

EARL OF
MANCHESTER

LORD
FAIRFAX

EARL OF
LEVEN

SIR THOMAS
FAIRFAX
(WITH SOME
SCOTTISH
HORSE)

Long
Marston

To York →

0   ¼   ½   ¾   1
Mile

Royalists
Horse
Infantry

Parliamentarians
Horse
Infantry

besides my Lord [it is his second wife who is writing] expected within two days Colonel Cleavering with above three thousand out of the North, and two thousand drawn out of several garrisons. . . .

Prince Rupert retorted that he had a positive and absolute command from King Charles to do battle at once. In fact, the King had given Prince Rupert no such order: what he had told him was that if he could relieve York only by fighting, then he must fight; but the letter was written in an involved and ambiguous manner, and those who knew Prince Rupert best rightly supposed that he would read it as instrucing him to fight at all hazards.

The Marquis of Newcastle was unable to depart from York immediately, for the men of his garrison took the view that after they had lived under siege conditions for so long they were entitled to rest, if not leave. It is said that the Marquis found it necessary to harangue and even bribe them in order to induce them to see their duty. He also inspected the spoils left by the hurried departure of the besieging armies: among the things abandoned in Lord Fairfax's tents were four thousand pairs of boots and shoes besides some small guns and ammunition. It was not until four o'clock in the afternoon of the battle that the Yorkshire grandee, who was now fifty-two, joined the young German prince.

As for the Parliamentarians, delicacies of seniority needed to be considered. The Earl of Leven, an unobtrusive officer who had served with distinction in the Thirty Years' War, was not only the most experienced of the three commanding generals, but his army was the largest, consisting of more than half the total force. It was on the Earl of Leven's advice that, after they had abandoned the siege of York and failed to cut off Prince Rupert, the Parliamentary armies marched toward Tadcaster. The purpose of the move was to meet reinforcements that were reported to be on their way from Chester, to prevent Prince Rupert from going south to rejoin the King, and to stop provisions reaching York from the East and West Ridings. But there had not been entire agreement at the Council of War when it met at Long Marston on the Tadcaster road. Moreover, its leaders had been misled by faulty intelligence, for the size of the Royalist army was overestimated. Nevertheless, Lord Fairfax and the Earl of Manchester (it may be supposed under Cromwell's influence) had been for fighting, but the Earl of Leven with professional caution wanted to retire to more favorable positions. Long Marston, at any rate, was overcrowded: "Our soldiers did drink the wells dry," related one of Manchester's chaplains, "and then were necessitated to make use of puddle water." So it had been decided to move towards Tadcaster, the infantry and artillery being sent in front, while the Cavalry under Cromwell covered the rear. However, on the morning of July 2 the commanding generals discovered that the enemy were on Marston Moor to the north of Long Marston. While they had been directing their movement west to Tadcaster, Prince Rupert had sent his men across the Ouse from Poppleton (today a suburb of York), where earlier he captured a bridge of boats, along the other road west of York that led to Boroughbridge. Another hasty council of war was called at Long Marston, and it was resolved to call back the infantry and artillery. So by the afternoon "both armies stood ranged in battle lines viewing each other and neither of them engaging."[6]

The three Parliamentarian armies were disposed roughly south of the York—Tadcaster road, between the villages of Tockwith and Long Marston, a distance of two miles. Their flanks were protected by water on one side and trees on the other. On the left of the line was the Earl of Manchester's cavalry commanded by Cromwell. Cromwell had offered to let the experienced Scottish officer, Major General David Leslie, hold this command, but since Leslie's poorly mounted cavalry was the smaller force and Leven was the senior officer on the field, it was thought politic to allow Cromwell to take charge of this wing. On its extreme left a regiment of Scottish dragoons was posted. In the center the infantry of all three armies was massed under the three commanding generals; on the right Sir Thomas Fairfax commanded the Yorkshire horse, supported, as Cromwell was also, by about eight hundred Scottish cavalry.

Opposite the Parliamentarian cavalry wings were stationed Royalist forces of about equal strength, each consisting of over two thousand horse interspersed with five hundred musketeers, according to the novel tactical plan that had been employed by the great Gustavus Adolphus, the King of Sweden, on the Continent. In the center was the Royalist foot, commanded by Lord Eythin, the Marquis of Newcastle's military adviser, with a group of horse in reserve. Prince Rupert was in full command, Newcastle with unusual modesty serving as a volunteer. Prince Rupert had himself drawn up the order of battle, siting his forward troops behind a ditch with most of his artillery massed in the middle. His, in fact, was a defensive layout. When Lord Eythin saw it, he remonstrated and remarked that they were too far forward. Prince Rupert offered to draw them back, but Eythin said it was too late.

While, in theory at least, the three Parliamentarian armies operated independently, the Earl of Leven evidently took the lead in arranging their dispositions. "We had," wrote the Earl of Manchester's chaplain, "double advantage of ground and wind":[7]

> Here the noble commander [Leven] exercised his martial abilities with unwearied activity and industry. He hasted from place to place, to put all his forces in battle array, which he did to the satisfaction and admiration of all that beheld it, the other two Generals acting also in their own armies. . . .

The Scottish infantry were distributed in orthodox pre-Swedish fashion, with the pikemen in the center and the musketeers on the wings. The Scots were to some extent intermingled with the English armies. But once the battle began neither commander in chief exerted any real control over the battle. After all, in those times there were no telephones or signaling system. It may be recalled that even two hundred years later, at the battle of Gettysburg, General Robert E. Lee had little control over the battle after he had sited his men and given the orders for the day. It is true that Gustavus Adolphus, who was a King and in unquestioned command, had controlled the battle of Breitenfeld thirteen years earlier.[8] But neither Prince Rupert nor the Earl of Leven had the authority or genius of Gustavus Adolphus, and neither could hope to exercise more than a rudimentary control when the largest armies that had been locked in battle in England since the Wars of the Roses met on the Yorkshire moor that summer evening.

The terrain favored the Parliamentarians. Their forces were disposed on gently sloping ground from which the cavalry might have a springboard for a devastating charge. Once the obstacle of the ditch had been overcome—and it can scarcely have been a serious obstruction—the moor lined by the Royalists was ideal for cavalry fighting, open ground sparsely furnished with hedges and trees. The Royalist Cavalry were outnumbered by about seven to five, and Prince Rupert by drawing up his men so close to the ditch had committed himself at least for the time being to a defensive action. In fact, he told Lord Eythin that he did not intend to go into battle that day. If his cavalry were surprised and beaten, the enemy's horse would have every opportunity in the wide open moorland to cut down the opposing infantry, who, except on the extreme left, were virtually devoid of cover.

The Parliamentarians were ready at two o'clock, and at once began a relatively harmless cannonade. By five a lull intervened. On one side, the Parliamentarians waited patiently amid the rye fields spattered by a gentle summer rain; on the other, the Royalists were still moving into position. "We may picture to ourselves," wrote the late Sir Clements Markham, "the long line of horsemen with their breastplates glittering in the afternoon sun; the solid masses of shouldered pikes . . . and the hundred of fluttering pennons above them all shapes and colours. The standard of Prince Rupert, with its red cross, was nearly five yards long."

A probing attack on the extreme left of the Parliamentarian line had been beaten off by the Scottish dragoons. By seven Prince Rupert decided that no battle would take place that day and went to his supper. The Marquis of Newcastle retired to his coach for a quiet pipe. But at half-past seven the Earl of Leven gave the signal for attack. Was that a stroke of genius? It seems more probable that some traitor from the other side had brought the news that then was the opportunity to surprise the Royalists. After all, "a summer's evening is as long as a winter's day," and when darkness came a harvest moon would light the moor. The whole allied line charged through the standing grain. On the left Oliver Cromwell himself led a division of three hundred men. "We came down the hill in the bravest order," wrote his Scoutmaster (or intelligence officer), "and with the greatest resolution that ever was seen. . . . Cromwell's own division had a hard pull of it, for they were charged by Rupert's bravest men both in front and flank." Prince Rupert himself, as soon as he heard the astonishing news, gave up all attempt to control the battle and galloped to the countercharge. "They stood at the sword's point a pretty while hacking one another, when at last (it so pleased God) he [Cromwell] brake through them, scattering them before him like a little dust." In the heat of the battle Cromwell was wounded in the neck, but David Leslie came up with the second line on his little Scottish nags and Prince Rupert was overthrown.

With this success achieved on their flank, the Earl of Manchester's infantry, led by Laurence Crawford, also moved forward, but on the right the tale was otherwise. Here were two lanes, protected by ditches and hedges beautified with wild roses, in which the Royalist musketeers, supporting their cavalry, commanded by the brave if drunken General George Goring, wreaked havoc, as the Swedish right wing had done at Breitenfeld. The Scots failed to restore the day, and Sir Thomas Fairfax himself received a saber cut which he bore on his cheek all his life. On their left the flower of the Scottish infantry were mown down, though five out of the ten regiments posted there stood their ground. Thus, while the Parliamentarian cavalry on the left was triumphant, so also was the Royalist cavalry on the opposite wing. Goring's troopers galloped uphill to plunder the baggage, and before them (as a Parliamentarian chronicler wrote) "it was a sad sight to behold many thousands posting away, amazed with panic fears."

It was at that crisis in the battle that Sir Thomas Fairfax showed his high personal courage. "Taking the signal [a white handkerchief or piece of paper that distinguished the Roundheads] out of my hat," he related afterwards, "I passed through [mistaken] for one of their commanders; and so got to my Lord of Manchester's horse in the other wing; only with a cut in my cheek which was given me in the first charge and a shot my horse received." It was a hard day for Fairfax, for his brother Charles was mortally wounded and his father fled the battlefield, believing that all was over. Cromwell had kept his men together after they had defeated Prince Rupert. One of the Royalists afterwards seized on this fact as being one of the principal reasons for his own side's defeat. "The enemy's keeping close and firm together in a body after they had routed the Prince's right wing," wrote the Governor of Scarborough (who had the facts directly from the fugitives), "though in that the active part must be imputed to Cromwell and his horse, yet it is thought that the ordering and advice to do so came from David Leslie, an experienced old soldier." That was mere speculation. Cromwell had done the same at Gainsborough. At any rate, he immediately answered Sir Thomas Fairfax's appeal and, as he himself said afterwards, "the left wing which I commanded, being our own horse, saving a few Scots in our rear, beat all the Prince's horse." He wheeled his troopers to the right and thrust across the battlefield, surprising the Royalist cavalry on the other side, catching them "at the same place of disadvantage where they had routed our horse formerly." "The enemy," observed another Parliamentarian account, "seeing us come over in such a gallant posture to charge them, left all thought of pursuit and began to think that they must fight again for that victory which they thought had already been got." The Royalists rode downhill from where the Parliamentarian lines had first been, and received Cromwell's charge exactly as they themselves had launched theirs upon Fairfax. After they were beaten, Cromwell's tireless cavalry, supported by the infantry of his own army, fell upon the Marquis of Newcastle's foot, Whitecoats and Greencoats alike. The Whitecoats were men clothed in uniform of undyed woolen cloth and known also as "Newcastle's Lambs," who had sworn to fight until their coats were stained red with the blood of their enemy. They fought it out to the last man and the last round, and died with their boots on. The Marquis himself, seeing no hope left, fled to York. Near the city he met Prince Rupert. According to his second wife's story, Newcastle was now asked by Rupert "how the business went?" Newcastle answered that "all was lost and gone on their side." And he told Rupert further that he himself intended to leave the country for Holland. Meanwhile David Leslie, who had tenaciously seconded all Cromwell's superb maneuvers, "seeing us thus pluck a victory out of the enemy's hands, professed Europe had no better soldiers."

It was indeed an extraordinary victory. It is true that from the start the Parliamentarians had all the advantages, larger numbers (some 27,000 against 17,000), higher ground, the initiative, the surprise, finer officers, and men with firmer morale. But the commander in chief never influenced the battle once they had ordered the dispositions. The Earl of Leven, after vainly trying to rally the Scottish infantry in the center, left the field disconsolate; Prince Rupert, having been completely defeated on the right wing, apparently did the same. What would have happened if Fairfax had not heroically penetrated the field in search of Cromwell's help and if Cromwell had not kept his troopers in check and thus been able to respond? The battle might have been as drawn out and indecisive as was Edgehill. Instead of that, at least three thousand Royalists were killed, many more were taken prisoner, including three major generals, and almost all their artillery was captured; and Oliver Cromwell was "crowned with never-withering laurels of fame and honour."

*   *   *

It was asserted by some of the Scots after the battle of Marston Moor, and the story was repeated in modified form by later historians, that Cromwell's share in the battle was exaggerated by himself and his friends, and that the credit for the victory was chiefly owing to Major General Leslie, whose countercharge at a critical moment saved the day. Denzil Holles, a Presbyterian M.P., had a different story in his posthumously published memoirs, averring that Major General Crawford took over the command of the Earl of Manchester's horse because Cromwell lost his nerve when he was wounded.

The story that Cromwell was saved by Leslie (or Crawford) at Marston Moor is paralleled by the story that he ran away (or was never present) at the battle of Edgehill. Great men always make enemies, and victories are invariably attributed to anyone but the commanding officer. But no one who reads Holles's memoirs can regard them seriously.

Cromwell's only surviving letter about the battle was a private letter of condolence to a friend and was by no means untruthful. He said the Scots were "few" and in the rear; and so they were: the accepted figures are that the Scots under Leslie were one third of the troopers under Cromwell, but they may have been even fewer, and they formed the reserve when the battle began. Neither Cromwell's Scoutmaster nor Manchester's chaplain mentions either the check or the flank attack of Leslie, and as their accounts were published immediately after the battle they challenged refutation. It is true that a civilian who was attached to Fairfax's army reported that "the Earl of Manchester's horse were repulsed by fresh supplies of the enemies, and forced to retreat in some disorder"; but such a report must be treated with caution. It is not clear why a civilian who was nowhere near that part of the battle should be trusted for what happened there, more especially as his narrative can be shown to be inaccurate in several other respects. David Leslie no more won the battle of Marston Moor than he won the battle of

Dunbar, where Cromwell was to beat him decisively with inferior numbers six years later.

Notes

1. For the Earl of Leven, see C. S. Terry, *The Life and Campaigns of Alexander Leslie, first Earl of Leven* (1899).

2. S. R. Gardiner, *The Great Civil War* (1886), I, 365.

3. See my *Cromwell's Generals* (1954), appendix.

4. *The Letters and Journals of Robert Baillie* (1841), II, 229.

5. For Sir Henry Vane, see the biography by J. Willcock (1913); a new biography of this capable administrator is overdue.

6. Bibliographies of the battle of Marston Moor are in Sir Clements A. Markham, *Life of the Great Lord Fairfax* (1870) and C. H. Firth, "The Battle of Marston Moor," *Transactions of the Royal Historical Society*, XII (1898). I am particularly skeptical of the value of Sir Hugh Cholmeley's narrative (Egerton MSS. 3884, f. 39). It is strange that neither Ash, a first-class authority, nor Watson mentions Cromwell's check and wound. Thomas Stockdale, M.P. (Firth, *op. cit.*, 75), is the civilian who mentions the check without referring to Cromwell. Lieut. Colonel Burne in his recent account, however, treats all this as if it were established fact. He may be right, but the authorities for it seem to me to be dubious.

7. Ash in Vicars, *England's Parliamentary Chronicle*, 271.

8. I am indebted to Mr. Michael Howard for drawing my attention to the battle of Breitenfeld.

Chapter 9

Cromwell the Statesman: The Self-denying Ordinance

"TRULY," WROTE CROMWELL after the battle of Marston Moor, "England and the Church of God hath had a great favour from the Lord, in this great victory given unto us, such as the like never was since this war began. It had all the evidences of an absolute victory obtained by the Lord's blessing upon the godly party principally." By "the godly party" he meant his own troopers. The question was how the victory was to be pursued. It was over this that differences of opinion first began openly to appear between Cromwell and his superior officer, the Earl of Manchester.[1]

Edward Montagu, second Earl of Manchester, was three years younger than Cromwell, having been born in 1602. Like Cromwell, he had been educated partly at Sidney Sussex College, Cambridge, under the Mastership of Dr. Samuel Ward. Even before his family had acquired Hinchingbrooke from Cromwell's uncle, he had three times represented Huntingdonshire in Parliament. But he had also been a friend of the first Duke of Buckingham, and King Charles I had raised him to the peerage as Viscount Mandeville before he succeeded his father in the earldom. He was in fact a pleasant man whom everybody liked. Clarendon wrote of him that "by his natural civility, good manners, and good nature, which flowed towards all men, he was universally acceptable and beloved." Dr. Burnet remarked that he was "of a soft and obliging temper, of no great depth but universally beloved, being both a virtuous and a generous man." Another contemporary called him "a sweet, meek man." Manchester married as the second of his five wives a daughter of Robert Rich, Earl of Warwick, the leading Puritan in the House of Lords. Under the Warwick influence and also, it is reasonable to assume, under that of Dr. Samuel Ward, he became a mild but consistent Presbyterian, and was anxious for the radical reform of the Church of England. When the Long Parliament met, John Pym and other Puritan statesmen frequently held consultation with him at his house in Chelsea. Earlier, he had been one of twelve peers who even before the signature of the Treaty of Ripon had urged the King to summon Parliament. He was recognized as a responsible critic of the Government in the House of Lords, and when King Charles I vainly attempted to arrest and inpeach five members of the House of Commons he planned to arrest Manchester, then confusingly known as Lord Kimbolton, along with them, although his name is said to have been added to the list as an afterthought. As soon as Parliament began to appoint its own Lords Lieutenant in the counties in preparation for the Civil War, the Earl of Manchester was a natural choice as Lord Lieutenant of Huntingdonshire. Thus Cromwell knew the Earl of old and, according to Clarendon, measured swords with him when enclosures of his lands for grazing cut across the customary rights of some of Cromwell's poorer neighbors. But Manchester bore Cromwell no grudge, and at first "always placed him in chiefest esteem and credit."

The contrast in character between the two men was extraordinary. No one could possibly accuse Cromwell of being a sweet, meek man. His temper was a byword both in the eastern counties and at Westminster. Though belonging to a branch of a once wealthy family, he had not been born to the purple and he had undergone a hard struggle as a farmer. He saw himself not as a reformer but as a crusader. John Pym had said in his famous speech to the Short Parliament: "There is a design to alter law and religion. The party that effect this are papists who are obliged by a maxim in their duty, that they are not only bound to maintain their religion but to extirpate all others." Cromwell believed, with his friend Henry Vane, that "the kingdom of God is within us." He saw no line of compromise between the aims of the "papist armies" that he believed he was fighting and the faith within him that urged him forward.

But to the Earl of Manchester, as to the Earl of Essex, the case was less clear-cut. On the eve of the battle of Marston Moor, Vane had gone up to Yorkshire to interview the three commanding generals, and to sound them about whether in the event of victory they would consent to reconstructing a government without King Charles I. Though engaged upon a contest to the death with the King's armies, they were appalled at the very notion of deposing him. From the beginning the commander in chief, the Earl of Essex, had equally favored negotiations at the earliest opportunity, and had sought plenipotentiary powers to come to terms to end the war. These Presbyterian magnates were monarchists to a man. So were their allies from Scotland. Had not King Charles as King of Scotland already conceded virtually all their demands? Let him accept the Solemn League and Covenant, and the two kingdoms could settle down under one ruler and one Kirk, advised by allied assemblies in London and Edinburgh. The Earl of Manchester never ceased to be a monarchist: he was to become Lord Chamberlain to King Charles II. Later in 1644, after the second battle of Newbury, he told his Council of War: "If we beat the King ninety-nine times he would be King still, and his posterity, and we subjects still; but if he beat us but once we should be hanged, and our posterity be undone." By posterity the Earl was thinking of the nobility to whom he belonged. On the other hand, once admit that the King could be dethroned or compelled to abdicate, then no established institution was safe. Hence Manchester's exceptional cautiousness as a commander.

It was unfortunate for this mild peer with his halfhearted views about war aims and his Presbyterian religion that he should have been assigned the command of the army of the Eastern Association. Though it was a splendid fighting machine, it was also an explosive one. When he assumed his appointment in the autumn of 1643, it was already filled largely with Independents, Baptists, and other sectarians. The principles on which Cromwell had recruited his own regiment had extended to others raised in the area. "In my own army," Manchester reluctantly confessed, were "many honest men, though differing in judgment to what I profess." It was estimated by a Scottish minister who came to London in 1644 that only one third of the Earl of Manchester's army were Presbyterians. To the rest the Solemn League and Covenant was anathema. The Independents and Brownists, wrote a contemporary as early as October 1643, were "enraged at the Scots Covenant which wholly blasted their hopes of a toleration or connivance, at the least, of the exercise of their own discipline," and added that three regiments would revolt for certain if Presbyterianism on the Scottish model was introduced into England.[2] Cromwell himself on one occasion told the Earl of Manchester that "he could as soon draw his sword against the Scots as against the King's army because of the way they carried themselves, pressing for their discipline." Some of the discontented English regiments, including Cromwell's own, regarded themselves as mobile Christian congregations, immediate servants of the Lord. "His officers," noted the Reverend Richard Baxter, who had been offered the chaplaincy of the Ironside regiment, "purposed to make their troop a gathered Church."[3] Cromwell came to think of himself and his men as together welded into an instrument of the Almighty, as truly a Church militant.

Cromwell was soon recognized after the Scottish alliance had been formed as "the great Independent" and "the darling of the sectaries."[4] It is scarcely true that he "packed" the Earl of Manchester's army with men of his own beliefs: it was already packed with them when the Earl assumed his command. But differences of temperament, opinion, and religious outlook ripened into antagonism once the immediate military crisis had passed away.

* * *

York surrendered a fortnight after the battle of Marston Moor, and a decision had to be reached about what the victorious armies were to do next. The battle had been a grueling one, and the commanders were far from anxious to undertake another. "My men, through want of clothes and other necessaries," complained Manchester at this time, "fall sick daily," and the Scots were said to be in like condition. They were also behindhand with their pay. The Committee of Both Kingdoms, under the leadership of Sir Henry Vane, wanted them to pursue Prince Rupert, who had retired into the northwest. But the three commanding generals replied in a rather incoherent way that what they desired was to establish a Presbyterian system at once and to settle with the King on that basis. That was their political counsel, for which they had not been asked; as to the war, they ignored the instruction to pursue Prince Rupert as pointless and determined to separate and go about their own business. Each did what was most congenial to him. The Scots departed north to secure Newcastle upon Tyne so as to clear their communications with their native land. The Fairfaxes proceeded to attack Scarborough and such other fortified places as still held out for the King in Yorkshire. And the Earl of Manchester returned to Lincolnshire and by easy stages to Huntingdon. On his way he somewhat reluctantly summoned and occupied Tickhill Castle on the Yorkshire side of the Nottinghamshire border, allowing the gentlemen who defended it to go home after handing over their arms and

horses. He also sent Major General Crawford to lay siege to
Sheffield, and himself paid a visit to Welbeck, where he had
an agreeable conversation with the Marchioness of Newcastle
and her daughters, and promised to allow them to go abroad
and to intercede with Parliament for their maintenance. The
Committee of Both Kingdoms was more than surprised at
the Earl's courteous and leisurely proceedings, and again
suggested that he should march against Prince Rupert at
Chester. That appeared to the Earl, who, according to Cromwell, was unusually angry at the suggestion, to be "so large
a commission and a work so difficult" that he summoned his
chief officers to help him draw up a paper explaining why
it was out of the question. It would take a month to besiege
Chester, he said, and, after all, summer was nearly over; in
any case, his forces were not big enough, his supplies were
insufficient, his communications were uncertain, his base
would be in danger from the Royalist hold on Newark, and
his men would infinitely prefer to stay near their own homes.
The Committee could but acquiesce in this impressive summary of the difficulties, but ventured to propose that if the
Earl himself did not feel like riding into Cheshire, he might
at least send some reinforcements there. The Earl promised
"to prepare a party," but explained that he must first consult
the neighboring counties about what they could provide. He
was still "preparing his party" at the end of August.

Meanwhile, in spite of Marston Moor the general military
situation was gradually changing back in favor of the Royalists. The Earl of Essex, like the generals in the north, had
ignored the orders of the Committee of Both Kingdoms,
which had been for him to combine with the army of Sir
William Waller in a central attack upon the King's headquarters at Oxford. Instead of doing so, the Earl, who was
extremely jealous of Waller, had marched his army away into
the west of England to seek glory by relieving Lyme in
Dorset and reconquering Devonshire and Cornwall for Parliament. Thus he left the King free to maneuver in his inner
lines. Waller was defeated by the King at the battle of
Cropredy Bridge in Oxfordshire, three days before Marston
Moor, and afterwards his soldiers, who were principally men
from the home counties, began to melt away. The Earl of
Essex, having successfully relieved Lyme, lengthened his
communications alarmingly as he plunged doggedly on towards hostile Cornwall, followed by King Charles's victorious
army. In this fresh crisis the Committee of Both Kingdoms

naturally looked to the unemployed army under the Earl of Manchester for assistance. It's plan was for Waller to go to the help of the Earl of Essex, and for the Earl of Manchester to move on Oxford.

The Earl of Manchester, who sat for a month at Lincoln doing nothing at all—even ignoring the advice of his own Council of War at least to besiege Newark—slowly made ready to obey his orders. Cromwell had become increasingly restive over the enforced inaction. The courtly habits of old-fashioned warfare were alien to his disposition. He learned with concern of the dangers being undergone by the Earl of Essex, and chafed to go to the west. "Truly," he wrote to a friend, "had we wings, we would fly thither." "Indeed," he added, "we find our men never so cheerful as when there is work to do." But there was no work found for them. "We have some amongst us much slow in action," he remarked meaningly. Not only had the Earl of Manchester rejected the advice of his own officers to besiege Newark, but he refused to call his Council of War again or to proceed with operations against the smaller Royalist garrisons in the neighborhood. So the remainder of the summer was wasting away in a welter of paralysis and indecision.

But in the first week of September even the Earl of Manchester was jolted out of his amiable lethargy. For the news reached him that the army of the Earl of Essex had been surrounded and compelled to surrender at Lostwithiel in Cornwall, while the commander in chief had escaped by sea to Plymouth. Essex had received no orders to desert his army, but he regarded his own survival as indispensable to his side. Manchester, who had now reached his home in Huntingdon, thought that "the Lord's arm was not shortened . . . though we be much weakened." He determined to act in obedience to his earlier orders, and obligingly promised the Committee of Both Kingdoms that he would "from time to time acquaint your Lordships with my marches." After five days he managed to reach St. Albans, but here he rested his army for more than a week. To make haste slowly was his motto, or at any rate his practice.

However, the Earl now enjoyed a far more satisfactory excuse than the sickness of his soldiers and their unwillingness to leave their own counties for the gentleness of his movements. His leading officers were quarreling among themselves.

Cromwell, as has been seen, had long objected to the

efforts of Major General Crawford to impose the Covenant on all and sundry. Crawford, for his past, had swollen the chorus begun by other Presbyterians, who had insisted that Cromwell and the Independents claimed more than their fair share of the glory for the victory of Marston Moor. Major Thomas Harrison of Colonel Fleetwood's regiment was said to have "trumpeted all over the City [of London] that Cromwell alone with his unspeakable valorous regiments had done all the service." Cromwell was accused of "attributing all the praise to himself of other men's actions." Crawford retorted by spreading the tale that Cromwell had acted the coward. The quarrel between these two fierce characters flared up as soon as Crawford returned from his spell of detached duty at Sheffield. It may well be that during his absence Cromwell had tried to undermine his position. At least Crawford thought so. "The said Cromwell," he asserted, "endeavoured to work Major General Crawford's ruin by dissuading the Earl of Manchester's army not to obey him, and giving his charge away to others." He added that Cromwell had spoken against him with such success that two regiments absolutely refused to obey him. Cromwell, realizing the unpopularity of this Presbyterian martinet with the largely Independent rank and file, had certainly attempted to have him removed. He went so far as to inform the Earl of Manchester that his colonels would resign in a body if a new major general were not appointed. Therefore, in spite of the urgency for military action by his army after the surrender at Lostwithiel, the Earl of Manchester took his two subordinates up to London and laid the matter before the Committee of Both Kingdoms. The Committee naturally adopted a patriotic line. It told the generals to stop quarreling and the Earl of Manchester to make haste to battle with King Charles I, who was returning as a conqueror from the west.

Cromwell was no ordinary soldier. He was himself a member of the Committee of Both Kingdoms (he took the oath of secrecy at this time) and of the House of Commons; and Vane, one of the most influential men in London, was his friend. While Cromwell was in London he took his place in the Commons and pleaded the cause of the sectaries. On his suggestion another friend, Oliver St. John, drew up a motion instructing the Assembly of Divines that in framing the new Church government they must find some way "how far tender consciences, who cannot in all things submit to the common rule which shall be established [i.e., the Presbyterian system], may be borne with according to the Word, and as may stand with the public peace." Not only was this important "accomodation order" accepted without a division, but at the end of the sitting the Speaker by the command of the House "gave thanks to Lieutenant General Cromwell for his fidelity in the cause in hand, and in particular for the faithful service performed by him in the late battle near York, where God made him a special instrument in obtaining that great victory." Thus Cromwell triumphed doubly: he had safeguarded the faith of the Independents who served with him in the Earl of Manchester's army and his own honor had been strikingly vindicated. In return he had waived his demand for Crawford's dismissal, and received the assurance that his commanding general would lay his doubts aside and go forward to fight the King.

The plan was for the armies of the Earl of Manchester and Sir William Waller to unite, and, strengthened by certain forces collected by the Earl of Essex and with some regiments from London, strike at the King and prevent his return to Oxford. Cromwell rode to Banbury, and on October 14 joined Manchester at Reading. The King was already moving on Salisbury, and, as Manchester was unwilling to push farther west, the three Parliamentarian generals met at Basingstoke on October 17. The combined army numbered about 19,000 men, and was under the command of a Council of War designed to inhibit jealousies and quarreling. A number of fortified places in Royalist hands—an outer ring guarding Oxford—had to be overcome before the Parliamentarian armies could maneuver freely, and they had not the strength to subdue them as well as to engage the King. King Charles, finding that these forts were closely besieged by his enemy, instead of coming on towards Oxford drew off to Newbury, with the intention of staying on the defensive until winter should put an end to all campaigning. The Earl of Manchester still hesitated to advance to meet the King and even contemplated staying at Basingstoke, but when the Council of War met he was overruled. On October 26 the Parliamentary army was posted at Clay Hill in Berkshire in full view of the Royalist positions.

The King's army was formidably posted. He had some 10,000 men, and they were marshaled along the eastern slopes of a hill between two watercourses, the river Kennet to the south and its tributary, the Lambourne, to the north. His right rested on the village of Newbury, and his left was protected by Donnington Castle, which was well furnished with artillery. The road to Oxford crossed the Lambourne river, and was protected by a fortified manor house, called Shaw, on the north bank. The Parliamentary commanders, recognizing that a mere frontal attack was out of the question, decided upon the bold expedient of dividing their army into two and sending a large detachment to assault the enemy's rear, which was held by a force under Prince Maurice, the younger brother of Prince Rupert. Cromwell's cavalry accompanied the detachment allocated for the purpose, and Sir William Waller, the most enterprising of the other generals, also served with it. But everything went wrong. The detached force carried out an elaborate detour of thirteen miles to avoid Donnington Castle, but the move was spotted and when the attack went in during the afternoon of October 27 Prince Maurice was ready. Cromwell's cavalry found itself on most unfavorable ground, intersected with hedges and coming under cannon fire from Donnington.[5] But the infantry pushed on bravely. It was at this time that the Earl of Manchester was expected to launch his frontal attack, and General Crawford, who was no coward, urged him to do so. But it was not until nearly dusk that Manchester was ready to assault Shaw House, and the attack was repulsed without difficulty as night came on. Meanwhile the King had thrown in his reserves in support of Prince Maurice, and the rear attack, though pressed courageously, was beaten off. Yet in a sense the battle had been won by the Parliamentarians, for when night fell King Charles resolved to withdraw. Though the moon lit the silent battlefield, he marched across Manchester's front and disappeared safely in the direction of Oxford. Next day Waller and Cromwell led the cavalry in pursuit, but the King made good his escape. Insult was added to injury when, less than a fortnight later, the King, accompanied by Prince Rupert, returned to Donnington Castle, reprovisioned the fortress, which had successfully defied a summons from the Earl of Manchester, and fetched away the artillery and stores of ammunition that had been left behind under the very noses of the victors of the second battle of Newbury.

Exceptionally bad weather brought the campaign of 1644 to a premature close. The Parliamentary cavalry was exhausted and the infantry sick and cold, while food and fuel were scarce. Even Cromwell, who felt bitterly about the conduct of his commander in chief both before and during the battle of Newbury, realized that no alternative remained but to retire into winter quarters.

*   *   *

The relief of Donnington Castle by King Charles I in the teeth of an army that claimed to have won the battle of Newbury caused perturbation in London. The Committee of Both Kingdoms wrote to the Earl of Manchester that "so long as the enemy continues in the field, we cannot advise that you should go to your winter quarters, but are very desirous that, keeping your forces together, you will use your best endeavours to recover the advantage the enemy hath lately gained. . . ." The same letter concluded:

That all your affairs may be managed with the greater unanimity and executed with the more cheerfulness, it is our desire that all your undertaking and enterprises be resolved upon by common advice of a Council of War, and from time to time give us frequent advertisement of your proceedings.

This was at once a reproof and a snub. But the Parliamentary armies had shot their bolt, and all that the Earl of Manchester did was to dispatch Sir Arthur Haselrigg, himself a member of the Committee of Both Kingdoms, to offer an elaborate explanation to the House of Commons why the campaign had ended in failure. The relief of Donnington had come at a most unfortunate time for the Parliamentary party, for at that very moment it was engaged in drawing up and tendering to the King a new set of exceptionally severe peace terms. When their commissioners reached Oxford they were brushed aside with contempt. "There are three things I will not part with," King Charles told them, "the Church, the Crown, and my friends."

While the peace commissioners were in Oxford, Cromwell resumed his seat in the House of Commons. The members were dissatisfied with Haselrigg's defense, and demanded explanations from the generals who had fought at Newbury. Sir William Waller and Cromwell both took part in a debate on November 25. Cromwell, now the politician and not the soldier, delivered a grave indictment of his commander in chief. Not only did he set out all the opportunities that Manchester had neglected throughout the year's campaign, but he put forward what he considered to be the explanation of the Earl's shortcomings. He said that he had reason to believe

> that his backwardness was not merely from dullness or indisposedness to engagement, but withal from some principle of unwillingness in his Lordship to have this war prosecuted unto a full victory and a design to have it ended by accommodation on some such terms to which it might be disadvantageous to bring the King too low.

The Commons referred the whole question to a committee appointed for army matters, under the chairmanship of a certain Zouch Tate, M.P. for Northampton. But the Earl of Manchester promptly defended himself before the remnants of the House of Lords, where he dubbed Cromwell a "factious and somewhat inert officer." Indeed, the commanding generals went much farther than that in their response to the accusation of the fiery cavalry leader. The Earl of Essex, still the commander in chief, called a meeting which included the Scottish commissioners in London, a number of the chief Presbyterians in the Commons, and some lawyers to discuss whether Cromwell could be brought to trial as an "incendiary." "Ye ken vary weel the Lieutenant-General Cromwell is no friend of ours," observed the Scottish Chancellor Loudoun in opening the proceedings; but the English lawyers doubted if there were proofs enough to arraign him, and stressed his popularity both in the Commons and in the country. Instead it was decided that a joint meeting should be held between the two Houses to debate these accusations and counteraccusations between the commander in chief of the Eastern Association and his second in command.

It would be easy to become bogged down in military detail if one attempted to sort out the arguments of the kind that were hurled backwards and forwards in the committees that had to investigate the truth about the campaigns of 1644. Basically the situation was a simple and even common one in war. After the battle of Marston Moor it had appeared as if final victory was near. But the commanders in the field had let their opportunities slip through excess of caution and want of leadership, and the Committee of Both Kingdoms had been too inexperienced and too remote to impress any unified strategy upon them. Consequently no such strategy existed, and the King was allowed to keep the initiative in maintaining his inner lines in the Oxford area, and successfully punching out from them when the chance was presented to him, in spite of the numerical inferiority of his armies. By the time that the Earl of Essex was cornered at Lostwithiel and the Earl of Manchester defied at Donnington Castle, it was obvious that something had gone radically wrong, that culprits must be found and a new system substituted. Yet the Earl of Manchester had recognized correctly that since, apart from the Scots, his was the only intact force in the field capable of meeting the enemy, he had no right to risk its destruction by any foolhardy enterprise. Caution in war is a question of degree rather than of principle. Cromwell himself saw that nothing more could have been done that season. Manchester was no traitor; he occupied a highly responsible position, and, like most soldiers, he did not believe that the civilians in Whitehall understood what was going on at the front. While he did not treat Cromwell as sharply as Cromwell treated him, he naturally resented the fact that his own once-trusted subordinate should come forward and accuse him of being idle and disloyal. If either man had then chosen to push matters to extremities, it would have been fatal to the Parliamentary cause. Manchester regarded Cromwell as a dangerous man because in a moment of anger he had told him that "he hoped to live to see never a nobleman in England." It is unlikely that Cromwell was being either humorous or entirely serious; it is more probable that he spoke in a gust of anger at the incompetence of the peers in the higher command. Cromwell had the sympathy of his friends like Vane and St. John, who had already perceived for themselves that neither the Earl of Manchester nor the Earl of Essex was a leader capable of winning the war for his side.

It was now that Cromwell, perhaps for the first time in his life, discovered the gifts of statesmanship of which the ingredients are restraint and magnanimity. Although Zouch Tate's committee upheld the accusations brought by him and his military colleagues about Manchester's slowness and incompetence, in a speech on December 9 Cromwell showed that he was prepared to let the matter drop. The important thing now, he said, was to save the nation from its desperate condition. Let them stop quarreling among themselves and admit that the chief causes of their divisions were pride and covetousness.

Therefore waiving a strict inquiry into the cause of these things, let us apply ourselves to the remedy, which is most necessary. And I hope we have such true English hearts and zealous affections towards the general weal of our Mother Country as no members of either House will scruple to deny themselves and their own private interest for the common good.

What was his remedy? It was no less than a clean sweep of the higher command. Tate (himself a Presbyterian) moved that for the remainder of the war no member of either House should hold a military or civil command. This motion was seconded by Vane who offered to lay down his own post as Treasurer of the Navy. Cromwell acknowledged the suspicion that had fallen upon them all, for he knew that people outside the two Houses were saying that they had shown favoritism in allocating well-paid commands to their own members. His own soldiers, he asserted in a second speech on the same day, would willingly fight and die in the cause of Parliament. "They do not idolize me," he insisted, "but look upon the cause they fight for." So a Self-denying Ordinance, prohibiting members of either House of Parliament from holding commands or offices, was passed by the House of Commons.

The Scots Commissioners watched with amazement the speed with which this measure was introduced and accepted. Undoubtedly the solution had been worked out behind the scenes since Cromwell had arrived in London. It was a compromise arranged in the public interest. If Cromwell had really wanted to destroy the power of Essex and Manchester and raise himself to the supreme command, he might have done so. But the Scots had just taken Newcastle-upon-Tyne, and they might equally have marched south to the aid of their friends in London if the quarrel had been pressed too far. In fact, it had already been proposed that they should be called south. The last thing that Cromwell wanted was to allow mutual recriminations at Westminster to play into the hands of the Scots. He recognized that all personal thoughts and even considerations about the future of the Church in England must be temporarily laid aside in the service of one overwhelming aim—an English Puritan victory. The army needed to be reorganized under a new general whom everyone trusted. For the moment nothing else mattered. Eventually the Earl of Essex and the Earl of Manchester came to see the position in a better light too. They resigned their commands with dignity and in the spring of the following year the House of Lords finally accepted the Self-denying Ordinance in a revised form.

Just as Cromwell had developed from being a dashing cavalry leader into a wise and skillful commander, so the irate and fanatical politician of early Caroline Parliaments had been transformed by wartime realities into a statesman. In his actions in the waning year of 1644 he exhibited a patriotism and single-mindedness that was the essence of his greatness.

Notes

1. For the Earl of Manchester's relations with Cromwell and with the Committee of Both Kingdoms, see *Documents relating to the Quarrel between the Earl of Manchester and Oliver Cromwell* (Camden Society, 1875) and *Camden Society Miscellany* (1883), VIII, from which the quotations are taken.

2. Robert Baillie, *Letters and Journals,* II, 170.

3. *Reliquiae Baxterianae* (1696), 50 seq.

4. Baillie, *op. cit.,* II, 230.

5. Lieut. Colonel Burne, *op. cit.,* 235, suggests that at Newbury Cromwell's heart was not in the affair. I cannot see any solid grounds for such a supposition. Again and again during the Civil Wars the cavalry was unable to operate in enclosed country if unsupported by infantry, and here the Royalists beat off the infantry under Sir William Balfour.

Chapter 10

Cromwell and the New Model Army: The Battle of Naseby

JOSHUA SPRIGGE, the Parliamentary chronicler of the events of 1645, began his account upon a somber note:[1]

> Two summers passed over, and we were not saved: our victories so gallantly gotten, and (which was more pity) so graciously bestowed, were put into a bag with holes; what we won one time we lost another; the treasure was exhausted, the countries wasted—a summer's victory proved but a winter's story; the game, however, set up at winter was to be new played again the next spring, and men's hearts failed them with the observation of these things.

Whoever may have deserved the credit for it, the King's strategy throughout the war had proved hitherto vastly more intelligent than that of Parliament. In 1642 he had nearly succeeded in thrusting his way to London after the battle of Edgehill. In 1643 the royal forces in the southwest and northeast had kept the initiative, and the Queen had brought timely succor from Holland to her husband in Oxford. Because of the setbacks of that year, John Pym had been obliged to call upon the help of the Scots. During 1644 King Charles I, recognizing that he was in an inferior military position, had adopted an offensive-defensive strategy. While maintaining his fortified base at Oxford, he had sent out Prince Rupert on daring expeditions to relieve threatened garrisons or to attack his enemies where they were weak. Although the battle of Marston Moor was fatal to his cause in Yorkshire, it remained formidable throughout the whole of the west from Chester to Cornwall. Only the seaports in that area (apart from Bristol) were in Parliamentary hands.

By contrast Cromwell's own side, though rich in resources, was feeble in strategy and even in morale. Instead of following a policy aimed at defeating the King's armies in the field, its efforts had been dissipated in attacking or defending scattered fortresses. Its generals had quarreled among themselves and ignored the orders of the high command, as represented by the Committee of Both Kingdoms in London. Its soldiers grew discontented partly because they were in arrears with their pay, partly because they were given nothing to do, and chiefly because, being for the most part local levies, they resented being led away from their home counties. The Scottish army had failed to make the conclusive contribution to victory that had been expected of it. Moreover, the Marquis of Montrose had reinvigorated the Royalist hopes in Scotland by rallying the Highlanders and falling upon the Covenanters. His successes shook the Scots in England. The Reverend Robert Baillie, one of their commissioners in London, wrote towards the end of 1644: "God help us! If God be pleased to settle Scotland and give us Newcastle, all will go well." But Cromwell and Vane had no intention of depending solely upon the Scots to conquer the King.

While the discussions on the Self-denying Ordinance were in progress, the House of Commons had also come round to the view that the wisest course was to enlist a "new model" army, which should be carefully officered, punctually paid, and enlisted nationally so that it should be free from those inhibiting local patriotisms that had so often disintegrated previous plans of campaign: "The customs of the soldiers here is woeful," noted Baillie, "they cannot stay from home a month together on any condition." The suggestion for forming a new army seems to have been put forward originally by Sir William Waller, but it was energetically taken up when Cromwell returned to Westminster in November 1644. A petition was then received from the Eastern Association complaining that it was no longer able to maintain the expense of supporting its troops and calling upon Parliament to find a remedy. The Committee of Both Kingdoms was instructed to "consider of a frame or model of the whole militia." The Committee, whose meetings Cromwell attended regularly, reported back on January 6, 1645, in favor of establishing a national army of over 21,000 men: it was to consist of ten cavalry regiments, twelve infantry regiments, and one regiment of dragoons. The Commons at once accepted these recommendations, all the more willingly because the House of Lords had refused to take any action on the Self-denying Ordinance unless the plan for a new army was first approved.

Ten days after the House of Commons had agreed to the

establishment of the New Model Army, it chose Sir Thomas Fairfax as the commander in chief and Phillip Skippon, an officer who had risen from the ranks and long been in charge of the London trained bands, as major general, but the post of lieutenant general was left vacant. Cromwell and Vane had acted as Tellers for the "yeas" when the vote was taken on the commanders, and Cromwell had assured the House that Fairfax was "very equal" to the post. On February 19 Fairfax came up to the House for an interview, when he modestly declined the chair that he was offered and preferred to stand.[2]

The House of Lords still jibbed both at the New Model Army and the Self-denying Ordinance. Cromwell, who was prominent in promoting these plans, serving assiduously on the committee which framed them, continued to show his new gift for tact and statesmanship. He had informed the Commons (perhaps with his tongue in his cheek) of a petition from some of the Earl of Manchester's officers asking that the Earl should be retained in his command.[3] Cromwell even proposed that while the New Model Army was forming the Scottish army should be brought south. That surely must have gone against the grain with him, but it may have soothed the fears of the Earl of Manchester and his friends lest the new army should be a force militating against the Presbyterian supremacy they thought so desirable. Cromwell and Vane, leaders of the Independents, were significantly reticent when peace negotiations were reopened with King Charles I, in which he was asked to take the Covenant, accept the abolition of the bishops, and set up a Presbyterian Directory. The breakdown of these negotiations reconciled the Presbyterian leaders to a renewal of the war and therefore to the recruiting of a fresh army. On February 15 the House of Lords agreed to the New Model Ordinance.

Cromwell himself had wanted the officers in the New Model Army to be appointed solely by the commander in chief and to be excused from subscribing to the Covenant. But he gave way over both these points. A compromise was arranged whereby the approval of Parliament was required for all the commander in chief's appointments, and while the Covenant was to be imposed in general terms, the officers and men of the new army were not bound in advance to any rigid Presbyterian system. A compromise was also eventually concerted over the Self-denying Ordinance. Instead of the members of the two Houses being absolutely excluded from all posts, it was enacted that members must lay down their existing posts forty days after the passing of the Ordinance, but they became eligible for future appointments. The House of Lords, which since it was a mere remnant of the original House, meant in effect the Earls of Manchester and Essex and their friends, agreed to this slowly and sadly, for it was virtually a censure upon their own conduct. It was only by a majority of a single vote that they confirmed the list of officers chosen for the New Model Army, and it was partly because the Commons threatened to revive the investigations into the Earl of Manchester's competence during the previous campaign that they came to heel over the New Model at all. A nicely judged blend of conciliation and aggression had thus achieved the purpose of those statesmen, led by Cromwell, who urged the reconstruction of the army. The New Model Army proved in the end to justify the personal and political sacrifices that he was making to procure its formation.[4]

But an army cannot be built in a day, and it was to the credit of its young commander-in-chief (Fairfax was now thirty-three) and the experienced General Skippon that it was so quickly organized. They set to work in the face of much foreboding and ill-humor. "When I went to take leave of a great person," Fairfax recalled in his memoirs, "he told me he was sorry I was going out with the army, for he did believe we should be beaten"; while "those who were disgusted at the alterations . . . sought by all means to obstruct my proceedings."[5] Baillie the Scot wrote home that "their new-modelled army consists, for the most, of raw, unexperienced, pressed soldiers. Few of the officers are thought capable of their places . . . if they do great things, many will be deceived." In fact, less than half the army consisted of pressed men, although impressment was used to fill the ranks. The infantry were partly men who had served in the former armies, while more than half the cavalry were drawn from the Eastern Association. But one characteristic distinguished the new body. Its officers were picked on merit and no religious test was applied. The Covenant was not imposed upon the common soldiers, while the officers could interpret it with latitude. Fairfax was not known to be either a Presbyterian or an Independent, while Skippon had a brand of Christian religion peculiarly his own. The cavalry officers were mostly country gentlemen of proved military skill, ranging from Cromwell's cousin Edward Whalley to Fairfax's uncle Thomas Sheffield. Thus it is not true to say that the

New Model Army was an organization designed by Cromwell to suit his own purposes and practice his own religion. Once the planning stage had been completed, Cromwell had nothing to do with its enlistment or training. That it contained a substantial number of officers and men—including his own former regiment, transferred to Fairfax—who had served under him in the Eastern Association was inevitable, since that was the one more or less intact and disciplined force left on the Parliamentary side. But it was intended to be a capable fighting machine and nothing more.

*   *   *

While General Fairfax, who took up his headquarters at Windsor, was recruiting the new army, Cromwell left London for the west of England. Here the Parliamentarian garrisons, isolated from each other except by sea, had fallen into difficulties. Weymouth for a time was recaptured by Dorsetshire Royalists, and Colonel Robert Blake, who had held out for many months in the inland town of Taunton in Somerset, was threatened by a Royalist army organized by General Goring. Sir William Waller had been chosen to uphold the Parliamentary interests there and to take Cromwell's regiment with him. But the news of the formation of the New Model unsettled the men still under arms, and even Cromwell's Ironsides grew restive. On March 4 therefore the House of Commons ordered Cromwell to join his former regiment, and Waller received peremptory instructions to move west.

Waller and Cromwell, both members of Parliament, threatened with the ax of the Self-denying Ordinance, got along well enough together. They had fought side by side at Newbury, and Waller now found Cromwell an obedient, modest, and quiet officer. As soon as Cromwell joined his own regiment, its anxieties subsided and it rode gallantly to its new task. Halfway to its objective, Weymouth, the Parliamentarian force captured a small group of Royalists, including a young lady disguised as a soldier, and at Amesbury, also in Wiltshire, a whole regiment was surrounded. But Waller had two difficulties: first, he lacked infantry (without whom the relief of Taunton was not possible), and secondly he soon outran his supplies in hostile territory. For a time he and Cromwell separated, Waller moving north towards

Bath and Bristol and Cromwell riding into Dorset. Then they rejoined and menaced Goring's headquarters at Bruton in Somerset, but Goring retreated into the enclosed country around Wells and Glastonbury, where they dared not advance without infantry. They fell back on Salisbury whence Cromwell wrote to Fairfax entreating him to send reinforcements lest they should be "put to the shame and hazard of a retreat," and thereby "lose Parliament many friends in these parts." But six days before Cromwell dispatched these urgent appeals for aid, the House of Lords had at last agreed to the Self-denying Ordinance, which required both Cromwell and Waller to lay down their commands within forty days. Thus, as so often happens in war, political considerations for the moment overrode military needs. The cavalry demonstration had given some relief to the Parliamentarian garrisons in the west, but on April 17, 1645, Cromwell received definite orders to return from Salisbury and deliver up his command to Sir Thomas Fairfax.

*　　　*　　　*

In war every battle has its repercussions on general strategy, no theater is entirely isolated, and the balance of forces may be unexpectedly altered by victory or defeat. Thus in the spring of 1645 the astounding victories of the Marquis of Montrose in Scotland had consequences which stretched as far as the south of England. The Earl of Leven, whose Scottish expeditionary force after the battle of Marston Moor and the capture of Newcastle had been expected to win the war for Parliament, was obliged to weaken his army in England in order to reinforce his beaten compatriots in Scotland, and he moved across from Yorkshire into Westmorland in order to intercept King Charles I or Prince Rupert in case they should try to bring an army from the Midlands to join Montrose. Such a plan had, in fact, been under consideration in Oxford, and while the New Model Army was forming and the available mobile forces of Parliament in the south had gone to the rescue of Taunton, the King prepared as a first step to leave Oxford and join Prince Rupert, whose main force was concentrated in the Worcester—Hereford area. Under these circumstances the Committee of Both Kingdoms thought it unwise to let go of Cromwell and the cavalry brigade he had brought back from the west. The very day after he had taken his leave of General Fairfax at Windsor, therefore, he was given orders to move on Oxford and do what he could to disrupt the royal plans.

He acted promptly. Leaving Reading on April 21 he ordered a rendezvous with other Parliamentarian horse in the neighborhood of Watlington in southeast Oxfordshire. Then, while he went to Wheatley, a few miles east of Oxford, his spies penetrated into the city on a market day. There they learned from the market people and some Oxford scholars that the Royalists were preparing for an immediate operation, since carriages and wagons were being collected to move artillery out of the city. He also learned that one Royalist cavalry regiment at least was posted at Islip to the north of the city on the river Cherwell. Cromwell immediately attempted to surprise the regiment, but his advance guard failed him and the Royalist regiment, commanded by the Earl of Northampton, withdrew. Cromwell kept his forces under arms at Islip throughout that night, and the next day a skirmish took place between his men and three Royalist regiments that came back to the attack. The Royalists were routed, losing 200 killed and 200 prisoners, and, as Cromwell reported to Fairfax, "the Queen's colours, richly embroidered with the Crown in the midst, and eighteen flower-de-luces wrought about in gold, with a golden cross on top." Some escaped to Oxford and Woodstock, but others got into the nearby fortified house of Bletchington, which had a garrison commanded by Colonel Windebank, son of a former Secretary of State. Cromwell summoned the house. The young commander was intimidated and surrendered. Cromwell regarded it as a divine act: "Though I have had greater mercies," he said, "yet none clearer. . . . I did much doubt the storming of the house, it being strong and well manned." But there was no mercy for the unhappy Windebank, whose decision to surrender was said to have been the work of feminine influence. He was condemned to death by his own side and shot in the castle garden at Oxford.

Cromwell now swept around to the west of Oxford, defeated another Royalist regiment at Bampton (between Witney and Faringdon), and then summoned Faringdon Castle on the Swindon road. But the governor was of sterner stuff than Colonel Windebank, and though Cromwell warned him that the garrison must expect to be slaughtered to a man if he was put to a storm, he was repulsed with loss. Later the tables were turned upon him, for General Goring, who

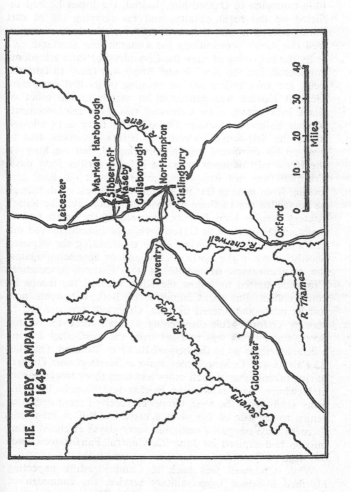

THE NASEBY CAMPAIGN 1645

Leicester
Market Harborough
Sibbertoft
Naseby
Guilsborough
Northampton
Kislingbury
Daventry
Oxford
Gloucester
R. Nene
R. Cherwell
R. Trent
R. Avon
R. Thames
R. Severn

Miles
0   10   20   30   40

had hurried from the west to his King's assistance, surprised Cromwell by a night attack on his headquarters at Faringdon, though in fact that did no more than interrupt his brilliant little campaign in Oxfordshire. Indeed, the losses he had inflicted on the royal cavalry, and his carrying off of cart horses needed to pull the royal artillery, effectively disorganized the King's preparations for a march into Scotland.

By the beginning of May the Committee of Both Kingdoms considered that the New Model Army was ready to take the field, and gave orders for the opening of its first campaign. General Fairfax was instructed to march to the relief of Blake in Taunton, while Cromwell was given reinforcements so that he could blockade Oxford. The forty days allowed under the Self-denying Ordinance before Cromwell had to give up his command had almost elapsed, but on May 10 the House of Commons extended it for a further forty days. Cromwell was not strong enough to prevent the King and Goring from leaving Oxford by the Woodstock road, though he controlled the southern approaches to the city. The King's strategy was to keep Fairfax occupied in the south and to maintain his garrison at Oxford, while he himself moved out of the Midlands with a view either to attacking the depleted Scottish army in the north of England or advancing against the Parliamentary stronghold of the Eastern Association. Cromwell started to follow the King with all the troops he could collect. But the Committee of Both Kingdoms now lost its nerve and altered its plan. Cromwell was ordered to stay by Oxford, after dispatching a small force to aid the Scots, and Fairfax was recalled from the west, after leaving a detachment to go to the help of Blake in Taunton. On May 22 Fairfax and Cromwell met again at Marston near Oxford, having taken leave of each other less than three weeks earlier at Newbury. And as soon as Fairfax had brought back his army safely from the west, Cromwell received fresh orders to return to the Isle of Ely with a mere handful of men, and there to stay on guard until his forty days' extended commission had expired on June 22. General Fairfax took over the siege of Oxford.

While Cromwell was back in Cambridgeshire expecting his final dismissal from military service, the campaign of 1645 suddenly flared towards its crisis. The opening weeks of service for the New Model Army had been unpropitious. The march to Taunton and the sudden recall had blunted its keenness, and the force it left behind suffered defeat. Then for a fortnight it laid siege to Oxford, only as suddenly to be withdrawn again. But General Fairfax's return had confused the King's plans. The scheme, such as it was, to go north was temporarily abandoned, and the King and his advisers vacillated between moving west, continuing north, and fighting Fairfax in order to save Oxford, whose garrison was dispirited and short of provisions. Finally the Royalists decided as a first move to relieve the pressure on Oxford by a surprise assault on the poorly fortified city of Leicester. At midnight on May 30 the city was stormed, hundreds of the defenders put to the sword, and the whole place given over to plunder. The King then retired to meet Prince Rupert in Daventry. The news of the storm and sack of Leicester jolted the Parliamentary authorities out of their amateurish strategies. Sir Thomas Fairfax was permitted to leave the siege of Oxford and given a free hand to advance against the enemy.

*   *   *

On June 8 General Fairfax, who had concentrated his army in the neighborhood of Newport Pagnall, summoned a Council of War. The King was known to be in Daventry, and it was resolved to follow him and compel him to battle. Fairfax had some 13,000 men under his command, and recognized that the best way to blood it was to use it to fight. One other thing was necessary. The New Model Army still had no lieutenant general. Should they not send for Cromwell, who, after his remarkable display as an independent commander in Oxfordshire, was eating his heart out in his birthplace of Huntingdon? On June 4 the House of Commons had received a petition from the City of London bemoaning the sacking of Leicester and demanding the reinstatement of Cromwell. The House had ignored this awkward request. But a petition from the Council of War was another matter. Fairfax's envoy reached Westminster on June 10 and the Commons assented to Cromwell's appointment without awaiting the concurrence of the House of Lords. Meanwhile General Fairfax himself without more ado sent for Cromwell to join the main army. He needed no urging. On June 13 he rode into Fairfax's camp at Kislingbury, eight miles east of Daventry, accompanied by six hundred mounted men. He was, recorded Joshua Sprigge ". . . with the greatest joy received by the General and the whole army. Instantly orders were given for drums to beat, trumpets to sound to horse, and all our army to draw to rendezvous. . . ."

While Fairfax was marching into Kislingbury, King Charles had left the Wheatsheaf Inn at Daventry to hunt deer in a park nearby.[6] He had reason to be in excellent spirits. A month earlier the Marquis of Montrose had defeated one of the two Covenanting armies in the field against him at the battle of Auldearn; General Fairfax had been compelled to raise the siege of Oxford and the New Model Army had appeared contemptible to its foes; and King Charles himself commanded an army of over 10,000 men surfeited with the plunder of Leicester, and another army of almost equal size under General Goring could be called up from the west. What should he do next? His civilian advisers wanted him to go over to the attack in the east; Prince Rupert advocated an expedition north to fight the Earl of Leven; another group of counselors recommended rallying all his forces in England to overwhelm General Fairfax. King Charles finally endorsed the third of these schemes. "I assure you that I shall look before I leap farther north," he told his Secretary of State, Sir Edward Nicholas, but he also assured him optimistically that "if we peripatetics get no more mischance than you Oxfordians are like to have this summer, we may all expect a merry winter."[7] The King's plan therefore was, after the plunder of Leicester had been digested, to move northeast towards Newark and Pontefract, and there recruit his army before turning upon the New Model Army.

But he underestimated his enemy. He was given no time to strengthen his army, which had suffered both actual and medical casualties in the Midlands. In the Parliamentary camp all hesitations were laid aside and it was determined to seek immediate battle. When Cromwell arrived in Kislingbury on June 13 a Council of War, which had been called for six in the morning, was already in session. The King was believed to be breaking up his camp outside Daventry, and Major Thomas Harrison, that stern man of God, was sent to obtain intelligence of the enemy's movements, while Colonel Henry Ireton was dispatched with a vanguard of horse to attack the Royalist flank if he could. That evening the Parliamentary army moved from its position at Kislingbury to Guilsborough, a village eight miles farther north, while Ireton, who was three miles in advance, ran into the Royalist rearguard as it was playing darts in the village of Naseby. General Fairfax thus learned that the Royalists had indeed departed from Daventry and were hastening away in a north-easterly direction, and he also received the satisfactory news that General Goring was unable at that moment to join his master. The Parliamentarians therefore pressed hard on the heels of their enemy. By three o'clock on the following morning they were on their way to Naseby, where Ireton had reported the Royalist rearguard on the previous day. Meanwhile the King himself, seeing that he could not get away as he intended, faced about and prepared to fight.

The battle of Naseby, which settled the first Civil War, was in some respects an extraordinary historical episode. The battle itself is not correctly named, for if we call the battle fought to the north of Long Marston in Yorkshire the battle of Marston Moor, then we ought to call the battle fought to the north of Naseby the battle of Broadmoor, for it was on that moor in the midst of a plateau halfway between the Northamptonshire villages of Naseby and Sibbertoft that the armies clashed. There was not a great deal to choose between the two sides in position or in generalship, in the widest sense, and even the wind dropped so that neither side had the dust blowing in its face. But as to number, while contemporary opinion was almost unanimous that the two sides were of equal strength, it seems certain that the Royalists were in fact considerably the fewer. But if they were outnumbered by two to one, as most modern historians suppose, then either the Royalist intelligence was appalling or their generals fool-hardy. And the casualty rate was fantastic. For at the end of the contest, which lasted nearly three hours, the Parliamentarians claimed to have captured 5,000 prisoners, killing only 700, and themselves losing only 200 men. Such figures, if they are to be trusted, reflect seriously upon the Royalist morale. No losses in any previous battle in the Civil Wars can compare with them. They mean that two men out of every three surrendered on the field of battle. It is known that the Yorkshire and Nottinghamshire cavalry on the left wing were discontented at being so far from their homes, and that the men of the right wing under Prince Rupert, after a successful charge, were given over to plunder, the kind of plunder that they had so recently enjoyed at Leicester and elsewhere. The infantry resisted enough, but in the end they were left to their fate. The Royalists must have expected an easier battle against the despised soldiers of the New Model

Army and when they found once more than the Cromwellian cavalry were unbreakable, panicked and surrendered.

The country where the battle raged was singularly suitable for cavalry. Broadmoor itself was open pasture land situated exactly between two gently sloping hills, Mill Hill to the south and Dust Hill to the north. The Royalists after a flank movement were deployed along Dust Hill, then, as now, covered with fields of golden grain, and the Parliamentarians, after twice shifting their positions, lay concealed behind the crest of Mill Hill. But because both armies were on open hillside both charged at the outset; neither awaited the other's attack. As usual, the cavalry in relatively small numbers was on the wings and the infantry in carefullly formed groups of musketeers and pikemen in the center. And, as usual, the cavalry decided the battle. On the Royalist right, Prince Rupert, who left such control as could be exercised to the King, charged against Henry Ireton, promoted on the eve of the battle to the rank of commissary general. Ireton was twice wounded and then taken prisoner, and his second line failed to stem the advance. Prince Rupert swept down into Naseby, and parleyed with the commander of the Parliamentarians' baggage train. On the Parliamentarians' right, General Fairfax also led the charge in person, supported by Cromwell. Although the ground on that side was uneven and the advance difficult, the Parliamentarians carried all before them, pushing back the swiftly demoralized enemy about a quarter of a mile. Fairfax, who lost his helmet in the heat of the struggle, then went across to rally the infantry who had been pushed back over the crest of the hill and whose commander, General Skippon, had been wounded but refused to quit the field. Cromwell took over the leadership of the right wing. As at Marston Moor and Gainsborough, Cromwell kept his men well in hand. Ordering three regiments to pursue the enemy, he directed the rest of his force in a series of waves to the aid of the infantry. Clarendon, the Royalist historian of the Civil War, remarked of the battle that once again it showed the superior discipline of Cromwell's men, who even if they were checked or beaten would rally and stand in good order while Prince Rupert's men could charge once and then never again.

Meanwhile on the extreme left the dragoons of the New Model Army, under the command of Colonel John Okey, had likewise performed their duty. Okey's orders had been to line the hedges on that side of the battlefield, and his men had done some execution as Prince Rupert swept by them. To their surprise they now found that part of the battlefield deserted. Okey, as the critics of the New Model delighted to point out, was no gentleman.[8] He had begun life as a stoker in Islington and was a keen Anabaptist. But he knew how to fight. He remounted his dragoons and directed them across the moor to attack the Royalist foot on its right flank. Thus the Royalist infantry was practically surrounded and overpowered on all sides, and by the time that Prince Rupert returned from the baggage train, all was over. The King himself had wanted to lead forward his reserve of horse and charge once more. But by that time Fairfax and Cromwell had entirely re-formed their line of battle, with their foot in the center and horse on either wing. The King was persuaded that discretion was the better part of valor, and watched as a pathetic spectator the surrender of his army before he rode away.

Robert Baillie thus summed up the course of the battle: "Rupert in his fury pursues too far; Cromwell comes on the back of the King's foot and Fairfax on their face and quickly makes them lay down their arms." In fact, arms for 8,000 men were captured, which again arouses the suspicion that more men fought on the Royalist side than is usually supposed. At any rate, it was a shattering victory.

Broadmoor lies in the very heart of England, in the center of the Midlands. From near the village of Naseby arise the sources of two rivers: one, the Avon, flowing westward into the Bristol Channel; the other, the Nene, eastward to the Wash. In this green and pleasant land, softer and bushier than the Yorkshire moors, where the previous and bigger victory had been won, the Royalist cause met its doom. No Scots were engaged on the winning side; no halfhearted generals mulled over the dangers of too full a victory; no Parliamentary commander fled in disorder from that battlefield. "Sir," wrote Cromwell on June 14, 1645, in a famous dispatch to the Speaker of the House of Commons,

> this is none other but the hand of God; and to Him alone belongs the glory. . . . The General served you with faithfulness and honour. . . . Honest men served you faithfully

Then came the essence of the dispatch, words that were to reveal the innermost thoughts and feelings in Cromwell's mind:

Sir, they are trusty; I beseech you in the name of God not to discourage them. . . . He that ventures his life for the liberty of his country, I wish he trust God for the liberty of his conscience, and you for the liberty he fights for.

Much of the work that Cromwell did in the years of his life that remained to him were to be an elucidation of the Naseby dispatch.

Notes

1. *Anglia Rediviva* (1854), 6–7.
2. Add. MSS. 31116, f. 194.
3. Add. MSS. 31116, f. 185.
4. Besides Sir Charles Firth's articles, "The Raising of the Ironsides" and "The Later History of the Ironsides," in *Transactions of the Royal Historical Society*, XIII and XV, see Sir Charles Firth and Godfrey Davies, *The Regimental History of Cromwell's Army* (1940), for the history of the New Model Army.
5. Fairfax's reference in his *Short Memoirs* (1699) is clearly to Denzil Holles; see his *Memoirs* (1699). Baillie is not reliable on the New Model Army, though his views are still sometimes accepted.
6. Recent accounts of the battle of Naseby will be found in J. F. C. Fuller, *The Decisive Battles of the Western World*, II (1955), Chap. 5, and A. H. Burne, *The Battlefields of England*, Chap. 25. Colonel Burne suggests that the Royalist infantry fought on until they were surrounded and their ammunition gave out. He may be right, but it is surprising how few were killed in the battle.
7. D. Nicholas, *Mr. Secretary Nicholas* (1955), 210.
8. For Colonel John Okey, see H. G. Tibbutt, *Colonel John Okey, 1606–1662* (Bedfordshire Historical Record Society, XXXV, 1954). From Okey's own account it appears that the dragoons charged on horseback.

Chapter 11

Cromwell the Politician: The Fight for Liberty of Conscience

THE KING'S ENEMIES now began to close in upon him. The Scottish army on English soil, relieved of its dread lest Charles I should attempt to thrust north and join the Marquis of Montrose in Scotland, turned to besiege Carlisle and, after this town surrendered, found that it had at last cleared its own lines of communication homeward and blocked the roads along which the King might come. Thus the Earl of Leven ventured to move south, and by the end of July 1645 laid siege to Hereford. Meanwhile General Fairfax, who was no Earl of Manchester, did not sit down to recuperate after the battle of Naseby, but, having retaken Leicester on June 18, gave order for the New Model Army to march southwest to attack the one large Royalist force left in the field, that under the command of General George Goring, which was still held fast by Colonel Robert Blake and the tireless defenders of Taunton.

Lieutenant General Cromwell accompanied Sir Thomas Fairfax to the southwest. His commission had been extended for three months after his services at Naseby. Fairfax and Cromwell got along admirably together. Fairfax found him, as Sir William Waller had done earlier, a subordinate as obedient as he was skillful. Both were popular with their troops; Fairfax, a man of few words, was the more aloof, more of the aristocrat; Cromwell, though always a disciplinarian, would on occasion besport himself with his men and indulge in practical jokes. He was then described by the chaplain of Colonel Whalley's regiment as "of a sanguine complexion, naturally of such a vivacity, hilarity, and alacrity as another man hath when he hath drunken a cup too much. . . ."[1]

General Goring's army was cornered at the battle of Langport on July 10. Fairfax had outmaneuvered him, compelled him to raise the siege of Taunton, and induced him to give battle to cover his retreat to Bridgwater. "We could not well have necessitated him to an engagement," Cromwell reported afterwards, "nor have stayed one day longer without retreating to our ammunition and to conveniency of victual." In other words, the Parliamentarians were hampered by the lie of the country (General Goring's army being protected by the Somersetshire rivers) and outran their communications. However, they were offered their opportunity, and a small number of cavalry commanded by Major Bethel, a Puritan of exceptional courage, and Major Desborough, one of Cromwell's brothers-in-law, turned the scale of the battle when they charged uphill, having forced a ford across a tributary of the River Yeo. The Royalists broke and fled, to be pursued by Cromwell through the burning village of Langport, which the retreating army had set on fire. A few troops and a handful of musketeers who crept through the hedgerows had defeated the bulk of Goring's army. "Thus you see what the Lord hath wrought for us," proclaimed Cromwell in a letter to a member of the House of Commons. "Can any creature ascribe anything to itself? Now can we give all the glory to God, and desire all may do so, for it is all due to Him."

The victory of Langport we followed by the successful siege of Bridgwater. The Parliamentarians' progress was interrupted by the activities of the "Clubmen," an ill-armed neutral body consisting mainly of peasants who tried to keep both the contending parties out of the West Country. Cromwell remonstrated with them and persuaded many that his intentions were good, but had to take firm action against others. Shaftesbury and Sherborne, the principal towns in north Dorset, were then occupied, and after General Fairfax had consulted the Council of War, the army turned north to Bristol. The town was infected with plague, and Prince Rupert, in command of the defense, did not have sufficient men to guard its long walls. Once breaches had been blown, the Prince, who had done all he knew to save it, surrendered.

Prince Rupert had already realized that militarily the royal cause was hopeless, and had advised his uncle to make what terms he could. But King Charles, who, after Naseby, went into Wales to try to recruit yet another army, was still obstinate and optimistic about Goring in the south and Montrose in the north. For his surrender of Bristol he unfairly condemned his nephew as a traitor. After Bristol, Fairfax divided his forces and sent Cromwell to take in succession Devizes in Wiltshire and Winchester and Basing House, known as "Loyalty House," in Hampshire. Three days later another Royalist stronghold, Langford House, capitulated to him. Here an incident occurred illustrative of Cromwell's discipline. Six soldiers, who had already been caught plundering contrary to orders, repeated their offense. One of them was hanged, and the other five sent to the Royalist Governor of Oxford to punish as he thought fit. By now the autumn had turned cold and wet, and Cromwell and his men rejoined General Fairfax at his headquarters outside Exeter.

In January 1646 Cromwell's commission was again renewed, this time for six months, and £2,500 a year, to be secured on confiscated estates, was voted him as a reward by Parliament. In the middle of March, Lord Hopton with the remnants of General Goring's army surrendered in Cornwall, and in the second week of April the siege of Exeter ended. A fortnight later Cromwell returned to Westminster to report on the campaign, and received the hearty thanks of the House of Commons for his services.

*   *   *

Oliver Cromwell had now just passed his forty-seventh birthday. He had lost his two elder sons: Robert, whose death, just before the Civil War began, he was to remember as he himself lay dying—it had been "as a dagger to my heart"; Oliver, whose death on active service he recalled when condoling with a brother-in-law about the death of his son after the battle of Marston Moor—"Sir, you know my troubles this way; but the Lord supported me with this: that the Lord took him into the happiness we all pant after and live for." Two other sons were left to him, Richard and Henry. Both of them joined the army after being educated at Felsted grammar school in Essex. Richard was at Lincoln's Inn, and like many of the better-class cadets was posted to General Fairfax's lifeguard. Henry entered the army at sixteen and was to become a captain in Colonel Thomas Harrison's regiment. Of their four sisters two, Bridget (Biddy) and Elizabeth (Betty), were wedded in that year. In January Elizabeth at the age of seventeen married John Claypole, son of an old family friend, a country gentleman in Northamptonshire. She received £1,250 as her dowry. Bridget married in June Commissary General Henry Ireton of Nottinghamshire, whom she first met when he was her father's deputy governor in the Isle of Ely. Both of them were religious women after Oliver Cromwell's own heart. Bridget was a woman whose soul was said to have acquired "the power of grace" and though "acquainted with temptations . . . breathed after Christ." Elizabeth, her father told Bridget in a letter that October when they had both married, "sees her own vanity and carnal mind, bewailing it . . . she seeks after that which will satisfy." Cromwell stirred their religious faith: "Dear Heart, press on," he told the newly wed Bridget, "let not husband, let not anything, cool thy affections after Christ." His two younger daughters, Mary and Frances, were nine and eight. He loved them all, although Elizabeth is supposed to have been his favorite. In the summer they moved with their mother and grandmother from Ely to a house in Drury Lane, where their father joined them at the end of the war.

At forty-seven most men's beliefs, principles, and outlook upon life are settled. Cromwell had discerned much during his time in the army, particularly during the past year in the New Model. He was to find wider experience later, first as commander in chief and afterwards as Lord Protector. For the man in position always has a different scale of values. He was to acquire in the end some control over his temper—though that was never complete and was to betray him more than once—and some measure of magnanimity. In the army he learned both how to command and how to obey. Though never a polished orator, he spoke and preached fluently: his "loquacity" was a matter of record, contrasting with the taciturnity of General Fairfax. His vigor was immense. At most times he thought carefully before he acted, but in the army he saw the importance of deciding quickly. He also perceived there the worth of unity and trust among men. If God had led the Puritans to victory, surely He would guide them also to a settlement in the spirit of unity and peace.

Religion had brought Cromwell into the war and sustained him in every battle. But it had not yet imbued him with that spirit of self-assurance which in statesmen as different as King Louis XIV and Otto von Bismarck was to make them despisers of public assemblies.[2] To him Parliament was the divinely inspired instrument that had managed the war and could achieve a just peace now the fighting was over. Cromwell himself was an old Parliament hand, having first been elected a member nearly twenty years earlier. Surely, he believed, this thoughtful, earnest body of men, purged of the Royalists, had a dedicated purpose to restore their country to the happiness it had known in the reign of the great Queen

Elizabeth when Cromwell himself had been born. Parliamentary differences, he thought, like other men of his generation, were to be avoided as far as possible. Better a select assembly than a quarrelsome one. In that forum of good Puritans the right solutions could be discovered and applied. During 1645 and 1646 most of the vacancies left in the House of Commons by the withdrawal of Royalists were filled, and a number of Cromwell's friends and fellow officers were elected, including his son-in-law, Henry Ireton, a future son-in-law, Charles Fleetwood, a brother-in-law, and a cousin. Although the social structure of the House was little altered by that influx, a number of Independents were chosen who might not have been elected earlier.[3] But in spite of that, the religious complexion of the House differed markedly from that of the New Model Army.

That was the fundamental political fact at the end of the war. The insistence of Cromwell and his friends that a Christian spirit and a willingness to serve were all that was necessary in the Parliamentary armies had achieved its effect. In the New Model, nearly every variety of the Christian faith (apart from Roman Catholicism) was to be found. The relaxation of the ecclesiastical authority in 1640 and the ultimate abolition of the bishops had damaged the idea of uniformity and spawned a profusion of sects. Hardly any of the famous figures of Puritanism, from Henry Burton to Hugh Peter or from Richard Baxter to John Milton, professed a precisely similar faith. But that did not prevent them from vigorously criticizing one another, while the more settled members of the middle classes, especially the tradesmen of the City of London, were aghast at the spiritual anarchy that was being engendered. Baxter, who served as a chaplain in the New Model Army after the battle of Naseby, is often quoted for his description of the mixture of beliefs and practices in that army, and of the way in which they were all tolerated by Cromwell. Yet Baxter himself was no model of orthodoxy and his acrimoniously critical attitude towards Cromwell's large-mindedness at this time (as reflected in his posthumous writings) was at variance with the more liberal position he adopted at any rate when the Restoration came. When he wrote that "a few proud self-conceited hot-headed sectaries had got into the highest places and were Cromwell's chief favourites," his remarks must be discounted by the consideration that Cromwell behaved coldly to Baxter, denying him the welcome and privileges which he fancied he deserved. Cromwell preferred chaplains like John Owen and Hugh Peter, who were as broad-minded as himself.

Even judging by Baxter's account, it does not appear that the New Model was overfull of fanatics. "Abundance of the common troopers and many of the officers I found to be honest, sober, and orthodox men," he wrote. But, he added, "the common soldiers" were "ignorant men of little religion," few of whom had taken the Covenant. Clearly what he witnessed was a genuine search for truth. Active discussions took place in camp on such subjects as church and state democracy, free grace and free will. Cromwell thought that varied opinions on these topics ought to be allowed. That did not mean to say that he was ceasing to be a true Calvinist who believed in the doctrine of election by grace. But each Christian man and woman, lit by the faith and hope that is inspired by an intimate relationship with God, should, he felt, have the right to seek Him after his own fashion. The troop that formed a gathered church, or the congregation that wished to be left alone to worship under its own chosen minister, was to him equally worthy of protection. Independency, of which he was the secular leader, defended the right of any society of godly persons to meet and pray without interference from the state. In essence it was a doctrine of liberty of conscience. Its advocates therefore urged that any church organization now set up in place of episcopacy should have the minimum of coercive power and should not constitute an exclusive establishment. To the Independents the conscience was sacrosanct; they recognized that "man is bound to God by individual ties which the state can neither cement nor loosen." The only limit upon toleration within the Puritan fold that Cromwell and the Independents were prepared to admit was that the public peace must not be disrupted by enthusiasts.

But outside the New Model Army this view was still displeasing to the majority. Cromwell's plea for liberty of conscience in his dispatch to the Speaker after the battle of Naseby was suppressed. After the siege of Bristol again he wrote:

Presbyterians, Independents, all had here the same spirit of faith and prayer . . . they agree here, know no means of difference. . . . All that believe have the real unity, which is the most glorious, because inward and spiritual in the body, and to the head. As for being united in forms, commonly called uniformity, every Christian will for peace' sake study and do as far as the conscience will permit; *and from brethren in things of the mind we look for no compulsion but that of light and reason.* In other things God hath put the sword into the Parliament's hand for the terror of evildoers and the praise of them that do well.

These passages were also omitted when the dispatch was printed.

Unquestionably Cromwell felt intensely about liberty of conscience at this period in his life. In one of his few private letters that have survived from the summer of 1646, he wrote a plea on behalf of a group of poor men who lived in a hamlet in Northamptonshire. Apparently they were in danger of being evicted because of their religious opinions:

The trouble I hear is they are like to suffer for their conscience [he wrote to their landlord]. And however the world interprets it I am not ashamed to solicit for such as are anywhere under a pressure of this kind; doing herein as I would be done by. Sir, this is a quarrelsome age; and the anger seems to me to be the worse *where the ground is things of difference in opinion; which to cure to hurt men in their names, persons, or estates will not be found to be an apt remedy.*

In another letter he interceded on behalf of the prince of unorthodox Puritans, Colonel John Lilburne, the future leader of the Levellers. But not even Cromwell could protect this disputatious visionary from the penalties of his indiscretions.

*   *   *

Throughout that year in the Assembly of Divines five ministers who represented the Independent point of view successfully fought a delaying action against the wishes of the Presbyterian majority. As late as November 1645, Cromwell's "accommodation order" had been renewed by the two Houses of Parliament. Hugh Peter came to London and preached in praise of "the godly, truly religious soldiers" of the New Model Army.[4] But powerful forces operated on the other side. The Scots demanded that the new English Church establishment should be co-ordinated with their Kirk. A petition to Parliament put forward by the City of London's Common

Council in the following May urged the repression of all the sects. King Charles I saw a chance of causing trouble among his opponents by offering to come to terms with the Presbyterians separately. Some of the Independents then contemplated the idea of removing themselves and their families to Ireland, as the previous generation had done to Holland and America, rather than submit to an all-embracing Presbyterianism of the Scottish kind. But Cromwell himself was not yet ready to advocate extreme measures either of withdrawal or compulsion. He still had hopes of his accommodation order. He was willing to accept any moderate Presbyterian establishment that permitted toleration outside it. Also he felt that he and his friends in the Commons could unite with politicians like John Selden, who were opposed to the church becoming a power beyond the control of the state, to defeat the aim of such Presbyterians as demanded the right of their hierarchy to occupy the place of the old bishops and to oblige all believers rigidly to adhere to their own set of rules. Such was Cromwell's liberal attitude of mind as the Civil War was ending.

*   *   *

One last task remained to the Parliamentarian army—to occupy Oxford. The King, desperately weaving schemes that he confided to no one, left the town before the end of April 1646 by way of Magdalen Bridge disguised as a servant. He had not yet made up his mind whether to go to London and throw himself on the mercy of Parliament, to wend his way to the east coast in the hope of escaping abroad, or to surrender to the Scottish army at Newark. Henry Ireton, who had been sent by General Fairfax in advance to Oxford, received two approaches from the King before he departed; but they were intended only to confuse the issue. Ireton informed Cromwell, who reported the matter to the House of Commons, publicly reproving Ireton for not sending his news direct to the Speaker. Then Cromwell left Westminster to take part in the siege of Oxford. The King's disappearance was soon known in London, but he was missing for no more than a few days before he turned up as a suppliant at the Scottish camp in the north.

The negotiations for the surrender of Oxford dragged on for nearly eight weeks, but on June 24 the defenders marched out and General Fairfax became governor. Meanwhile the

Scots withdrew from Newark to Newcastle-upon-Tyne, taking the King with them. Thus the first Civil War came to its close.

*   *   *

During 1646 Parliament concentrated on four problems arising out of the end of the war. It had to come to some arrangement with the King, to pay off the Scottish army, to demobilize or at least reduce the size of its own army, and to subdue Ireland. All these problems were complicated by the continuing division of opinion between the Presbyterians and Independents among the victorious Puritans.

Cromwell had always regretted the decision to invite the Scots to England to help win the war. And in fact, except at Marston Moor, the Scots under the Earl of Leven had done very little towards winning it. That was admitted by the Scots themselves. If their army had contributed more towards victory and had dared to come farther south than it ever did, the Presbyterian cause would have been infinitely exalted. Indeed, Independency might easily have been crushed at the outset. But as things were it was Oliver Cromwell and not the cautious Earl of Leven who gained a reputation in the war. After the battle of Naseby, Robert Baillie, the Scottish minister, had written from London to the Earl of Lauderdale: "As yet our army has done nothing. . . . Cromwell's extraordinary success makes that party here triumph." The only hope of defeating the Independents, as Baillie saw it, was for the Scottish army to march up to London, but it never did. Cromwell, "the great independent,"[5] remained therefore a figure dominating the military scene. In April 1646 Baillie reported the rumor that the Parliamentarians had "belaid all the ways that they may catch the King if he should essay to go anywhere out of Oxford till Cromwell come and take him up." Why Cromwell? Why not Fairfax? The answer is that Cromwell was the general whom the Scots feared most. When King Charles gave himself up to the Scots they acquired a temporary political advantage, but they did not exploit it for religious ends. Their army in the north wanted to go home, and they thought it wiser to leave the religious settlement to their Presbyterian friends at Westminster. So after the King had rejected the propositions sent to him at Newcastle—proposals that would have made him little more than a ceremonial monarch or "a Duke of

Venice," to use the phrase then in vogue—and the English Parliament had voted £400,000 to pay off the Scots, they recrossed the Tweed at the end of the year and handed over the King. Parliament ordered that he should be assigned a place of honorable and indeed palatial custody at Holdenby House in Northamptonshire pending a decision as to his fate.

When Cromwell's commission expired at the end of June, he came to live in London and resumed his seat in the House of Commons. He had engaged in the last stages of the siege of Oxford (during which he had attended the marriage of his eldest daughter to Henry Ireton), and had signed the propositions of Newcastle, which the King rejected. Afterwards, however, he was to confess that he was glad the King did reject them, for they would virtually have meant a Presbyterian supremacy. He watched with growing distress the attitude of Parliament hardening against the army. As usually happens when wars end, those who had once been thought heroes were given shabby treatment. Demobilization was pressed for with little regard either to justice or reason, and an attempt exerted to fob off the soldiers on the cheapest terms. Cromwell found all that distasteful and ungrateful. On August 10, 1646, he wrote to Fairfax: "Things are not well in Scotland; would they were in England! We are full of faction and worse." The Commons were now divided over many questions—military, religious, and political. For example, Cromwell and Henry Vane believed that the Great Seal of the Realm ought to be in the custody of the two Houses, were at first defeated on the matter and then had the vote reversed. The episcopacy was at last abolished, but neither the Assembly of Divines nor the Commons, after months of disputation, agreed about what to put in its place. The Scottish army was paid off, but no conclusion was reached regarding the future of the English army. The London City authorities, who were the trumpeters of English Presbyterianism, were eager to be rid of the New Model Army for religious as well as financial reasons. On December 19 they put forward another of a number of petitions asking Parliament to disband the army because of the favor it showed to "heretics." Cromwell reported on that to Fairfax:

We have had a long petition from the City. How it strikes at the army and what other aims it has, you will see by the contents of it; as also what the prevailing temper is at present, and what is to be expected from men.

As yet, however, he acquiesced in events. For although the Independent representation in the Commons was not large, it was powerful enough to prevent any extreme measures from being taken either to suppress the sects or bilk the army. In the long run he trusted that all would be well:

> This is our comfort, God in heaven, and He doth what pleaseth Him; His and only His counsel shall stand, whatever the designs of men, and the fury of the people be.

But during the winter of 1646–47 Cromwell was taken seriously ill and was away from the House of Commons. His absence was a grave loss to his friends. But in any case members (particularly a number of lawyers) who had voted with him on religious questions had no love for the New Model once the Scots were gone and the King was a prisoner. While Cromwell was not present a scheme was propounded by the Presbyterian leaders to reduce the size of the army in England and to send an expeditionary force to Ireland under the command of generals sympathetic to the Presbyterians. Just after Cromwell's recovery from his illness the Commons passed a resolution pointedly excluding him from any new command. He was upset at the snub, but did not retort in public. Behind the scenes he spoke of ingratitude, and possibly thought of taking service in the Protestant cause abroad. He did not doubt that if the English army were paid its arrears it would disband peaceably.

The evidence that remains about Cromwell's behavior and feelings immediately after the end of the first Civil War is tenuous in the extreme. Apart from the record of isolated activities in the House of Commons after his illness, the only entirely reliable information is a number of letters that he wrote to his former commander in chief, Sir Thomas Fairfax. To Fairfax he was loyal and devoted. "I can say in the simplicity of my heart I put a high and true value upon your love," he wrote to him, "Which when I forget, I shall cease to be a grateful and honest man." Sir Thomas Fairfax, like any good general, was ready to obey the orders of the civil authorities, but was determined that his men should be decently treated. But his health was never good, and he also was taken ill at this time. Both Cromwell and Fairfax were pained by the thankless treatment of the New Model Army. "There want not in all places men who have so much malice against the army as besots them," Cromwell told Fairfax.

"Never were the spirits of men more embittered than now. Surely the Devil hath but a short time." Yet, he added: "Sir, it's good the heart be fixed against all this. The naked simplicity of Christ, with that wisdom He please to give, and patience will overcome all this." Though his sympathies lay with the army in which he had served, Cromwell was still too much of the parliamentarian himself to question the authority of the House of Commons. His aim was to resist passively, standing firm for the rights of the soldiers as to pay and freedom of conscience, and not to intrigue against the civil power. As to General Fairfax, he would gladly have laid down his command.

But now the extremists on both sides came into the open, and in the summer of 1647 tempers flared and passions beat high.

In the House of Commons the direction of affairs was now largely controlled by Denzil Holles, an old enemy of Cromwell, and Sir Philip Stapleton, a vigorous Yorkshireman who, according to the Reverend Robert Baillie, had persuaded the Scots to leave England "upon assurance that this was the best means to get that evil army disbanded and the King and peace settled according to our [Scottish] minds." In March these Presbyterian leaders sent a deputation to the New Model Army, which was being reorganized at Saffron Walden in Essex, to raise volunteers for service in Ireland. The officers told the deputation that they required assurance about the names of the commanders, the pay, and the settlement of their arrears before they could induce the soldiers to enlist. (The pay of the infantry was eighteen weeks in arrears and that of the cavalry forty-three weeks.) The parliamentary delegation took offense at what they regarded as conditions being imposed upon them. But the officers, led, among others, by Cromwell's son-in-law Henry Ireton, and his cousin Colonel Edward Whalley, stuck to their guns. Moreover, the soldiers themselves drew up a petition to General Fairfax asking in more violent terms not only for the payment of arrears but for pensions for war widows and compensation for personal losses during the fighting, as well as for a gratuity on disbandment. The Presbyterians in the Commons were furious at these importunities; Ireton was called to the Bar of the House, and it was even proposed that Cromwell, who had nothing to do with any of these demands, should be put under arrest, and Holles drew up a declaration that "all those who shall continue in their distempered condition, and go on advancing and promoting that petition shall be looked upon and proceeded against as enemies of the state and disturbers of the public peace." "Thus we see," wrote an M.P., "there is nothing constant in the world's affairs. The Parliament, having conquest and success after their own desires, yet are now miserably encumbered with the multitudinousness of their army on one side and with the petulancy of pamphlets and with discontented persons on the other side."

Denzil Holles's declaration against the army, accepted by Parliament, provoked the soldiers to a threat of mutiny. Already they had been warned by Hugh Peter that they might be crucified if they did not idolize the Covenant. The former Colonel John Lilburne, though a prisoner in the Tower of London, poured out virulent pamphlets stirring up the men, and eight cavalry regiments elected agents or "Agitators" to represent their point of view. Cromwell brooded, but still did not publicly take the army's part. Indeed, he expressed his disapproval of the soldiers' petition, while absenting himself from the Commons and from the Committee of Both Kingdoms that still functioned in a desultory way. When in the middle of April another parliamentary commission went to Saffron Walden, the officers asked why they could not go to Ireland under their old generals: "Fairfax and Cromwell," they cried, "and we all go!" The indignation of the army at its treatment sobered the Commons. Instead of trying to enforce Holles's declaration, it decided to send four of its military members, headed by Cromwell and including Ireton, who was M.P. for Appleby, to quieten the army by promising the soldiers an indemnity and a small part of their arrears in cash.

At Saffron Walden, Cromwell did his utmost to persuade the army to obey Parliament, though at the same time he reported back to the House that both officers and men were suffering from a deep sense of grievance.[6] While the Presbyterian leaders held out an olive branch to the army, they also prepared to defend themselves: the City militia, an effective force, was purged of Independents, and a coalition was secretly negotiated with the Scots with the aim of restoring King Charles I as a Presbyterian ruler. After three weeks of discussions at Saffron Walden, Cromwell and his fellow commissioners informed the House that the soldiers would not volunteer for Ireland, but would disband quietly if their arrears were paid. But the most that the Commons would do was to offer minor concessions. On May 25 a plan was framed to break up the army, starting with General Fairfax's own regiment (formerly Cromwell's, and the standard-bearers of liberty of conscience), and give the soldiers the alternative of service in Ireland or instant disbandment. That, indeed, was to invite mutiny. Officers and men had become exasperated. "Is it not better to die like men than to be enslaved and hanged like dogs?" asked the private soldiers. On May 29, 1647, two hundred officers conferred and resolved upon a rendezvous of the whole army, to be held at Newmarket.

Up to that point Oliver Cromwell had been a loyal member of Parliament who accepted the votes of the majority on all questions, however distasteful they were to him. He had used his whole influence to delay the imposition of an exclusively Presbyterian church system, but he had more than once agreed to Presbyterian supremacy provided that toleration was allowed to the sects. He had disapproved of the soldiers' petition to General Fairfax, and exercised all the appeal of his popularity in the army to induce it to accept the disbandment proposals of the House of Commons. In a speech to the officers on May 16 he had asked them to persuade their regiments to accept the concession about their arrears, and "work in them a good opinion of that authority that is over both us and them." "If that authority falls to nothing," he continued, "nothing can follow but confusion." But when on May 27 both Houses of Parliament insisted upon immediate disbandment, he had to choose whether he should continue rigidly to obey the majority or be loyal to the army where he was loved and trusted. It was the first difficult political crisis of his life.

Nothing is more fascinating in Cromwell's character than the length of time that he spent in thought and prayer before suddenly, as it seemed, coming to a crucial decision. While he did so he often vanished completely from the public gaze. But a choice of loyalties had to be taken at last. He was aware that he now counted for little in London, while if he went to the army he could at least help to restrain and guide its deliberations. But first he realized one overwhelming danger—that the fruits of victory might be wasted. The King, though nominally a prisoner, could hope to play off the Parliament against the army. He had already conceded the right of the Presbyterians to rule the Church for three years. If he should now come to London and if the Scottish army returned south to assist their fellow Presbyterians in

Westminster, then the cause of Independency, the right of Christians like Cromwell and his fellow soldiers to seek God in their own way, would be imperiled. Secret meetings were held in the last days of May 1647 at Cromwell's new home in Drury Lane. Cornet Joyce, a junior officer in General Fairfax's lifeguard, and a cavalry detachment went, apparently without orders from the commanding officer, to seize the artillery in Oxford and then to secure the King at Holdenby House. On the same day that Joyce arrived at Holdenby on his mission, Cromwell left London for Newmarket. Had he not done so, it is possible that the Presbyterian leaders would have sent him to the Tower. Whether he approved Joyce's mission except retrospectively is uncertain. Nevertheless, his purpose was not to overthrow the Parliament, of which he was a member, but rather to mediate between it and the army in the cause of peace, reconstruction, and religious freedom.

Notes

1. *Reliquiae Baxterianae*, 57. Besides the book on Fairfax by Sir Clements Markham, there is a biography by M. A. Gibb (1938); see also my *Cromwell's Generals*, Chap. 1, where I wrongly state that Fairfax was of Scottish descent.

2. I was struck by the contrast with Bismarck when reading Mr. A. J. P. Taylor's excellent biography.

4. For the "recruiters" to the Long Parliament, see Brunton and Pennington, *op. cit.*, Chap. 2.

4. R. P. Stearns, *The Strenuous Puritan* (1954), Chap. 10, describes Hugh Peter's activities at this time.

5. The phrase "the great Independent" is Baillie's, probably used in an opprobrious sense.

6. The Saffron Walden meetings are reported in *Clarke Papers* (Camden Society, 1891), I, 20 seq.

Chapter 12

Cromwell the Conciliator: "We would have healed Babylon, but She would not."

DURING THE SECOND TWO WEEKS of June 1647, events moved fast towards a climax, and a new civil war threatened to engulf the victors of the old. Cromwell's aim was to hold the New Model Army together and to come to terms with Parliament. As soon as he reached army headquarters near Newmarket, he arranged for the establishment of a Council of the Army, in which the generals were joined by representatives of the commissioned officers and private soldiers from each regiment, so that political questions might be referred to them, although the Council of War remained responsible for giving orders and imposing discipline. The army as a whole solemnly swore to remain united, but at the same time assured Parliament that it did not intend to overthrow the existing government, to prevent the organization of a Presbyterian Church, or to permit disorder under the guise of "liberty of conscience." As soon as the Presbyterian leaders at Westminster realized how impregnable was the position of the New Model Army with Cromwell as its effective political head and King Charles I its prisoner, it began to offer concessions. But, as so often happens in times of revolutionary pressure, the concessions came just too late. As more was given, more was asked.

The army moved forward from Kentford heath near Newmarket to Triploe heath near Cambridge on the road to London. Here commissioners arrived from Parliament on June 10 to meet the representatives of the army and explain to them the concessions that they were now prepared to grant, which included the payment of their arrears in full, but these were in effect rejected and the New Model Army came on through Royston and St. Albans, menacing the very heart of government.

Why did Cromwell and the New Model Army refuse the concessions of June 10 and advance upon London? The matter has never been entirely explained. There are three clues. The first is the story (the source is a letter written to

Cromwell nearly ten years afterwards)[1] that "the violent and rash part of the army"—that is to say the Agitators—"peremptorily told" him that if he "would not forthwith, nay presently, come and head them they would go their way without him." The second clue is that before the regiments were drawn up on Triploe heath to listen to the proposals from the parliamentary commissioners they were warned of the danger of a Scottish invasion; in other words, they were already given reason to suspect, what was true, that while these concessions were being dangled before them, the Presbyterian leaders were actually planning to recall the Scots in order to impose their will upon the kingdom. Lastly there is the letter, supposed to have been drafted by Cromwell and certainly signed by him along with General Fairfax and the other principal officers, addressed to the authorities of the City of London, in which they claimed the right not merely to have their "just demands" as soldiers met but also "as Englishmen" to see before they disbanded that a constitutional settlement was concluded in accordance with the objects laid down when they first took up arms. In his letter Cromwell and his fellow officers asserted that they had no desire to alter the existing government, to meddle with the setting up of Presbyterianism, or to open a way to "licentious liberty under the pretence of obtaining ease for tender consciences." The letter continued:

> We profess, as ever in these things, when the state have once made a settlement, we have nothing to say but to submit or suffer. Only we could wish that every good citizen, and every man that walks peaceably in a blameless conversation, and is beneficial to the commonwealth, may have liberty and encouragement, it being according to the just policy of all states, even to justice itself. These are our desires, and the things for which we stand, beyond which we shall not go. And for the obtaining of these things, we are drawing near your city. . . .

The general feeling in the army was that Parliament was not to be trusted either to fulfill its promises or to guarantee individual liberty, and that the only way to ensure these ends was a show of force. Indeed, as soon as the proposals at Triploe heath were rejected, the parliamentary leaders tried everything possible to raise troops to fight the New Model Army. Both sides were swept forward as passions rose and fears took root. The New Model ceased to have faith in Parliament ever since it had unwisely declared its soldiers to be public enemies, while Parliament, once menaced by mutiny, could scarcely avoid seeking means to defend itself. Cromwell still believed that it was the business of Parliament and not of the army to frame a constitutional scheme, and insisted that all he wanted was that the soldiers should receive fair treatment both as to their pay and their religious freedom. Yet within another four days his point of view again shifted. For on June 14 when the New Model Army was at St. Albans he assented to a declaration of the army in which it began to prescribe how a constitutional settlement ought to be attained.

Here was an even more startling change in attitude. As late as June 13 Cromwell had signed a letter again repeating the assurance that the army did not wish to "meddle with matters of religion or church government," and saying "we desire as much as any to maintain the authority of Parliament and the fundamental government of the kingdom." But on the very next day the officers of the New Model—including Cromwell—signed a declaration which sought the "purging" of Parliament and the choice of an entirely new House of Commons. This declaration was drawn up by Commissary General Ireton and embodied his political principles. In it Denzil Holles and ten members of the old House were proscribed as enemies of the state. Holles himself wrote that "here they first took upon them openly to intermeddle with the business of the kingdom." Thus the New Model Army had advanced from a mutiny over pay and conditions towards a *coup d'état*. First it had objected to disbanding until it had received better terms; then, offered better terms, it had refused to disband until it was assured of the kind of constitutional settlement it approved; lastly it demanded not only the right to endorse a settlement but even to dictate its terms.

Though Ireton was Cromwell's son-in-law, it is reasonable to suppose that Cromwell himself had come reluctantly to acquiesce in the last position. Great men, it is said, are those who guide events and are not submerged by them. But in those days of anger and suspicion, what could Cromwell do? He had left London as late as he dared; he had used all his influence to prevent the rank and file of the New Model Army from becoming completely out of hand; he had at the outset expressed his disapproval of the political activity of the army; he had insisted that what was won by force was unlikely to last; he was later bitterly attacked by extremists for offering to negotiate and compromise. All his authority was in fact thrown upon the side of restraint. He has been accused of not appreciating that he was exerting force to impose his will upon Parliament, or at any rate of deluding himself about his conduct and policy. But is that realistic? The Civil War itself was a display of force aimed, so far as Cromwell was concerned, primarily at securing liberty of worship for the Puritans. The New Model was for him the microcosm of the ideal society in which that liberty was preached and practiced. Cromwell would have been unfaithful to himself if he had not continued to use every means to uphold the principles in which he believed. Nevertheless, he wanted to retain the parliamentary system, provided only that it did not endanger what he regarded as being the essential freedom of the individual to seek God in his own fashion. He was, in fact, already struggling with that mighty dilemma that was to haunt him all his life—how to reconcile liberty with order.

It was therefore with reluctance that Cromwell agreed to the march on London to overawe Parliament or to the army propounding by itself a scheme for a constitutional settlement.

*　　　*　　　*

On June 23, 1647, the House of Commons refused the demands put forward in the "Declaration of the Army," and the New Model Army advanced its headquarters to Uxbridge and was master of London. Next day the eleven proscribed Presbyterian leaders voluntarily retired from the House of Commons, which became so much more acquiescent that the New Model Army withdrew to Reading. All the while Sir Thomas Fairfax and Cromwell controlled the movements of the King, who was comfortably housed at Windsor and then at Caversham.

Cromwell had met the King for the first time at Childerley, near Cambridge, on June 7. It had not been on Cromwell's instructions that the King had been removed from Holdenby,[2] but Joyce had thought it safer to do so, and the King himself afterwards insisted that he did not wish to go back there. General Fairfax, as soon as he had heard of Joyce's exploit, had at once ordered up three regiments to protect the King and escort him back, and Cromwell had supported him. Joyce's original intention may well have been only to seize the King's person in the army's interest, but he decided to move him south when he found that the King's Presbyterian guard was likely to put up a fight. All that appears to have been explained by Cromwell to the King at Childerley. Later he conversed with him again, both at Windsor and at Caversham. Cromwell was anxious to discover how far Charles I would be willing, if he were restored to formal authority, to guarantee religious freedom. Cromwell liked the King as a man (both were profoundly religious after their own manner) and was touched by his affection for his family, but thought, as everyone else did, that he was lacking in frankness and narrow in outlook. He informed the King's advisers that Henry Ireton was employed in drawing up detailed proposals for a constitutional settlement which would be submitted to the consideration of Parliament. Ireton saw the King, and actually modified a number of the draft proposals to meet his wishes. But both he and Cromwell were adamant about liberty of conscience (which they themselves appear to have been willing to extend, up to a point, even to Roman Catholics) and about the need to restrict the rights of the monarchy in the future. But the King, naturally enough, was noncommittal until he learned the outcome of the conflict between the army and Parliament.[3]

On July 13 the London apprentices, who had just been granted a monthly holiday, took advantage of it to present to the Houses of Parliament a petition calling among other things for the suppression of the sects and the disbandment of the army. This demonstration aroused the indignation of the rank and file of the New Model Army, which also continued to believe that a Scottish invasion was being planned and that the Commons, where the Presbyterians retained a majority, were trying to raise forces in the north of England to attack them. The Council of the Army met at Reading on July 16, and the Agitators and others demanded that they should at once enter London. Cromwell explained that Ireton was still perfecting his proposals and argued cogently that it would be wiser to negotiate than to coerce. If these proposals were agreed to, he urged, they would be "firm and durable," and of benefit to posterity: "We shall avoid that great objection that will lie against us, that we have got things out of Parliament by force." What they must seek, he said, was a general settlement; what they must avoid was a second civil war "and the defeating those things that are so dear to us." After some discussion the Council of the Army agreed to the scheme, known as the "Heads of the Proposals," and to the postponement of their march into London.

The "Heads of the Proposals," drafted by Ireton and the able young Yorkshireman Major General Lambert, and approved in principle by Cromwell, provided for the holding of Parliaments once every two years for sessions lasting at least 120 days, for "free" elections and a redistribution of seats upon a more equal basis. The army was to remain under the control of Parliament for ten years, and Royalists were to be excluded from office for five. A Council of State was to administer military affairs and foreign policy under the direction of Parliament, which was also for ten years to make appointments to all the principal offices of state. Religious liberty was to be guaranteed (the Book of Common Prayer being abolished along with the Covenant), and the remedying of a number of grievances, ranging from the imposition of the excise to the high cost of litigation, was promised. It was never likely that this constitutional scheme, drafted by the New Model Army, would meet with acceptance from either King or Parliament as it stood. But it was intended only as a basis for discussion (Cromwell himself criticized the clauses relating to the method of dissolving Parliament), and a copy was now officially sent to the King. Before it could be forwarded to Parliament, however, anarchy had broken out in London and Westminster. The House of Lords now consisted of only nine members and the House of Commons of about 120. A mob invaded the Commons, and the Speaker was pinioned in his chair. Later all the Independent members vanished from the House, along with the Speaker. The group of Presbyterians that was left bloated itself up like a bullfrog, elected a new Speaker, re-formed a Committee of Safety, collected a disheveled sort of army under a Presbyterian general, and defiantly told General Fairfax to stay away from London. But the situation had become farcical or tragic, according to the way it was looked at. Even the City authorities did not relish the idea of their shops and warehouses being given over to the plunder of a promiscuous horde of excited apprentices, ex-soldiers, and riffraff; they preferred the lesser evil of the disciplined New Model Army. Thus at last on August 6 Oliver Cromwell, who had been more than reluctant to enter London in armor, rode at the head of the cavalry that had served under him at Marston Moor and Naseby, to restore order, reconstitute Parliament, and procure a settlement of the kingdom.

*　　　*　　　*

The position of the House of Commons had been weakened first when, after the soldiers of the New Model had jibbed at the unreasonable terms of disbandment offered to them, it had declared them to be public enemies and, secondly, when it allowed itself to be bullied by the London mob. Its prestige had been further tarnished when the Speaker and Independent members had withdrawn from Westminster. It had continued whistling to keep up its courage even after the New Model Army entered London and Cromwell's cavalry bivouacked in Hyde Park. Until Cromwell had exercised pressure, the Presbyterian majority refused to admit that its actions during the absence of the Speaker and of half its members were null and void, and though Holles and Stapleton fled abroad, the remaining Presbyterian members still clung to the belief that they could impose their form of Church government upon the whole of England in the teeth of the Independents in the army.

Under these circumstances Cromwell, desperately seeking a settlement, looked to the beaten King for help. He hoped that if he would accept the constitutional proposals drafted by Ireton, Parliament might be induced to accept them too. According to Sir John Berkeley, the most trustworthy of the Royalist memoir writers, Cromwell said to him before the march into London:

> That whatsoever the world might judge of them, they would be found no seekers of themselves farther than to have leave to live as subjects ought to do, and to preserve their consciences; that they thought no men could enjoy their lives and estates quietly without the King had his rights, which they had declared in general terms already to the world, and would more particularly very speedily, wherein they would comprise the several interests of the Royal, Presbyterian, and Independent parties, as far as they were consisting with each other. . . .

Berkeley himself strongly pressed King Charles to agree to Ireton's proposals. "Never was a Crown so near lost, so cheaply recovered, as His Majesty's would be, if they agreed upon such terms," he assured him. But the King blew hot and cold, tried to bribe Cromwell with the promise of an earldom, and thought he might be rescued from his captivity by a Scottish army.

The King's vacillations handicapped Cromwell's patient efforts to secure peace. At the same time the army was not united behind him. Fairfax had washed his hands of politics (his wife was a secret Royalist); the Agitators were demanding a "purge" of Parliament; John Lilburne, who had now founded his Leveller movement, which sought a democratization of Parliament and a written constitution replete with fundamental rights, stirred up the rank and file with his flaming pamphlets, and a republican movement was beginning to form among some of the officers, headed by Colonel Thomas Rainsborough. Cromwell did all he could to preserve unity. He interviewed Lilburne in the Tower of London and begged him not to incite the army to mutiny while negotiations were in progress, and he assented to Parliament's once more offering the King the "proposition of Newcastle," although he did not conceal from the royal advisers his hope that the King would prefer Ireton's "Heads of the Proposals."

In the second week of September it seemed as if Cromwell's and Ireton's plan for a pacification was going to work. The King sent a letter to Parliament rejecting the Presbyterian "propositions" and recommending them to take into instant consideration the army's "proposals," with their regard for "liberty to tender consciences." On the same day that the letter was dispatched an officer was expelled from the Council of the Army for maintaining that there was "now no visible authority in the kingdom but the power and force of the sword," and a week later the Army Council met at Putney and agreed to invite Parliament to proceed to a settlement by drawing up bills to implement the "Heads of the Proposals."

But Cromwell was beset by difficulties on every side. He was accused of intriguing with the King against the interests of the nation, and the cloud of suspicion that centered over his actions became so dark that when the King was lodged in Hampton Court Palace after the army withdrew to Putney he no longer dared openly to negotiate with him. King Charles I, on the other hand, rejoicing in the divisions among his former enemies, patently boasted: "You cannot be without me; you will fall to ruin if I do not sustain you." Doggedly Cromwell kept to the course he had set for himself. When on September 22 Henry Marten, the republican spokesman in the Commons, moved that no further negotiations should be carried on with the King, Cromwell resisted the motion, acted as teller at the division, and procured its defeat by a sizable majority. Later he persuaded the Army Council to let him begin fresh talks with the King at Hampton Court, but Charles I, imagining that everything was coming his way, was stiffer than ever.

Meanwhile the extremists in the army, profiting by the virtual breakdown of negotiations, were refreshed. The cavalry regiments, including Cromwell's and Fairfax's own, elected new Agitators, and a young attorney named John Wildman came to the army to press Lilburne's democratic ideas upon the soldiers.[4] Cromwell moved backwards and forwards between the House of Commons and army headquarters at Putney, while keeping in touch with the King. At one time he wrote to Fairfax: "I pray excuse my non-attendance upon you. I scarce miss the House a day, where it's very necessary for me to be." He tried to persuade the Commons in a long speech that even if republicanism were now growing in the ranks, he and General Fairfax were firm for a settlement that would preserve the monarchy. But the King himself was not convinced of this. One of his favorite advisers, Jack Ashburnham, a relative of the dead Buckingham, asserted that "Cromwell had made a long discourse to him of the happy condition the people of this kingdom would be in if the government under which they in Holland lived were settled here [i.e., a republic]." If Cromwell said any such thing, it must have been intended to make the King see reason. For certainly the winds of republicanism were blowing hard over Putney heath, and men like Marten and Rainsborough were convinced that Charles's instability and insincerity precluded his restoration. But during those summer days Oliver Cromwell remained unshaken in his hope that a constitutional settlement might be attained with a reformed monarchy and a reformed Parliament. In spite of the vituperations poured upon him in pamphlets, speeches, and underground mutterings, he did not depart from the role he had chosen as a conciliator or attempt to impose any narrow political aim by the pressure of his sword.

At the end of October and the beginning of November 1647 the Army Council, together with one or two outsiders, including John Wildman, met in Putney to debate the constitutional scheme of the Levellers known as "An Agreement of the People," and to consider whether it might be dovetailed with Ireton's "Heads of the Proposals" and presented as an agreed scheme to Parliament. Broadly the Levellers sought manhood suffrage, constituency reform, regular Parliaments, frequent elections, and unalterable Bill of Rights, and the abolition both of the monarchy and the House of Lords. These were indeed revolutionary alterations, and it is a proof of Cromwell's open-mindedness that he was able to contemplate them without rancor. Fairly full accounts of some of these debates were discovered seventy years ago, and have since been exhaustively analysed on both sides of the Atlantic. Cromwell took the chair at them in place of General Fairfax, who was ill. Here he continued to act as a conciliator; he defended his conduct in the Commons and his dealings with the King, and he showed a tolerant outlook about a political solution, being willing to examine any plan that provided for liberty of conscience, did not promise anarchy, and was consonant with the genius of the English people.

As a conciliator he strove for unity. He tried to damp the sparks of wrath that flew between his son-in-law, Ireton, and Wildman, Rainsborough, and other democrats. "Really for my own part," he exclaimed at one point, "I must needs say that while we say we would not make reflections, we *do* make reflections. . . ." Yet "we are all here with the same integrity to the public." "Let us be doing, but let us be united in our doing." "Perhaps God may unite us and carry us both one way." He denied that he was committed to the King or to anyone else. "I thank God I stand upon the bottom of my own innocence in this particular; through the Grace of God I do not fear the face of any man." "We are . . . as free from engagements to the King as any man in all the world." He had never told anybody that it was the will of the army that the King should be restored; what he had said in Parliament was as a member and not as the spokesman for the army. Monarchy, he believed, was no more a divinely ordained institution than any other form of government. "I think that the King is king by contract, and I shall say, as Christ said, 'Let him that is without sin cast the first stone.'" Any scheme that aimed at "peace and safety" and was "for the good of the people" was welcome to him. The Jews had been equally happy under kings, judges, and heads of families. He was not "wedded and glued to forms of government."

The Levellers, directed by the able and pertinacious John Wildman, profoundly impressed the Army Council. Yet Cromwell and Ireton doubted the wisdom of manhood suffrage: "The consequences of this rule," Cromwell averred, "tends to anarchy, must end in anarchy; for where is there any bound or limit set if you take away this limit, that men that have no interest but the interest of breathing shall have no voice in election?" Later he repeated: "The first particular of that which they called the 'Agreement of the People' did tend very much to anarchy." Nevertheless, a joint committee of the two sides, Ireton's followers and Wildman's, was set up and the "Head of the Proposals" were modified in a democratic sense. While it was agreed that the monarchy and the House of Lords must be retained, their authority was to be greatly reduced, and even the House of Commons was to be subjected to the will of the constituencies and limited by a Bill of Rights.

But all Cromwell's travail for unity and conciliation, his astonishing patience, his attempts to save the King from himself, were in vain. While he was still contending at Putney with men who wanted to abolish the monarchy and even put the King to death as "a man of blood," King Charles was plotting his escape from his honorable captivity in Hampton Court Palace. He still imagined he might secure his restoration to the throne on his own terms by playing off the English against the Scots, and wished to acquire larger freedom to negotiate out of the reach of the New Model Army. Three Scottish commissioners, who were in close touch with him, urged him to make for Berwick, where he would be at liberty to seal a bargain with them. The King excused his breach of parole on the ground that he was afraid for his life, though Cromwell had given strict instructions to his cousin Colonel Whalley to guard him closely. Once again Charles I vacillated over where he should go. He took a dangerous if understandable decision. Instead of going to Berwick to join the Scots or sailing overseas to his Queen, he fixed upon the Isle of Wight as a place of refuge, where he believed he would cease to be in the power of the New Model Army and be able to put up his crown for auction. But Colonel Robert Hammond, the new Parliamentarian governor of the island, was related by marriage to Cromwell and was a man of conscience. Though a monarchist by conviction, he was not prepared to betray his duty in response to Royalist blandishments. Cromwell himself felt that Hammond was tempted, and in a number of fascinating letters fought for his soul. The governor hated his fate. He compromised by allowing the King a measure of freedom, until once again he attempted to escape. But Charles I's flight in mid-November to Carisbrooke Castle, where he was lodged, was to prove the first stage on his road to the scaffold.

The King's flight set the army aflame. It had already been restive when, after the Putney debates, Fairfax and Cromwell had suspended the meetings of the Army Council pending the sittings of a constitutional committee. Two regiments mutinied, but Cromwell faced it out with his sword in his hand. Only one man was summarily executed. The army was quietened. But the King's escape from Hampton Court had another dire consequence. Cromwell now recognized that they could negotiate with him no longer. In January 1648 he supported the vote of an exasperated House of Commons that no further addresses should be made to him. In the early spring, as soon as campaigning became possible, the second Civil War broke out. Cromwell must again have reflected, as he had done earlier during the debates in the Army Council, that "whosoever would have gone about to heal Babylon when God was determined to destroy her, he does fight against God, because God will not have her healed."

Notes

1. *Thurloe State Papers,* VI, 54.
2. The evidence that Cromwell gave Joyce his orders to seize the King is tenuous (see Gardiner, *History of the Great Civil War* (1893), III, 266–8). Sir John Berkeley remarked: "Cromwell stayed very long in London, for one that had been the author of the design." Mr. Christopher Hill has persuaded me that there is a good case for believing that Joyce acted without Cromwell's authority under pressure from the radicals in the army; afterwards he acquiesced (cf. p. 184 above).
3. The best authority on the Royalist side for Cromwell's meetings with King Charles I is Sir John Berkeley, *Memoirs* (1699). It is to this period that the famous phrase attributed to Cromwell: "No one rises so high as he who knows not where he is going" belongs. The source is Cardinal Retz's *Memoirs,* and in my view the story is doubtful.
4. For Wildman and the Putney debates, see my *John Wild-*

man: Plotter and Postmaster (1948). The Putney debates have been reprinted and edited by A. S. P. Woodhouse under the title of *Puritanism and Liberty* (1938). Of the many books on the Levellers three of the best and most recent are W. Haller and G. Davies, *Leveller Tracts, 1647–1653* (1944), M. A. Gibb, *John Lilburne* (1947), and Joseph Frank, *The Levellers* (1955).

Chapter 13

Cromwell the Avenger: the Second Civil War and the Execution of King Charles I

WHEN KING CHARLES I fled to the Isle of Wight, hoping to free himself from the grip of the English army, he abandoned all expectation of coming to terms with Cromwell, but still believed that he could win back his throne through negotiation either with the Scots or with the English Parliament. His consistent aim was to preserve his crown, his church, and his friends. He thought of himself as a master of diplomacy, but in fact floundered in a morass of doubledealing. "Many things," he observed on one occasion, "may be offered to obtain a treaty that may be altered when one comes to treat." He was not in the least concerned over liberty of conscience. On another occasion he had written to the Scots Commissioners:

> I send you here enclosed the answer which I have resolved to send to London; wherein you will find a clause *in favour of the Independents,* to wit, the forbearance I give to those who have scruples of conscience: and indeed I did it purposely, to make what I send relish the better with that kind of people. But if my native subjects [the Scots] will so countenance this answer that I may be sure they will stick to me in what concerns my temporal power, I will not only expunge that clause but likewise make what declarations I shall be desired *against the Independents,* and that really without any reservation or equivocation. . . .

That letter was written at the end of 1646.[1] In the winter of 1647 the King was maneuvering along the same serpentine lines. On November 16 he wrote to Parliament offering toleration outside a Presbyterian system (woven in with episcopacy), but a month later he told the Scots he was ready to suppress all the sects. There lay the essential difference between Charles I and Cromwell. For one liberty of conscience was a mere bargaining counter; for the other it was the main cause of the war and condition of peace. It was no wonder that Cromwell had come to recognize the

197

impossibility of treating with a man so different from himself.

On January 3, 1648, Cromwell stated his position clearly in the House of Commons: he observed that the King was "an obstinate man, whose heart God had hardened." On the same day he wrote to Colonel Hammond, who was responsible for guarding the King in the Isle of Wight, that "the House of Commons is very sensible of the King's dealings. . . . You should do well, if you have anything that may discover juggling, to search it out and let us know. . . ."

But though Cromwell thus felt that to negotiate further with Charles I was valueless, he still believed that in order to construct a fresh constitutional system he had to employ existing foundations. In one of his speeches at Putney he had insisted that the army needed to have some civil authority to support it—"if it have but the face of authority, if it be but a hare swimming over the Thames," he explained, he would "take hold of it rather than let it go." Now he turned back to Parliament in search of that basis of authority, and, as for monarchy, he contemplated the idea of replacing Charles I by his eldest son. Vigorously he explored all these possibilities. He gave dinner parties at which the army chiefs and parliamentary leaders met. He worked on the Committee of Safety, which replaced the Committee of Both Kingdoms as the provisional executive authority in England. He conversed with the republicans and tried to reconcile the Independents with the Presbyterians. On the Puritan side he stood out as the one man who might restore order and peace. A contemporary ballad, "O Brave Oliver," that appeared at this time contained the verse:

> For Oliver is all in all,
> For Oliver is all in all,
>   And Oliver is here,
>   And Oliver is there
>   And Oliver is at Whitehall.
>   And Oliver notes all,
>   And Oliver votes all,
> And claps his hand upon his bilbo. . . .

But his failure to find a solution benefited the King and the Royalists. On December 26 Charles I had come to an agreement, known as "the Engagement," with the Scottish Commissioners in England in which a compromise over religion had been arranged: the Presbyterian system was to be set up for three years, pending a final Church settlement, the sects were to be suppressed, and certain privileges conferred upon Scottish subjects following a union of the two kingdoms. In return the Scots were to promise the King to restore him control over the English army, the right to veto bills in Parliament, and an act of oblivion for his adherents. If the English Parliament were to refuse peace on these terms, a Scottish army would be sent to England to enforce them. The King undertook, once war began, to do everything he could to obtain men and arms from abroad and at home to assist the Scots in their campaign. With this agreement secretly concluded, the Scots Commissioners left England in January 1648, but they had yet to induce their fellow countrymen to accept it.

Meanwhile, though nothing was known for certain at Westminster, Cromwell and his friends in London had a shrewd idea of what was happening. They learned that the King had twice tried to escape from the Isle of Wight (where he had now been placed under close arrest), and they perceived all around them Royalist stirrings stimulated by the failure of either Parliament or the army to procure a settlement. In April the City of London was lit with bonfires in celebration of the King's accession to the throne twenty-three years earlier, and the streets were filled with crowds drinking his health and demanding his return. At Pembroke Castle in Wales the governor had refused to give up his command when ordered to do so and was declared a traitor. In Scotland the adherents of the King were trying to persuade the Committee of the Estates to honor the Engagement. Cromwell was perturbed and distressed. At the end of April he appeared at a prayer meeting at Windsor, where army headquarters were, and "did press very earnestly on all those present to a thorough consideration of our actions as an army, as well as our ways particularly as private Christians, to see if any iniquity could be found in them. . . ." While the Council of the Army was praying and examining its conscience, the news came that South Wales was in a state of revolt. Thus the second Civil War began.

By signing the Engagement and inviting a Scottish army to invade England, and by giving the signal for a universal Royalist uprising, the King had thrown his last dice. His motives were easy to comprehend. Plainly many of his subjects wanted him back on the throne. Though he had given some qualified promises about the establishment of Presbyterianism, he had not violated his fundamental principles or beliefs. Once restored, he could hope—and did hope—to recover for the Crown much of its ancient glory. Yet he had miscalculated both in terms of politics and of war. Many of the Scottish Covenanters, fully sustained by the ministers of the Kirk, were dissatisfied with his promises and refused to support the invasion. The "Engagers" alone, headed by the Duke of Hamilton and his only brother, the Earl of Lanark, were committed to the hilt. Moreover, the Royalist revolt in England and Wales exploded too soon, well before the Scottish army was ready. And few of the Scots or the English Royalists were sufficiently trained or armed to overcome the soldiers of the New Model Army.

Cromwell thought that the revival of the Civil War by the King was "a prodigious treason," a deliberate affront to the Almighty. After all, most of the Royalists when they surrendered in 1646 had promised to fight no more. King Charles had given his parole at Hampton Court, and evaded it by dubious means. When the second war was under way, even a general as merciful as Lord Fairfax ordered the execution of two of the Royalist commanders for breaking their parole and causing useless bloodshed. After the battle of Preston, Cromwell urged that "they that are implacable and will not leave troubling the land may speedily be destroyed." The rank and file of the New Model Army felt even more resentfully than their generals that the new war was a breach of faith by the King that should be visited with retribution.

* * *

At the beginning of May 1648 General Fairfax ordered Cromwell to South Wales. He concentrated his troops in Gloucester, whither he had dispatched his artillery by water, and rode to the head of each regiment reminding the men of their former triumphs and promising to live and die with them. After urging upon Fairfax that Bristol should be reinforced with a garrison, he entered Wales to learn that the insurrection had already collapsed. It only remained for him to lay siege to Pembroke Castle, where a former Roundhead officer, Colonel Poyer, had declared for the King. Here Cromwell showed his immense organizing ability. He was short of artillery, and sent to Carmarthen for "shells for our mortar piece the depth of them we desire may be fourteen

THE CAMPAIGN OF 1648

Line of March →

Berwick

Newcastle

Carlisle

Kendal

Hornby

Knaresborough

Skipton

Gisburn

Preston

Leeds

Pontefract

Wigan

Winwick · Manchester

Warrington

Uttoxeter

Nottingham

Warwick

Carmarthen

Gloucester

Pembroke

LONDON

20   0   20   40   60

Miles

inches and three-quarters of an inch." He scraped up a "few little guns," with the aid of his chaplain, cut off the garrison from all food supplies, and burned a number of houses. But meanwhile the rest of the country was afire. In districts even where the Parliamentary cause had formerly been popular, Royalist risings took place, especially in the southeast of England. General Fairfax, after surprising Maidstone, was confronted by prolonged resistance at Colchester. Part of the navy changed sides, and young Prince Charles collected a fleet to block the Thames and try to blackmail London. In the north the Royalists took the strategic towns of Carlisle and Berwick, Pontefract was gained by the agency of a turncoat, and Scarborough was occupied later, while Major General Lambert, with a small force, could only fight a delaying action. Cromwell, however, who lacked guns rather than men, was able to spare reinforcements both for Lambert and for Colonel Whalley in Essex. And as he sat down before the formidable castle of Pembroke he wrote to Fairfax with cheerful piety reminding him that "these things that have lately come to pass have been the wonderful works of God; breaking the rod of the oppressor, as in the day of Midian, not with garments much rolled in blood but by the terror of the Lord." In fact, he interpreted the second Civil War as a "providence" rescuing men from their bondage. He had no doubt that the Lord would "yet save His people and confound His enemies." Eventually, on July 11, Pembroke surrendered and Cromwell sternly exempted from mercy Colonel Poyer and other former Roundhead officers, who had "sinned against so much light and against so many evidences of Divine Presence going along with and prospering a righteous cause, in the management of which they themselves had a share."

As soon as Pembroke castle had fallen Cromwell hurried to the aid of Major General Lambert. John Lambert, who was not yet thirty, was a natural military genius, second only to Cromwell and Fairfax. While Cromwell was at Pembroke, Lambert had contained Sir Marmaduke Langdale, a Yorkshireman like himself but a Roman Catholic, in the city of Carlisle, guarding the route by which the Scottish Engagers were to advance into England. Lambert had only about twenty-three troops of cavalry under his immediate command, and could do little but indulge in harassing movements until he was reinforced.[2] But he was an aggressive general, and Cromwell thought it wise to instruct him not to fight a battle before he came up. Cromwell was advancing rapidly towards him. His infantry covered 260 miles from Pembroke to Pontefract, via Gloucester, Warwick, and Nottingham, in twenty-seven days, stopping on the way only to pick up shoes and stockings to clothe their ragged feet. On August 12 Cromwell's and Lambert's forces met near Knaresborough. Cromwell took over the command of the combined army, which amounted to about 9,000 men.

Meanwhile the Scots, headed by James, Duke of Hamilton, had crossed the border. Hamilton was a strange character, proud, restless, ambitious, perverse.[3] He was a cousin of King Charles I, became his Master of the Horse, and was appointed Royal Commissioner for Scotland at the time of the first Bishops' War. His loyalty to the King had survived a spell of unjustified imprisonment in Oxford. With some difficulty he had recruited an army of over 10,000 men, although he had been opposed by the astute and mighty Marquis of Argyll and the ministers of the Kirk. But his army was poorly trained and ill-equipped. It lived on plunder. Sir Arthur Haselrigg, now the Parliamentarian governor of Newcastle, wrote: "The Scotch take all—movables, cows, sheep and all household stuff to the very pothooks; they take children and make their parents pay ransom for them, and force women before their friends' faces." Hamilton's biographer wrote of the Scottish army:[4]

> The regiments were not full, many of them scarce exceeded half their number, and not the fifth man could handle pike or musket. The horse were the best mounted that ever Scotland sent out, yet most of the troopers were raw and undisciplined. They had no artillery, not so much as one field-piece, very little ammunition, and very few horse to carry it. . . . Thus the precipitating of affairs in England [by the Royalist risings] forced them on a march before they were in any posture for it. . . .

The summer was an excessively wet one, clogging the roads and damaging equipment.

Thus there was a contrast between a large army compounded of different contingents—for in addition to Langdale's Royalists, Hamilton was joined by 3,000 Scots brought over from Ireland under Major General Sir George Monro—

inadequately armed and trained, and a small but "fine, smart army, fit for action," as one of the captains in it described Cromwell's army.[5]

The Duke of Hamilton, after entering England on July 8, moved south in a leisurely way. He had put a Scottish garrison into Carlisle and, sending Langdale forward as an advance guard, marched via Kendal in Westmorland to Hornby, north of Lancaster. Here the decision was taken to continue through Lancashire and not to turn into Yorkshire. The various Scottish officers were at odds with each other and with the English. Nevertheless, the main motive for going into Lancashire was to pick up more English Royalists. The intelligence on the two sides was indifferent. General Lambert seems to have had a fixed idea that the Scots would come into Yorkshire, perhaps to join their Royalist friends at Pontefract (Cromwell had stopped to inspect the arrangements for the siege of that town on his way north), while the Scots had no conception of the nearness of Cromwell's army; they even thought part of it had gone to Manchester. In one way the Parliamentarians had the advantage, for the Pennine range acted as a screen concealing their strength and dispositions from the enemy, and it was possible for them to debouch and assault the Scots in the flank through one of the three or four roads that crossed the hills to the west.

While Cromwell and Lambert were consulting near Leeds, the Duke of Hamilton went on slowly to Preston. More by accident than design, Langdale had now become a cover to his flank instead of his advance guard. Hamilton's forces were strung out over a distance of some fifty miles: Lieutenant General the Earl of Callander with the Scottish horse was now ahead, then came the Scottish infantry, next Langdale's men, and, trailing far to the rear, Major General Monro with the Scots from Ireland. On August 16 Cromwell, having crossed the Pennines by way of Skipton and Gisburn, sacrificing on the altar of speed the artillery he had collected with such difficulty, held a Council of War to determine whether to make straight for Preston or to cross the River Ribble to the south and try to intercept the Scottish advance through Lancashire. It was resolved, since it was believed that Hamilton would need to wait for General Monro, to go on to Preston; for Cromwell felt that the enemy would stand and fight, and he wanted a battle. Evidently at this time Cromwell's intelligence was superior to that of the Royalists. But what is not clear is whether Cromwell knew, when he ordered the attack on the morning of August 17, if he was going to confront the main Royalist army or only a portion of it. His dispatches after the battle suggest he thought he was fighting the bulk of Hamilton's army. In fact, he had to contend only with some 4,000 men under Sir Marmaduke Langdale. At any rate, knowingly or not, he had achieved the ultimate in war of concentrating an overwhelming force at a decisive point. It was a lucky strike, owing its success to aggressiveness on one side and stupidity on the other. For Langdale was unable to persuade the Scottish high command that Cromwell himself was upon them—Hamilton himself was incredulous, and even fancied the enemy were the local Lancashire militia—and he was left to fight alone while nearly the whole of the Scottish cavalry rode on towards Wigan, and the infantry remained immobile on the other side of the river six miles from the moor where the battle was waged.

Sir Marmaduke, a gallant if austere Cavalier, fought bravely enough—and the Duke of Hamilton, to his credit, joined him in the last phase of the battle with a small body of horse, compensating in some small degree by his personal courage for his all-round incompetence as commander in chief. In the beginning it was an infantry battle, Cromwell's men trying to overcome or outflank the Royalist foot, who were excellently protected in enclosed fields covered with hedge. At the critical moment Parliamentarian levies from Lancashire, under Colonel Ralph Assheton, kept in reserve, were thrown in, and after four hours of struggle Langdale was compelled to fall back into Preston itself, where the Duke of Hamilton came up with his guard of horse. Four troops of Cromwell's own cavalry regiment, supported by Colonel Thomas Harrison's regiment, charged the Royalists in the town and, though Hamilton thrice countercharged, succeeded in clearing the streets. To escape capture, Hamilton himself had to swim a ford across the Ribble.[6]

The battle of Preston was largely a soldiers' battle, a prolonged infantry melee dictated by the lie of the ground: the foot, as Cromwell reported to the Speaker of the House of Commons, "often coming to push of pike and close firing, and always making the enemy to recoil . . . the enemy making, though he was worsted, very stiff and sturdy resistance." But before that the Royalists had been outmaneuvered strategically and completely surprised, and Cromwell, as always, kept a good reserve in hand, and ordered it up at the time of crisis. The charges of his seasoned cavalry concluded a battle whose consequences far outranged its scope. Never until Dunbar did Cromwell's military genius shine more vividly than in this campaign.

The Scots were left in an appalling state of confusion. Their major general of infantry was fourteen miles away with the cavalry in Wigan. Their main body of foot had stood helplessly in the rain while their allies were overwhelmed on the other side of Preston. Monro's experienced contingent, still miles to the rear, made no attempt to come to Langdale's rescue. Sir James Turner, a Scottish colonel, confessed that "want of intelligence help to ruin us, for Sir Marmaduke was well near totally routed before we knew that it was Cromwell that attacked us." As night fell the Duke of Hamilton and his commanders took hasty counsel together. Should they make a stand where they were, posted on a hill, recalling the cavalry from Wigan, or should they march on through the night and join the cavalry? They felt insecure where they were: six hundred musketeers had tried to protect the bridge across the Ribble, only to be swept aside by Cromwell's infantry. The Scottish commanders, after arguing with each other on horseback, decided that retreat was the better part of valor. The Scots foot soldiers, wet, weary, and dispirited, set off on their "drumless march" through the night in foul weather, and were compelled by lack of transport and the poverty of the roads to leave behind their ammunition save for what they could carry in their belts. Orders were given that the rest of the ammunition should be blown up three hours after their departure, but it fell intact into Cromwell's hands.

So the Scots straggled miserably onwards through the mire to Wigan moor, but nearly half of them fell out upon the route. The "faint and weary soldiers" who "lagged behind," wrote a Scottish officer, "we never saw again."[7] To add to the general muddle, the Scots cavalry came back from Wigan to look for their infantry and missed them on the way. However, in the end the cavalry provided an effective rearguard, even though it was constantly attacked by Cromwell's skirmishers. When the Scottish army at length reached Wigan moor, it was discovered that it was hopeless as a battleground and another march was ordered to Warrington, ten miles farther on. "There," wrote Sir James Turner, "we conceived we might face about, having the command of a town, a river, and a bridge. Yet I conceive there was but few of us thought we might be beaten before we were masters of any of them." Thus Cromwell's shadow, seemingly gigantic behind them, oppressed the Scots with a sense of impending doom.

In fact, Cromwell's small army was also tired out after the battle of Preston. Cromwell had ordered three cavalry regiments to push on as fast as they could and harass the Scots. The leader of this vanguard. Colonel Thornhaugh, a friend of Ireton's from Nottinghamshire, did his duty so eagerly that he was slain by the Scottish lancers. But Cromwell brought the rest of his army on through the wet and mud, and caught the Scots three miles short of Warrington at Winwick Pass. After a long contest "at push of pike and very close charges," the Scots foot were broken and in Warrington surrendered to a man. Four thousand prisoners were taken at Preston and six thousand at Wigan and Warrington. The Duke of Hamilton, after deliberately leaving his infantry to capitulate, rode off with his cavalry in a final despairing attempt to reach the shelter of Pontefract castle. Cromwell sent Lambert after him with four brigades of horse. Hamilton got as far as Uttoxeter in Staffordshire—"the weather being rainy, windy and tempestuous and we came thither in great disorder," wrote one who was with him.[8] The local trained bands came out to attack him, and Lambert was soon on his heels. At a pleasant house, where Mary, Queen of Scots, had once been a prisoner, the Duke of Hamilton surrendered on August 25. Cromwell treated him with every courtesy and consideration, but he was to die for the master whom he had served faithfully if without inspiration. Colonel Sir James Turner wrote the epitaph of the Scottish invasion of 1648 in these words:

> The weakness, rawness, and undisciplinedness of our soldiers, our want of artillery and horse to carry the little ammunition we had, the constant rainy, stormy and tempestuous weather which attended us, which made all highways impassable for man and beast, our want of intelligence, our leaving our Irish auxiliaries so far behind us, and our unfortunate resolution to waive Yorkshire and march by Lancashire, all . . . made us a prey to Cromwell's veteran army.

And he added, "what was intended for the King's relief and restoration posted him to his grave."

*　　　　*　　　　*

At the end of August 1648 Cromwell received orders from the Committee of Safety to retake Berwick and Carlisle and to prevent the formation of a new Royalist army in the north of England. The remaining English Royalists were soon mopped up, but Sir George Monro with his three thousand Scots from Ulster got away across the border, where they joined the Earl of Lanark in Stirling. Cromwell arrived at the Scottish border near Berwick in the middle of September and thence demanded from the Committee of the Estates the surrender of the two English towns in Scottish hands. The defeat of the Duke of Hamilton and the proximity of Cromwell with his victorious army brought about a revolution in Scotland, the Marquis of Argyll and the Covenanters seizing power in Edinburgh, while the Engagers glared at them from Stirling. The English army found it impossible to subsist in the Berwick area and, partly for that reason and partly in order to compel the Scots to withdraw their garrisons from England, Cromwell rode into Scotland on September 21 and next day interviewed Argyll. The Marquis accepted the inevitable, and so did the Earl of Lanark. Orders were sent for the surrender of Berwick and Carlisle, and the Engagers agreed to lay down their arms. After that Comwell was invited to Edinburgh, where he arrived with a substantial force of cavalry on October 4. During the next day or two Cromwell continued to negotiate with Argyll and the Covenanters, who had now obtained control of the Committee of the Estates. Cromwell explained that he was not satisfied with the mere disbandment of the Engagers, but required their exclusion from all offices. That was to push against an open door. The Covenanters were delighted to oust their rivals, and Cromwell reported home that Scotland was now likely to become "a better neighbour." At Argyll's requests he left behind Major General Lambert with two cavalry regiments and some dragoons to support the Covenanters while they were recruiting their own army. After barely a fortnight, Cromwell returned to England.

The Covenanters were not, however, at heart grateful for the assistance that Cromwell gave them. After all, he had defeated their fellow countrymen and come to Edinburgh as a foreign conqueror. Nor was Cromwell's diplomacy without its critics in England. It was said, at any rate among the Independents, that he let off Argyll far too lightly. Ought he not to have established "liberty of conscience" among the Scots? But Cromwell took the view that the Scots were entitled to their own religion, if they would only be good neighbors. Was he supposed to subdue Edinburgh, he demanded, in order to deprive the Scots of the form of church government in which they believed? That was not his idea of toleration.

* * *

Two days after the battle and rout of Preston, Colchester had surrendered to General Fairfax and the second Civil War was virtually at an end. In the north, after the reoccupation of Carlisle and Berwick by Parliamentary forces, only Pontefract and Scarborough held out for the Royalists. Cromwell did not hurry back to London, but stayed in the north, personally supervising the siege of Pontefract. He had been filled with a sense of wonder and humility at the swiftness and completeness of his victories. In less than two months since he joined General Lambert in Yorkshire, he had broken the Royalist revival in the north and completed the discomfiture of the Scottish Engagers. It seemed to him to be "the great hand of God" that enabled him to beat his enemies piecemeal instead of meeting at Preston, as he might have done, a concentration three times the size of his own little "handful." A letter he wrote to his friend Oliver St. John soon after his victory was instinct with awe. In it he expressed his consciousness of the mercies that God had vouchsafed. They were but "poor, weak saints" and "our rest we expect elsewhere: that will be durable." They were sanctified as the agents of the Lord's "righteous witnessing" in this "unjust war." And God "who is not to be mocked or deceived," took vengeance upon the "profanity" of their enemies "even to astonishment and admiration." But though he recognized the miracle, what did these "outward dispensations" portend? He was perplexed about the future of his country.

While he had been away in the north many of the excluded members of Parliament, led by the irrepressible Denzil Holles, had returned to Westminster, repealed the "vote of no addresses," and reopened negotiations with the King. Still resilient, King Charles had gone to Newport in the Isle of Wight, and offered concessions to Holles and his colleagues. Yet nothing came of these negotiations, though it is hard to understand why they failed when both sides had so much to gain from their success. The King himself ingenuously confided to his friends that if the other side could be induced to believe that he dared deny them nothing, they would be less careful about guarding him and thus give him another opportunity to escape. Perhaps the Presbyterians realized the King's insincerity.

The Independents had long known the King's untrustworthiness, and the New Model Army was seething with anger at the very idea of renewing negotiations with him. The Levellers were openly demanding the trial and deposition of the King. Cromwell himself hinted at his own position in a private letter of November 6. He suggested that to negotiate further with the King was to meddle with "an accursed thing." He defended his own treaty with the Scots, and urged the need for "union and right understanding between all godly people." He contraverted the view that "the enthroning of the King with presbytery" would "bring spiritual slavery" while "with moderate episcopacy" it would work "a good peace." "I trust there's no necessity of either," he said. But at the time he wrote this letter he was still uncertain about what the next step ought to be. He was not yet advocating the deposition of the King. It is likely that he deliberately stayed away from London (for he could easily have left the siege of Pontefract to Lambert, as in fact he did later) in order to profit from the opportunity for meditation and prayer. "We wait upon the Lord," he wrote then, "who will teach us and lead us, whether to doing or suffering." He soon realized that the negotiations at Newport were useless, and that no agreement was likely to be reached with King Charles that would promise the Christian freedom for which the Ironsides had fought.

During the first half of November, while Cromwell was lingering at Pontefract and wrestling with his conscience, the army in the south was taking action. On November 18 General Fairfax forwarded a "remonstrance" to Parliament demanding the trial of the King as "the grand author of our troubles" and the bringing to justice of other men who had been "the chief instruments" in the two civil wars. Two days later Cromwell wrote to Fairfax to inform him that the northern army agreed that "impartial justice" must be done on "all offenders," and added, "I do in all, from my heart, concur with them."

Thus, during his stay in the north of England Cromwell at last came to the end of his mental striving. The army, he recognized, must punish the instigators of war and blaze the path to a peaceful settlement. No longer could he turn trustfully either to the King or the King's children, to the existing Parliament, or even to a "purged" Parliament, to furnish the basis of authority in the state. The army had, he felt, been elected to that task and must no longer flinch from its duty. By the events of that summer the Lord had completed His revelation: He had shown him that the army was the chosen vessel of His vengeance and His justice: "Let us look into providences; surely they mean somewhat," he wrote. "They hang so together; have been so constant, so clear and unclouded." Was not the army "a lawful power, called by God to oppose and fight against the King upon some stated grounds"? Was not "the people's safety," for which they had contended "a sound position"? Did not they, as God's soldiers, alone honor the cause of Christian liberty when they took up arms? Were they not alone capable of ensuring that "the whole fruit of the war" should not be frustrated? Thus when Cromwell at last came back on orders from General Fairfax to London, where he arrived on December 5, he had convinced himself that Providence had directed that the King must be tried (and, by implication, deposed), and that the army was the providential means to fashion good government in England.

* * *

Cromwell's political feelings at this time in his life, though clothed obscurely in the Puritan language of his time, were neither hypocritical nor absurd. It was a wrench for a man born under the Elizabethan monarchy to recognize that Charles Stuart must be deposed before peace could be reestablished. But he had learned from personal experience the impossibility of negotiating with such a king because of his evasiveness, stubbornness, and duplicity. Cromwell may well have discovered that in 1647 some of the King's own advisers had urged him to come to terms with the army and to consent to liberty for the sects. But, instead of agreeing, the King had renounced the idea of religious freedom, relaid and relit the fires of war, and again seen his followers crushed. If one translates the phrases "outward dispensations" and "remarkable providences" into the "plain lessons of experience," Cromwell's conclusions become clear. Yet, as he meditated in Yorkshire, away from the current of affairs in London, he still hesitated. Others in the New Model Army, notably his son-in-law, Ireton, had seen the logic of events earlier than he did. While Cromwell was still opening his mind in a number of revealing letters to Colonel Robert Hammond, Hammond himself was deprived by General Fairfax of his command in the Isle of Wight and of his responsibility for guarding the King. King Charles was removed to the isolation of Hurst Castle in Hampshire, where he was momentarily left to contemplate the shingle, the silence, and the Solent. On December 6 the southern army also took the incisive step, so long contemplated, of "purging" the House of Commons of its Presbyterian members, whose leaders had voluntarily absented themselves during the previous summer, only to return to press the reopening of negotiations with the King when the second Civil War broke out. Cromwell expressed his approval of both the decision to remove and try the King and the purge of the Commons.

On December 7 Cromwell took his place in the much attenuated House of Commons, and attended three meetings of the Council of the Army later in the month. The army was now committed to the trial of the King, and Cromwell concentrated upon that question. Apart from interesting himself in the detailed arrangements for guarding the King, preventing his escape, and bringing him to London, Cromwell was concerned over two wider issues: one was whether the lesser offenders, like the Duke of Hamilton, ought to be put on trial first; the other was whether the punishment of the King as instigator of war might be waived if now, at the eleventh hour, he would concede all the constitutional demands that were put to him. During December Cromwell actually visited the Duke of Hamilton on two or three occasions, though what they said to each other is not known, and about Christmas the Earl of Denbigh, who was a relative of the Duke and one of the few peers who still attended the House of Lords, tried to see the King at Windsor and open the way to a last-moment compromise, but Charles I refused even to talk to him.

It was natural enough that Cromwell should still hesitate before pressing through the trial of the King. He accepted his personal responsibilities, for he knew that General Fairfax was at best half-hearted. Cromwell was sufficient of a realist to understand that a trial would mean condemnation and that deposition or banishment would raise more problems than they would solve; and that the probable result of a trial would be the King's execution. On the other hand, he would indeed have been a poor judge of character if he had imagined that Charles I, having spurned so many opportunities to regain his throne on terms and having always refused his consent to any proposals that would have meant the permanent diminution of his powers as head of church and state, would at last, under the threat of death, yield to his enemies. If, as has been suggested, Cromwell approved of the Earl of Denbigh's "mission" and awaited its outcome before finally committing himself to the immediate trial of the King,[9] then surely he can scarcely have expected that it would do more than prove King Charles's steadfast determination to be martyred rather than give way.

On January 2, 1649, an ordinance for the King's trial was considered in the House of Commons. On that occasion Cromwell was reported to have said:

If any man whatsoever hath carried on the design of deposing the King, and disinheriting his posterity, or if any man had yet such a design, he should be the greatest traitor and rebel in the world, but, since the Providence of God hath cast this upon us, I cannot but submit to Providence, though I am not yet provided to give advice. . . .

Both the army and Independents in the Commons were divided over the wisdom and righteousness of trying the King; nearly all the Presbyterians were opposed to it, and the House of Lords, or what remained of it, refused to assent to the ordinance. But Cromwell, whatever his previous thoughts about postponement may have been, was now fixed upon his course. Justice must be done and the road opened to peace and a settlement. Perhaps Cromwell, like the republican Ludlow, convinced himself "by the express words of God's law": "That blood defileth the land, and the land cannot be cleansed of the blood that is shed therein, but by the blood of him that shed it." He was aware that there were no legal or constitutional means by which the King could be tried and condemned. But he brushed aside the scruples of the lawyers, and was contemptuous of men who demanded the King's death and sat at his trial and then in the end tried to evade signing the death warrant.

The story of how King Charles I was tried in Westminster Hall and how he perished on the scaffold in Whitehall and of how Oliver Cromwell helped to bring it about has frequently been told. It is one of history's immortal tragedies, the last confrontation of two sincere and obstinate Christian gentlemen engaged in a conflict of ultimate values. When Cromwell was long dead and buried, Royalists, republicans, and Presbyterians wrote their memoirs or made their speeches, and out of them historians have reconstructed often contradictory accounts of how Cromwell thought and acted between December 6, 1648, when he returned to London from the north, and January 30, 1649, when King Charles's head was severed from his body upon the block. Much is speculation and, as Lord Morley wrote,[10] a "hunt for conjectural motives for conjectural occurrences is waste of time." Only one thing is certain, and that is that once Cromwell had made up his mind that the King must die, he went forward relentlessly. In the Preston campaign he had seen himself as the instrument of God's vengeance. When he returned to London he felt sure that sooner or later the King would have to stand his trial for renewing the civil war, even if that meant the army taking the matter into its own hands and Parliament being forcibly dissolved. It is sometimes said that Cromwell regarded the King's death as a "necessity," but no authentic words of his have survived to this effect;[11] and if he did think it a necessity, it was only because he defined necessity as God's law. When he spoke of King Charles I's death in later life, as he did once or twice, he referred to it as an act of "justice"—not justice in any narrow legal sense (for, after all, a minority had engineered the whole proceedings against the wishes of the many), but of God's justice, the transcendental justice that Cromwell had learned in his youth at Cambridge and in the books of Ralegh and Beard. The wicked were always to be punished for their sins, not merely in the afterlife but here below. And though they could expect no abiding resting place, the saints, the Chosen People, were the divinely appointed agents and witnesses of retribution, and were intended by the Lord of Hosts to inherit the earth.

Notes

1. Gilbert Burnet, *The Memoirs of the Lives and Actions of James and William, Dukes of Hamilton and Castle-Head* (1852), 381.

2. There is a life of Lambert called *Cromwell's Understudy* (1938), by W. H. Dawson. I have taken the quotation by Haselrigg from this. For Langdale, see, *inter alia, Tracts relating to*

military proceedings in Lancashire during the civil war (Chetham Society, 1844).

3. Recent characterizations of Hamilton will be found in David Mathew, *Scotland under Charles I* (1955) and C. V. Wedgwood, *The King's Peace* (1955).

4. Burnet, *op. cit.*, 450.

5. *Memoirs of Captain John Hodgson* (1806), 114.

6. Gardiner's account of the battle of Preston still remains as good as most. See also E. Broxap, *The Great Civil War in Lancashire* (1910).

7. Sir James Turner, *Memoirs* (1839), 65.

8. Sir Marmaduke Langdale's account in Burnet, *op. cit.*, 459.

9. Gardiner, *History of the Great Civil War* (1893), IV, 285–87. Gardiner's view of what Cromwell thought about Denbigh's "mission" is conjectural in the extreme. Once Cromwell made up his mind that the King must be put on trial he was a committed man. Gardiner's evidence about his hesitations is tenuous.

10. John Morley, *Oliver Cromwell* (1900), 275.

11. I still maintain the view that the story of Cromwell lifting up the coffin lid, gazing into the face of King Charles I, and muttering "cruel necessity," which was virtually accepted by both Gardiner and Abbott, is incredible.

Chapter 14

Cromwell and England in 1649

EVERY MAN, IT has been said, is a genius at twenty-five; the difficulty is to be one at fifty.[1] Oliver Cromwell was nearly fifty when King Charles I was executed, and the nine fullest years of his life lay ahead of him. Up till then he had shown himself, above all in the campaign of 1648, to be a superb commander; he had proved himself a statesman from the time when he took part in the debates of the Self-denying Ordinance, he had worked ceaselessly as a conciliator during the confused revolutionary period that intervened between the end of the first Civil War and the trial of the King; and he had become acknowledged as chief of the Independents and the standard-bearer of liberty of conscience. Now that a new state was being formed—and it was inevitable that it should be a republic since no Stuart could return to the throne on Puritan terms—Cromwell and Lord Fairfax were believed to be its real leaders. The Dutch ambassador, Pauw, who had come to England on a mission to plead for the King's life, praised Fairfax of his "great civility," but Cromwell for his "ability and eloquence."[2] One of the many Royalist journalists whose work was published that winter wrote hopefully:

> *Black Fairfax can climb no further*
> *Than heaven will give him leave;*
> *Red Cromwell no more can murder*
> *Nor the saints more deceive . . .*

thus pinpointing the two men who had conquered.[3]

But Lord Fairfax remained anxious to keep outside politics, and was willing to serve the commonwealth only as a soldier and administrator; he had withdrawn from the trial of the King and repudiated his execution. Cromwell, on the other hand, in a speech to the Council of the Army in March, asserted that "the execution of exemplary justice upon the prime leader of all this quarrel" had been the will of God. Though he was not without family cares, he faced all his public responsibilities. His mother, now over eighty, was taken so ill that for a time he did not want to leave her. He was energetically negotiating the marriage settlement of his eldest surviving son, a young man much in love ("My son has a great desire to come down and wait upon your daughter," Oliver wrote to the prospective father-in-law, "I perceive he minds that more than to attend to business here.") He did not contemplate leaving the future of his country to others. His only concern was to feel certain where his duty called him.

Cromwell's place in the state had been confirmed by the course of the wars. Two years earlier John Lilburne, who was to become one of his most determined critics, had written a striking letter to him:[4]

> God hath honoured you . . . not only in giving you extraordinary large room in the affections of thousands and tens of thousands of his chosen ones, but in hanging upon your back the glory of all their achievements, by means of which you have been made mighty and great, formidable and dreadful, in the eyes of the great ones of the world, and truly myself and all others of my mind that I could speak with have looked upon you as the most absolute single-hearted great man in England, untainted or unbiased with ends of your own. . . .

This back-handed testimony to Cromwell's popularity and integrity was, in fact, but a prelude to an attack upon him, but it showed how sincerely many of the Independents and soldiers had admired and trusted him. A pamphlet entitled *The Rest of Faith*, dedicated to him by one of the colonels in the army in February 1649,[5] proved that he was believed by other officers as well as himself to be the appointed instrument of God in all that had gone before.

Now, however, Cromwell found himself with the virtually impossible task, not merely of helping to constitute a new government and to defend it against all its enemies, but of reconciling the many factions born of the revolution. He was no bigot or narrow Puritan; "he cared deeply for what was called godliness of spirit"; he distrusted all dogmas and genuinely loved toleration. But how were both order and freedom to be established? For example, at that very time the Lord was "opening Himself" to George Fox, founder of the Society of Friends, in Leicestershire. Fox then went into Nottingham, entered the Church of St. Mary, and shouted down the preacher in his pulpit, telling the startled congregation that "God did not dwell in temples made with hands."[6] He was put under arrest and thrust into prison. The question of how to allow liberty to so great a Christian leader as Fox and his disciples while at the same time maintaining the public peace proved insoluble, and it was to perplex Cromwell for the rest of his life. Yet before it could even be considered, peace had to be established both at home and abroad beneath the flag of the new republic that was finally hoisted on May 15, 1649.

* * *

London was free from disturbances on the day that King Charles I perished. The shops had been open as usual. Next day was the monthly fast. And while the Royalists hastened to paint the portrait of a martyr who had died for his people, the republicans recalled the words of John Bradshaw, who presided at the trial, that the king had been punished "in the name of the people" for betraying his trust. After seven years of civil strife, there was a general longing to have done with it at all costs. But that was not so simple. In Scotland the Presbyterian rulers averred that they had never sought the blood of their King and they condemned his execution, and were ready to proclaim Prince Charles if he would but accept the National Covenant. In Ireland the King's Lord Lieutenant, the Marquis of Ormonde, was feverishly building a fresh military coalition which, if it could subdue the island, might afterwards invade England. Abroad even the Dutch, themselves republicans, favored Prince Charles, and most of the foreign ambassadors were indignantly withdrawn from London. In Yorkshire Pontefract Castle still held out against General Lambert, though it was soon to capitulate. Throughout the north frost and snow lay thick upon the ground. The governor of Newcastle was warned to allow no horses to be sent across the Scottish border, and as soon as Pontefract surrendered to John Lambert, he received orders to dispatch guns thence to Berwick to guard the frontier. Lambert was popular in Yorkshire and received a declaration "from the northern counties" promising support and asking—in broad optimism —for the ending of "all injustice." But at the same time the new Council of State was sent a petition from Yorkshire requiring that Pontefract Castle should forwith be demolished and "free quarter" taken off.

Lancashire was also discontented by the free quartering of the 2,500 horse and foot stationed in that county, and a report came from Manchester of "great expectation of some sudden disturbance." From Chester it was reported (incorrectly) that Prince Rupert was in the Isle of Man and Prince Maurice at Wexford. From the Midlands a petition was received in London demanding the settlement of the militia, the abolition of tithes, and the relief of Ireland. The officers of the Hull garrison asked that February for new parliamentary elections and the prompt reform of the law. From Hereford came another petition likewise seeking the abolition of free quarter, the paying off of the army, and "the settlement of the kingdom." Down in Devonshire, as in distant Manchester, rumors were rife of Royalist preparations based not only upon Ireland but upon the Scillies. In Cornwall, while some were declaring themselves to be loyal to Parliament and the army, an appeal from Lord Hopton, aboard ship, was circulated begging his former officers, the Cornish gentlemen, to rally in revenge for the murder of their King, done "to satisfy libidinous bloodthirsty appetites."

In the capital itself all sorts of proposals were being put forward. The complaint was heard that food and clothing were dear, unemployment growing, and the relief of the poor an urgent necessity. A widespread demand was also raised for the relief of men in prison for debt, so strident that the House of Commons took it into immediate examination. Pamphlets tumbled from the presses defining the new Zion that was to replace the fallen Tower of Babel. By the extremists, lords and lawyers were described as "the vermin and caterpillars of the Commonwealth." Others more moderate (not Royalists) were inveighing against toleration or urging the enthronement of a new king. Thus these early weeks of 1649 were filled with whirling agitation, as the oligarchy in London, with Cromwell one of its chiefs, was struggling to maintain order, restore peace, and defend the Commonwealth.[7]

*   *   *

The executive body of the new government was a Council of State consisting of forty members, whose every act was subject to the approval of the House of Commons. The House of Lords was abolished (although Cromwell does not seem to have agreed with that). The Council of State (which succeeded the former Committee of Both Kingdoms and the Committee of Safety) would have been an unwieldy body if all its members had been present regularly. But in fact the average attendance was only fifteen. It was a sober enough group of men. Cromwell's intelligent son-in-law, Henry Ireton, and the fire-eating Fifth Monarchy man, Colonel Thomas Harrison, were pointedly excluded from membership, and when it held its first meeting, with Cromwell as chairman pro tem, it was found that only thirteen members were willing to subscribe to an engagement approving the trial and execution of the King and the abolition of the monarchy. Consequently, a new engagement had to be drawn up inviting members merely to concur in the establishment of a republic. Then General Fairfax and a number of peers and lawyers consented to sit on the Council. Two thirds of the councillors were members of Parliament, and it originally met at eight o'clock in the morning before the Commons assembled. Later it decided that it could not continue sitting after nine o'clock on the days when the House met. Thus the statesmen who first guided the halting steps of the Commonwealth of England arose to their work bright and early.

While the Council was settling down Cromwell three times acted as its chairman, but he was only one among the conclave who governed the country. (It should not be imagined, whatever foreigners may have thought at the time, that civilians like Vane, Bradshaw, and Haselrigg were mere ciphers.) To begin with, Cromwell was fairly assiduous in his attendances, arriving early forty-four times during February, March, and April, and only eight times late; but in May, June, and July, when war was again looming ahead, the total number of his attendances fell to twenty-nine.[8] Matters of policy as well as administration were examined by committees of the Council. Questions were tossed backwards and forwards between committee, Council, and Parliament, a procedure which scarcely made for efficiency, especially as the remnant or "Rump" of Long Parliament was touchy about its rights. The new constitutional structure was completed by the formation of a High Court of Justice whose first task was to try those whom Cromwell called "divers persons of very great quality" who co-operated with Charles I "in the destruction of this kingdom," including the first Duke of Hamilton, vanquished by him at Preston. This Court was again presided over by Bradshaw. The Duke of Hamilton and two others were executed, and later Colonel Poyer, who had surrendered to Cromwell at Pembroke, was tried by court martial and shot. Other principal Royalists had their estates confiscated. After Hamilton's trial, Bradshaw was appointed President of the Council of State. The new rulers recognized that they were a small group whose practices hardly squared with their pretensions to be the guardians of "a Free State." But they were realists. They saw that they must first establish order at home and peace abroad before fresh elections to Parliament could be held and the Commonwealth be settled upon a more permanent basis. Thus the members of the Council of State were appointed for only one year, and promises were given of the ultimate reformation of Parliament.

But first things had to come first. The Lord High Admiral, the Earl of Warwick, was the brother of one of the Royalist peers who was put on trial for his life, and had perforce to be replaced by three Commissioners or Generals at Sea, including the squat Somerset hero, Colonel Robert Blake. Prince Rupert had collected a fleet in Holland, and was soon harassing the trade routes from a base at Kinsale. Cromwell was at once appointed to committees to consider the question of Ireland, to act in liaison with the Navy Commissioners, and to inquire into the existing state of the armed forces and the numbers necessary to keep the peace in England and reconquer Ireland. This last committee reported that there were over 44,000 horse and foot under arms, of whom only 2,500 could be disbanded (as unfit for service), while the rest were still needed. An expeditionary force of 12,000 men for Ireland was recommended, and it was reckoned that the sum of £120,000 a month was wanted for the upkeep of the army. Parliament accepted this report, and asked on March 9 that General Fairfax and his Council of War should consider which commanders and regiments should be sent to Ireland.

A fortnight earlier the Council of the Army had discussed the question, and decided that Cromwell ought to lead the expedition to Ireland. Lord Fairfax promptly told the Council of State that no preparations for the Irish expedition could be made until a commander in chief had been officially nominated. On March 15 (the same day on which John Milton was appointed "foreign secretary" of the Council of State) Cromwell was named commander in chief by the Council. But for some time he hesitated over accepting. He explained how he felt in a speech to the General Council of the Army on March 23. Was it indeed his duty to go? "It matters not who is our commander in chief if God be so," he told his audience. He pointed out, in effect, that Ireland was not the only center of danger to the new Commonwealth; there was a "very angry, hateful spirit" in Scotland also; and the Royalists, under the future Charles II, constituted a threat both at home and abroad. But he thought that the Irish peril was in reality the greatest: "I had rather be overrun with a Cavalierish interest than a Scottish interest," he said; "I had rather be overrun with a Scotch interest than an Irish interest; and I think of all this is most dangerous." Thus he disclosed that he was willing to serve as commander in chief in Ireland provided that he was given the force that he required. He asked for 8,000 foot, 3,000 horse, and 1,200 dragoons—more than the numbers recommended by his own committee. He wanted £3,000 for his outfit; pay of £10 a day while he was in England organizing the expedition, and £8,000 a year once he was in Ireland. All that was conceded by Parliament. But it was not until he was entirely satisfied that the expeditionary army would be fully armed and supplied and punctually paid that he agreed at the end of March to take up the new post.

Cromwell's reasons for considering with care whether he should or should not go to Ireland were obvious. To leave London then, to abandon his duties in Parliament and in the Council of State, and thereby give up his part in the direct government of the new state so soon after its inception, was a grave resolve. Only his belief that Ireland represented the most immediate menace to the Commonwealth induced him to go. Like a wise general, he took advantage of the need for his services there to ensure that the conditions which he regarded as indispensable for the success of the expeditionary army were guaranteed to him before he consented to command it.

The situation in England was still precarious. Before Cromwell sailed to Ireland, he found it necessary to impose order upon the army and ensure that the regiments selected for service in Ireland were disciplined and loyal.

*　　　*　　　*

Cromwell knew that discontent had pierced the army, and that was why he had insisted on first-class conditions for his expeditionary force. "I think there is more cause of danger from disunion among ourselves," he told the Council of the Army, "than by anything from our enemies." The officers were shaken by a wave of agitation that had swept through the army within a month of the execution of the King. It was decided that petitioning by the soldiers must be regularized through proper channels, and that Parliament should be asked to prescribe severe penalties upon civilians who tried to stir up unrest in the ranks. Various hopeful or subversive movements had been created by the conditions of the revolution. The Fifth Monarchists, who believed in the swift coming of Christ to reign on earth, disapproved of both the religious and political arrangements. A group of "Diggers" urged and tried to practice a form of primitive agrarian communism. But the most effective and dangerous critics of the regime were the Levellers with their dream of democracy next week.

At first John Lilburne, the Leveller leader, was apathetic. He contemplated buying a shop or a farm, going to Holland, or collecting by mild blackmail compensation for the wrongs done to him in the past. His colleague, John Wildman, appears to have sought a commission to serve in Ireland.[9] But both disliked the new government, which was not after the pattern they themselves had designed. Soon Lilburne was publishing a string of pamphlets lambasting both the Council of State and the "Rump" Parliament. Cromwell was pressed by the regimental officers to prevent the corruption of discipline. For a time it looked as if under the spur of Leveller propaganda the army might become out of hand. Early in March five troopers, who had taken part in a Leveller demonstration, were cashiered and their swords broken over their heads. Later in the same month Lillburne and three others were arrested and brought before the Council of State. Lilburne uttered the wildest threats, saying that he would raise a mutiny and burn Whitehall to the ground. No government would stomach that kind of defiance. But though he was committed to the Tower of London, he was allowed to continue writing pamphlets there, including an "impeachment" of Oliver Cromwell for treason. In April a troop mutinied over pay. Strong action was taken and after a court martial the ringleader was shot. Another soldier, who had been cashiered for taking part in a tavern brawl, succeeded in provoking a mutiny in the Midlands, and after killing an officer fled with a number of sympathizers to Salisbury, where he persuaded some 600 men to join his revolt. Cromwell and

Fairfax were anxious to quash this rising with as little bloodshed as possible. In a speech to regiments collected at Andover, Cromwell reminded them that he had fought with them against "the common enemy" and was resolved to live and die with them, but expected their loyalty against "those revolters which are now called by the name of Levellers." The mutineers were cornered at Burford, and four of them shot. Thus, after three months of turmoil, discipline in the army was restored at the price of five lives.

While army discontents came to a climax in mutiny and Lilburne and his friends fired the land with heady literature intended to undermine the government, Royalists were punching the Commonwealth with a profusion of lampoons and broadsheets, and Presbyterian ministers were denouncing from their pulpits the murder of the King and the very notion of religious toleration. For several months complete freedom of the Press was maintained. While *The Moderate* promulgated Levelling doctrines, papers like *Mercurius Elencticus* put the Royalist case. Readers were offered "a handkerchief for loyal mourners or a cordial for drooping spirits, groaning for the bloody murder and heavy loss of our gracious King." *Mercurius Pragmaticus* warned that "the King-choppers are as active in mischief as such thieves and murderers need to be." A song was sold that could be sung to the tune of "Fain I would" entitled "A Coffin for King Charles: a Crown for Cromwell: a Pit for the People."[10]

Under the circumstances it was surprising that Parliament held its hand as long as it did. Eventually in May it was asked to suppress "scandalous books," but it was not until September that the licensing of books and pamphlets was introduced, with a maximum penalty of £10 or forty days' imprisonment for offenses. As to the muzzling of preachers, although in July Parliament resolved to punish ministers who preached or prayed against the existing government, Cromwell and Ireton characteristically acted as tellers against it.

Thus Cromwell, although firm, was temperate. No commanding officer could tolerate mutiny, whatever its cause. General Fairfax was as much responsible as his lieutenant general for the shooting of mutineers after trial by court martial. Cromwell was not and never had been a Leveller. He had befriended Lilburne in the reign of King Charles I and been willing to discuss and examine the Leveller proposals. He was by no means unsympathetic to reforms so far as they were practicable and timely. But once Lilburne exerted his influence to incite the army to overthrow the new Commonwealth, Cromwell had no alternative but to act against him. Yet remarkably few executions marred the early days of the new Republic. Only a handful of Royalist leaders and army mutineers were put to death. Lilburne was not even brought before the new High Court of Justice, but was tried and acquitted by a London jury. Compared with the holocaust offered up by the terrorists of the French, Russian, German, and Chinese revolutions of a later age, Cromwell is seen as a sober, fair, and even lenient man.

*   *   *

It was not until midsummer day that Parliament finally approved Cromwell's commission as commander in chief and Governor General of Ireland. The appointment was for three years, and later his title was altered to the old-established royal designation of Lord Lieutenant. In that capacity he received pay at the rate of £10 a day, as well as a salary of £3 a day as lieutenant general. When he reached Ireland his total remuneration, with allowances, was about £13,000 a year, an impressive figure. But he was less concerned about his own salary (out of which others' salaries had to be found) than with the pay of his soldiers. He was determined that the expedition should not sail until it was completely supplied and equipped. He had had painful experiences during both the first and second Civil Wars of the threat to army morale when pay was permitted to fall in arrears. Some of the regiments that were picked by lot for service in Ireland were restless, and mutinies had been caused as much by discontent over pay and conditions as by democratic propaganda. Cromwell's letters during June and July were therefore filled with financial questions; and he made it known that he required as a war chest £100,000 in bullion, and not in promises, before he would leave England.

The Commonwealth government found it hard to raise the money. But an act was passed charging the excise with payment for the army; another source was the sale of Church lands; and borrowing from the City on the security of such funds was authorized. But the Common Council, though pleased with the suppression of the Levellers, was unwilling to lend as a corporation, even though Cromwell himself went in deputation to try to borrow £150,000. Gradually, however, the required sum was provided in installments by the Council of State. Cromwell busied himself in collecting and dispatching artillery, horses, and ammunition in advance. His headquarters was Milford Haven; but he also sent three regiments ahead from Chester to Dublin.

On July 10 he left London after a farewell dinner and a number of sermons (one of which he preached himself) in a coach drawn by six Flanders mares and surmounted by a milk-white standard and accompanied by a life guard of seventy officers. At Bristol he was welcomed by the mayor and presented with a butt of sack. He delayed in that part of the country for nearly a month, collecting his supplies and convoy, his military intelligence, and his army surgeons, and still awaiting his promised £100,000. Most of the guns and ammunition was sent in advance to Dublin, and the transports had to return to England before the force could be embarked. Every available vessel was requisitioned and still there were not enough. It was the middle of August before everything was ready. But Cromwell's patience was rewarded. Altogether about 130 ships, carrying more than 10,000 men, then bore down upon the Irish coast. Colonel Richard Deane directed the naval arrangements and Commissary General Ireton was second in command of the expedition. Cromwell later vainly tried to induce Colonel Robert Blake, one of the three generals at sea, to accept the post of Major General of Foot under him, but he did succeed in persuading Roger Boyle, Lord Broghill, a former Royalist of capacity, to take charge of the ordnance.[11]

"Not since the Armada," it has been said, "had there been such a formidable expedition in that quarter of the world." It had long appeared as if it might be frustrated, first by the mutinies, then by the difficulties in collecting money to pay for it. Up to the last moment bets were being taken in London on whether Cromwell would go or not. Apart from the difficulties of supply, dared he leave his country beset by internal convulsions? His departure has been compared with that of Caesar from Rome or of Napoleon to Egypt. No doubt he was ambitious, as many then thought. But no inkling exists of any conscious impulse other than a high sense of dedication to duty: "a man is born for public services," he wrote aboard ship. His last thoughts were of his family: the wife who had seen him off, the elder son who he feared was a little idle and pleasure-bound, a grandchild stillborn. The crossing from Milford Haven occupied two days over a choppy sea. One of Cromwell's chaplains, the omni-present Hugh Peter, noted that the commander in chief was "as seasick as ever I saw a man in my life" before they were out of harbour. But, as Cromwell announced on his arrival, when he was greeted by the roar of the cannon around Dublin, God had "brought him thither in safety" to under-take "the great work against the barbarous and bloodthirsty Irish."

Notes

1. The saying is attributed to Degas.

2. *Calendar of State Papers (Venetian), 1647–1652,* 90.

3. *Mercurius Elencticus,* Thomason tracts E545.

4. *Jonah's Cry,* reprinted in W. Haller and G. Davies, *Leveller Tracts,* 12.

5. February 19, 1649: written by Colonel Robert Tichborne, E544.

6. *The Journal of George Fox,* a revised edition by John L. Nickalls (1952), 45.

7. This section is based on the *Calendar of State Papers (Domestic), 1649* and *1649–1650,* and Thomason tracts E541–48.

8. Cromwell's attendances at the meetings of the Council of State are given in the *Calendars of State Papers (Domestic).*

9. M. A. Gibb, *John Lilburne the Leveller* (1947), Chap. X, and Maurice Ashley, *John Wildman* (1947), Chap. V.

10. April 23, 1649, E550.

11. Cf. my *Cromwell's Generals,* 124, for Cromwell's relations with Blake.

Chapter 15

Cromwell in Ireland

THE IRISH REBELLION of 1641, a nationalist and Roman Catholic outbreak against alien Protestant masters, was influenced and later transmuted by events in England. During the early part of the seventeenth century the Irish had enjoyed a measure of prosperity, and while the Earl of Strafford ruled in Dublin the exercise of their religion had been tolerated, if not approved. Their relative well-being made them all the more conscious of the political, religious, and economic disabilities from which they suffered. After Strafford had left Ireland and the Long Parliament had engineered his execution, the very weakness of King Charles I had encouraged aspirations of Ireland for the Irish beneath the standard of God and Our Lady. The Irish knew that the King had been compelled to grant the Scots religious independence, and at the same time they feared that unless they promptly struck a blow for their own freedom the English Puritans, now in the ascendancy, would try to root the Catholic religion out of their country.[1]

The rebellion began in the late autumn. Its leaders hoped that the winter weather and the general confusion in England would prevent the authorities at Dublin Castle from receiving succor in time from across the Irish sea. Although the rebels failed to capture Dublin, large parts of the country were soon overrun by the Old Irish, who represented the bulk of the inhabitants, and later were joined by the Catholic "Lords of the Pale." It was guerrilla warfare of a pattern that was later to become familiar in Irish history, and many cruelties were practiced. English settlers were robbed, driven from their homes, and their cattle seized or scattered, and altogether some three to five thousand English men and women were killed outright. The news, exaggerated in transmission, sent a thrill of horror through the hearts of English Puritans. They even suspected that King Charles I had connived at the rising, more especially since one of the Irish leaders, Sir Phelim O'Neill, had flourished a document which suggested it. While they were unwilling to allow the King to command an army in Ireland to suppress the rebellion, lest they should

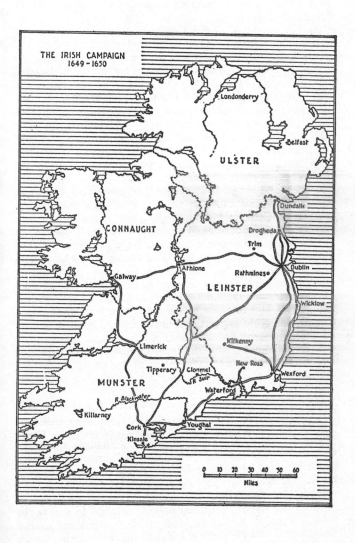

THE IRISH CAMPAIGN
1649 – 1650

find it later turned against themselves, they were equally determined ultimately to exact vengeance and restore English Protestant supremacy.

At Kilkenny a Catholic Confederacy was set up seeking to re-establish the Church in its pre-Reformation position and secure legislative independence for the Irish Parliament, and thence it virtually ruled the country for nearly a decade.[2] James Butler, Marquis of Ormonde, who in 1644 was appointed the King's Lord Lieutenant in Ireland, did not fight insurgents after the opening years of the rebellion, but tried, on the contrary, to induce them to furnish the King with military support against the English Puritans in return for promises of favors when the civil wars were over. The Irish were divided, but after much maneuvering, at the beginning of 1649, a treaty was drawn up to which the Old Irish and Anglo-Irish acceded, whereby they agreed to back the Royalist cause in return for religious concessions. Nine Irish Catholic bishops urged their followers to "fight fiercely against sectaries and rebels for God and Caesar" since "under those banners you may well hope for victories." The alliance was cemented by the news of the King's execution, and during 1649 the Marquis of Ormonde succeeded in gaining military control of much of Ireland apart from Londonderry and Dublin itself. He proclaimed King Charles II and invited him to come to Ireland. For a brief spell Prince Rupert, smoothly converting himself from a general into an admiral, maintained a naval base at Kinsale until his squadron was forced out by Robert Blake. Ormonde, after capturing Drogheda, twenty-three miles north of the capital, encamped outside Dublin, which was held for the English Commonwealth by Major General Michael Jones.

Such was the perilous situation as Cromwell was embarking his troops. Jones, reinforced by the three regiments dispatched by Cromwell from Chester, with enterprising opportunism fell upon the Royalist camp at Rathmines and broke Ormonde's army asunder. This victory invigorated Cromwell's expedition, and when he arrived in Dublin on August 15 with his formidable army the Royalists were still licking their wounds from that unexpected defeat.

Cromwell stayed in Dublin only a fortnight to survey the scene, organize his army, and publish directions against drunkenness and plundering. Little of the campaigning season was left, and it was a tribute to his administrative competence that he could move forward so quickly and bring up an impressive train of artillery to besiege Drogheda, into which Ormonde had thrown the flower of his remaining troops.

Drogheda was a towered and walled city lying athwart the River Boyne. Its garrison consisted of 2,000 foot and 300 horse under the command of Sir Arthur Aston, a Roman Catholic who had once been governor of Oxford. Most of his men were Irish. Cromwell had mustered some 8,000 men as well as his batteries, which he brought into position on the south side of the town. As soon as they started firing on September 10 he received a summons from Cromwell in these words:

> Having brought the army belonging to the Parliament of England before this place to reduce it to obedience to the end effusion of blood may be prevented I thought fit to summon you to deliver the same into my hands to their use. If this be refused, you will have no cause to blame me.

That evening Aston informed Ormonde in the last letter he ever wrote:[3]

> Since the summons I heard no answer but by the mouth of the cannon which hath ever since without intermission played upon our walls and works. They have eight pieces of battery, the least throwing shot 12 lb., one of 30 lb. bullet. They have made a very great breach near the church [of St. Mary]. . . . Speedy help is much desired. . . . Living I am and dying I will end, my Lord, Your Excellency's most faithful and most obliged humble servant. . . .

According to the rules of war, the defenders of a fortress who failed to surrender after a breach had been blown in had no claim to quarter. Before ordering the assault Cromwell removed the white flag from his quarters and substituted a red ensign, and it was clear from the tone of Aston's letter that he knew he had sealed his fate. Nevertheless, even after two or three hundred shot had effected two large breaches in the south wall, Aston continued to resist. Twice Cromwell's men were repulsed with loss as they advanced to the assault, but finally they thrust their way across the enemy's earthworks and into the Church of St. Mary, from the tower of which the Irish had first fired upon them. Cromwell himself led the critical charge on September 11. "Being thus entered," Cromwell reported laconically to the President of the Council of State, "we refused quarter; having the day before summoned the town." Aston himself and a number of his officers and men retreated to the Mill Mount, an artificial mound close to the southwest angle of the wall. Here they made their last stand. Cromwell ordered the garrison to be put to the sword and forbade his soldiers to spare any found in arms in the town. Next day the defenders of two towers in the wall were also compelled to give in. In one of them every tenth soldier as well as all the officers were killed, but the rest of the soldiers were spared their lives and shipped to the Barbados. Lord Inchiquin reported to Ormonde on September 15:[4] "Many men and some officers have made their escapes out of Drogheda . . . some of every regiment have come in to me." Still the greater part of the garrison must have been slain in the fighting or put to the sword for defending the breaches.

Cromwell resolved to put the garrison to the sword primarily for military reasons: "Truly I believe this bitterness will save much effusion of blood," he wrote; and again, "It will tend to prevent the effusion of blood for the future." In that purpose it was successful: "It is not to be imagined," wrote Ormonde to King Charles II, "how great the terror is that these successes and the power of the enemy has struck into these people. . . ."[5] "If Cromwell has taken Drogheda by storm," declared Sir Phelim O'Neill, "if he should storm Hell, he will take it." The garrisons of Trim and Dundalk quitted them in panic, leaving their guns and stores behind them. The governor of Ross surrendered when summoned, and the garrison of Wexford was demoralized. War is relentless, and similar acts of calculated terror are to be found throughout modern history: the siege of Munster in the Thirty Years' War, the sack of Leicester by the Royalists, the devastation of the Palatinate by Turenne and of Bavaria by Marlborough, the "obliteration" bombing of British and German towns in the last war, and finally the dropping of atomic bombs on Hiroshima and Nagasaki. The great Duke of Wellington wrote in 1820: "The practice of refusing quarter to a garrison which stands an assault is not a useless effusion of blood."

Sir Winston Churchill wrote in 1953 of the nuclear bombing of Japan:

The nightmare vision [of the loss of a million and a half American and British lives] had vanished. In its place was the vision—fair and bright it seemed—of the end of the whole war in one or two violent shocks. . . . To avert a vast, indefinite butchery, to bring the war to an end, to give peace to the world, to lay healing hands upon its tortured peoples by a manifestation of overwhelming power at the cost of a few explosions, seemed, after all our toils and perils, a miracle of deliverance.

All these episodes must be seen in proportion. To Sir Winston the atom bomb was a "miracle of deliverance"; to Cromwell the slaughter of the Drogheda garrison was "a marvelous great mercy." Cromwell believed that the example of two thousand Irish killed in Drogheda—in accordance with the rules of war—would save the lives of his large army and of all the English settlers in Ireland.

Cromwell was a humane man. His letters are filled with concern for widows, bereaved parents, and the destitute. "He was naturally compassionate," wrote his steward, John Maidstone, "towards objects in distress, even to an effeminate measure; though God had made him a heart wherein was left little room for fear but what was due to Himself . . . yet he did exceed in tenderness towards sufferers."[6] Of the execution at Drogheda Cromwell wrote: "It will tend to prevent the effusion of blood for the future, which are the satisfactory grounds to such action, *which otherwise cannot but work remorse and regret.*" Cromwell, it has been observed justly, "was probably the only man in the victorious army who imagined what had taken place needed any excuse at all. When Monck's storm of Dundee in 1651 was followed by a massacre, he said nothing in his own justification."[7]

A phrase in one of Cromwell's letters about the siege of Drogheda in which he said: "And indeed being in the heat of the action, I forbade them to spare any that were in arms in the town" has been misinterpreted as meaning that he took his decision to give no quarter "in the heat of the action," that it was a sadistic outburst. But it is clear both from the terms of the original summons and of his later summonses at Dundalk, Ross, and Wexford that he had made up his mind before the assault was delivered in favor of severity if the garrison continued to resist once the breaches had been entered. It was a grave and deliberate act of policy after full warning had been given (as at Hiroshima and Nagasaki); and Cromwell explained it and defended it as such.[8]

It is necessary to set this story in perspective because it has so often been used to picture Cromwell as a monster of cruelty, differing from other generals and statesmen in English history, and secondly because it is frequently assigned as a main reason for the poisoning of Anglo-Irish relations in modern times. In fact, Cromwell's Irish policy—wrongheaded as it may have been—was identical with that of Queen Elizabeth I, King James I, Strafford, and Pym. All of them sponsored the colonization of Ireland by Protestant settlers. To the Puritans Ireland was a nearer alternative to Massachusetts or Virginia and the natives as capable of absorption or extrusion as the Indians. Irish history is stocked with the horrors of civil war, from the rising of the peasant mob in 1641 to the guerrilla campaigns of the 1920s. And it cannot be supposed that, if Cromwell had shown mercy to the garrison of Drogheda, that war or any other war in Irish history would have been the less shocking.

Cromwell offered one other explanation for his severity at Drogheda, namely that the garrison had "imbrued their hands in so much innocent blood." Cromwell and all who fought under him had heard exaggerated accounts of the rising of 1641, which they thought of as a vast massacre of harmless families. It has been urged that, in fact, the bulk of the defenders of Drogheda could not be held responsible for the ill-treatment of the English settlers eight years earlier. On the other hand, the decision taken by the Protestant Marquis of Ormonde, on the instructions of King Charles I, to come to terms with the Irish Catholic leaders who had directed the revolt condoned the original rising and invited the Irish nationalists to repeat their guerrilla tactics with all the suffering that flowed from them. The Royalists were ready to use any methods, from the exploitation of Irish or Scottish nationalism to the hiring of assassins to murder republican agents, in order to win back their heritage in England. Honorable men like Aston or Sir Edmund Verney, who forfeited their lives at Drogheda, paid the price for their loyalty to an unscrupulous leadership.

*   *   *

After taking Dundalk and Trim, Cromwell sent Colonel Robert Venables north with a force to link up with Sir Charles Coote, who commanded for the English Parliament in Ulster. Owen Roe O'Neill, the Irish hero who led the Ulster Catholics but had changed sides more than once, was dying, and Coote and Venables overran much of the north, only three fortresses in Ulster remaining under Royalist control. Cromwell himself turned south with the aim of capturing Wexford, a port that had long been a hotbed of privateers who preyed on English shipping. Arklow was taken on September 28, and the next day General Deane arrived in Wexford harbor with twenty ships carrying food and ammunition and began a blockade. Throughout his Irish campaign Cromwell was sustained by the assertion of the sea power of the Commonwealth.

The weather was wet and stormy when the army drew up before Wexford on the first day of October 1649. But the defenders of the town were divided among themselves and, but for the pressure of Ormonde, would undoubtedly have surrendered through dread of Cromwell's name. On October 3 Cromwell dispatched a summons to Colonel David Sinnott, the governor. He warned him that if he rejected the terms, which would prevent the effusion of blood and preserve the town from ruin, the guilt would lie upon him should the innocent suffer. Sinnott, hoping for reinforcements, tried to spin out time, although Cromwell refused an armistice since his tents afforded poor protection to the besieging army in the inclement weather. When the winds abated Cromwell landed his cannon, and placed his batteries at the southeast corner of the town trained on the castle. Michael Jones, now promoted lieutenant general, who had come with him from Dublin, had succeeded in clearing a fort that commanded the entrance to the harbor so that the siege train and provisions could be brought up from the ships. After the batteries began to play, the governor's "stomach came down" and he offered to surrender if he were granted the liberal conditions that he required. Cromwell answered that he would do no more than spare the officers, let the soldiers return to their homes, and guarantee the town against plunder. But before that answer was sent one of the commissioners who had been sent by the governor to treat, a certain Captain Stafford, who was in charge of the castle, agreed to betray it to the besiegers. The Parliamentarian soldiers thereupon clambered up into the castle and turned its guns on the town's garrison. In the market place the Irish fought gallantly behind barricades, but were eventually overwhelmed and slaughtered, together with a number of the townsfolk and Catholic priests. Many were drowned as they attempted to escape by boat. For a time the English Puritan soldiery got completely out of hand, killing, plundering, and wreaking their revenge on those whom

they regarded as pirates and idolators. Cromwell refused, or
at any rate failed, to intervene. "We intended better to have
this place than so great a ruin," he reported home, "I could
have wished for their own good, and the good of the garrison
that they [the soldiers] had been more moderate." But he
thought that the defenders of Wexford had brought their
fate upon themselves, not merely because they had rejected
his summons in the first instance, but because they had earlier
overloaded a vessel with "seven or eight score poor Protestants" and let them drown in the harbor, while others had
been starved to death. Unlike at Drogheda, the Irish had not
sought quarter, but determined to sell their lives dearly, and
in trying to exact a toll from their foes had perished to a
man—many of the innocent to whom Cromwell would have
been merciful being killed along with them in the confusion.

Once Wexford fell, Cromwell had good reason to hope that
the whole of the south would be speedily subdued. For many
of the English Royalists there, like the wretched Stafford,
were read to betray their own cause. Two days later the English garrison at Cork rose and declared for Parliament, and
others throughout Munster deserted. At New Ross the
governor surrendered after a summons from Cromwell in
which he reiterated his wish to avoid "effusion of blood," and
insisted that it was his principle "that people and places where
I come to *may not suffer except through their own wilfulness.*"
The garrison of Ross was allowed to march away with their
arms, bag and baggage, drums beating, colors flying, bullet
in mouth, bandoliers full of powder, and match lighted at both
ends, and the inhabitants were protected against violence. As
soon as the town surrendered, Cromwell set about building
a bridge of boats across the River Barrow to give access to
the interior. The swiftness with which the bridge was constructed over the boisterous tidewater profoundly impressed
the Irish. Cromwell purposed to prolong his campaign into
the winter. But he himself fell sick and his lieutenant general
died. His army was laid low by dysentery and malaria. Moreover, owing to the need to garrison captured towns, its numbers, despite the arrival of reinforcements, were much reduced.
When, having recovered from his illness, Cromwell laid seige
to Waterford, after it had been cut off from the sea, his army
was down to a mere three thousand infantry—"a crazy company" he called it—and on December 4 the siege had to be
abandoned and winter quarters occupied in the neighbourhood
of Youghal and Cork.

*   *   *

Writing to the Speaker before he took up his winter quarters, Cromwell had observed: "Although God hath blessed you with a great tract of land in longitude along the shore, yet it hath but a little depth in the country." Most of the north, east, and south coasts of Ireland were held by the English Parliamentary forces; only Waterford, Galway, and one or two other small ports were still open to Irish shipping, and they were subject to blockade. Ormonde had some ten to twenty thousand men under his command, but they were demoralized, scattered, and disunited, and by propaganda Cromwell played upon the differences between the Protestant Royalists and the Catholic Irish. Nevertheless, the Ulster Catholics, now under the command of Hugh O'Neill, an old soldier with experience in Spain, joined Ormonde in the south, and Cromwell was anxious to strike inland and scarify the heart of the resistance that remained. The southern ports occupied by his own army were cut off by rivers and mountains from the fertile tableland of Tipperary and the ancient town of Kilkenny, former capital of the Irish confederacy. As soon as his men had recovered their health and strength, Cromwell directed two columns northward in a converging movement across the Rivers Blackwater and Suir. Lord Broghill was left to protect his left flank against Lord Inchiquin, a young soldier of fortune who had leapt to fame in Munster. After taking a number of forts, Cromwell's two columns rejoined. Colonel John Hewson, who succeeded General Jones in Dublin, was called up from the east, and Cromwell's son Henry arrived at Youghal with reinforcements from England. Thus Kilkenny was surrounded on all sides and was summoned on March 22.

My coming hither [announced Cromwell] is to endeavour, if God so please to bless me, the reduction of the city of Kilkenny to their obedience to the state of England, from which, by an unheard of massacre of the innocent English, you have endeavoured to rend yourselves.

The governor, Sir Walter Butler, a cousin of Ormonde, was at first defiant, although his garrison was infected with the plague. Cromwell's men occupied Irishtown, which lay outside the city walls, and brought up batteries first on the west and then to the south. Butler then capitulated. Cromwell again granted generous terms, partly because he was anxious to get his men away from the plague spot. "I believe the taking of the city of Kilkenny," he wrote home, "hath been a great discomposing of the enemy, it's so much in their bowels." Soon afterwards Inchiquin's men, advancing from the west, were routed by Broghill and Henry Cromwell at the battle of Macroom, and Oliver Cromwell turned in comfort to the siege of Clonmel, the largest town in Tipperary. It was brilliantly defended by Hugh O'Neill, who inflicted heavy losses both on Cromwell's infantry and cavalry as they attempted to assault the breaches. After O'Neill's supplies and ammunition had given out, he slipped away with his soldiers, much to Cromwell's annoyance. Nevertheless, Cromwell spared the townsfolk from reprisals. According to Whitelocke, "they found in Clonmel the stoutest enemy this army ever met in Ireland; and that there was never seen so hot a storm, of so long continuance, and so gallantly defended, either in England or Ireland."

Clonmel fell in May and immediately afterwards Cromwell left Ireland forever. In spite of the jolt he had received, his Irish campaign ended in triumph. For while he was engaged upon his fighting in Tipperary, he had also entered into successful armistice talks with the Royalists. Though Ormonde and Inchiquin refused to negotiate with him, a number of their principal subordinates had done so, and had even accepted safe-conducts on their behalf. Cromwell's victories had dispirited the Protestant Royalists, who, no longer liking or trusting their Catholic allies, were ready to give in. Ormonde, an able statesman but poor general, ceased to exert any influence on either the English or the Irish, and wanted King Charles II to recall him. At the end of the year he handed over to a Catholic deputy. The defense of Ireland against England was then assumed by the Irish clergy.

Meanwhile the English Council of State and Parliament had been clamoring for Cromwell's return to London. As early as January 8 the Commons had voted in favor of his recall. King Charles II, observing from Holland the blasting of all his hopes in Ireland, had reluctantly turned to meet the demands of the Scottish Covenanters, and a Scottish invasion was feared. Hence the urgency of the need for Cromwell's services in England. But Cromwell himself, though he heard rumors of his recall, received no official intimation before he left his winter quarters, and he deliberately decided for the time being to shut his ears. He wished to clear the south and make terms with the Royalists before he left. But at Clonmel he learned that a frigate had been sent to fetch him. So, handing over his command to his son-in-law Ireton, now President of Munster, whom he loved and trusted, but retaining for himself the title and authority of Lord Lieutenant, he set sail from Youghal on May 26. He and Ireton were never to meet again.[9]

Cromwell's Irish campaign had been masterly. Some critics, it is true, claimed that the Irish had been beaten before he arrived, when Michael Jones won the battle of Rathmines. But commanders in chief are not expected to win every battle themselves. In the deployment of his forces (to which the victory of Rathmines owed much), the use of political warfare in dividing the Protestant Royalists from the Catholic Irish leaders, the achievement of co-operation between the army and the fleet, the organization of supplies, the effective movement and siting of his siege artillery, even in the frightening example set at Drogheda, Cromwell proved that he knew all the arts of generalship, and could practice them in a terrain very different from that over which the civil wars had been fought. When he first arrived at Dublin there were still large Royalist forces in the field against him and the Irish were universally hostile. Yet he maintained discipline, preserved the health and morale of his men, and manipulated his different columns with skill, in spite of heavy medical casualties and shortages of pay about which he constantly complained to Parliament. In this complicated and at times obscure pursuit of siege warfare, his military genius was manifest.

Politically he voiced the feeling of Puritan England. Ingrained in his mind was the belief that the Irish were savages who during the 1640s had spilled seas of innocent blood. To him also they were the servants of Antichrist, the victims of proud and grasping prelates, far removed from the apostolic brethren of primitive times. "Your covenant," he told the Catholic clergy, "is with death and hell." The Irish, he claimed, had "barbarously massacred" the English, who had "lived peaceably and honestly" among them, and in days of peace and prosperity had broken the union and campaigned for men of blood. He urged that he himself was contesting against civil and ecclesiastical tyranny and arbitrary rule. Thus he would countenance neither a Catholic hierarchy nor the public exercise of the Mass. He fancied that the economic advantages conferred by a true union between England and Ireland, and the introduction of justice "freely and impartially administered," would draw the Irish over to the Puritan way of life, emancipating them from corruption and poverty. It was no ignoble view. He was not the first or the last Englishman to believe that orderly colonial government, Protestant missionaries, and economic assistance would reconcile discontented nationalists to political subjection. Had he been able to remain in Ireland he might at least have afforded the inhabitants the same kind of material benefits that they had received from the benevolent despotism of the Earl of Strafford. But ten years of internecine war, of murder and rapine, of ambush and robbery, of death and destruction in all their forms, were a poor prelude to government by even the most generous of Christian conquerors and the most enlightened of colonial administrators. The blame for the historical failure of England's policy in Ireland does not lie at the door of any one party or any one man.

Notes

1. For Cromwell and Ireland, see *inter alia* D. M. Murphy, *Cromwell in Ireland* (1875); J. T. Gilbert, *Contemporary History of Affairs in Ireland* (1880); Richard Bagwell, *Ireland under the Stuarts and during the Interregnum* (1916), II; *Memoirs of Edmund Ludlow* (ed. Firth, 1894), I, and *Perfect Diurnall*.

2. A recent book from the Irish point of view is Thomas L. Coonan, *The Irish Catholic Confederacy and the Puritan Revolution* (1956).

3. J. T. Gilbert, *op. cit.*, II, Pt. 2, 259.

4. *Ibid.*, II, Pt. 1, xxviii.

5. *Ibid.*, II, Pt. 2, 269.

6. *Thurloe State Papers*, I, 766.

7. S. R. Gardiner, *History of the Commonwealth and Protectorate* (1901), 138, note 3.

8. Those interested in the siege of Drogheda should read the articles in *The Nineteenth Century* of 1912 and 1913.

9. For Ireton, see R. W. Ramsey, *Henry Ireton* (1949) and *Cromwell's Generals,* Chap. IV.

Chapter 16

Cromwell in Scotland: Dunbar and Worcester

SELDOM HAS EUROPE been in a state of darker political turmoil than it was in the middle of the seventeenth century. France was at war with Spain, and Cardinal Mazarin, who governed during the minority of King Louis XIV, was tormented by a civil war exploited by irresponsible elements of the aristocracy. In the United Netherlands conflict raged between the supporters of the House of Orange and the merchant republicans. Germany and the Scandinavian countries lay prostrate after the horrors of the Thirty Years' War. To that combination of circumstances the English Commonwealth owed its survival, for Charles II and his mother were able to enlist little more than expressions of sympathy from their friends and relations on the Continent. To regain his throne the young King had therefore to rely upon his adherents in Britain and Ireland. But after Cromwell's campaign, Ireland could be written off.

In Scotland, as in Ireland, confusion reigned: ancient loyalties to the throne were obscured by religious excitement and nationalist ideals. But one man, relentless and formidable, stood out above the ruck of clans and visionaries: Archibald Campbell, Marquis of Argyll.[1] Argyll, at forty-three, held sway like a princeling in the western Highlands, where he had rebuilt his family fortunes and become the wealthiest nobleman in the land. A small, florid man with red hair, a cast in his eyes, and a minimum of charm, he had an astute and lucid mind, was a splendid organizer and an avid Christian. Converted to Presbyterianism in about 1638, he rose every morning at five and prayed until eight. At his castle in Inveraray he wrote the sermons for his minister to preach and studied the political scene. His representative in Edinburgh was his kinsman John Campbell, Earl of Loudoun, and after the defeat of the first Duke of Hamilton at the battle of Preston, Argyll, Loudoun, and another implacable Presbyterian, Archibald Johnston, Laird of Waristoun, had virtually ruled Scotland. Through their influence an Act of Classes had been passed by the Scottish Parliament excluding Hamilton's supporters from political life; and for good Puritan measure all who were "given to uncleanness, bribery, swearing, drunkenness, or deceiving or . . . otherwise scandalous in their conversation or who neglected the worship of God in their families" were also banned from office. This act was aimed primarily at the Royalists, who were dubbed "malignants," yet, ironically, within a month of the execution of King Charles I this very same Parliament proclaimed his son, "the greatest malignant of them all," to be King of Great Britain, France, and Ireland. For whatever rivalries might exist within the country, Scottish patriotism was affronted by an English Parliament doing to death a Stuart king. In his pursuit of power, Argyll is said ever to have swum with the tide. And he soon realized that should Charles II bind himself to the Kirk, then Scotland would have to serve his cause. Thus it was recognized by the Government in London that, after the suppression of the Irish rebellion, the next threat to the English Commonwealth would come not from the monarchies of Europe but from their fellow Puritans in Scotland.

Negotiations between Charles II and the party of Argyll continued throughout the early part of 1650. The King at first had hopes of the crushing of Cromwell in southern Ireland or of an expedition organized by the Marquis of Montrose in Scandinavia. But in April Montrose's tiny force was cut to pieces by his countrymen in an ambush at Carbisdale; he himself was taken prisoner and executed as an outlaw, and Argyll and his family witnessed the last degradation of the other "great Marquis" in the streets of Edinburgh. King Charles bowed to the terms demanded by Argyll and the leaders of the Kirk, repudiated his beaten servant, and in June signed in Heligoland a treaty that made him a Covenanted King. A fortnight earlier Cromwell had landed in England.

* * *

The Lord Lieutenant had been welcomed at Bristol with a triple salute of guns after another bad crossing, when he was again seasick, and he rode thence to Windsor, where he was greeted by his wife, friends, and some colleagues. He was "affable and courteous to all," and declared that he had no wish to enter London in pomp. Nevertheless, the warmth of his reception and the multitude of officers and M.P.'s who came out to salute him on his way to the capital testified to the gladness that was felt that a great English soldier had come home again.

During his absence the Council of State had toiled manfully to maintain order and sponsor reform. Acts had been passed to assist poor creditors and to put down highway robbery; a number of Puritan measures had also been enacted, and a licensing system had been introduced to stop Royalist and Leveller propaganda. The reform of Parliament and a new election had been contemplated, but in view of the many dangers at home and abroad the general feeling was that a period of firm and stable government was necessary before constitutional changes could be adopted. Above all, what was urgently needed was the formulation of a military plan to fight off the Scots should King Charles II direct an invasion from the north.

Oliver Cromwell's reputation had been enchanced by the Irish campaign. His dispatches had been read from the pulpits, and his victories had invigorated the English Government. Thus his return was widely acclaimed. The Cockpit (on the site of the present Treasury) which formed part of Whitehall Palace, was put at his disposal as a residence, and he was voted an income of £2,500 a year in land. On June 1 he was welcomed by General Fairfax on Hounslow Heath "with a great train of members of Parliament and Council of State, divers companies and troops of foot and horse, and many thousands of the well-affected, so that the ways were thronged down to Westminster." Thus reported the official news-sheet, *Mercurius Politicus*. But the printer of the Royalist organ, *Mercurius Pragmaticus*, which described Cromwell as "Copper Nose," was thrown into prison. On June 4 the Speaker of the House of Commons gave the returned general eloquent thanks for his services, and the House postponed the consideration of an act against women painting their faces, or wearing black patches or immodest dresses. And Cromwell went into conference in the Council of State to examine the danger from Scotland.

Undoubtedly there were members of the new governing classes who now wanted Lord Fairfax to be superseded by Cromwell. Since 1649 Fairfax had never concealed his Royalist and Presbyterian sympathies, although he himself was neither a Royalist nor a Presbyterian. While Cromwell was away rumors were heard of plans to give him the command against the Scots and to retain Fairfax in a more or less honorary capacity. Though tongues were wagging freely, it is not known exactly what went on in the Council of State. But under Cromwell's impulse arrangements for a campaign against the Scots were accelerated, and on June 10 the Council voted that General Fairfax should have the command and that Cromwell should go with his in his old post of lieutenant general. This scheme was approved by Parliament two days later. On June 13 both Fairfax and Cromwell accepted, and a solemn fast was ordered. But within ten days everything had been changed. On June 20 the Council of State passed a resolution that the invasion of Scotland was the only means of preventing a Scottish invasion of England. General Fairfax did not agree. He urged that there was no clear evidence that the Scots intended such an invasion and that a preventive war would be a breach of the Solemn League and Covenant concluded with the Scots over six years earlier. Cromwell argued and pleaded with Fairfax, both on moral and military grounds. War, he asserted, could not be avoided. He reminded him of the misery that had been caused in the north of England by the Scottish invasion of 1648, and urged that it was wiser to fight—if fight they must—"in the bowels of another country." Fairfax would not be moved; his conscience would not admit the justice of what he saw as a war of aggression; he preferred voluntarily to give up his command rather than to change his mind. Cromwell did all he knew to conciliate or persuade him. Eventually Fairfax loyally agreed to submit his resignation on the nominal ground of ill-health. On June 26 Parliament appointed Oliver Cromwell to be captain general and commander in chief. Major General Henry Ireton was confirmed as Cromwell's Deputy in Ireland.[2]

It is a measure of Cromwell's patriotism and devotion to the Commonwealth that he and his friends struggled to induce Lord Fairfax to keep his post. Cromwell was ready enough to take over himself. His experiences in Ireland had convinced him of his own capabilities. But just as in 1647 he had labored to reconcile Parliament and the army, so now he wanted to avert a split between the English Presbyterians and the Puritan sectaries whom he led. There is no jot of evidence that Cromwell was other than sincere. His lack of jealousy or animosity is illustrated by his treatment of Edmund Ludlow. Colonel Ludlow was a gruff, incorruptible young republican who on more than one occasion had publicly criticized Cromwell's conduct. Yet at this very time Cromwell personally begged him to go to Ireland as Ireton's second in command and to serve on the Irish Council. In talking to Ludlow, Cromwell appealed to his ideals as well as to his sense of duty. England's policy in Ireland, he told him, must be thoroughly to reform the clergy and the law. Ireland was "a clean paper" on which such reforms might be written, a land where justice could be impartially administered, thereby setting "a good precedent to England itself." When, however, Ludlow protested that he had just married and could not take up a post abroad "without hazarding my family and estate," Cromwell answered sternly that "men's private affairs must give place to those of the public." By that same sense of duty Cromwell himself was animated when, after less than a month's reunion with his wife and children, he again left London on the road north.

Elaborate preparations had been made for the campaign. Muskets, pikes, tents, and supplies of food had been collected at Newcastle-upon-Tyne and Berwick-on-Tweed, which were to be the rear bases of the army. A naval squadron had been formed to support the land forces, and artillery was sent by sea from London. Sir Arthur Haselrigg was in command at Newcastle, and for some time new regiments were being raised in the north, including a cavalry regiment for Cromwell from Lancashire. Charles Fleetwood, an officer of Independent persuasions from the Midlands, was appointed Lieutenant General of Horse and John Lambert, also a young man in his early thirties, a Yorkshireman of proven military ability, commanded the infantry and acted as chief of staff. Major General Thomas Harrison was left in England to guard against threats from abroad and to enlist a new militia. In fact, apart from the army in Ireland, the Commonwealth had as many men on garrison duty in the south as served in the expeditionary army, which, on its entry into Scotland, consisted of about 16,000 soldiers, many of them veterans of the first Civil War.

While Cromwell during his short stay in England had helped to work out these arrangements and had been concerned in selecting officers—he had created a regiment, the forerunner of the Coldstream Guards, for the taciturn Devonian, Colonel George Monck—he also set store, as he had done in Ireland, on political warfare. He had been on the committee which drew up the declaration of war, and before he crossed the border he ordered the publication of an exceedingly long document—"A Declaration of the Army of England upon their March into Scotland to All that are Saints and Partakers of the Faith of God's Elect in Scotland." This document defended the execution of the King, which, it observed, was no breach of the Covenant. It emphasized that the English had fought and were fighting for religion and liberty. It argued that their signature of the Covenant had not meant that the Presbyterian religion was to be imposed by force, but merely that it was to be respected. The gravamen of the charge against the Scots was that they had taken their "grand enemy," King Charles II, "into their bosoms," and by promising to restore him to power in England and Ireland had sown the seeds of perpetual war. It was un-Christian dealing to commit themselves to a monarch with a popish mother, a popish army in Ireland, and popish servants who had shed innocent Protestant blood.

That declaration, which was published on July 18, and other later pronouncements by Cromwell had their repercussions upon the Scots. Though King Charles II was allowed to land in Scotland, he was treated in a derogatory way, and not permitted to direct the army or concern himself with policy or strategy. The King was warned by the Earl of Leven that if he came to the army "we should not keep trenches." The Earl of Loudoun went about the Scottish camp telling all and sundry that theirs was the cause of God and was not to be marred by wicked men: "such," it was reported, "they accounted all Cavaliers, Montrosians, and such as engaged with Hamilton, that is to say their best soldiers." Not only was the King's household purged, but up to the eve of the battle of Dunbar the Committee of the Estates were "going through all the regiments of horse and foot putting out and placing in officers." Finally ministers of the Kirk and high-ranking Presbyterian civilians interfered in the running of the war. Johnston of Waristoun proposed to Lieutenant General David Leslie that "a sub-committee with general officers and Council of War ought to consult how to dispose of their forces." The Lieutenant General," noted Waristoun, "gave a sharp answer and I as free a reply, and they shifted it."[3] Had Leslie been left to run things in his own way and to employ the best men available, as Cromwell used officers ranging from the unbending Ludlow to the ex-Royalist Monck, it might have gone hard with the invading army.

The day before the "Declaration to the Saints" was published Cromwell wrote to inquire after his first grandchild. "I could chide both father and mother for their neglects of me," he observed. "I know my son is idle, but I had better thoughts of Doll." "He is in the dangerous time of his age," he remarked to his son Richard's father-in-law, "and it's a very vain world." Did Oliver's thoughts go back to his two sons who had died during the early Civil War? At least he found no joy in his new position: "Great place and business in the world is not worth the looking after," he said. "I should have no comfort in mine but that my hope is in the Lord's presence." It was in a subdued and dedicated spirit that, on July 22, 1650, he led his army across the Scottish frontier.

*   *   *

The Scottish command had emptied the country between Berwick and Edinburgh of all able-bodied men, cattle, and stocks of food, and had destroyed the grain. A fortified line extended from Holyrood Palace in Edinburgh to the waters of Leith, which was protected by entrenchments—or "flankered" as Cromwell called it—and manned by a numerous if incompletely equipped army. Cromwell moved forward rapidly through devastated East Lothian along the coast road that led from Berwick by way of the ports of Musselburgh and Dunbar to the outskirts of Edinburgh. At Dunbar supply ships had landed stores, and supporting warships were ordered to bombard Leith. But Cromwell found the Scottish defences impregnable, and he soon had to withdraw his tired, dirty, and hungry army first to Musselburgh and then to Dunbar in order to collect provisions. The Scots harassed the retreating English rearguard, but were beaten off and let Cromwell's men reach their Dunbar base unmolested, the Presbyterian ministers preaching from the text: "The wicked flee where no man pursueth. . . ." Cromwell soon advanced again and vainly attempted to outflank the Scottish capital, but at the end of August he was once more compelled to draw back through lack of supplies. At Musselburgh Cromwell called a Council of War, and it was decided to march into Dunbar and fortify the town. Thus the English army would obtain an excellent base, magazine, and hospital, and also hope to provoke the Scots to battle.

Lieutenant General David Leslie, who was the real Scottish commander, had adopted Fabian tactics with success, though he was condemned by the armchair critics on his own side. His skill in stripping the occupied territory of all resources, his superior knowledge of the topography, and his handling of his hastily raised troops were masterly, and he had natural hopes that because of Cromwell's losses through sickness and the tempestuous weather he would be obliged, before winter

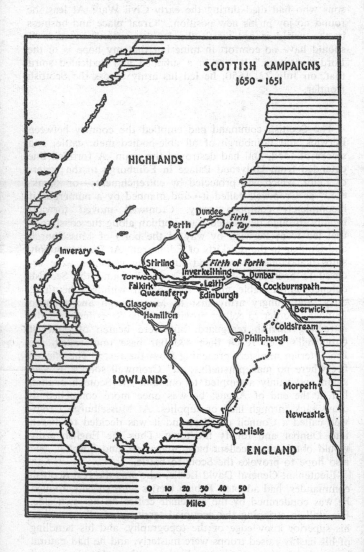

SCOTTISH CAMPAIGNS
1650 - 1651

HIGHLANDS

Dundee

Perth

Firth
of Tay

Inverary

Stirling

Firth of Forth

Torwood
Falkirk
Queensferry

Inverkeithing
Leith
Edinburgh

Dunbar
Cockburnspath

Glasgow
Hamilton

Berwick

Coldstream

Philiphaugh

LOWLANDS

Morpeth

Newcastle

Carlisle

ENGLAND

0 10 20 30 40 50
Miles

closed in, to retreat into England. But Leslie was misled about his enemy's intentions. Neither Cromwell nor any of the capable group of generals who served under him—Fleetwood, Lambert, Monck, and Edward Whalley—had any immediate thought of retreat. But the shipping away of some of the sick and wounded, the double withdrawal to Dunbar, and the failure of Sir Arthur Haselrigg to send up reinforcements from Newcastle, all contributed to the Scottish command's belief that it had only to apply the final pressure upon the English to see them try to break out and hurry home along the road by which they had come in such high hopes six weeks earlier.

When Cromwell returned to Dunbar at the end of August, Leslie followed him along a parallel line and encamped his army upon Doon Hill, a high point two miles to the south of Dunbar. He also detached a force to block the supposed English way of retreat at the narrow pass of Cockburnspath between the Lammermuir hills and the sea. In military theory Cromwell's army was trapped. The Scots outnumbered it by more than two to one. Doon Hill appeared to be unassailable, while the Scots could at any moment come down and attack the English in Dunbar, either from the west or the southeast. On September 2 Cromwell wrote post-haste to Haselrigg:

> We are upon an engagement very difficult. The enemy hath blocked up our way at the Pass at Copperspath [Cockburnspath] through which we cannot get without almost a miracle. He lieth so upon the hills that we know not how to come that way without great difficulty, and our lying here daily consumeth our men who fall sick beyond imagination.

But Leslie also had his difficulties. The bad weather that had distressed Cromwell's retiring troops made the Scots miserable as they lay exposed on the slopes of Doon Hill. Their Commissioners grew increasingly impatient with his Fabian tactics and "called on him to fall on." Whatever his exact motives, whether he was incited by his critics, by the complaints of his men, or—most likely of all—by the notion that he had Cromwell at his mercy, on September 2 he began to bring down his army and put it out in a three-mile arc reaching from the foot of the hill across the Berwick road almost to the sea.

On the afternoon of Monday, September 2, the day on

which Cromwell wrote his letter to Haselrigg, Cromwell and Lambert rode out to Broxmouth House, in the center of a deer park, which stood to the left of the English position less than a half a mile from the sea, in order to inspect the new Scottish line. They had no doubt that their enemy intended to attack them or at any rate to block their road home. But after they had examined the Scottish positions both Cromwell and Lambert were convinced that, although they were much inferior in numbers they had been afforded the opportunity to take the offensive themselves. They sent for Colonel Monck and told him what they thought. He agreed with them, and a Council of War held that evening concurred in Cromwell's resolution to attack.

The Scottish army, after its descent from Doon Hill, evidently presented a target at which the more compact and better disciplined army of the English Commonwealth could aim. The probability is that the Scottish command had unwittingly left openings between their forces as they were strung out towards the sea which the English felt that they might hope to exploit if once they effected a surprise. Between the two armies ran a "great ditch" or flooded burn, known as the Brox, which was a minor obstacle. But if this obstacle could be surmounted before dawn the next day surprise might be achieved. Six cavalry regiments under Lambert, Fleetwood, and Whalley were allocated for the initial assault, supported by a brigade of three and a half infantry regiments under Monck. Cromwell was determined to control the battle himself by keeping a reserve under his own hand consisting of his own cavalry regiment and three regiments of foot. From the time when he had a hasty meal in Dunbar at four o'clock on the afternoon of September 2 until the moment of victory next day he never relaxed his exertions.

The Brox burn was crossed without mishap before dawn. The night had been black and stormy; because of the wet the Scots had extinguished the match they kept ready to fire their muskets; the Covenanting soldiers tried to shelter from the continuous rain amid the shocks of grain, and many of their officers sought and found refuge in the neighboring farmhouses. But the English were alert throughout that short summer night, during which their forward troops drew up to the edge of the burn and their officers prepared indefatigably for the supreme moment of the attack. Once across the Brox burn the cavalry charged; on the left Lambert met with stiff resistance from the Scottish cannon and the lancers. Monck's foot soldiers were also checked at first, but recovered. When, however, the second wave of English foot was also repulsed by superior numbers, Cromwell threw in his reserves. That was the climax of the battle. "My own [foot] regiment," he related, "did come seasonably in; and, at push of pike, did repel the stoutest regiment the enemy had there." "I never beheld a more terrible charge of foot than was given by our army," reported an eyewitness. The English cavalry rallied and "after the first repulse given," the Scottish horse and foot were—in Cromwell's words—"made by the Lord of Hosts as stubble to our swords." Once General Leslie's right had been routed, the victorious English cavalry turned on the main body of Scottish infantry who, after less than an hour's struggle, panicked and fled. Three thousand Scots were killed and 10,000 taken prisoner. Fifteen thousand arms were left to be picked up on the field of battle.

The victory of Dunbar was a triumph for organization, surprise, and discipline. The Scots never expected to be attacked by a foe whom they believed to be demoralized and much reduced in numbers (Cromwell had indeed only 11,000 effectives left out of the 16,000 he had brought across the border). Leslie wrote afterwards: "It was the visible hand of God, with our own laziness, and not of men that defeated them, notwithstanding of orders given to stand to their arms that night."

Loudoun thought it "a sad stroke" revealing "God's great anger."[4] For his part Cromwell wrote to Ireton in relief: "The Lord upheld us with comfort in Himself, beyond ordinary experience." And to the Speaker he preached a sermon on the text of God's mercies.

> Disown yourselves, but own your authority, and improve it to curb the proud and insolent, such as would disturb the tranquility of England, though under what specious pretences soever; relieve the oppressed, hear the groans of poor prisoners in England; be pleased to reform the abuses of all professions; and, if there be anyone that make many poor to make a few rich, that suits not a Commonwealth.

If in his Naseby dispatch Cromwell proclaimed the Independent cause, it seemed after Dunbar almost as if he had become a Leveller.

*　　　*　　　*

The consequences of Dunbar were ample but not decisive. General Leslie offered his resignation to the Committee of the Estates, but it was refused. He was, however, compelled to change his strategy. He abandoned the Edinburgh–Leith line, and withdrew across the Firth of Forth to Stirling, which became in effect the new Scottish capital. Argyll and his friends were now obliged to treat the young King with less haughtiness. For he commanded allegiance in the Highlands from which reinforcements for the depleted Scottish army were needed. Charles II was appointed nominal commander in chief, and Argyll's rival, the second Duke of Hamilton, was called to his counsels. The King was enthusiastically welcomed at Stirling, but later retired to Perth, whence on January 1, 1651, he went to Scone to be crowned. Thus he was not entirely distressed over the defeat at Dunbar. The Scots, who had humiliated him, had in their turn been humiliated by Cromwell. King Charles never cared for the Covenant. Indeed, he is said to have murmured when he accepted it that he could never look his mother in the face again. Still he concealed his emotions and told Argyll that he would continue to be guided by his advice. But many Covenanters, impressed by Cromwell's propaganda, disliked these closer dealings with the "malignant" King. They attributed Dunbar to the wrath of God because they had fought for him. They remonstrated at the proceedings of the Committee of the Estates, and in the southwest a more or less independent Scottish army, under Colonel Gilbert Kerr, entered into secret communication with Cromwell.

Immediately after Dunbar, Cromwell occupied Leith, which became his chief support port, and the town of Edinburgh, although the well-fortified castle remained in Scottish hands and gave the English soldiers uncomfortable nights. As soon as reinforcements had joined him, Cromwell marched towards Stirling on reconnaissance. But the roads were so bad that he was unable to bring up his full complement of artillery. Leslie had collected 5,000 men as a garrison, and after a Council of War had been held Cromwell determined not to storm the town, largely because he believed that even if it were taken it could not be held in view of the supply difficulties. He concentrated instead upon clearing the line of communications with England and attempting to win over the remonstrating Covenanters. For that purpose he paid a short visit to Glasgow in mid-October. But the negotiations broke down, and at the end of November General Lambert and General Whalley defeated Kerr at the battle of Hamilton near Glasgow and took him a prisoner. Negotiations with the governor of Edinburgh Castle, who also sympathized with the Remonstrants, were, on the other hand, a success. An attempt to mine the rocky heights on which the castle stood had been frustrated, and Cromwell was pleased to permit its evacuation on generous terms. On the day before Christmas the garrison marched out, much to the fury of the King. Thus most of southern Scotland came under English military control during the winter of 1650.

Oliver Cromwell was never a strong man. When he was young, he was often affected by boils and bad blood. The Irish campaign, when he had suffered from malaria and dysentery, undermined his health, and the continuous campaigning gave him no opportunity to recuperate. After Dunbar[5] he wrote to his wife: "I grow an old man, and feel the infirmities of age marvellously stealing upon me." In February of the next year he was forced to take to his bed, with a recurrence of either dysentery or malaria, and in March he was reported to be so ill that the doctors kept his letters from him. On March 24 he wrote to the President of the Council of State that "I thought I should have died of this fit of sickness, but the Lord seemeth to dispose otherwise." In early April, Lady Waristoun when she saw him remarked that "he seemed to her dryer than before."[6] In mid-May he was again down with a serious attack of malaria. He was still weak at the end of June, after doctors had been sent from London by the Council of State to attend him. "My sickness," he wrote at this time, "was so violent that indeed my nature was not able to bear the weight thereof." Once again he could exclaim: "The Lord . . . hath plucked me out of the grave." Though Cromwell worked on throughout these six months and he had a competent second in command in John Lambert (Charles Fleetwood had returned to London), his constant illness helped to prevent the completion of the Scottish campaign. Scarcity of food, horses, and forage were among other reasons for its delay.

It has been said that Cromwell's ill-health frayed his temper. It is true that his temper was never mild, but there is no proof that it then influenced his conduct or policy. On the contrary, his letters testify to his humanity, patience, and devotion to his family and friends. When one of his colonels died, he wrote to the Speaker on behalf of the widow and seven small children. On petition from their wives he offered to exchange various officers, who were prisoners, with the Scots. He guaranteed Lady Lothian, whose house and park were behind the English lines, against molestation. And he showed his modesty when he asked that the medal commemorating Dunbar should not be inscribed with his own name but that of his army and the Lord of Hosts. Often he wrote to his wife assuring her of his love but worrying about the family. His favorite daughter Elizabeth had recently married. He asked his wife to remind "poor Betty" of the dangers of being "cozened with worldly vanities and worldly company, which I doubt she is too subject to." As to "Dick" Cromwell, his father learned with disappointment that he had exceeded his allowance and was in debt. He loved him dearly and also his wife, who was again with child. But "God forbid," he exclaimed, "that his being my son should allow him to live not pleasingly to our Heavenly Father, who hath raised me out of the dust to what I am!" In Ireland his second son Henry was loyally serving under his brother-in-law, Ireton. "In the same house," commented Carlyle, "one works, another goes idle." Yet for all his reproofs Oliver's deepest affections appear to have rested on the idle Dick and the charming and un-Puritanical Betty—an understandable ambivalence.

During Cromwell's illness the Scots recovered the initiative and marched out to the hills of Torwood near Bannockburn, where Robert Bruce won the battle three hundred years before. It was not until the end of June that the convalescent commander in chief reconnoitered the Scottish entrenchments there and tried to provoke David Leslie again to battle. But not even the storming of the frontier fortress of Callander House, which the Scots had retaken, and the slaughter of its valiant governor and most of its garrison before the very eyes of the main Scot army, could lure Leslie from his defensive strategy. Afterwards Cromwell described how "we did say one to another we know not what to do." How to get Leslie or push him out, that was Cromwell's problem. Evidently one plan that he examined was to occupy Glasgow and overrun the whole of the southwest of Scotland with his cavalry. Another scheme was to outflank Stirling from the west. A third, and the most promising idea of all, which he had long contemplated, was to exploit his command of the sea by an amphibious operation across the Firth of Forth.

The danger that attached to all these plans was that they would afford an opportunity for the Scots to break out and march into England. Should that grave risk be taken? Cromwell knew from spies and captured Royalists that King Charles II, who had been champing at the bit and was quite ready to hazard his own life, was eager to thrust across the border. The Marquis of Newcastle from his impecunious retirement on the Continent had recommended that move to his master. At this time Major General Harrison and been ordered up from the northwest with 3,000 reinforcements, and Cromwell had reasonable hopes that, with the military garrison of Carlisle on the one side and of Newcastle on the other, he could hold up any attempt by the Scots to push far southward into England. Finally in mid-July Cromwell succeeded in sending Colonel Robert Overton with a brigade across the Firth at Queensferry. By doing so he risked their being crushed by a detachment from Leslie's army moving more rapidly backwards over Stirling bridge. But Leslie did not react or did not act quickly enough. So Cromwell then sent over Major General Lambert with a bigger contingent in Overton's wake, and by Sunday, July 20, 4,000 men had been ferried across the Forth and were drawn up at the village of Inverkeithing on the Queensferry peninsula. Now Leslie was obliged to detach men to deal with the menace to his flank, but he dared not dispatch too large a force as Cromwell was demonstrating against him at Torwood. Major General Lambert won the battle of Inverkeithing, and Cromwell at once reinforced his victory. He threw the bulk of his army over the Firth and cut the Scottish communications with the Highlands. Leslie, who withdrew to Stirling, was presented with the alternative either of fighting where he stood or gambling all upon a march across the border into England. For weeks Cromwell and the young Charles II had glared at each other across the river line. Now the moment of decision had come. While Cromwell was directing the siege of Perth, Charles II's former place of residence, the King with Leslie and the second Duke of Hamilton, but without the somber and doubtful opportunist Argyll, was heading southwest towards Cumberland and Lancashire.[7]

On August 4 Cromwell wrote to the Speaker from Leith in a typically English understatement: "I do apprehend that if the enemy goes for England, being some days before us, it will trouble some men's thoughts, and may occasion some inconvenience. . . ."

But he defended his strategy by observing that he could not have averted another winter of war in Scotland except

THE WORCESTER CAMPAIGN
OF 1651
Showing Cromwell's line of Advance

by acting as he had done. The Council of State was understandably alarmed and alerted the militia throughout England, while King Charles II optimistically hoped to lead southward an ever-swelling army upon a defenseless capital. Cromwell, however, knew what he was doing. Major General Harrison, who had been waiting that very turn of events at Newcastle-upon-Tyne, made a forced march across the Pennines, and Major General Lambert with the cream of the cavalry rode forward from Leith. By the time these two generals had joined at Hasselmoor in Lancashire on August 14, they had an army about the same size as the King's and were scarcely a day's ride behind him. On August 6 Cromwell himself had left Leith with the infantry, the artillery, and the rest of the cavalry, and advanced at the remarkable speed of twenty miles a day, allowing his men to march in their short sleeves, while country horses were impressed to carry their doublets and arms. He left behind him Lieutenant General Monck to reduce Stirling and Colonel Overton to complete occupation of Perth, while Lieutenant General Fleetwood came up from London with a force of militia. Lambert regarded it as his duty not to fight the King, but "to amuse the enemy and to flank and front them till the General came to us."

Marching by the eastern route through Newcastle, Ripon, Doncaster, and Warwick, Cromwell finally concentrated the Parliamentary armies at Evesham on August 27. Four days earlier King Charles II and the Scots, who had been hemmed in and harried along the western route, had found shelter in Worcester. Few English Royalists even in Lancashire swelled their numbers as they came, and they were exhausted after marching three hundred miles in three weeks.

Cromwell had a big enough army assembled from north and south to be able to surround Worcester.[8] He planted his artillery two miles east of the city, and sent Lieutenant General Fleetwood to Upton-upon-Severn, ten miles to the south, after the village had been surprised by Major General Lambert. Colonel Robert Lilburne was ordered north to Bewdley bridge to cut the road back to Scotland. Cromwell's plan was for Fleetwood to attack the city from the south while the rest of the army converged upon the Royalists from the east. He himself, as at Dunbar, fully controlled the battle, having a reserve consisting of his lifeguards, one cavalry and three foot regiments. Fleetwood launched his assault on the afternoon of September 3, crossing the River Teme, a tributary of the Severn, by a bridge of boats. Here the Scots resisted skillfully, and Cromwell had to come up and throw in his reserve near the angle where the Teme joins the Severn. While the battle swayed doubtfully along this river line King Charles II led an attack upon the Parliamentarians east of the city. Though his numbers were inferior, the young King and his men struggled heroically against their disciplined enemies. In the end they were driven back downhill into the city, and many were trampled to death in the streets. Some of the Scots apparently took little or no part in the battle, including David Leslie, who played an ambiguous role: they tried to escape but were intercepted and taken prisoners.

Oliver Cromwell had trapped his enemy by dividing his army. For as late as August 29 he expressed the misgiving that they might "avoid fighting and lead us a jaunt." Afterwards he told the Speaker that "this hath been a very glorious mercy and as stiff a contest for four or five hours as I have seen." "Both your old forces and the newly raised [Fleetwood's militia]," he continued, "have behaved themselves with very great courage." So, too, had the Royalists under a brave King. Fighting each other in the last big battle of the civil wars, British soldiers on both sides acquitted themselves with honor.

Once again Cromwell's thoughts, as he penned his second dispatch to the Speaker, stretched out into the future. Surely, he reflected, Parliament would now be guided "to do the will of Him who hath done His will for it and the nation."

On September 12 he came to London, to be congratulated by the Speaker, the Lord Mayor, and the Council of State. He was agreeable and modest, "and in all his discourses about the business of Worcester would seldom mention anything of himself but of the gallantry of the officers and soldiers and gave (as was due) all the glory of the action unto God."

Notes

1. For Argyll see David Mathew, *Scotland under Charles I,* Chap. XV; J. Willcock, *The Great Marquis* (1903).

2. Cf. *Cromwell's Generals,* Chap. I.

3. For the Scottish side, see P. H. Brown, *History of Scotland* (1911); *Correspondence of Sir Robert Kerr of Ancram* (1875), II; *Diary of Sir Archibald Johnston of Wariston* (1919), from which quotations in this chapter are taken.

4. *Correspondence of Sir Robert Kerr,* II, 282.

5. For a more detailed account of Dunbar, see *Cromwell's Generals,* Chap. II; for a more traditional view of the battle and the alleged flank attack, see John Buchan, *Oliver Cromwell,* 371, seq.

6. *Diary of Sir Archibald Johnston,* II, 36.

7. For Cromwell and Scotland, see *inter alia* C. H. Firth, *Scotland and the Commonwealth* (1895), and W. S. Douglas, *Cromwell's Scotch Campaigns, 1650–1651* (1899).

8. Recent accounts of the Worcester campaign are in *Cromwell's Generals,* Chap. III, and A. H. Burne, *op. cit.,* Chap. XVIII; I agree with Colonel Burne that "it is surprising that the battle is not better documented or more fully dealt wih by historians" and that "the full story of Worcester has yet to be told."

Chapter 17

The Foundation of the Protectorate

HUGH PETER, one of Cromwell's chaplains who had served with the army, exhorted the soldiers in the autumn of 1651: "When your wives and children shall ask where you have been, and what news, say you have been at Worcester, where England's sorrows began, and where they are happily ended."[1] Certainly it seemed as if at last the English republicans had subdued all their enemies; and ordinary Puritans aspired to peace and the "glorious reformation in Church and State." Oliver Cromwell, who was acknowledged as the architect of victory with awards of money and houses, was also widely regarded as destined to direct the postwar reconstruction. A few months later John Milton hailed him as "our chief of men":

> . . . *who through a cloud*
> *Not of war only, but distractions rude,*
> *Guided by faith and matchless fortitude,*
> *To peace and truth thy glorious way hast ploughed,*
> *And on the neck of crownèd Fortune proud*
> *Hast reared God's trophies, and His work pursued*
> *While Darwen stream, with blood of Scots imbrued,*
> *And Dunbar field, resounds thy praises loud,*
> *And Worcester's laureate wreath: yet much remains*
> *To conquer still; Peace hath her victories*
> *No less renowned than War. . . .*

Like George Washington, when he farmed Mount Vernon after the surrender at Yorktown, Cromwell was aware of the need for a strong central government and a new constitution. But like him, too, he hesitated to accept his call to leadership. Four years after he left the army Washington became President of the Philadelphia Convention; more than two years after Worcester Cromwell was appointed Lord Protector under the "Instrument of Government."

But at first Cromwell was doubtful where his duty lay. In October the Tuscan agent in London reported that though he was zealous and popular "there cannot be discovered in him any ambition save for the public good, to which he brings all his spirit and power." In a self-revealing letter written about the same time to John Cotton, pastor to the church at Boston, he showed that while he was conscious of his own shortcomings he also owned his call:

> I am a poor weak creature . . . yet accepted to serve the Lord and his people. Indeed . . . you know not me, my weaknesses, my inordinate passions, my unskillfulness and unfitness to my work. Yet, yet the Lord, who will have mercy on whom He will, does as you see.

But the way ahead was obscure. "How shall we behave ourselves after such mercies?" he asks. "What is the Lord a-doing?" For the time being at least he was content simply to do what was required of him by his colleagues in the Government. He had duties enough. Besides commanding the army and supervising the redistribution of its forces and the demobilization of the militia, attending meetings of the Council of State and taking his seat in Parliament, he was still Lord Lieutenant of Ireland, and served upon many committees, including the admiralty and ordnance committees and the committees on Scottish and Irish affairs. He had also been chosen Chancellor of Oxford University. He was particularly concerned with disposing of the many prisoners of war taken in the last two campaigns, and with the reduction of the Isle of Man. But after Worcester, his immediate intention appears to have been to model himself on the behavior of the previous commander in chief, Lord Fairfax, loyally performing the administrative tasks assigned to him and bowing to the civil power, in which, after all, he shared.

Yet, unlike Fairfax, Cromwell had been a politician for more than twenty-five years, and was closely associated with the Independent army which, as he and his friend Henry Ireton had claimed before the execution of the King, was in itself no mere mercenary force, but a body of men representative of all that was finest in the Puritan community. The November after Worcester Ireton died of fever in the Irish bogs, and Cromwell was left sadly aware of his loss and of the brevity of life. "What is of this world will be found transitory," he wrote to his sister, "a clear evidence whereof is my son Ireton's death."

Cromwell was anxious for a settlement to conserve the revolution and yet open the way to reforms. After the punishment of the Royalist leaders and the discharge of the prisoners, he wanted an Act of Pardon and Oblivion to be passed, though he appreciated that some time must elapse before the former Royalists could be absorbed into the new state. Nevertheless, he urged that the "Rump" Parliament should be dissolved and a new one chosen in its place. As early as September 25 he acted as a teller in the House of Commons in favor of a motion to bring in a bill for that purpose. This bill for a "new representative" received its second reading on October 10 and the House went into committee on it four days later. A month afterwards the Committee of the whole House voted by a majority of only two to set a date for its dissolution, Cromwell again acting as teller for the majority. Clearly this Parliament of fewer than a hundred active members was exceedingly reluctant to give up its authority. On November 18 those who opposed Cromwell and his friends in their desire for a new assembly effectively blocked them by securing a vote that the Rump should not be dissolved for another three years.

How did Cromwell respond to his defeat? He recalled afterwards that when he and his fellow officers and soldiers returned from Worcester they "had some reasonable confidence" that their expectation of reforms "should not be frustrated." Here indeed was frustration of a high order, and Cromwell does not seem to have known where to turn. Ireton was dying; Lambert, who had been his second in command in Scotland, had returned there for the time being; Sir Henry Vane, who had once been Cromwell's intimate friend and was described as being "within the House what Cromwell was without," was now on the other side. Two factors counted heavily with Cromwell: first, he was, like Washington, convinced of the need to strengthen a government vitiated by the lack of an effective executive, and secondly he felt that he himself had been elected both by God and men to help direct the fortunes of the new state and could not stand aside forever. The very day after his reverse over the proposed dissolution he had been unanimously returned at the head of the annual poll for membership of the Council of State, and at the same time he was being approached by foreign powers with offers of military alliances and thereby virtually recognized abroad as the chief of the new state. Still he neither contemplated a personal dictatorship nor did the other republican leaders as yet fear it. "His ambition" was "for the public good." But it was natural that Vane and his friends should be jealous of Cromwell's pre-eminence and popularity, and it is likely that a decision taken at that time to have no permanent chairman of the Council of State reflected that jealousy.

Cromwell, though always by nature a passionate man, had come, as men do in their early fifties, to practice patience and ignore provocation. He held his fire and did not exploit the excellence of his position. The next two years were not to disclose impetuous scheming, but only caution, self-examination, and prayer. Ambition—at least personal ambition in its crudest form—should be made of sterner stuff. Cromwell, if one interprets his letters and sayings rightly, was subconsciously aware of a power of leadership burning inside him that could carry him, if he exercised it, to the highest place in the land. But in a broad sense, within the ambit of the existing republic, he already held that place. A modesty of intellectual approach—what a modern historian has described as his "back-bench" frame of mind[2]—what a psychologist might call defensiveness—and a hesitant or opportunist attitude to constitutional questions prevented him from forcing his opinions upon his colleagues until he was slowly persuaded of their validity. Thus it was not until December 10, three months after Worcester, that he first made a move openly. He then called an informal meeting at the Speaker's house of lawyer M.P.'s, including his old friend Oliver St. John, now Chief Justice, and of a number of officers to examine the problems of government.

Cromwell was then worried about the weaknesses of the executive. That was what he meant when he told the conference—"Really I think, if it may be done with safety and preservation of our rights, both as Englishmen and as Christians, a settlement with somewhat of monarchical power in it would be very effectual." All the lawyers agreed, but the soldiers boggled at the word "monarchy." So nothing was decided, and Cromwell, temporarily laying aside the constitutional question, turned to other aspects of reconstruction, including an amnesty and church reform.

Though in the first flush of victory Cromwell had urged that "some severity" ought to be shown to men "as well of quality as meaner ones" who had again taken up arms against the Commonwealth in the last stages of the campaign in Worcestershire, he soon perceived that mercy was an essential ingredient of the permanent settlement he craved. He therefore warmly advocated an Act of Oblivion. Other members of Parliament were less enthusiastic than he. He "pressed it," wrote the critical Ludlow in his later memoirs, "with so much importunity, though some members earnestly opposed it bearing date till after some months . . . yet nothing could prevail upon the General; and so the act was passed: the Parliament being unwilling to deny him anything for which there was the least colour of reason." In fact the act, passed on February 24, 1652, was clogged with exceptions, and while Cromwell tried to mitigate hardships upon the Royalists, it contributed less than he had wished towards pacification.

As to the question of religion, the situation remained confused. The rights of private patronage and the payment of tithes were acquiesced in, but an ordinance of 1648 which ordered the establishment of a Presbyterian system was never generally effective, partly bcause the Independent Churches were so strong, partly because most Englishmen disliked the idea of the old episcopal discipline over the morals of laymen being at once replaced by the discipline of Presbyterian elders. Parliament appointed a committee early in 1652 to formulate plans for ecclesiastical reform and its leadership fell upon Dr. John Owen, a dapper Independent minister, who was Dean of Christ Church, Oxford.[3] Cromwell later appointed him Vice Chancellor of the University, and even delegated to him some of his powers as Chancellor. Dr. Owen favored a state church in which all Protestants who accepted certain broad fundamentals might unite. Owen's scheme for limited toleration under a state umbrella had Cromwell's full support.

During the first half of 1652, however, the prospects of a political and religious settlement of the Commonwealth were clouded by difficulties overseas. Ireton had, it is true, almost completed the subjection of Ireland. In January the Council of State had nominated Major General John Lambert as his successor as Lord Deputy. But when later in the year financial embarrassments arose, Parliament abolished the post of Lord Lieutenant, held by Cromwell, and Lambert's office went along with it. Cromwell was troubled to "see honest John Lambert so ungratefully treated," and gave up the balance of pay due to him as Lord Lieutenant to reimburse the major general for the money he had laid out on his equipment. On July 8 Cromwell, now demoted to commander in chief, Ireland, selected Lieutenant General Charles Fleetwood, who had just married Ireton's widow, as his deputy there. Fleetwood's weakness alienated the Irish without pleasing the English. In Scotland the English commanders had been unable to subdue the Highlands, and most of the Scottish leaders, except Argyll, resisted a proposal that Scotland should forthwith be incorporated into the English Commonwealth. A similar, and more sensational, offer of incorporation had also been extended to the Dutch Republic in 1651. When, as was hardly surprising, that was rejected, relations between the two republics rapidly deteriorated. In October of that year the Rump passed a Navigation Act which forbade the importation of goods from abroad (other than from the countries of their origin) except in English ships. This was a blow aimed at the Dutch carrying trade, which during the civil wars had obtained a virtual monopoly even in taking provisions out to the English colonies and bringing back their produce. As Cromwell was now in London, presumably he acquiesced in it, although he was away when it was framed. Cromwell's old friends Vane and St. John both wanted a war against the Dutch, with whom England had long-standing colonial and commercial rivalries and who had aided the Stuarts. The idea of such a war was also approved by English shipowners and some trading companies and merchants.[4] The army, on the whole, was opposed to it, for it feared that being a naval war it would damage its interests; indeed, because of the war the soldiers' pay was later reduced and that of sailors increased. Cromwell's advice is not known. But once the war began, he exerted himself to achieve a speedy peace. "I do not like the war," he is reported to have said, "I will do everything in my power to bring about peace." But the war arose almost accidentally when the Dutch fleet under Tromp clashed with the English under Blake off Dover, and evidently Cromwell thought it had been forced upon them by the Dutch. As commander in chief and a member of the admiralty committee, he was involved from the outset, visiting Dover to investigate the reason for the engagement (he laid the blame on the Dutch), sending infantry to serve in the fleet, planning coastal defenses from Scarborough to Deal, and helping to man and conscript the merchant ships to reinforce the navy.[5]

"That Cromwell had no liking for the war," wrote Dr. Gardiner, "is beyond doubt, and, according to one witness, he was only reconciled to it by the assurance that it would be quickly over." So hope all reluctant warriors. But the Dutch were tough and resilient, and although the English fleet outnumbered theirs and was capably commanded, setbacks were suffered both in the Baltic and in the Mediterranean, while the fortunes of war ebbed and flowed in the Channel and North Sea. This war, the failure to pacify the Scots, the high taxes exacted to supply the armed forces, and the continued interruption of foreign trade, all combined to arouse discontent against the Rump Parliament.

Inevitably that discontent was focused in the army, where the center of opposition lay. In August the Council of Officers held a number of private meetings, where Cromwell was urged to press for the dissolution of Parliament and the summoning of a new one. Cromwell used all his influence to modify the political ardor of his officers, and when an army petition was presented to Parliament by his cousin Commissary General Edward Whalley, it omitted the demand for an immediate dissolution; instead, it advocated a number of reforms and outlined old grievances, including the perennial arrears of army pay. The lawyer M. P. Whitelocke remonstrated with Cromwell that the officers ought not to petition "with their swords in their hands." Cromwell brushed that aside. After all, even his critics admitted that he had successfully "stifled" the agitation for the time being, but he could scarcely eradicate the causes of discontent or silence its expression.

Parliament was galvanized into activity by the petition from the army. The petition was referred to a committee, of which Cromwell was appointed a member. That committee suggested, among other things, that the bill for elections, buried in the Grand Committee of the House for six months, should be taken into fresh consideration, and the House agreed that the bill should now be referred to this same committee, while a blank should be left for the date of dissolution.

But the dissatisfaction of the army was intense. Rightly or wrongly, officers and soldiers believed that members of the Rump Parliament were self-interested, bent upon perpetuating their own power, and guilty of nepotism and corruption. They were convinced that their cherished hopes of reforms—in the law, in the Church, in public finance—were being deliberately obstructed, and Cromwell, though himself a member, was gradually coming to feel the same. "My lord," he told Whitelocke in November, "there is little hope of a good settlement to be made by them, really there is not." Whitelocke admitted that Cromwell had answered his former complaint, that he had done his utmost to keep the army in obedience to Parliament. But what was the key to the future? Should a figurehead of a king be brought back to grace a strengthened executive power? The boy Duke of Gloucester, youngest son of King Charles I, was still a prisoner in England. Should he be elevated? Cromwell, ever eclectic, seems to have played with that idea. Alternatively ought he himself now to seek the office of chief executive? Whether he asked at that time, as Whitelocke claimed he did: "What if a man should take upon himself to be King?" or whether Whitelocke invented the phrase and inserted it in his memoirs after the Restoration we shall never know. But unquestionably Cromwell wanted a change of government, the abandonment of the makeshift committee system, some new constitutional arrangement that would provide for reform and reconstruction as soon as the Dutch war was over. He could not expect to suppress the ferment in the army indefinitely. Yet he remained patient and inscrutable. And for another eight months after the August petition he managed to control the Council of Officers and check the ambitions of rival generals who would have ousted him and themselves directed a *coup d'état* against the Rump.

For generals come and go. Cromwell had replaced Fairfax, as Fairfax had replaced Essex. Cromwell in his turn might be superseded. Since his retirement Fairfax had been the darling of the Presbyterians: Thomas Harrison, distinguished by his services in the Worcester campaign, was the acknowledged leader of the Fifth Monarchy men who were eager to overthrow the Rump and rule themselves until the Lord came again; John Lambert, as clever a political thinker as the dead Ireton and almost as superb a general as Cromwell himself, was affronted by the snub he had received from Parliament, and was exceedingly popular with the soldiers. Thus Cromwell was subjected to many pressures and rivalries in the winter of 1652–53. In loneliness he struggled with his conscience. The lawyers told him that what was needed was the restoration of a monarchical system, and warned him that to allow the army to coerce the Rump would mean anarchy. Many officers urged upon him the need to set up a new representative. The Council of Officers met and prayed nearly ever day, and a dozen meetings were held at which both officers and M.P.s were present. In January a letter was dispatched to the armies stationed in Scotland and Ireland as well as in England advocating "successive [i.e., short] Parliaments consisting of men faithful to the interests of the Commonwealth, men of truth, fearing God and hating covetousness." Yet Cromwell himself headed a group in the army which was ready to maintain the existing House for the time being, provided it kept its promise of September 1652 to dissolve itself soon. But Harrison and Lambert were insisting on the corrupt character of its members and the critical need to take power out of their hands. By March pressure from the rank and file had reached fever pitch. On March 7 Cromwell and the major generals were asked "to consider what is fit to be done by them in relation to a new representative either by petition *or otherwise*." A news-letter of March 11 from London reported that "the Council of Officers at St. James's had resolved to turn them out . . . had not the General and Colonel Desborough [his brother-in-law] interceded." It was at that time that Cromwell told Quartermaster Vernon that "he was pushed on by two parties to do that, the consideration of the issue whereof makes my hair stand on end." One party, he explained, was led by Major General Lambert, who wanted to revenge himself on Parliament by engineering a dissolution; the other was directed by Major General Harrison, who, "from impatience of spirit," would not—as Cromwell himself did—"wait the Lord's leisure." The Venetian envoy reported home that "so much bad blood exists between Cromwell and Harrison, who both covertly and openly seeks to deprive the former of his command of the army." It was said that Harrison had a following in Wales capable of revolt. As to Lambert, no one knew what he had in mind. But he was young and ardent. The Royalists were told that March how "Fairfax and Lambert were both in town, but both disgusted by the General. He will not vouchsafe to see either of them and calls Lambert bottomless . . ."[6]

Cromwell's own story of what happened was given later in a speech to Parliament (of the divergent pressures upon him naturally he said nothing):

> Finding the people dissatisfied in every corner of the nation . . . we divers times endeavoured to obtain meetings with divers members of Parliament. . . . And in these meetings we did, with all faithfulness and sincerity, beseech them that they would be mindful of their duty to God and men, in the discharge of the trust reposed in them.

The last of these meetings was held on April 19 in Cromwell's lodgings in Whitehall, as the Dutch war appeared to be drawing to its close. Sir Henry Vane and his friends had prepared a scheme by which only partial elections were to be permitted: they themselves were to retain their seats, but new members were to be recruited and allowed, subject to their approval, to enlarge the House; Cromwell and the army, on the other hand, wanted a clean cut, a temporary body, consisting of M.P.s and officers, to govern pending the working out of a new constitution. Nothing was decided, but Cromwell understood that the discussion of some kind of compromise between the two plans would be resumed next day, and that meanwhile both sides should refrain from any action. On the following morning, however, messages were brought to him that a number of members inspired by Sir Arthur Haselrigg were, after all, trying to hurry Vane's plan through Parliament. Now at last Cromwell's patience deserted him—the stopper was out, the censorship raised. Dressed in plain black clothes and gray worsted stockings, he came and took his seat in the House, but left a file of musketeers at the door and in the lobby. Divergent eyewitness accounts have survived of how Cromwell behaved. He took off his hat, rose in his place, and spoke. After commending his fellow members for their early efforts for the public good, he reproached them for their recent slowness in righting injustices. Then he put on his hat, left his seat, and walked up and down the middle of the House angrily blaming individual members by name: some he aspersed as drunkards, others as whoremasters; and lastly he confronted his old friend Vane whom he called a "juggler": "Oh, Sir Henry Vane! Sir Henry Vane! The Lord deliver me from Sir Henry Vane!" He has justly been compared with an Old Testament prophet rebuking the wicked. His anger was terrible, his language unparliamentary. But he retorted to those who tried in vain to stem the torrent of his wrath—"You are no parliament. I will put an end to your sitting." And he called in the musketeers. Major General Harrison, who was by his side throughout, pulled down the Speaker by his gown from his chair, and Cromwell then turned to the table on which lay the mace and other emblems of the House's authority, saying, "Take away these baubles." Thus the Long Parliament, to which he had come as member for Cambridge thirteen years earlier, was brought by violence to its close. The same afternoon Cromwell also dissolved the Council of State. After prolonged hesitations, thrust forward by the army, he had completed the second revolution.

*   *   *

On the whole, what Cromwell did was popular. The Speaker—who had been the nominal head of the republic—was accused of having been corrupt and Parliament as a whole of lacking firmness and energy. "The dissolution," reported the Venetian envoy, "is viewed with admiration rather than surprise and gives general satisfaction." At Wolverhampton a maypole was set up to celebrate the event. "The people are very calm and pleasant," said the writer of a newsletter, "expecting great things to be speedily done for the nation." Two considerations had inspired Cromwell to the deed over which he had so long hesitated: the first was his conviction that the Rump had failed to "proceed vigorously in reforming what was amiss in government"; the second, that having so signally failed, it still intended to extend indefinitely its own "arbitrary" power. It seemed to him as if the cause of the revolution had been betrayed, that the Commonwealth had not been settled on a foundation of justice and righteousness, and that people were weary of being ruled by the same little group of politicians in perpetuity. To assert that he had destroyed or even intended to destroy the Parliamentary system as such is nonsense. What he planned was a short interregnum during which a carefully selected body of men of integrity should draw up a new constitution in church and state, and after passions and jealousies had subsided fashion a new executive and a fresh Parliament.

But what was the first step to be? The old Council of State was too intimately linked with the Rump to govern alone. Ought he, Cromwell, as commander in chief, to assume full authority and appoint a few men he could trust to advise him? He resisted the temptation. The decision that he ultimately reached was to invite the Independent churches in each county to forward a list of names from which the Council of the Army could make the final choice of an "assembly of notables." This select body was to be entrusted with "the peace, safety, and good government of the Commonwealth." To these "saints," not without some misgiving, Cromwell surrendered all power. He gave them to understand that he hoped that in due course a wider representative would replace them. Significantly he observed that "never was there a supreme authority consisting of so numerous a body"—thereby showing that he had called them together as a sovereign government and not as a mere debating chamber.

It has lately been argued that this "Assembly of Saints" ought in fact to be pictured both as "a party congress and a constituent assembly," based upon "a relatively democratic electorate" and constituting "a high point of the revolutionary movement."[7] Translated into modern terms, that was indeed much how Cromwell himself regarded it. Though the Royalists waxed sarcastic at the expense of "pettifoggers, innkeepers, millwrights, stocking-mongers and such rabble as never had hoped to be of a Grand Jury," the members were for the most part sober merchants, tradesmen, lesser gentry or professional men, "honest and well-meaning persons," as General Ludlow called them, ranging from the Highmaster of St. Paul's School and the venerable Provost of Eton (who became Speaker) to a number of local religious enthusiasts. George Monck, Charles Fleetwood, Robert Blake, and Henry Cromwell were nominated, though soldiers on the active list were in a minority. Few lawyers were chosen members, though there were included thirty justices of the peace and the Recorders of Colchester and Canterbury. Thomas Barbon, after whom the Assembly was nicknamed "Barebones' Parliament," was a respected City leather merchant. Cromwell himself, together with Lambert, Harrison, and two others, was co-opted.[8]

Cromwell afterwards called this "Little Parliament" "a story of my own weakness and folly." Yet the summoning of a constituent assembly of Puritan revolutionaries lay in the logic of his life. "Own your call," he told the members. In a sense they did so. While the Rump had delayed to reform the laws, ignoring even the recommendations of its own committees and entangling itself in legal abstrusities every Friday, the new assembly plunged recklessly into the reform and codification of the law. Had not Cromwell himself set them an example when a few days after the dissolution of the Rump he had given an order remitting the death sentences on ten men, announcing that in future only murderers should receive capital punishment? The Assembly of Saints ruled that pickpockets and horse thieves were not to be executed for their first offense, that women were not to be burnt alive, that genuine bankrupts were to be released from prison. They passed an act for the relief of creditors and poor prisoners. They framed a law for civil marriages and introduced one for the speedier probate of wills. They examined schemes for the advance of learning and the protection of tenants. They resolved that the Court of Chancery should be abolished, and proposed the ending of tithes and lay presentations to benefices without, however, providing for any considered alternatives. The rate of reform was breath-taking, contrasting strikingly with the sluggishness of their predecessors. "Business came on fast from committees," wrote Barbon himself, "which did cause striving which should be first heard, and much time lost thereby." Altogether twenty-six acts were passed in just over five months, sometimes at the rate of more than one a day.

That was too much for Cromwell and Lambert, and in general for the better-off section of the community. To them the Saints drove too fast and furiously. "What did the Convention of your choosing?" Cromwell asked the army officers four years later. "Fly at liberty and property, insomuch as if one man had twelve cows, they held another that wanted cows ought to share with his neighbour. Who could have said that anything was their own if they had gone on?"

While the radical majority of the Assembly of Saints challenged many vested interests, it gave offense in other ways. Cromwell's influence in domestic questions was small (though he succeeded in defeating the first proposal to abolish tithes), but he still took a principal part in the conduct of foreign affairs. Ever since his return from Worcester he had been intimately involved in them. As a soldier he was anxious to secure a foothold on the Continent, partly as a means of checking piracy in the Channel but chiefly so as to exert Puritan influence abroad. His heart was set on obtaining for England the port of Dunkirk—long a center of piracy—which belonged to the Spanish Empire but was being fought over between France and Spain. Proposals to surrender it to him on terms had come to him from various quarters in 1651 and 1652, and at one time he had contemplated an alliance with France or even with Spain, according to which kingdom made him the better offer. But then supervened what he regarded as the unfortunate complication of the naval war with the Dutch. Before the Assembly met he had been appointed to a committee assigned to negotiate peace with the Dutch, and he helped to draw up far-reaching proposals for union between the two republics. (He had also interested himself in opening negotiations for a treaty with the Protestant Swedes.) The Dutch, however, still regarded the suggestion of union with aversion, as an attempt to absorb and subject their nation to its more populous and mightier neighbor. Rather than accept that, they preferred to renew the war. Thus Cromwell achieved no progress. And the Assembly was firm in refusing to moderate the peace terms.

Gradually also the Assembly alienated most Londoners. First it caused the arrest of the Leveller hero, John Lilburne, who had been outlawed by the Rump and had returned home in search of his pardon. He secured acquittal by a friendly City jury in spite of his breach of outlawry, but was immediately cast into the Tower of London. William Walwyn, the Socrates of the Leveller movement, was also arrested.[9] Many of the City aldermen were irritated by the attacks on property launched in the Assembly, while the extreme religious views of its more active members, tending to millenarianism and general irresponsibility, alienated the Presbyterians. The treatment of Lilburne, religious confusion, and heavy taxation led to rioting in the City, while at the other end of the island the Scottish Highlands were once more aflame.

Cromwell himself was perturbed, not only by the extremism of the radicals and their neglect of his counsels and by their persistence with the Dutch war, but also because he felt that they had conferred on themselves an authority that had never been intended. He had envisaged the Assembly as a constituent body that would not sit for more than eighteen months at the outside. Instead of that, it had arrogated to itself the name of "Parliament"—though smaller in number even than the Rump—and proceeded to turn the Law and the Church as well as social institutions upside down. General Harrison was the prophet of the new order, though when things went wrong Cromwell received all the blame. The Venetian envoy, who had earlier noted that Cromwell "is moving with careful circumspection" and that "he had been relieved of the vast responsibility of directing everything," yet referred to the Parliament as his "dependent." The Levellers accused him of violating fundamental laws and public liberties. Fifth Monarchy and Anabaptist preachers denounced him as the "Old Dragon" and "Man of Sin" because he favored a state church. Harrison was fanatically opposed to Cromwell's religious ideas and to his efforts to secure peace with the Dutch, and stood out again as a candidate to supplant him as commander in chief.

On November 1, 1653, Cromwell was again unanimously elected at the head of the poll for members of the Council of State, far ahead of Harrison. Rumors had been rife during the summer of Cromwell being given a new title, but not until the middle of November was there any inkling of a positive move to that end. The agent of the new *coup d'état* was not Cromwell himself but John Lambert. This able Yorkshireman was leader of the moderate party in the Assembly which, when it could rally its full complement of supporters, slightly outnumbered the radicals under Harrison. How long Lambert had been preparing his scheme for a Protectorate is not known. But in the middle of November he presided over a meeting of army officers after he had succeeded in halting the radical steam roller at Westminster. The crux came on December 10 when Harrison and his adherents managed to reject a sensible scheme for ecclesiastical reform sponsored by Dr. Owen. Now, in Cromwell's words, "they laid the axe at the root of the ministry," preferring religious anarchy to the mildest form of order. On the morning of December 12 the moderates met very early, and as soon as the Speaker took the chair carried a vote to resign their powers to the Lord General from whom they had first received them. Then Major General Lambert, following the precedent set by Cromwell, sent along a contingent of musketeers to close the House. Afterwards he presented the "Instrument of Government" which he and his friends had drawn up to the Council of State. Four days later Cromwell was proclaimed Lord Protector.

Cromwell always denied that he had any part in Lambert's conspiracy, though he must have suspected what was on foot, and was possibly consulted by Lambert about the new constitution. Virtually nothing is known of what Cromwell said or did that early December. But "I can say it," he observed later, "in the presence of divers persons here who know whether I lie, that I did not know one tittle of that resignation, till they all came and brought it, and delivered it into my hands." Patient, selfless, perplexed, and disappointed, and deeply concerned over the good of church and state, in the end he recognized an obligation to assume an office he had been genuinely reluctant to seek. But at last he saw the event as the clear manifestation of God's will, as much a "providence" as the victories of Preston or Dunbar. He now believed that when he had appointed the Assembly of Saints and handed over all power to it, he had willfully and weakly denied his own call. He dared no longer divest himself of what he regarded as his duty—to heal and settle the nation. He felt the urge to govern. As the constitutional head of the republic, he solemnly undertook the task of making peace, establishing order, and promoting considered reforms, after more than a decade of civil strife and political chaos.

Notes

1. *A Perfect Diurnall*, E641.

2. H. R. Trevor-Roper: see his essay on "Oliver Cromwell and his Parliaments" in *Essays presented to Sir Lewis Namier* (1956).

3. Anthony Wood, *Athenae Oxoniensis* (ed. Bliss, 1820), IV, 98–102; W. Haller, *Liberty and Reformation in the Puritan Revolution* (1955), 336 seq.

4. Cf. M. P. Ashley, *Financial and Commercial Policy under the Cromwellian Protectorate* (1934).

5. Abbott, II, 551, seems to question the accepted view that Cromwell was opposed to the Dutch war. The evidence is slight, but I incline to the opinion that Cromwell disliked it from the beginning.

6. *Cromwell's Generals*, Chap. V, for Cromwell's relations with Lambert and Harrison at this time.

7. Christopher Hill, "The Barebones Parliament," *The Listener*, July 23, 1953.

8. Henry A. Glass, *The Barebone Parliament* (1899) contains a list of members.

9. For Walwyn, see W. Schenck, *The Concern for Social Justice in the Puritan Revolution* (1948), Chap. III; Perez Zagorin, *A History of Political Thought in the English Revolution* (1952), Chap. II; and Joseph Frank, *The Levellers* (1955). These are among the best of the numerous books on this topic.

Chapter 18

The First Months of the Protectorate

THE FIRST INTENTION of General Lambert and the officers who carried out the coup of December 1653 had been, according to Oliver Cromwell himself, to offer him the title of king. As late as December 2 the Venetian agent in London reported how "some private persons and even preachers had suggested the nomination of a king." But when on December 12 Cromwell was discussing the future constitution with John Lambert, he made it clear that he would not accept the honor. On December 14 and 15, during further discussions, the title of Lord Governor was proposed, but in the end that of Lord Protector, already familiar in English history, was selected. The title had originally been given by Parliament to the Duke of Gloucester in 1422. Afterwards the protectorship had "put on weight," and the Duke of Somerset in the reign of King Edward VI had exercised wider authority than had the Duke of Gloucester during the minority of King Henry VI.[1] Cromwell was not, however, to govern on behalf of any king, but as Lord Protector for life. Nevertheless, the protectorship was conceived to be an elective institution, and its powers were circumscribed, as they had been over two centuries earlier, both by Council and by Parliament.

Indeed, in many ways the new constitution was a conservative and restrictive document. Cromwell willingly acquiesced in the reduction and definition of his authority, which he regarded, after the ingeniously devised resignation of the Saints, as being as "boundless and unlimited" as after he had dismissed the Rump. "I was arbitrary in power, having the armies of the three nations under my command, and truly not very ill beloved by them, nor very ill beloved then by the people, by the good people." He repudiated any desire to preserve "arbitrariness" and he craved a "settlement."

And after many arguments, and after letting of me know that I did not receive anything that put me into any higher capacity than I was in before, but that it limited me and bound my hands to act nothing to the prejudice of the nations without consent of a Council until the Parliament met and then limited me by the Parliament as the Act of Government expresseth, I did accept it.

Thus he recognized himself to be a constitutional ruler, and he was modest about his capacities, though he acknowledged his call to service.

The "Instrument of Government" was an amalgam of many paper constitutions that had been compiled and circulated during the previous ten years, ranging from the "Nineteen Propositions" offered to King Charles I to the "Agreements of the People" drawn up by the democratic Levellers. It was "an attempt to combine ideas suggested by the old constitution and by recent experience."[2] For example, the executive was now again separated from the legislature, but subjected to the control of the Council of State. The Lord Protector was to be responsible for the administration and for the direction of the army and navy and of foreign affairs, with the assistance of the Council. Membership of the Council of State was defined by the Instrument, vacancies by death or resignation being filled by a choice from names submitted to the Protector. The Lord Protector and the Council of State were given the right to publish ordinances until Parliament was in session, but these had then to be approved by it. When it was sitting (at least once every three years) Parliament alone had the right to make laws, and the Lord Protector could not veto parliamentary bills, though he might withhold his consent for twenty days.

A revenue was granted to the Lord Protector sufficient to maintain a modest army and navy and to meet his household expenses, but for further taxation he had to apply to Parliament. Liberty of conscience was guaranteed in the Instrument, for while "the Christian religion, as contained in the Scriptures" was to "be held forth and recommended as the public profession of these nations . . . to the public profession held forth none were to be compelled by penalties or otherwise." Everyone might practice his own brand of Christianity "provided this liberty" were "not extended to popery or prelacy nor to such as, under the profession of Christ, hold forth and practice licentiousness." All this bore the impress of Cromwell's own Independent frame of mind.

As to the electoral franchise, that was restricted, so far as the counties were concerned, to owners of property, real or personal, to the value of £200. The borough franchise was not defined. But, as compared with the Long Parliament, the county representation was quadrupled and the borough representation halved.[3] And while Scotland and Ireland were both allotted thirty members, the choice was in effect limited to nominees of the English Government. It was a new and possibly not very carefully thought-out pattern, but its intention was to provide for stability and a fairer distribution of constituencies.

The "Instrument of Government" was deliberately meant to establish a system of constitutional checks and balances which would prevent either the executive (as with King Charles I), or the Parliament (as with the Rump or the Assembly of Saints), or the Council of State (as in contemporary Venice), from becoming omnipotent. It looked back to the reigns of Queen Elizabeth I and King James I when the idea of "sovereignty" was virtually unknown. In less theoretical terms, it was no mere façade to preserve the power of the New Model Army, though its officers had framed it and were an important (though not dominant) element in the new Council of State. And it was certainly no scheme for autocracy. Oliver Cromwell himself was entirely indifferent about forms of government. To neither a monarchy (if it were limited) nor an Upper House (if it contained no bishops) was he opposed in principle. What he wanted was a workable constitution. In accepting the "Instrument of Government" on December 16, 1653, he announced:

I do promise in the presence of God that I will not violate or infringe the matters and things contained therein, but, to my power, observe the same, and cause them to be observed, and shall in all other things, to the best of my understanding, govern these nations according to the laws, statutes, and customs thereof, seeking their peace, and causing justice and law to be equally administered.

Here spoke no latter-day dictator, but the first servant of a Commonwealth of Nations.

*   *   *

In Cromwell there mingled the quick intelligence of a practical ruler of men and the deep-rooted strains of a Protestant idealist who saw in the spread of a liberal Christianity the right aim of government throughout the world. That was why he had been attracted, and even misled, by the burning evangelism of Thomas Harrison and the Welsh radical demagogues who had initiated the Assembly of Saints. But the practical side of his nature had been affronted by their romantic behavior and had brought him in the end to accept the more realistic blueprint of John Lambert. Lambert was a hardheaded and exceptionally able Yorkshireman, and yet he had shared, and had been influenced by, the political ideas of Cromwell's dead son-in-law, Henry Ireton, a Puritan thinker of the highest order. Together Ireton and Lambert had drawn up the "Heads of the Proposals" in the days before King Charles was executed. The "Instrument of Government" was in effect the "Heads of the Proposals" adapted to the needs of a republic. Thus Cromwell and Lambert were far from being counterrevolutionaries when they launched the Protectorate. They believed, with no less ardor, if with more caution, than the Fifth Monarchists, on the one side and the Levellers on the other, in the need for reforms. In that sense they had no wish to call a halt to the English revolution, let alone to destroy it, but they saw the necessity of first making the Commonwealth secure before refurbishing the framework of church and state.

Peace was the urgent need. In Scotland the Highlands were still aflame, and Colonel Robert Lilburne, the brother of "Freeborn John," who had been left with the military command after General George Monck had been transmuted into an admiral, was unable to cope with the unrest there. In spite of a series of naval victories, the Dutch war was still raging, the Dutch nation having defied the demand, adumbrated in the grimmest terms by the Assembly of Saints, to submit themselves to a humiliating peace. An undeclared state of naval warfare also existed against France, whose ruler, Cardinal Mazarin, had hesitated to recognize the regicide republic. Portugal, like France and the United Netherlands, had given aid and comfort to Prince Rupert when he directed his guerrilla sea warfare upon English commerce. But the very establishment of the Protectorate held out hopes of a general pacification. Within two months of the day when Cromwell took the oath, Dutch ambassadors had returned in force to London on a mission of peace, and the French and Spanish monarchies began a competition for an English alliance. The appointment of the Dutch plenipotentiaries carried with it the recognition of the Protectorate, and within two months of their arrival a draft treaty was signed. This provided for a defensive agreement between the two republics, for the expulsion from their territories of enemies or rebellious subjects belonging to each other, and for freedom of trade between the two countries, though the Dutch were obliged to acquiesce in the Navigation Act. They also promised compensation for damage done to English merchants and to the East India Company, and that their own men-of-war would salute the British flag in British waters. During the negotiations Cromwell had, with the assent of the Council of State, waived certain more extreme demands, such as that the Dutch should furnish heavy reparations, acknowledge their war guilt, limit the size of their navy, and even pay for the right to fish. On one condition, however, Cromwell did insist, and that was that William, Prince of Orange, the three-year-old grandson of King Charles I, should be permanently excluded from high office in the United Netherlands. Eventually, and secretly, John de Witt, the Grand Pensionary of Holland, succeeded in forcing through this Act of Exclusion; then the Anglo-Dutch treaty was completed.

The terms of the treaty were of a kind that only a conqueror could impose and profoundly impressed the rulers of Europe. It is true that in retrospect Cromwell's republican critics declared this act of statesmanship to have been weak-kneed: "We never bid fairer for being the masters of the world," they said; "we might have brought them to oneness with us."[4] But the terms were still stiff and were resented by the majority of the Dutch people, who later strove for more acceptable trading arrangements and were ultimately to reverse the Act of Exclusion (but not until after Cromwell was dead). Cromwell, for his part, rejoiced that the two Puritan republics were now again friends, if not united, as he had desired, in the service of Protestantism.

He dispatched envoys to Switzerland and Sweden, and came to terms with the King of Denmark, who had been the ally of the Dutch. He had faith in the young and autocratic Queen of Sweden, Christina, daughter of the Protestant hero Gustavus Adolphus. The Queen, a bluestocking but not lacking in the insatiable curiosity of her sex, showed a flattering interest in the character of the Puritan ruler, and indeed expressed herself to be an enthusiastic admirer of his. Sweden was a great Protestant power which had humbled the Danes and gained a foothold in Germany. As soon as the Dutch treaty was completed, Cromwell told his ambassador extraordinary to yield concessions in order to procure a treaty of friendship with the Swedish monarchy. Unfortunately for his fondest hopes, no sooner had the treaty been signed than Queen Christina abdicated, declaring herself—of all things—to be a Roman Catholic. The twenty-five reindeer which she had sent the Lord Protector as a present appropriately died en route.

A treaty with Portugal was also concluded in dramatic circumstances. The brother of the Portuguese ambassador in London, a youth of nineteen, had been involved in an affray in a fashionable shopping center on the south side of the Strand during which an innocent onlooker had been shot dead. He was arrested in the embassy and cast into Newgate prison. Diplomatic immunity was vainly claimed for him—all the envoys in London rallying in professional indignation—but the Lord Protector was adamant. And on the very same day that his brother was beheaded on Tower Hill, the Portuguese ambassador signed the treaty and left England forever.

Once these treaties were signed, Cromwell and the Council of State had to decide whether they would agree to an alliance with France or Spain, both of whom were eager to enlist the support of the strongest naval power in the world, the conqueror of the Dutch. Since the Thirty Years' War had ended, these two nations had been locked in apparently ceaseless struggle, while the French had since 1648 been divided by civil wars, half tragic and half comic, known as the Fronde. Prince Condé, an arrogant and formidable prince of the blood royal, was actually in command of Spanish troops. Cardinal Mazarin, adviser and lover of the French Queen Regent, had twice to leave Paris, and the French armies fighting in the Spanish Netherlands were forced upon the defensive. But in February 1653 Mazarin had returned to Paris in triumph, and by the beginning of 1654 the Fronde was over. Still, Dunkirk had been lost, and Mazarin's long-term aim of buying Cromwell's alliance was sharpened.

A French envoy who had been sent to England without instructions to recognize the republic had been rebuffed in 1652. At the end of that year an able young member of the French merchant class, Antoine de Bordeaux, arrived to spy out the land.[5] He made himself comfortable in London, found himself an English mistress, and wrote lucid reports home. Spain was represented capably by Alonso de Cárdenas, and while the two foreign envoys awaited the close of the Anglo-Dutch war they amused themselves by bidding against each other for art treasures, such as rare tapestries and masterpieces by Raphael on sale in the London market. In January 1654 Bordeaux was joined by Paul, Baron de Baas, a musketeer officer descended from Dumas's hero, D'Artagnan, a proud and excitable character, as a special envoy. Bordeaux was promoted ambassador, and in April was officially received by the Lord Protector. Meanwhile Cárdenas had been sounded about what he had to offer, and John Thurloe, Cromwell's Secretary of State, explained to the Spanish ambassador that his King would be expected to furnish a large sum to grease a military pact. But the Spaniards, as usual, had no ready money, and could offer only a meager contribution of £120,000 a year. Cardinal Mazarin had no difficulty in capping that.

In the early spring the English Council of State began earnest deliberations about which alliance should be preferred. John Lambert headed a minority which was inclined towards a Spanish alliance, partly because of long-standing grievances against the French, whose privateers preyed on English commerce, and partly because they regarded the French monarchy, which sheltered and subsidized Queen Henrietta Maria and her son, as the fount of Royalist support: they saw the French coasts as a springboard for a Royalist invasion; above all, they regarded Spain and her empire as a profitable market they did not want shut. Sir Gilbert Pickering and the majority of the Council favored a war with Spain. This appealed in a peculiarly convenient way both to Protestant zeal and imperialist motives. Pickering, a cousin of the poet John Dryden, spoke French fluently, and acted as Cromwell's interpreter during the negotiations with the French envoys. John Thurloe, although thought by the French to incline towards Spain, was neutral in his views, a top-ranking civil servant in advance of his age.[6] Cromwell himself listened to both sides, talked affably to everybody, studied the various arguments and, as always, was slow to make up his mind.

A principal factor in the situation was the campaign in Scotland. In February 1654 Lord Middleton had arrived there with the task of organizing and inspiriting the highland chieftains against the republican government, and had enlisted the aid of Lord Lorne, heir to the Marquis of Argyll. Cromwell offered the Scots peace and prosperity. On April 12, 1654, an ordinance of union with Scotland was passed by the English Council of State promising free trade, fair financial treatment, and representation in the Parliament at Westminster as defined in the Instrument of Government. Major General Monck, as soon as the Dutch war was over, was sent back to Edinburgh to replace the incompetent Lilburne, and with instructions to implement the union and suppress the Royalist rising. Monck demanded money and men, and until the Scottish campaign was finished Cromwell and his Council had neither the intention nor the resources to commit themselves to a new war on the continental mainland, though they did not object to finding employment for thirty or forty of the warships released by the Dutch peace. The Scottish situation also entered into the question in another way: there was a tradition of friendship between France and Scotland stretching back into the Middle Ages, and Middleton was directed and aided by King Charles II from France. Therefore the problem to be solved was which was wiser—to fight the French as the ally of Spain, or to come directly to terms with the French Government, thereby knocking away the principal prop of Royalism? For intelligent statesmen only one sensible answer was possible, and that is why there was an air of make-believe about the complicated negotiations that went on in London during the summer of 1654. Early in May Cromwell stated the English terms for a French alliance. These included, besides the repudiation of King Charles II, compensation to English merchants for their losses at sea, a promise that the French Protestants would be well treated, the handing over of Dunkirk in the event of the English joining in the war against Spain, and a payment of £200,000. These terms angered the proud musketeer de Baas, who, provoked by what he regarded as double-dealing, became involved in intrigues with a group which was conspiring against Cromwell. His indiscretion was betrayed, and in the middle of June he was summoned before the Council of State and ordered to leave England forthwith. But just as the affair of the Portuguese ambassador's brother did not prevent a treaty with Portugal, Cromwell did not allow his justifiable indignation with de Baas to interrupt the French negotiations. In July Bordeaux received new instructions from Cardinal Mazarin, and victories won by the French Marshal Turenne helped to persuade the majority of the Council of State that war against France would be too hazardous an undertaking. On the other hand, Monck was still having a tough time in Scotland, and the English Government, restricted in its financial resources by the Instrument of Government, finally recognized that it could not engage at once in a full-scale Continental war against Spain. At the same time, the Spanish ambassador had at length made clear that his King was unwilling either to permit free trade to British merchants in the

West Indies or liberty of worship for them in the Spanish dominions. So, as Thurloe wrote afterwards:[7]

> It was resolved to take all the opportunities to maintain a good understanding with France, and to send a fleet and land forces into the West Indies, where it was taken for granted the peace was already broken by the Spaniards contrary to the former treaties; and not to meddle with anything in Europe until the Spaniard should begin, unless the American fleet should be met with, which was looked upon as a lawful prize.

Such was the conclusion ultimately reached by the Council of State, whose advice on foreign affairs Oliver Cromwell was obliged to follow. The decision was a compromise between the two sides in the Council: between those who wanted a full-scale war against Spain and those who, like Lambert, thought even a colonial war too costly and risky.[8] Cromwell has sometimes been accused of hypocrisy and slyness in negotiating with Spain at all. But there is little evidence that he ever seriously contemplated a military pact with the old foes of Elizabethan England. He had, however, to provide the pro-Spanish party in his Council with evidence that such an alliance was totally impracticable.

On August 18 Cromwell gave instructions to a committee, managed by Martin Noell, a prosperous merchant and financier (a friend or relative of Thurloe), to prepare a squadron of warships to carry an expeditionary force to the Spanish West Indies. A month earlier General Robert Blake had been directed to lead a squadron into the Mediterranean in order to assert the majesty of the Commonwealth against the Bey of Algiers, who had impounded English ships and imprisoned English subjects. The presence of Blake's fleet in the Mediterranean was evidently also intended to divert the attention of Spain from the design against the West Indies and to impress the French with the punishing powers of the Commonwealth navy. At the same time Cromwell informed Bordeaux that he did not desire a close alliance but merely a general treaty of friendship with France. So the die was cast and Cromwell's foreign policy formulated: peace and friendship with the Protestants of Europe; the neutralization of France as a springboard for English Royalists (and, as Thurloe astutely remarked, if King Charles II were now forced to turn for help to Spain the traditional enmity for the home of the Inquisition would damage him in Presbyterian eyes); and a naval war in support of commerce and pursuit of treasure "beyond the line." Meanwhile the pacification of Scotland could be completed, and Cromwell might meet his first Parliament in an aura of peace and prosperity, laying claim to triumphs gained at the outset of his Protectorate.

*   *   *

By May 1654 the Protectorate seemed fully to have justified its existence. On the 23rd a public thanksgiving was held for the Dutch peace. At home the new Government had shown itself to be extraordinarily clement. No engagement was exacted to compel men to swear loyalty to the new constitution. Royalists were, so far as possible, conciliated, and Cromwell chose his officials with little regard for their past political histories. It is true that Major General Harrison had been banished from London to his father's home in Newcastle-under-Lyme, and that his friends, the leading Fifth Monarchist preachers, had been placed under arrest without trial, but Harrison made no complaint about his treatment, and the Fifth Monarchists might under the Instrument of Government have been condemned to death for treason had they been brought to trial. Cromwell gave orders that over sixty persons imprisoned for a variety of crimes punishable by death should be released and transported to the colonies. He pardoned a Welsh minister sentenced to have his hand burned for manslaughter. His opinions were consistent and exemplified in his conduct as ruler. Five years earlier he had said that "the law as it is now constituted serves only to maintain the lawyers and to encourage the rich to oppress the poor." To his first Parliament he was to say that: "To see men lose their lives for petty matters is a thing God will reckon. . . ."

Thus, at home, once two abortive plots against the Protector's life had been thwarted, an air of calm progress prevailed. Major General Monck's drive against the Scottish Royalists progressed successfully, and in Ireland Charles Fleetwood's authority was enhanced with the title of Lord Deputy. In the thanksgiving proclamation, which Cromwell clearly drew up himself, gratitude was also extended to the Lord God for the warm spring rains which relieved a drought that had threatened the crops: "That this hath been a nation of blessings in the midst whereof so many wonders have been wrought forth by the outstretched arm of the Almighty, even to astonishment and wonder," he asked "who can deny?" At that propitious moment writs were issued for a general election.

Meanwhile Cromwell, with the assistance of his Council, labored upon domestic affairs. He had at his disposal a new class of administrators, impartial and competent, with something of a civil-service cast of mind. He selected able and distinguished lawyers to be judges, with scant regard for their party affiliations. A committee was appointed to draft an ordinance for the reform of the Court of Chancery, which the Assembly of Saints had summarily abolished without providing for an alternative equity jurisdiction. The ordinance aimed at simplifying, cheapening, and speeding the functioning of the court. Two of the Commissioners of the Great Seal and the Master of the Rolls, however, objected to it both on practical and personal grounds. Cromwell insisted that it must be worked, and the Master of the Rolls obeyed. But the two Commissioners had to be replaced, and after 1657 the ordinance was allowed to lapse. Thus the conservatism of the lawyers proved weighty enough to overcome the reforming zeal of the Puritans. Yet (as Sir William Holdsworth wrote) "many of the reforms which the Commonwealth statesmen had proposed deserved to be carried out, and have in fact been carried out in the course of the succeeding centuries." A new High Court of Justice was also set up on June 13.

The question of religious organization was now settled at last after over ten years of argument. The right of private patrons to present to benefices was confirmed and the payment of tithes retained. But a commission of "triers" for the whole of England and Wales was nominated to sit in London and approve all such presentations on the basis of local certifications of worth. Later other bodies of commissioners were chosen to meet in the counties or in groups of counties, with power to eject incompetent or scandalous ministers and schoolmasters. Provided therefore that a qualified minister was selected each parish was left to manage its own affairs, and the form of service might be Presbyterian, Congregational, or Baptist, or any other in tune with the truths of Christianity regarded as fundamental by the Puritan mind. The use of the Book of Common Prayer was forbidden. But no one was compelled to attend any particular church or to accept the discipline of any particular minister. If members of a congregation objected to their minister's ways or his form of service, they were free to leave their parish church and form a new one for themselves. It was a flexible system.

Although Roman Catholics and Anglicans were excluded from the new order, Cromwell's own belief in liberty of conscience was illustrated at every level, and in office he grew more and not less tolerant. No new laws were passed against Roman Catholics, and the old ones were not much pressed. During the year Cromwell had a number of mysterious interviews with the wealthy and eccentric Roman Catholic virtuoso, Sir Kenelm Digby, who afterwards expressed his obligation to the Lord Protector for his courteous treatment. It is believed that what Digby sought was an undertaking that Roman Catholics should not be persecuted for the private celebration of the Mass.[9] Later Cromwell was to write to Mazarin, saying that while he could not publicly proclaim toleration for the Cardinal's fellow religionists he thought that under his government "Your Eminency, in behalf of Catholics, has less reason for complaint as to rigour upon men's consciences than under the Parliament." The French ambassador reported home in September 1656 that "the Catholics find their position better than under former kings who did not allow them freedom of worship."[10] Equally services conducted according to the Book of Common Prayer were left undisturbed if they were held in private. In January 1654 an Anglican squire had been informed by a correspondent in London: "The news is very current about the town that the Protector expressed thus much —that the ministry would discreetly use the Common Prayer." After the Restoration, Church of England clergy recollected how they "took the confidence, being partly emboldened by the higher powers that were, to fall to the exercise of our ministerial function again in such poor parishes as would admit us."[11] In many parts of London the Communion was administered and services held in accordance with the old liturgy. John Evelyn, the Royalist author and amateur scientist, who returned to the capital from his travels abroad in 1652, found that during the Protectorate a number of congregations met regularly for Anglican worship, which he and his wife frequently joined, and neither he nor his friends ever had any serious difficulty in arranging for services of any kind —whether for christening, Communion, weddings, or funerals —conducted with all the customary rite. Far from being a despot, Cromwell "connived at liberty."[12]

Finally the Jews were allowed to resettle in England. This was owing very largely to the persistent support of Cromwell. It seems that the matter was first raised when John Thurloe went with a mission to Holland in 1651, and there met the famous Rabbi Menasseh ben Israel. The question was discussed in the Assembly of Saints, but no decision was reached. Cromwell later suggested to a crypto-Jewish merchant who had settled in London that if Menasseh were to come over to London in person to treat it might be helpful. He duly came, and on November 12, 1655, Cromwell brought his petition before the Council of State. The Council recommended that outside opinion should be consulted, and on December 4 Cromwell presided over a conference of lawyers, theologians, and others. The lawyers said there was no bar to the readmission of the Jews, but the theologians objected and so did the merchants of the City of London. Cromwell, realizing that no help was to be obtained from the conference, referred the matter back to his Council of State. In March 1656, during the opening stages of the Spanish war (when Jewish intelligence proved valuable), he again pressed for reconsideration of the question, and eventually, on June 25, permission was granted by the Council for the Jews to hold private services (as the Anglicans and Roman Catholics), and to purchase a cemetery outside the city. In December a house was rented as a synagogue and a cemetery opened at Mile End. Thus four times Cromwell attempted to persuade his Councilors to agree to the admission of the Jews before they reluctantly consented.[13] The episode exemplified his liberal attitude of mind on matters of religion and also the limitations of his own influence as Protector.

During the Protectorate education flourished.[14] It was a golden age for the grammar schools, where Oliver Cromwell and his friends were brought up. In addition there was a large number of private schools offering much the same education as did the endowed schools. Eton and Winchester, Westminster and St. Paul's, Repton and Felsted were among the thriving establishments. Cromwell sent all his four sons to Felsted. Trustees for the maintenance of ministers were empowered to make grants towards the cost of schoolmasters, under the immediate supervision of the Lord Protector and the Council of State, and did so on a fair scale. The qualifications of schoolmasters were the concern of the Commissioners, who were responsible for ejecting "scandalous, ignorant, and insufficient ministers." Most of the schoolmasters passed muster, but the heads of Bedford and Reading grammar schools were dismissed. An ordinance was also approved for the regulation and government of the universities and one or two famous schools, and in general the Protectorate showed itself enlightened in its treatment both of the grammar schools and the old universities. Later Cromwell was to approve the foundation of a university college at Durham. As Chancellor of Oxford he presented the Bodleian Library with twenty-five ancient manuscripts and arranged for an annuity to meet the salary of a Reader in Divinity.

Altogether between December 1653 and September 1654, eighty-two ordinances were published, covering not merely the reform of the law and the control of religion and education, but the reorganization of the Treasury, the banning of dueling and cockfighting, and the discouragement of swearing by porters. But the more extreme measures that are often associated with Cromwell's name, such as the tightening of the Puritan Sunday and the punishment of wandering minstrels as rogues, were introduced not by him and his Council but by the free Parliament once it met. Although the list of ordinances contained much routine matter, it does not compare unfavorably with the feverish legislative activity of the Assembly of Saints.

When he published his biography of Oliver Cromwell more than fifty years ago, Sir Charles Firth wrote that "nothing could be farther from the truth" than the statement that Cromwell, unlike Napoleon, failed to display any interests in social reform or leave any evidence of a legislative mind. Yet that view has persisted. Cromwell showed in fact in his speeches, his actions, and his ordinances a genuine desire to reform the law, to make its processes cheaper and more accessible, and to render it more merciful. In religion he gave liberty to Protestant Christianity, which was subjected to state discipline only in so far as it was necessary to prevent public disorder or disloyalty. In matters of education he was helpful and generous. That some of the things he wanted to do for the Commonwealth were not completed and that all traces of the Protectorate's legislation were erased from the statute book at the Restoration was scarcely his fault. He was granted only a bare five years to govern, and throughout them he was handicapped by the restrictions imposed upon him by the circumstances of the revolution and the control of his Councils and Parliaments, which were often less liberal than he was. If his was largely an opportunist approach, he also had a generous and merciful attitude of mind, a large view in which he strove to comprehend order and liberty. Those who have blamed him for not driving faster or more furiously towards social reconstruction or a Puritan millennium can hardly have understood the art of government.

Notes

1. J. S. Roskell, "The Office and Dignity of Protector of England" in *English Historical Review*, LXVIII (1953).

2. W. S. Holdsworth, *A History of English Law,* VI (1924), 155.

3. H. R. Trevor-Roper, "Oliver Cromwell and His Parliaments" in *Essays Presented to Sir Lewis Namier* (1956).

4. *Diary of Thomas Burton,* III, 111; *Ludlow Memoirs* (ed. Firth), I, 378, note 1.

5. *Recueil des Instructions, etc.: Angleterre, 1648–1665* (ed. J. J. Jusserand, 1929), VI.

6. Cf. S. F. Bischoffshausen, *Die Politik des Protectors Oliver Cromwell in der Auffassung und Thätigkeit seines Ministers des Staats-Secretärs John Thurloe* (1899).

7. *Ibid.,* 199. The appendices contain three versions of John Thurloe's own survey of Cromwell's foreign policy.

8. See Edward Montagu's notes of council meetings in *Clarke Papers,* III, 203 seq.

9. R. T. Petersson, *Sir Kenelm Digby: The Ornament of England 1603–1665* (1956), Part III, Chap. IV, "Cromwell's Catholic Favourite."

10. P.R.O. 31/3/100 f. 361.

11. Robert S. Bosher, *The Making of the Restoration Settlement, 1649–1662* (1951), Chap. I.

12. *The Diary of John Evelyn* (ed. E. S. de Beer, 1955), III, 77 seq.

13. Cecil Roth, *A History of the Jews in England* (1949) Chap. VII, corrected by Cecil Roth, "The Return of the Jews to England" in *The Listener,* July 5, 1956. I dissent from the view there expressed by Dr. Roth that the main credit lay with "the attitude of the man in the street." Cromwell appears to have pushed through the resettlement in face of widespread opposition.

14. W. A. L. Vincent, *The State and School Education, 1640–1660, in England and Wales* (1950).

Chapter 19

Cromwell and the First Protectorate Parliament

THE FREE ELECTIONS promised by the "Instrument of Government" were held during the summer of 1654. In a number of constituencies—in spite of the restriction of the county franchise to owners of £200 of property—lively contests took place. Accounts have survived for example, of the election in Wiltshire.[1] Here ten members had to be chosen, and two lists were drawn up, one headed by a young Councilor of State, Sir Anthony Ashley Cooper, to be known in future history as the first Earl of Shaftesbury, Father of the Whigs, and the "Achitophel" of John Dryden's satirical poem, and the other by Lieutenant General Edmund Ludlow, that indomitable and humorless republican who, having reluctantly gone to Dublin at Cromwell's request, had repudiated the Protectorate as soon as it was established. General Ludlow was still in Ireland when the election took place, but his supporters in Wiltshire were noisy and energetic. Cooper and his friends canvassed busily pointing out that the return of conservative-minded M.P.'s ready to sustain the Protectorate was more likely to contribute to peace and prosperity at home than that of disgruntled republicans. Cooper had the backing of most of the local ministers. When the deputy sheriff (the writs were sent to the sheriffs) tried to conduct the election in Wilton too many voters arrived to allow orderly proceedings in the county court. So both parties adjourned to Stonehenge. Here, amid the megaliths, a poll was taken, and Cooper's list won a narrow victory.

Such was a county election. Whether it was typical or not nobody knows. But it is unlikely that there were contests in the majority of constituencies any more than there had been for earlier Parliaments. It does not seem that the abolition of many of the smaller boroughs— the "pocket boroughs" of a later age—made any difference to the results. For most of the local gentry, who had formerly represented these boroughs in Parliament or whose families had more or less prescriptive rights to such seats, had little difficulty in obtaining their election in the counties. Altogether a quarter of the members who had represented constituencies in England and Wales in the Long Parliament were elected again to the first Protectorate Parliament. In fact, Cromwell's first Parliament was markedly similar in complexion to the Long Parliament after the Royalist members had withdrawn from it.

The new Parliament contained groups of lawyers, merchants, and professional officers, but the bulk of the members were country gentlemen of Puritan persuasions, as Cromwell himself had been. A few Royalists were elected in Wales and some of the western counties. The Government had a useful block of supporters: including the members of the Council of State, officials of one kind or another, and Cromwell's own relatives and friends, it numbered in all some sixty members from England and Wales, apart from the officers named for Scotland and Ireland, not all of whom attended. Balancing them were about forty experienced Presbyterian M.P.s, who had been excluded by the army or had withdrawn at the time of "Pride's Purge" in 1648. In addition, there were another forty irreconcilable republicans who regarded the Protectorate as a betrayal of the "good old cause." The republican leaders were Sir Arthur Haselrigg, who was elected both for Newcastle-upon-Tyne and for Leicestershire, and Thomas Scot, M.P. for Wycombe in Buckinghamshire. Haselrigg more than any other man had been responsible for provoking Cromwell into dissolving the Rump, since at the very last moment he had repudiated the compromise that was in the process of being reached between Cromwell and the followers of Sir Henry Vane. When the Protectorate Parliament met, Haselrigg at once rallied round him both the out-and-out republicans and many of the Presbyterians, who still smarted at the way they had been treated by the army since 1648. But Haselrigg's following numbered only eighty as compared with over one hundred members of the court party. The rest of the House consisted of the independent gentry, who in every Parliament from that time onwards for more than a century determined the character and conduct of the British House of Commons.[2]

But an analysis of the membership of the House of Commons, however complete one can make it, does not in itself explain the relations between Parliament and the executive. Cromwell in calling Parliament naturally hoped that the creditable record of the Protectorate Government during the first nine months of its existence would speak for itself, and that the obvious failure of both the Rump and the Assembly of Saints to provide anything like such efficient government as his would induce the members to work with him in garnering the fruits of the Puritan revolution. This may be described as intellectual optimism, and passion rather than reason was to rule.

Parliament, as soon as it met, recalled its privileges, its traditions, its dignity, and above all the victory it had won over the Stuart monarchy. It re-elected the Speaker of the Long Parliament; it reappointed the Clerk of the Long Parliament; it ordered the mace to be brought in by the former Sergeant at Arms—that very symbol of the House's authority that had been so insultingly treated by Cromwell when he broke the Rump. The phalanx of nearly one hundred former members of the Long Parliament who awaited his opening speech on Sunday, September 3, could not, with all the good will and patriotism in the world, have forgotten or forgiven the humiliations inflicted upon them in earlier days by Cromwell's army. The first thought of most of the members was not only that the House of Commons had now to be restored to its rightful place in the state, but that here was an opportunity for revenge upon the army leaders who had been the authors of the "Instrument" under which they had been called to Westminster.

That was the practical situation; but to turn for a moment to theory: Ever since the time of the Grand Remonstrance English political thinkers had been feeling their way towards a doctrine of "sovereignty." Sir Robert Filmer, a Royalist, had written in 1648: "We do not flatter ourselves if we hope ever to be governed without an arbitrary power, whether one or many." Albertus Ward in *Eight Reasons Categorical* (1653) wrote: "The question never was whether we should be governed by an arbitrary power, but in whose hands it should be."[3] Henry Parker, one of the ablest political writers of his generation, is said to have been the first man to realize that a struggle for "sovereignty" was in progress. He argued that whereas before the Civil War the king in Parliament was sovereign, once the king withdrew Parliament had become sovereign.[4] All this was quite alien to the traditional views in which Cromwell himself and many of his friends had been brought up during the reigns of Queen Elizabeth I and King James I; they still thought in terms of a "balanced constitution," and the checks and balances of the "Instrument of Government" were congenial to that frame of mind. Thus even had they all loved one another as Christians should, a clash of ideals could be expected when the first Protectorate Parliament met.

Of the 400 or more members actually elected and approved over 300 were present when they gathered at Westminster on September 3, 1654. The day had been chosen because it was the anniversary of the battles of Dunbar and Worcester, and the new House of Commons was thus reminded of the services that the Lord Protector had performed for the Commonwealth. But it was a Sunday, and therefore a curious day on which to hold an opening session. In fact, the members did not assemble until five o'clock in the afternoon after attending the evening service. Then Major General John Lambert, himself a member elected for two different constituencies but also a Councilor of State and author of the "Instrument of Government," entered the House and told his fellow members that Cromwell wished to see them in the Painted Chamber. John Bradshaw, who had presided over the trial of King Charles I and was understandably an ardent republican, led a defiant cry of "Sit still!" Nevertheless, the members duly went to hear what the Lord Protector had to say. He merely gave them a formal and Christian welcome, and explained that as it was the Sabbath he would postpone his political address until the morrow. At nine o'clock the M.P.s adjourned until nine the next morning.

Cromwell then drove in a coach of state from Whitehall Palace to Westminster Abbey. In his coach were his second son Henry and Lambert. The Master of the Horse, John Claypole, who had married Cromwell's favorite daughter, led along the Protector's war horse, and the procession included members of the Council of State, officials and functionaries, and soldiers of the lifeguard. The French ambassador reported that Cromwell was "very modestly clothed and attended to the Parliament," and the Venetian representative that "his external demeanor was always very humble and modest." One must be careful of accepting later accounts of extravagant royal grandeur, for any trappings even faintly reminiscent of the old monarchy would naturally have affronted—and did affront—the more austere republicans.

Cromwell's speech had been written and arranged with care. He defended the Protectorate as the organ of conservative reform, whose program was to protect liberty of conscience, liberty of subjects, and liberty of property. He criticized the Puritan extremists—the Levellers and the Fifth Monarchy men—as authors of political destruction. The Levellers, he urged, would have brought economic communism, the Fifth Monarchy men have promoted spiritual chaos. His own policy was "healing and settling," his Biblical precedent that day when the Israelites had been brought out of Egypt through the wilderness into the promised land of Canaan. Having presented the case for his Government, he turned to commend its achievements in foreign policy, the reform of the law, the reorganization of Church, and the reduction of taxation. He spoke simply as "one that doth resolve to be a fellow servant with you, to the interest of these great affairs and of the peoples of these nations," and he assured his audience that they were a "free parliament" called "to put the topstone" to the work of pacification "and make the nation happy."

How did the members receive this skillful speech? Thurloe reported that "as often as he spoke in his speech of liberty and religion the members seemed to rejoice."[5] On the other hand, they plainly disliked their dependence upon him. They did not care to be reminded that they owed their very existence as a "free parliament" to the good will of the army. Pride in their past, resentment at the treatment of the Long Parliament by the army, and a corporate sense of dignity gave an emotional edge to their early debates. Haselrigg, a wealthy man "of morose and haughty temper,"[6] felt the mantle of John Pym wrapped around him. To him Oliver was another Charles I writ large. When the Cromwellians in the House suggested, on September 5, that they should at once take the "Instrument of Government" into consideration, he perceived his opportunity, for in Grand Committee the new constitution might be torn to shreds. What the new courtiers had in mind was that the House should approve the constitution as a whole or in principle, and it was on that basis that the matter was first debated. Sir Matthew Hale, an eminent judge, at once proposed a reasonable compromise, namely that they should agree that "the Government should be in the Parliament of the people of England . . . and a single person, qualified with such instructions as Parliament should think fit." At first a majority was willing to accept that formula, but the republican leaders prevented its being put to the vote, and on the following day "the differences seemed so wide, the contest so hot, and the struggling so violent on both sides, as there seemed no hope of a fair agreement." The republicans argued vehemently for the sovereignty of Parliament, for a return to the committee system of Pym's time, in which so many of them had taken part.

The officials of the new regime were driven bluntly to retort that it was essential to maintain Cromwell's detached position, that he could not now be expected to lay down the civil sword he had girt on and become again the unquestioning servant of a Parliament sitting in perpetuity.

Next day (September 9) tempers in the House cooled. Though the case for approving outright the words "government by one person and the people assembled in Parliament" lost ground, the general inclination was to confer on Cromwell an "honourable status" which "might render him very conspicuous to the world and testify the great obligations which the English nation had to his virtues." In other words, he was to be offered the ceremonial place designed in the last stages of the first Civil War for King Charles I. The Cromwellians would no more consent to this than the Royalists had done—and they spoke for their master. They feared the tyranny of a sovereign Parliament claiming all power in the state, as the Rump under Vane and Haselrigg had done. They insisted instead on the need for the "co-ordination" of executive and legislature. The republicans replied (unhistorically) that the supreme power was originally in the people, whom Parliament alone represented—and that they could not set up "two supremes," for one would always quarrel with the other and never be at peace. Thus an impasse was reached. It was a genuine conflict of principles, and if Hale's compromise was rejected or sidestepped, one side or the other had to yield.

Yet it was a strange thing, which has never been satisfactorily explained, that, according to Guibon Goddard, M.P. for King's Lynn, who was present and is our chief authority for these debates,[7] when the House rose at eight o'clock on the evening of September 11 the general feeling was that, after all, Hale's compromise ought to be accepted. Why then did Cromwell and his advisers take the drastic step they took next morning?

A possible solution is that by that time they had received intelligence that the divisions in Parliament were leading not merely to unrest in the capital but revolt in the country. Major General Harrison, who alone of Cromwell's critics had a sufficient following to divide the army against him, and was piously indignant about the whole nature of the Protectorate and its religious policy, had been sounding a trumpet to the extreme sects in the north of England and in Wales. It was said that he actually collected 20,000 signatures to a petition against the Protector. Orders were sent from Whitehall that he was to be arrested at his home in Staffordshire and brought up to London. A Leveller movement was also on foot organized by John Wildman, that saturnine figure from the conspiratorial underworld, who had been elected M.P. for Scarborough but had been forbidden by the Council of State to take his seat. Early in September, Thurloe as Secretary of State had received reports that a number of discontented colonels, including John Okey, commander of the dragoons in the New Model Army and an M.P. for Scotland, had been conferring with Wildman at his London house and in the City taverns. Among those who had attended these meetings was Vice Admiral John Lawson, another Leveller leader, who carried great weight in the fleet that was preparing to sail for the West Indies. Cromwell must have felt that unless the authority of the Protectorate was at once publicly asserted, the loyalty of the armed forces would be undermined. A second factor may well have been that action was being taken in Parliament to reverse the tolerationist policy of the Protectorate which lay so close to Cromwell's heart. As the price of Presbyterian support, Haselrigg had offered to "suppress the sects." On September 11 the House had voted to call into being another Westminster Assembly, which might have meant the fastening of Presbyterianism on the country, and thereby a return to the rigid ecclesiastical policy in favor before Pride's Purge.

Such must have been the reasons that induced Cromwell on the morning of September 12 to affirm his authority by force. After ordering the Lord Mayor of London to surround the Parliament house with guards, he came by water from Whitehall again to address the members in the Painted Chamber. Cromwell spoke with emotion. So far as the argument of his speech was concerned, he merely repeated what had already been set out by his own supporters in the House. He declared that he had been called to his office by God and the nation, and had received the explicit approval not only of the army, the City of London, which had ceremoniously entertained him, the judges and justices of the peace who had acted under his commissions, but also many cities and counties which had thanked him for assuming office. These reasons were less specious than they have appeared to later democratic readers. For, after all, Parliament itself was neither democratic nor fully representative. Cromwell then went on to claim that he must appeal to Parliament to accept four "fundamentals"— government by a single person and a Parliament, a guarantee that Parliaments should not be perpetual, liberty of conscience in religion, and the division of the control over the armed forces between the "single person" and Parliament. The last was essential because it was a guarantee against absolutism. According to the Venetian representative in London, Cromwell spoke with more feeling about it than any of the others:[8]

> He said he had no intention of resisting the authority of Parliament, in proof of which he meant it to be free, all members being at liberty to speak and propose, and, where necessary for the commonweal, to remonstrate. During the session of Parliament the power of legislating and reducing or imposing taxes was vested in the House, which had the right of disposing of the revenue, to supply the wants and secure the tranquility of the state. But the army had been entrusted to him alone. . . .

Such was a foreigner's impression of what Cromwell said.

Cromwell did not think of himself as a dictator, even when he exerted, as he did now, the power of the sword, selecting like any good strategist the objectives for which he proposed to fight. "I appeal to the Lord," he said, "that the liberty of England, the liberty of the people, the avoiding of tyrannous impositions, either upon men as men, or Christians as Christians, is made so safe by this act of settlement that it will speak sufficiently for itself." Even then Cromwell did not require that the M.P.s should concede his four fundamentals, only that they should, according to the terms of the indentures by which the sheriffs had returned them, undertake not to alter the government "as it is settled in one person and a parliament."

Cromwell was no more a consistent political thinker than any of the other great statesmen in English history. He did not want government to be tidy in theory, but to be effective in practice. He was neither a democrat in a modern sense nor a tyrant in the classical mold. His approach was Elizabethan, and yet in his own way he was groping towards a doctrine of the "separation of powers" that was embodied during the next century in the constitution of the United States of America. Parliament, for its part, was equally groping towards another future constitutional form, that of the direction of the nation by leadership within the House of Commons. Had the Protectorate been firmly established and survived, had Cromwell himself lived longer than he did, the evolution of the British constitution might have been very different. As it was, neither side was really prepared to compromise. Haselrigg and the republicans preferred to withdraw from the House rather than confer any approval upon the Protectoral system as originally conceived by the army. The rest of the members of Parliament—about 300 of them—agreed in the end to sign the recognition demanded of them, but afterwards returned with fresh appetite to their self-appointed task as a constituent assembly, altering and expanding the "Instrument of Government" to ensure parliamentary sovereignty, half-forgetful of the fact that across the sea the young King and his court were awaiting their opportunity to profit from the quarrels in London and return to destroy the political and religious privileges they had lost in battle.

*   *   *

In spite of distant rumblings of unrest in the Commonwealth, it appeared momentarily as if Cromwell's intervention might result in an understanding between him and his Parliament. In a short time 240 members had signed the recognition, and they began to consider how they could induce others to do so. The problem was solved (a solution plausibly attributed to Sir Anthony Ashley Cooper) by the House of Commons itself voting that the recognition or subscription should not be construed to prevent members from examining or altering any of the forty-two articles of the "Instrument of Government" except the first. Thus the members preserved their *amour propre* and stressed their independence. On September 22 three of Cromwell's "four fundamentals" were approved in principle, and while the House was debating the fourth fundamental, the control of the armed forces, Cromwell held out an olive branch by writing a letter to the Speaker volunteering to acquaint the members with his military plans, that is to say, the aims of the two naval expeditions that were about to sail. After a brief debate he received the polite reply that for security reasons it was thought wiser that such plans should not be divulged and that "the design should be wholly left to the management of the Lord Protector." The Venetian representative, who was anxiously following events, reported that Cromwell's gesture "won over the Parliament, who told him they knew his zeal for its service."

A week later Cromwell had a nearly fatal accident while driving a coach and six horses in Hyde Park. The horses, gray Frieslands, which had been presented to him by the

Count of Oldenburg, got out of hand and threw him so that he caught his foot in the reins and fell, a pistol in his pocket exploding as he did so. He was out of action for a fortnight, and Parliament realized that, after all, worse things might befall the country than having Cromwell for its chief executive. At any rate, it struck a foreign observer that though Parliament met every day to revise and approve the "Instrument," it was "now offering no opposition to the present Government, but was rather seeking to consolidate it."[9]

Yet that November was a trying month for Cromwell. He was lame after his accident. On the sixteenth his mother died at the age of eighty-nine, after giving him her last blessing. Pamphlets critical of the regime were circulating freely, including the remonstrance of the discontented colonels who had been cashiered. The navy had to be placated, for while General Blake's expedition had set sail the previous month, the West India force was still in port, and its chief officers, General Penn (the naval commander) and Colonel Venables (the military commander) were quarreling over their relative spheres of influence and complaining about their supply officer, General Desborough. Eventually the inter-services dispute was settled, and a meeting of the Council of Officers held in Whitehall on November 29 swore to maintain the "Instrument of Government" and to live and die with the Lord Protector.

The news of this last meeting, however, provoked the House of Commons, sensitive to a new threat of military dictation. Rumors that an immediate dissolution was intended shook the members. Thus, in spite of the continued absence of the extreme republicans, it was only after violent debates that on December 6 the House voted by a majority of two (83 to 81) to confirm the powers and position of the Lord Protector broadly as they were originally constituted. Meanwhile the opposition of the independent gentry was vigorous enough to limit the control exercised by the Protector over the armed forces by tightening the purse strings. Members of the court party were offended by these maneuvers, so that some of them said "they cared not ever to come into the parliament house again." Cromwell himself had to make it clear that unless taxes were voted by Christmas Day the army would have to resort to "free quarter," that is to say, requisitioning.

After two months debating the House of Commons had gone back on its own decisions. Not only was it attempting to wrest control of the army from Cromwell, thus defying his fourth fundamental, but it began to irritate him over the question about which he felt most keenly of all—that of religious toleration. It demanded the sole right to legislate against atheism, blasphemy, and "popery." It ordered the arrest of several religious extremists, including John Biddle, a Unitarian, and appointed a committee to examine his offenses. Cromwell showed a different temper when at about the same date he had an interview with two Fifth Monarchy men, who had escaped from their prison at Windsor and resumed their agitation in the City of London. One of them, Simpson by name, told Cromwell to his face that he was a traitor who had broken his vows by abandoning the causes of true republicanism and religious liberty. Cromwell ordered Simpson's release, after dismissing him with "an exhortation to carry [himself] soberly." Later, after Parliament was dissolved, Cromwell saved Biddle's life by releasing him on bail. "Where," Cromwell demanded, "shall we have men of a universal spirit? Everyone desires to have liberty, but none will give it." He recognized that those who tried to uphold religious liberty, as he did, laid themselves open not to gratitude—he received no thanks from the Fifth Monarchists or the Quakers, whom he treated with a tolerant understanding as long as they did not preach sedition or organize disturbances—but merely to abuse from every side: "so that," as he wrote to a friend, "whosoever labours to walk with an even foot between the several interests of the people of God for healing and accommodating their differences is sure to have reproaches and anger from some of all sorts."

In that same letter Cromwell poured out his heart, as he seldom did:

> My exercise of that little faith and patience I have was never greater. . . . And truly this is much of my portion at present, so unwilling are men to be healed and atoned, and although it be thus with me, yet the Lord will not let it always be so. If I have innocency and integrity the Lord hath mercy and truth and will own it.

While Parliament continued its work of revising the constitution to the neglect of almost everything else, Cromwell carried on with his administrative duties. He held the French ambassador in play, watched the progress of Blake's Mediterranean expedition, discussed the final details of the West

Indian plan, and examined with his Council of State the question of naval dispositions when winter ended. He wrote letters aimed at promoting the reopening of commerce following the end of the Dutch war, and offered the new Swedish King his mediation in a dispute that had broken out between Sweden and the Duchy of Bremen. He emphasized that he regarded it as his duty as head of the English Commonwealth to work for the common safety and peace of Protestants everywhere. In view of reports of Royalist and Leveller plots, he strengthened the garrison of the Tower of London. And he nominated a new Professor of Greek at Cambridge University.

During January 1655 the attitude of the majority of the Commons hardened against Cromwell. The revenue, although at last voted, was reduced to such an absurdly low figure that it would have been quite impossible for him to supply the navy, protect the sea routes, maintain the policing of England, garrison Scotland and Wales, and guard the coasts against invasion. In a series of votes, all carried by narrow margins, the House defiantly repudiated every one of Cromwell's "fundamentals." It omitted his office from the title of the constitution when its revision had been completed; it retained the sole right to define penalties for atheism and blasphemy; it twice rejected a proposal by Cromwell's supporters that the army should come under the joint control of Protector, Council, and Parliament, and voted that "the militia of this Commonwealth ought not to be raised, formed, or made use of, but by common consent of the people assembled in Parliament." The financial arrangements finally approved meant reducing the pay of officers and men, the disbanding of a large part of the army, and the starvation of the navy. On January 10 the House rejected by 107 votes to 95 a motion to hold a conference with the Lord Protector about the new constitution before it was engrossed, and a week later decided that if Cromwell refused to accept the whole constitution exactly as it had been rewritten by Parliament, then every article in the bill should be deemed null and void. In other words, Cromwell was told he must acquiesce in the sovereignty of Parliament or resign.

How did it come about that whereas in November it had looked as if a *modus vivendi* between Parliament and Protector would be found, by January every hope of an understanding had vanished? It has been suggested that the real explanation was that Oliver Cromwell had proved himself to be incapable of managing Parliament as Queen Elizabeth I had done,[10] although he was himself an experienced parliamentarian and many members of the first Protectorate Parliament were his old friends and colleagues. Yet contemporary foreign observers did not think that Cromwell was unreasonable. As late as January 19 the Venetian representative in London wrote: "His Highness . . . had handled it all along with tact and dissimulation rather than by violent methods."[11]

One difficulty was that he was inadequately served by his ministers. If Cromwell lacked the personality of a Tudor queen, John Thurloe was no William Cecil. The Government party, if capably led, might easily have kept its majority (as an analysis of the membership and the closely contested votes shows), but first John Lambert had offended the House by proposing in October that the office of Lord Protector should be made hereditary, and then young Ashley Cooper had gone further and brought in a motion during December that Cromwell should be offered the crown. Cromwell actually instructed his friends and relations to vote against Cooper's proposal, but the damage was done, and on January 5 Cooper resigned his membership in the Council of State.[12] Cromwell's generals, like Lambert and Desborough, were extraordinarily flat-footed in the House; they did not understand its traditions and uttered veiled threats. In the second place, the non-military members feared the army, remembering, as so many of them did with personal rancor, the episodes of Pride's Purge and the breaking of the Rump. What they failed to appreciate was that mere paper guarantees would not enable them to snatch the power of the sword from Cromwell unless he were willing to surrender it. When they refused to consult him over the proposals for revising the constitution and ordered him to take it or leave it as it stood, they were saying in effect that the country could be governed without a chief executive as it had been in the time of the Long Parliament.

Cromwell did not believe, and never had believed, that this was true. He thought that the provocation of the armed services, the absorption in constitutional minutiae, the trend towards religious intolerance, the failure by the House over a period of five months to attend to urgent legislative questions, all showed Parliament's incapacity for government. He knew that the quarreling between Westminster and Whitehall had fomented unrest and heartened the Royalists. Above all, he thought that Parliament was betraying the causes of the revolution. When on January 15 the House resolved that the Unitarian Biddle had been guilty of "horrid, blasphemous and execrable opinions," and had ordered that a bill should be brought in for his punishment, he saw that far from "liberty of conscience" being realized under the Protectorate, the intention was to kill and persecute for religious opinions.

Is there not yet upon the spirits of men a strange itch? [he asked]. Nothing can satisfy them, unless they can put their fingers upon their brethren's consciences to pinch them there. To do this was no part of the contest we had with the common adversary. . . . Is it ingenuous to ask liberty, and not to give it? What greater hypocrisy than for those who were oppressed by the bishops, to become the greatest oppressors themselves, as soon as their yoke was removed?

So as soon as he felt himself entitled to do so, Oliver Cromwell dissolved his first Parliament. On January 22 he addressed its members in a speech compounded of sorrow, anger, contempt, and disappointment. He claimed that he had been patient and had left them alone, but that their conduct had paved the way to a renewal of civil warfare. The Cavaliers and Levellers had grasped their chance to conspire. The conduct of the Commons had been inimicable to religious liberty, had undermined the discipline of the army, and had contributed nothing constructive to the welfare of the Commonwealth. For his part he was willing to consent to any reasonable scheme for a balanced government, and he had rejected more than once any proposal that his office should be hereditary. He recognized that government "was not a patrimony," and that nobody knew whether a ruler "may beget a fool or a wise man." Yet he was convinced that he himself had been chosen by God to lead a people blessed by God. He denied that he was responsible for creating the situation in which he found himself as chief executive. "I say this, not only to this assembly but to the world, that that man liveth not that can come to me and charge me that I have in these great revolutions made necessities. . . ." He was guiltless of cunning, but they had labored to destroy his government, and the army was now upon free quarter. He concluded by bluntly saying that he did not think it was for the common or public good that they should continue to sit.

It was a rambling and bitter speech. His temper, so long under duress, had conquered him, his disappointment in the fervid hopes he had felt when Parliament first met had disarmed him, robbing him of the tact he had once displayed. He may have been pushed on by soldiers like Lambert and Desborough so abruptly to dismiss a group of men, many of whom were, after all, not unfavorable to his Government, but the decision was his own. Yet, thinking in terms of things as they were and not as they might have been in the age of democracy, the historian may ask: would the Commonwealth have survived if Cromwell had resigned his office in January 1655? For no statesman of any strength or character or consciousness of his own quality could have agreed to stay in power on the restrictive terms inexorably laid down by a very small majority of the House of Commons. Would not anarchy have followed, as it was to do later when he died?

General Robert Blake, as brilliant a sailor as Cromwell was a soldier, was then at sea exalting the prestige of Britain as a Great Power by proclaiming her naval might in the Mediterranean. Blake was a patriot without blemish and a religious and honest republican, who had served alike in the Rump and in the Assembly of Saints and had been elected M.P. for Bridgwater in the Protectorate Parliament. When he learned the news of the dissolution he wrote as follows to John Thurloe:[13]

> You inform me of the dissolution of Parliament, with the grounds and consequences of it. I was not much surprised with the intelligence; the slow proceedings and awkward motions of that assembly giving great cause to suspect it would come to some such period, and I cannot but exceedingly wonder that there should remain so strong a spirit of prejudice and animosity in the minds of men who profess themselves most affectionate patriots as to postpone the necessary ways and means for the preservation of the Commonwealth, especially in such a time of concurrence of the mischievous plots and designs, both of new and old enemies, tending all to the destruction of the same.

Obsessed by its desire for political supremacy, Parliament

had forgotten that the country desperately needed governing.

Notes

1. *Ludlow Memoirs*, I, 388–90, and Appendix V.

2. I have analyzed the members of this Parliament with the aid of the official *Return* (1878) and the list given in *The Parliamentary History of England* (1763), XX. I have compared the names with those given in Bruton and Pennington, *op. cit.*, and Keeler, *op. cit.* My conclusions differ from those of Abbott, but of course the latter books had not been published when he wrote. Although my calculations are necessarily rough and will be superseded when the official history of Parliament appears, I think they are not likely to prove seriously wrong.

3. I owe these quotations to George L. Mosse, *op. cit.*

4. For Parker's views, see W. K. Jordan, *Men of Substance* (1942).

5. *Thurloe State Papers*, II, 588.

6. Add. MSS. 27990, f. 42.

7. *Diary of Thomas Burton*, Vol. I introduction; the quotations from the parliamentary debates given in the chapter are taken from this.

8. *Calendar of State Papers* (*Venetian*), *1653–1654*, 267.

9. *Ibid.*, 271.

10. Mr. Trevor-Roper emphasizes this point in his essay, *loc. cit.*

11. *Calendar of State Papers* (*Venetian*), *1655–1656*, 15.

12. L. F. Brown, *The First Earl of Shaftesbury* (1933) attributes Cooper's withdrawal to his having been refused the hand of Mary Cromwell in marriage and to jealousy of Lambert. But the more likely explanation was the rebuff to his proposal to offer the crown to Cromwell.

13. *Thurloe State Papers*, III, 232.

Chapter 20

The High-water Mark of the Protectorate

IT IS HARD for the historian confidently to interpret the mind of Oliver Cromwell from the records that remain of the Protectorate. Very few of his private or personal letters have survived. His official correspondence appears rarely to have been dictated by him: it was usually drafted by his Secretary of State or some other official, and although the drafts were approved by him and embodied his policies, the language is scrupulously diplomatic and the meaning becomingly wrapped up. In the case of Napoleon Bonaparte, we can follow what he did and thought every day of his life during his period of supremacy, and we know that his decisions were his own, sharply revealing the majestic ambitions of an Italian *condottiere*.[1] In spite of all the researches of a hundred years of scientific history, no such body of evidence lights up Cromwell. Nor have we more than occasional indications of what went on when the Lord Protector met his Council of State or his chosen advisers independently. It has recently been suggested that a clearer view of Cromwell's policy, methods, and even character can be obtained from the dispatches of the foreign envoys then in London than from his letters and speeches. But, in the first place, these envoys, however conscientious they were, were strangers who spoke no English and had few contacts with Englishmen; secondly, they rarely saw the Lord Protector himself, and their observations seldom are of assured value except in assessing Cromwell as a diplomatist. Thus we are still compelled to rely chiefly on Cromwell's own writings and sayings —such as they are—and upon the accounts of him by Englishmen who talked to him and knew him in the days of his supremacy.

It may be argued that the very paucity of personal letters and memoranda by Cromwell reflects upon his administrative abilities; that he was a steersman whose hands were not constantly upon the tiller, a ruler who failed to harry his officials or throw out ideas for reform. But every statesman has his own way of governing. Some statesmen—Lloyd George was an example—prefer interviews to reading papers; others, like

Sir Winston Churchill, have kept up a stream of notes, criticisms, suggestions, and instructions. It is probable that Cromwell's method was to examine questions in detail with his Councillors of State (he often attended council meetings), and he was always prepared to meet both his friends and his critics face to face. Not only was that his custom, but it was his deliberate practice to consider, to consult, and to meditate. On most questions he made up his mind very slowly. From his experiences in political life he realized that there must always be a source of authority in the state and constitutional forms that ought to be followed. About what that source was and which those forms should be he had an open mind. When he was commander in chief he had long adhered to the authority of the Rump Parliament. Now that he was a Protector, who had failed to come to terms with his first Parliament, he clung to the "Instrument of Government" as the foundation of his authority: the "Instrument" had prescribed consultation with his Council of State both on domestic and foreign affairs, and, as he explained to foreign envoys, he was not prepared to reach any decisions without its concurrence. In those consultations all expressed their opinion fearlessly.

Yet Cromwell was troubled that his integrity and dedication to the service of his country were not more widely appreciated by the men who had acted with him in the Long Parliament and fought with him in the civil wars. "The wretched jealousies that are amongst us and the spirit of calumny," he wrote to his son-in-law Charles Fleetwood, "turns all into gall and wormwood." An earlier letter (of April 1656) to his son Henry illustrates the value he attached to upright behavior and a conciliatory outlook:

> Study to be innocent [he wrote] and to answer every occasion, roll yourself upon God which to do needs much grace. Cry to the Lord to give you a plain single heart. Take heed of being overjealous, lest your apprehensions of others cause you to offend. Know that uprightness will preserve you. . . . Take care of making it a business to be too hard for the men who contest with you. . . .

In that letter, written in intimacy to his ablest son, one comes closest to Cromwell in undress. We know how he struggled in private conversations to measure the motives and spirit that drove men like the republican Edmund Ludlow, the Quaker George Fox, and the Fifth Monarchy man Thomas Harrison, forward along what appeared to be tortuous and dangerous paths. John Rogers, the Fifth Monarchy preacher, who had long interviews with Cromwell during February 1655, said that the Lord Protector often gave men with whom he had conversed the impression that he agreed and sympathized with them. What is, at any rate, certain is that Cromwell was always "tender towards the Saints," that he imprisoned his fellow Puritans with reluctance and released them with relief, and that those who had interviews with him—like John Tillinghast, for example, another Fifth Monarchist—were never afraid to "speak their minds" before "the great man" or "bear testimony to his face." George Fox instructed Cromwell to "lay down his crown at the feet of Jesus" and to "Mind the crown that was immortal." Cromwell thanked him for his advice and invited him home. Thomas Harrison, who had plotted against him, was asked to dinner at Whitehall, where Cromwell expressed his affection and esteem for him, and kept him in prison only when he refused to give his word not to endanger the public peace. Whereas General Monck thought that the Lord Protector had no alternative but to be "severe" with all disturbers of the peace, Cromwell himself always disliked showing unkindness towards saintly men whose Christian ideals differed from his own.[2]

No tinge of purely selfish aims cast a shadow over Cromwell during the Protectorate. It is true that according to the "Instrument of Government" a sum of £200,000 was allowed him for the costs of civil government, but out of that he had to pay for the administration of justice and to maintain his diplomatic service. When his younger daughters married he was able to provide them with a dowry of £15,000 each, a startling contrast to the meager dowry that his own wife brought him. But the Protectress lived in a modest way, and even Royalist critics sneered at her economies rather than her extravagances. Bonaparte refused to draw on his private fortune in the desperate days after the Russian campaign. Cromwell on more than one occasion waived a part of his salary to help the public service. When Bonaparte was very young, his own brother wrote: "I have always discerned in Napoleon a purely personal ambition which overrules his patriotism." When Oliver Cromwell's mother was dying her last words were: "The Lord . . . enable you to do great things for the glory of the Most High God and to be a relief unto His People."

* * *

Cromwell in these years suffered from ill health; indeed, he never recovered from the bout of malaria with which he was struck down in the Irish bogs. Punctually every week end he left Whitehall by coach for Hampton Court, and took exercise by riding or playing bowls. His fondness for horses was famous, and foreign potentates vied with one another to present him with their finest breeds. (The Sultan of Morocco was an exception: he sent him a lion.) At Hampton Court he had installed an organ from Magdalen College, Oxford, where it was played by his favorite musician, John Hingston. He delighted in Latin motets, and would entertain his guests with music and wine. Two choristers who sang Latin motets for him in Hampton Court were among the official mourners at his funeral. Although the theater still lay under the Puritan ban, during the Protectorate the ingenuity of Sir William Davenant contrived the performance of the first operas in London. *The Siege of Rhodes* performed "after the Italian manner" was given in 1656. According to some accounts, the first actress ever to appear on the English stage, Mrs. Coleman, took part in this opera.[3] Though neither literature nor art flourished under Cromwell as it had done under King Charles I, it was by no means a philistine age. John Milton, who had been appointed Latin Secretary to the Council of State, went completely blind in 1652, but Cromwell retained him in a similar post during the Protectorate at the same salary, and employed him in nobly translating many of his state letters. At Milton's suggestion another younger poet, Andrew Marvell, was also engaged by John Thurloe in 1657; while Edmund Waller, a former Royalist, received a grave and modest compliment from the Lord Protector when he wrote a poem in his honor, and was appointed by him to the Committee for Trade. The Court patronized English portrait painters: Robert Walker was no Van Dyck though John Evelyn thought him "excellent," but Samuel Cooper was a miniaturist of genius. Though the Protectorate did not have the gaiety or abandon of the Restoration Court, it was not a world without culture. The Lord Protector, smoking his pipe and listening to music in Hampton Court, devoted to his wife and children, and seeing life *sub specie aeternitatis,* was a man none could despise.

But he lived in a land full of enemies. Inevitably the Royalists took advantage of the dissensions between the Government and the first Protectorate Parliament to plan a restoration by arms. King Charles II was despairing of active help from abroad, for neither France nor Spain, which competed with each other for Cromwell's alliance, was willing to risk their resources in an oversea invasion. Thus the King, bored and poverty-stricken, and compelled to leave France first for a stay with his sister in Holland and then for Cologne, was ready to snatch at straws. His more staid counselors, like Hyde and Sir Edward Nicholas, were no believers in rash projects, nor were the members of the Sealed Knot, the official Royalist conspiracy group in England. But other advisers, notably those who took their lead from the King's mother, Queen Henrietta Maria, and included the Earl of Rochester, dangled before him hopes of an internal rising that would overthrow the Protector in a discontented Commonwealth. Elaborate plans were drawn up for a concerted insurrection in many counties: the date first chosen was February 6, after the House of Commons had risen. The King gave the scheme his grudging blessing, or at least he did not forbid it. However, Thurloe had organized a highly efficient system of counterespionage. Cromwell brought over troops from Ireland, reinforced the garrison of London, and had artillery posted at strategic points. An intercepted letter from King Charles II gave him the final warning. Meanwhile the date of the operation was twice postponed by the Royalists. And while they were havering, other dissatisfied elements were rounded up by the Government. Colonel Robert Overton, formerly governor of Hull, who, thwarted of his ambitions for promotion, had dipped his fingers in lukewarm waters of treason, was promptly arrested by General Monck in Scotland and sent under escort to London. John Wildman, the Leveller conspirator, who had made tools of some of the disloyal colonels, was arrested near Marlborough, and a number of Royalists leaders were put in custody. On February 13 Cromwell himself addressed the Lord Mayor, Aldermen, and Common Council of the City, produced evidence of the plotting against the Government, and told them that he would rely upon them to guard the capital if the troops he had concentrated there had to be dispatched to the provinces. Major General Harrison, whose attempts to suborn the army had long been known, was packed off to Carisbrooke Castle, and a proclamation issued prohibiting the holding of horse races for six months on the ground that they were obvious centers for conspiracies. Two days before the date ultimately selected by the Sealed Knot for the insurrection, Cromwell sent a member of his Council, Colonel Philip Jones, up to Shrewsbury to watch the frontier with north Wales. On the same date he alerted the local government at Newcastle-upon-Tyne.

These precautions proved successful. The Royalist rising, planned upon a national scale—"the one general effort by the English Cavaliers between their defeat in war and the fall of the Protectorate to overthrow the revolution without recourse to Scottish or foreign arms"[4]—failed utterly. In Yorkshire a hundred men gathered on Marston Moor, only to disperse leaving their arms behind them. At Newcastle the would-be assault force numbered eighty. In Nottinghamshire three hundred Cavaliers gathered at Rufford Abbey, while their leaders remained hidden in London. Only in Wiltshire did the conspiracy awake into the realm of action, but after its courageous commander, Sir John Penruddock, had surprised Salisbury, capturing the assize judges in their beds, he was unable to recruit supporters in Dorset or Devonshire, and was finally taken prisoner by the captain of a regular troop stationed in Exeter. King Charles II, who had secretly moved from Cologne to Middelburg to await a call back to his throne, had his hopes inflated by rumor only to be pricked by reality. On April 23, after a fair trial, Penruddock was condemned to death in Exeter, and on May 3 Cromwell signed the warrant for his execution. But altogether only about fifteen Royalists perished for their part in the insurrection.

No informed historian today imagines that the Royalist plot of 1655 was manufactured by Cromwell to strengthen himself in power. The evidence from Royalist sources is far too complete and detailed. But the argument is still sometimes put forward that Cromwell, Thurloe, and his other advisers exaggerated its scope for their own ends. There can, however, be little doubt, as a modern historian has written, that "the Wiltshire rebellion of 1655, like that in Cheshire four years later, was only a small visible appearance of a vastly greater mass of conspiracy which remained below the surface."[5] Nor is it true that inadequate precautions were taken, that the conspiracy was allowed to ripen deliberately.

On the contrary, Cromwell's actions in London, his dispatch of Jones to the Welsh borders, his warning orders to Newcastle, and his reinforcement of danger points throughout the country, all testify to the effectiveness of his military machine and the competence of his command. On March 3 the Venetian representative in London reported that "Cromwell neglects nothing for putting a stop to evil designs." The Royalists were demoralized before their D-day came. The manner in which the insurrection was constricted and then stamped out impressed foreign rulers and heightened the prestige of the British Government everywhere.

The rising confronted the Lord Protector with a number of financial and constitutional problems. Hitherto the army had been paid largely out of the monthly assessments which during the first six months of the Protectorate had been levied at the rate of £120,000 a month or £1,440,000 a year. This tax was proportioned among all the counties of England and Wales, and levied there by a pound rate upon real and personal property. Thus, though in fact it was principally a land tax, it was also a local rate falling upon all property owners. On the eve of the meeting of Parliament, the Government had reduced the assessment to £90,000 a month, and it was then proposed in the Commons that it should be further reduced to £60,000 a month and finally abolished altogether.[6] To achieve this it was essential to cut down the size of the army. The "Instrument of Government" had stipulated an establishment of 30,000 men (roughly half the existing size), but large garrisons were still needed in Scotland and Ireland, a land force had been sent with the West India expedition, and the Salisbury rising was evidence that substantial garrisons were still required for police purposes. Furthermore, as every government in history has discovered, a strong foreign policy cannot be pursued without the backing of considerable armed forces. Had Cromwell been a ruthless dictator of the stamp of Napoleon or Stalin, he would have had no difficulty. The army would have been enlarged and the money been found. But Cromwell and his Council of State were conscious both of the terms of the constitution under which they governed and of the express wishes of the House of Commons. Thus, by an order of February 1655, Cromwell lowered the monthly assessments to £60,000 and proceeded to decrease the establishment of his infantry regiments and cavalry troops, reduce their pay, and pare down the garrisons of Scotland and Ireland. Though small revenues were obtained in Scotland and Ireland, the Government discovered (as has often been the case in the British Empire) that these dependencies cost more than they produced. Lieutenant General Monck was given money to pay off the arrears of his forces, and ordered to bring down his establishment in Scotland to seven cavalry regiments and thirteen infantry regiments. Lieutenant General Fleetwood, Lord Deputy of Ireland, was brusquely informed that only £17,000 a month could be allowed from England to pay for his army, and he must do what he could to garrison the country out of that and the local revenue. To compensate for the reduction in the size of the establishment in England, a committee of army officers recommended, and the Council of State approved, the formation of a horse militia as a reserve that could be called up when needed in an emergency for the defense of the country. As Parliament had sponsored the idea of such a militia (indeed the control over it was one of the causes of dissension between Cromwell and his first Parliament), this scheme was soon introduced. It was adopted in principle at the end of May 1655, and the reduction of the regular army was begun in the middle of the summer.

As an experiment in linking the militia with the old regular army, Cromwell's brother-in-law Major General John Desborough was at once put in command both of the existing forces in the six western counties and also of the new militia. But by the autumn the original militia scheme had been completely altered and expanded. Instead of using the militia as a reserve force, training at intervals and called up as required, it was decided to embody cavalry troops permanently and pay them and have them ready to serve outside their own areas when necessary. Although the men were to live in their own homes and therefore were less expensive to maintain than regular soldiers, the new militia was expected to cost £80,-000 a year, and it therefore constituted an added burden upon the Exchequer. To meet the expenditure a capital levy was imposed on all former Royalists at the rate of ten per cent on land of rentable value of £100 a year or more and £10 on every £1,500 of personal property.

The "decimation," as the levy was called, was difficult to justify in view of the Act of Oblivion, which Cromwell himself had been forward in promoting, and the articles of war on which Royalist officers had surrendered. An elaborate manifesto, said to have been written by Nathaniel Fiennes, one of the Commissioners of the Great Seal, but signed by

Cromwell, was published on October 31, 1655, arguing that all the former Royalists had been implicated in the plan for revolt and must therefore "pay for securing the state against the danger which they are authors of." The King's friends were quick to point out the logical weaknesses of the case; they urged that to single out one class of citizens for punishment was to affront the rule of law. Yet as a political action such a step has not been uncommon in the history of "emergencies": a modern parallel is the collective fines imposed in Cyprus in 1956, three hundred years afterwards.

To control the new militia and collect the decimation, the country was divided into eleven Associations (groups of counties), each under the command of a major general.[7] These major generals, headed by Charles Fleetwood, recalled from Ireland, and John Lambert, were Cromwell's most trusted commanders, all known personally to him, and most of them his relatives and close friends. Their duties were not only to prevent plotting and unrest, but to "promote godliness and virtue" by enforcing the existing laws against immorality and blasphemy. The main impulse for the system has plausibly been attributed to John Lambert, and the Puritan aspect of it to Cromwell himself. It is sometimes said that the introduction of the major generals—those Puritan Pashas—was intended to supersede the local government of England, that ancient method of voluntary government manned by sheriffs, justices of the peace, and borough councils, which had served the country not unhappily for generations. But that must not be exaggerated. In those days before the invention of modern transport and communication England could never he highly centralized: local traditions were too strong, the local gentry too influential. The major generals could not hope, and indeed were not instructed, to brush aside the time-honored arrangements. Most of them were in fact local figures of some standing themselves. They were sent out to police the country and to strengthen the hands of the existing authorities in a time of crisis. In every modern emergency in western Europe some such system has been necessary, from the French Intendants to the Regional Commissioners established in Britain during the war of 1939. The system of major generals was an expedient to ensure national security after an abortive insurrection and at a time when war was still in progress at sea both with Spain and France. Once granted that Cromwell and his Council were right to respect the wishes of Parliament in reducing the size and cost of the regular army, it is hard to see what alternative security arrangements would have worked.

While the army was largely paid out of the monthly assessments, the cost of the navy, whose splendors were making England into a formidable power, was met from the customs and excise. In November 1654 a merchant named George Cony had refused to pay duty on a quantity of imported silk, and had resisted the Customs Commissioners who attempted to seize his goods in payment. Parliament was sitting at the time under the terms of the "Instrument of Government." When the matter was finally brought before the Court of Upper Bench (the former King's Bench), Mr. Serjeant Maynard argued that the ordinances under which customs duties were imposed were illegal, that is to say, the "Instrument of Government" had no validity. To argue thus was to attack the very foundation of the Protectorate. If Cromwell and the Council of State had permitted the arguments of Cony's counsel, they might as well have resigned. So the three lawyers concerned were summoned before them and sent to the Tower to think it over. Mr. Serjeant Maynard was no Oliver St. John and George Cony was no John Hampden. In the end all of them submitted. But the Chief Justice of the Upper Bench had qualms and resigned. Earlier two other judges, engaged upon the trial of insurgents captured in the north, had questioned the validity of the ordinance of treason, which again was based upon the "Instrument of Government," and were dismissed from their posts. These events, disclosing as they did the legal weakness of the Government's position, were most damaging to it. It was simple for Cromwell's critics to draw a comparison between life under the Protectorate and that under the "eleven years' tyranny" of King Charles I. In both cases, it was said, taxes were levied illegally, judges dismissed, and the rule of law defied. But the comparison was not exact. When King Charles I reigned, it was a period of perfect peace, and the idea of a "balanced polity" had been accepted for many decades. When Cromwell ruled, England had undergone civil war and revolution, and an entirely new constitutional system had become unavoidably necessary. Neither Charles I nor Cromwell thought in terms of nineteenth-century democracy. Nor did Cromwell's republican critics. Moreover, the country now was at war, was restless, unsettled, and liable to disintegrate into anarchy. By summoning Parliament, by reducing his army, by refusing to publish fresh ordinances, Cromwell tried to keep within the framework of government provided by the "Instrument" which was a written constitution that anybody could read. Had he now renounced it and ruled by the naked sword, he would have abandoned forever any claim to be a constitutionalist and repudiated the beliefs and avowals of his own past. Did he not once say of the importance of having some accepted form of government, "if it have but the face of authority . . . he would take hold of it rather than let it go"? Without such a basis there could be no order and no government. Cromwell still believed passionately in individual liberty—above all, in "liberty of conscience"—but in the emergency of 1655 he was compelled to put order first. His was the eternal dilemma of statesmanship.

*   *   *

Financial difficulties were among the factors that shaped the foreign policy of the Protectorate. Scarcity of funds restricted enterpise. That was not because the country could not afford to pay taxes, but because constitutional inhibitions prevented Cromwell from increasing them other than by means of the "decimations." During the summer of 1655 he anxiously awaited the outcome of the two naval expeditions. Had they yielded rich prizes, the Government would have gained a freer hand. We do not know exactly what General Blake's original instructions were,[8] but he was on the lookout for prizes as well as aiming at the rescue of ships and sailors captured by the Moors off North Africa. On March 19 he was sent positive orders to attack the Spanish treasure fleet on its return from South America, and in June he was instructed to prevent the Spanish Government from sending any help to the West Indies where the other British naval force was operating. The directions given to this other expedition were broader and clearer: a commission of five was put in charge of general strategy, consisting, besides the two commanders, the governor of Barbados (which had been recovered from the Royalists in 1650), of Edward Winslow, who had formely been governor of the colony at Plymouth (Massachusetts), having sailed there in the *Mayflower,* and of Captain Gregory Butler, who was said to be a bad-tempered nonentity. They were told to attack the Spaniards at sea or on land, and "make way for the bringing in the light of the Gospel and power of true religion and godliness into those parts." To attain that they were "to gain an interest" in the Spanish West Indies (Britain already possessed Bermuda and Antigua as well as Barbados), and occupy islands and forts with the ultimate object of intercepting treasure fleets and even gaining access to Cuba and Cartagena.[9] Thus Cromwell hoped to fulfill the grandiose purpose of destroying Roman Catholic supremacy in the New World and becoming master of the gold of Peru. Much of Britain's naval resources were absorbed in these two expeditions, and the army, about to be reduced in size, was devoted to guarding the British Isles against invasion. While the envoys of France and Spain, of Prince Condé and King Charles X of Sweden, were competing for Cromwell's military aid, they had to be fobbed off until the outcome of the naval operations was known.

The outcome was disappointing. The West India expedition, as it proved, was inadequately organized. The land forces, consisting of drafts from English regiments and of men hastily enlisted in Barbados, were ill-disciplined and untrained. They were not equipped—and there General Desborough may have been to blame—for campaigning in the tropics, and their tossing in the Atlantic diminished their efficiency. The naval and military commanders were at loggerheads, and the committee of five proved incompetent in taking decisions. Although altogether some 9,000 men were recruited to fight on land, they were repulsed in attempting in May to capture their first objective, the island of Santo Domingo or Hispaniola, and later occupied the ill-defended Spanish outpost of Jamaica farther west as a *pis aller*.

The news of the failure at Hispaniola was slow to reach London. Meanwhile the King of Spain, still eager for a treaty with Cromwell, and perhaps, un-Spaniardlike, ready to stomach an insult or two at sea or in his far-flung islands, had sent a special ambassador to Whitehall with fresh proposals, while Cardinal Mazarin, who was equally hankering after an offensive alliance with Cromwell, had been irritated by the extensive English demands. If Cromwell expected to be treated like a king, he said sharply, then let him assume the title.[10] Once, however, Cromwell had dispatched secret instructions to General Blake to capture the Spanish plate fleet and once he learned, to his profound disappointment, that the West India expedition had succeeded only in occupying what was thought to be the barren island of Jamaica, he was committed to reaching agreement with France and to a war with Spain. Obliged to retrieve failure, he had to abandon any thought of protecting the French Huguenots against their sovereign or giving active support to the successor of Gustavus Adolphus, let alone to succoring the Venetians in their war against the Turks. The Puritan crusade against Antichrist had been transformed, through practical necessity, into something less idealistic and strangely akin to Elizabethan venturing—a splendid instance of the comparative immutability of national foreign policy.

In July King Charles X of Sweden assaulted Poland, and the news of the failure in the West Indies at last reached London. Thenceforward it was only a question of time before a general treaty was concluded with France; this provided, apart from the usual conditions relating to friendship and commerce (Hamburg was appointed the arbitrator over naval disputes), for secret clauses whereby France agreed to expel the Royalists except Queen Henrietta Maria, herself a French princess, and the British to have no more dealings with the agents of Prince Condé, still in arms against his native land.

The signature of the French treaty was delayed by the incident of the attack on the Protestants in the Duchy of Savoy. These Protestants, known as Vaudois, after Peter Waldez, a twelfth-century ascetic, had lived in the valleys of the Savoy Alps for five centuries, and had recently become Calvinists. Being inhabitants of a Roman Catholic dukedom, attempts had been made to convert them and, when these were unsuccessful, the Vaudois became overconfident of their independence and spilled out and even counterattacked the missionaries. In January 1655, the Duke (or rather his mother the Duchess) ordered the Vaudois to return to their original homes at once on penalty of death unless they became Catholics; when they refused, a military expedition was sent against them from Turin, which resulted in death and destruction for many desperate peasants. Oliver Cromwell, who regarded himself as the European protector of all Protestants, was deeply moved by their fate, and he spoke for his country. Yet he acted in a diplomatic way to save them. He sent envoys to Switzerland and Savoy; he pressed the other Protestant rulers of Europe to join him in protest, and he suspended negotiations with the French court all the more definitely since French troops were involved. Cromwell's exertions were rewarded. Cardinal Mazarin was indifferent about the sufferings of the Vaudois, but wanted a British alliance. He brought pressure to bear upon the Duchess of Savoy, and by the treaty of Pignerol the Vaudois were pardoned and restored to most of their former rights.[11]

By the autumn of 1655 therefore the Protectorate had reached the high-water mark of its achievement. At home the Royalists and other enemies of the Government had been crushed; abroad the influence of the British Commonwealth was paramount; and although Cromwell was disappointed over the modest gains by his naval expeditions, he was determined at all costs to convert Jamaica into a permanent and flourishing colony, the first ever to be won by conquest, a dagger to the heart of the Spanish Empire, and a stepping-stone to British imperial advance.

By contrast with these stirring events, the winter of 1655-56 contained little of interest; it has been described as the "dullest and most depressing period in the history of the Commonwealth." Cromwell himself was taken ill again, and his foreign policy suffered setbacks. Blake failed to capture the Spanish plate fleet and, owing to a misunderstanding of his instructions, refrained from destroying the Spanish navy. When Penn and Venables returned from Jamaica without orders, they were both put in the Tower of London after being unable to defend their behavior convincingly before the Council of State. Cromwell tried to induce the Swedes to enter into a joint anti-Catholic alliance with him, arguing that as King Charles X was campaigning in Poland and he himself was committed to a war against Spain, their interests were mutual. The Swedes, who were anxious to convert the Baltic into a Swedish lake, were unwilling to embark upon far-reaching adventures against the House of Austria. Moreover, it was represented to Cromwell that if he threw in his lot with the Swedes he would be violating the Anglo-Dutch treaty of 1654; the Dutch ambassador made that plain. Even the King of Portugal was defiant, and it was not until Cromwell sent General Blake back to Lisbon for a third time that he ratified the treaty of 1654 and paid the sums due under it. Blake was further ordered to attack Gibraltar or Cádiz. Both proved impregnable. And Cromwell found that a large part of the naval and financial means at his disposal had to be consumed in maintaining the conquest of Jamaica—where no fewer than six harassed governors died one after another —for its loss would have been a shock to British prestige.

The war against Spain—it had broken out finally in October 1655—was now in full flow. It was clear that it could not be sustained for long if the Protectorate Government was unable to increase taxation. At the end of May 1656, Cromwell summoned his major generals to a conference in London and discussed with them as well as with his Council the question of finance and the advisability of calling a new Parliament and invoking its help. We do not really know what went on in the inner councils of the Protectorate Government at that time, and it is unwise to depend on foreigners' reports of rumors they picked up.[12] At any rate, early in July Cromwell and his Council of State finally decided to hold a general election at the end of August. Until Parliament met and the Government was provided with fresh funds, it was hard for the Protector to fix upon the next move in his foreign policy, in particular to determine what he should say to the envoys of France and Sweden, both seeking his military assistance. Just as financial exigencies had restricted and shaped what he could do in 1655, once the war with Spain began his enterprises abroad could not be pursued to a triumphant end unless fructified by fresh resources.

But it was not the poverty of the English people that prevented progress overseas: indeed, such evidence as we have—from customs returns and the movement of prices, for example[13]—suggests that the country was more prosperous between the end of the Dutch war and the beginning of the Spanish war than at any other time during the Interregnum. The difficulty was that the Lord Protector and his Council of State were reluctant to exercise arbitrary powers to raise money, other than by the "decimation" of the Royalists, which did not even meet the full cost of the horse militia. Cromwell imagined that the part he had assumed of the Protestant leader of the world—the ally of the United Netherlands, of Sweden, Denmark, and Switzerland, the declared foe of the Pope and of the Habsburgs, the champion of the Vaudois and the Huguenots, could not fail to appeal to the Puritan community over whom he ruled. He forgot that his enemies were legion, that he had affronted earlier Parliaments, and that a clear conscience and a sense of Christian integrity were poor instruments of persuasion. No longer was he able to settle his policies in secret and in a rational way with a group of trusted and sympathetic councilors and officials. Political passions would once more be animated and his own position again disputed.

Notes

1. Cf. J. M. Thompson, *Napoleon Bonaparte: His Rise and Fall* (1952), an excellent up-to-date account.

2. John Browne, *History of Congregationalism, etc.* (1877), 295; E. Rogers, *The Life and Opinions of a Fifth Monarchy Man* (1867), 173–74; *Cromwell's Generals*, 141–42.

3. Cf. Percy Scholes, *Puritans and Music* (1934).

4. A. H. Woolrych, *Penruddock's Rising, 1655* (1955), 3.

5. *Ibid.*, 3.

6. M. P. Ashley, *op. cit.*, Chap. VIII.

7. For a detailed account of the major generals, see *Cromwell's Generals,* Chap. IX.

8. For Blake, see J. R. Powell, *The Letters of Robert Blake* (1937).

9. A. P. Watts, *Les Colonies anglaises aux Antilles* (1924), reprints the instructions to the commanders of the West India expedition.

10. *Recueil des Instructions,* 205.

11. Cromwell's critics sometimes make the point that it was the French Government and not the English Government that saved the Vaudois from persecution, neglecting to notice that Cardinal Mazarin would never have acted had it not been for Cromwell's pressure upon him. This is a remarkable instance of the way in which the petty-minded will try to denigrate a statesman.

12. Both Firth and Gardiner, it seems to me, relied unduly on the reports of the Venetian representatives in London for their interpretation of Cromwell's views at this time. I am inclined to doubt whether these reports should be accepted except where they are confirmed by other good evidence. They can frequently be shown to have been inaccurate and I fancy that their informants were sometimes Royalists. Francesco Giavarina gets even Cromwell's age wrong when he died. Bordeaux (P.R.O. 31/3/99, ff. 288 seq.) does not confirm Giavarina's stories of what went on between the Lord Protector, his Council, and the major generals in the summer of 1656.

13. M. P. Ashley, *op. cit.,* Chap. XIV. The evidence is admittedly tenuous, but food prices certainly fell and customs returns increased in value during the period 1655–57.

Chapter 21

Cromwell and The Second Protectorate Parliament

"I HAVE LIVED the latter part of my age in the fire," said Cromwell in March 1657, "in the midst of troubles." His troubles culminated in the general election of 1656. The Lord Protector himself had been opposed to having an election at all, but his advisers were allowed to overrule him. The measures taken to win the war against Spain and prevent Royalist risings required, in their view, parliamentary approval and grants of money. So orders went out that polling should take place on August 20.

The election was closely and fiercely fought on something akin to party lines, though the opponents of the Government were by no means united. "The day of the election draws near," wrote John Thurloe to Henry Cromwell on August 12, "and here is the greatest striving to get into the Parliament that ever was known. All sorts of discontented people are incessant in their endeavours." Most of the major generals had evidently advocated the election, for Cromwell later, in speaking to his principal officers, said: "I gave my vote against it, but you were confident by your own strength and interest to get men chosen to your heart's desire. . . ." Some of them, Fleetwood's deputy, Major Hezekiah Haynes, for instance, wanted the horse militia to be paraded on polling day so as to overawe the voters, but Cromwell would not allow it. Others hoped that he would publish a proclamation, when the writs were distributed, to support his Government's case. Eventually he did send a letter on August 12, but it was thought to have arrived too late.

However, the major generals exerted what influence they could. "Notwithstanding all the endeavors of the old dissatisfied party," wrote Major General John Desborough to Cromwell from Cornwall, "I shall make it my business to encourage the honest sober people, and strengthen their hands as much as in me lies; and leave the issue to the Wise Disposer." From Cheshire, Major General Tobias Bridge announced: "With the advice of some honest persons I have taken the best course we could think of to engage the gentle-

323

men to bestir themselves to procure the election of persons of the most sober and suitable spirit to the present work." From Kent Major General Thomas Kelsey assured him: "We will stand by you with life and fortune."[1]

According to Thurloe, Cromwell did not intend originally to interfere with the elections, but to rely upon inspecting the qualifications of those chosen and insisting upon their again signing a "recognition" of the Protectoral form of government. But during July he interviewed some of his leading republican critics, notably his old friend, Sir Henry Vane, who had published a cloudy pamphlet entitled *A Healing Question,* as well as Chief Justice John Bradshaw, Colonel Edmund Ludlow, and the Fifth Monarchy Colonel Nathaniel Rich. Vane was temporarily imprisoned in Carisbrooke Castle and Rich at Windsor, but Bradshaw and Ludlow were left at liberty, though neither of them got into Parliament. Cromwell also wrote last-minute instructions to the major generals. In spite of all these precautions, the activities of the mixed opposition aroused misgivings in Whitehall. Before polling day the French ambassador reported in a series of dispatches home his opinion that things were going against the Government, and that while both sides were taking pains the Lord Protector was "finding an entire repugnance to his plans," for many of his friends were being rejected in the counties, as well as in the boroughs.[2] The major generals confirmed that there was a widespread agitation against "swordsmen." "decimators," and the court.

Yet in general the election results were less dismal for the Government than the pessimists feared. Major General Goffe, who had been very gloomy, wrote on August 29 from Winchester that: "Though they be not so good as we could have wished them yet they come not so bad as our enemies would have had them." In Wiltshire, where, as we have seen, in the election of 1654 there had been a straight fight between two lists, one headed by Ludlow, and Ludlow's list had been beaten, this time out of the ten elected four members obnoxious to the court were chosen, even though the sheriff, appointed by the local major general, had done what he could to help by shifting the county poll from Wilton to Devizes.[3] That was a fairly typical maneuver and result.

Of the 400 members elected in England and Wales, fewer than half had been members of the former Parliament. Over a quarter were officials and regular army officers. At least eighteen were Cromwell's own relations.[4] All the major generals except one and all the members of the Council of State except two found seats. The members for Scotland and Ireland were entirely Government nominees or supporters—"all staunch men." The French ambassador, who had at first been anxious about the outcome, was later noncommital, and finally admitted that "the storm had passed" and thought the Lord Protector should be pleased, and his power increased.[5] On a close analysis, the Government had some reason for dissatisfaction in that in areas which had once been strongly Puritan—such as Norfolk and Suffolk—a good number of candidates critical of Cromwell were returned. Even in the West Riding of Yorkshire, John Lambert's own stamping ground, four out of six members elected were unfriendly to the Protectorate.

Cromwell and his Council took every care to prevent unrest or revolt when Parliament met. Known Royalists were ordered out of the capital for six months, nine regiments were brought up to strength, and ten days before the opening of Parliament the Lord Protector addressed a meeting of field officers warning them of the danger of an invasion from Flanders and of the Royalists linking up with Levellers and Fifth Monarchy men. Finally the Council of State examined the returns and granted certificates of membership only to those of whom it did not disapprove. Cromwell himself doubted the wisdom of this last extreme measure, but he enforced it—reluctantly perhaps, for afterwards he told the leading officers "when they were chosen you garbled them, kept out and put in whom you pleased by the 'Instrument,' and I am sworn to make good all you do. . . ." Still the fact remained that unless the Council of State had actually named the members of Parliament—as it had done largely in the Assembly of Saints—the House of Commons that finally functioned at Westminster in the autumn of 1656 could scarcely have been more friendly to the Cromwellian Protectorate.

*　　　*　　　*

While the election was being decided upon, held, and its results retailored, progress in foreign affairs was interrupted, although the Spanish war was being fought at sea. Cromwell had insisted upon sending an ambassador to France, a move disagreeable to Cardinal Mazarin, who was not keen to guarantee his safety from assassination. Colonel William Lockhart, a capable Scotsman who married a niece of Cromwell, was selected for this post of danger and arduousness, and the Anglo-French negotiations were shifted from London to Paris, where Mazarin pressed for British troops to come over and serve with the French armies against Spain. When on July 16 Marshal Turenne was defeated by Prince Condé at Valenciennes, the French Government became even more anxious for a military alliance with Cromwell. But the negotiations hung fire. Cromwell's primary interest was to thwart King Charles II. For when war broke out between the English Commonwealth and Spain, the exiled King had naturally been able to come to terms with the Court of Madrid, which in April promised him 6,000 men to assist him to regain his throne. Cromwell was not afraid of assault from Spain itself, which was effectively blockaded by General Blake's fleet, but he did fear an expedition launched from Belgium (the Spanish Netherlands).[6] Hence he demanded an agreement with France that would give him early possession of Dunkirk, thereby enabling him to frustrate a Royalist invasion. The English Government was also concerned about the safety of commerce. Apart from the inevitable loss of profitable business with Spain, trade had been hit by the war because the Spaniards had resorted to the normal practice of the weaker naval power in attacking British merchant shipping by licensing privateers, and the corsairs of Dunkirk and Ostend, ports always nests of pirates, collected many rich prizes in the Channel. Here was another reason why Cromwell urgently wanted Dunkirk in his own hands.

In midsummer the English fleet was divided. Blake sailed into the Mediterranean to punish attacks on British merchant vessels; he left a force to watch Cádiz, and other warships were detached from the Mediterranean fleet to reinforce the Channel squadron. Meanwhile yet another squadron had been sent to the West Indies under Admiral Goodson, while Colonel Brayne had been dispatched with an expeditionary force to strengthen the garrison of Jamaica. The combined pressure upon the Spanish Empire won its first notable success in September. While Blake was away, Vice Admiral Stayner, whom he left in command off Cádiz, intercepted a plate fleet from South America. The battle was on a small scale. Stayner had only three ships in action, the largest carrying sixty-four guns, and the Spaniards only two galleons, apart from armed merchantmen. Nevertheless, several Spanish ships were sunk or captured, and at last the English navy touched golden pieces of eight. Considering that the Exchequer was in such straits that no money had been coined by the Mint for eighteen months,[7] the news of the victory was like a shower in a parched summer. It did not reach London until after the new Parliament met.

*   *   *

When Oliver Cromwell drove in state to open his second Parliament on a hot September day, he was accompanied in his carriage by his two principal major generals and military advisers, John Lambert and Charles Fleetwood, men of radically different characters, and rivals for his favor. Lambert, hardheaded, versatile, ambitious, with a beautiful wife, whom Cromwell admired, was the author both of the "Instrument of Government" and of the system of major generals. Fleetwood, equally ambitious after his own fashion, had no such originality of mind, but he was, unlike Lambert, a Puritan of Cromwell's own kind, was married to his eldest daughter, and was an able administrator, but of a shifty, impressionable, and rather nervous character.

Cromwell delivered a well-arranged, luminous speech to the members gathered once again in the Painted Chamber. He came at once to "facts" or "necessities." He was clearly aware that, according to the terms of the "Instrument," he ought to have consulted Parliament about the war against Spain, and he justified it at considerable length. The Spaniard, he explained, was historically and in religion their "natural enemy" ever since the time of Queen Elizabeth I of honored memory. The Spaniards were agents of the Pope, tools of the Jesuits, instruments of the Counter Reformation. They were in alliance with the Royalists, who were in turn linked with the Levellers. These alliances were not imaginary. Cromwell had ample information from traitors or spies in the Royalist camp, while John Wildman, once John Lilburne's bosom friend, was a dark and impenetrable adventurer who purveyed intelligence to all sides. Cromwell envisaged the King of Spain as the head of the Catholic interest in Europe, as he himself was the head of the Protestant interest. The only Catholic nation with which the English Commonwealth was allied, he explained, was France, "and it is certain they do not think themselves under such a tie to the Pope" as the Spaniards, "their greatest enemy." In England the papists were "Spaniolized," and they and the Cavaliers "shook hands."

So Cromwell defended the war and the institution of the major generals, whose increasing unpopularity he recognized.

Next he turned to domestic affairs, expounded his religious policy—toleration for all peaceable Christians and the payment of ministers by tithes until a better way could be found —and urged the reform of manners and of the law. Finally he asked for a grant of money to pay for the upkeep of the forces fighting upon the seas and to ensure home defense. The state, he pointed out, was "hugely in debt," since all the casual revenues raised by selling the lands of the King and the Church after the civil wars were practically exhausted. He begged his new Parliament to set to work against the Pope, the Spaniard, and the Devil, so that peace might be restored, mercy and truth meet together, and the City of God made glad.

Such a speech grated upon later ears, whether of the eighteenth-century philosophers or twentieth-century cynics. But it was in the language of his own time, of Puritan England. It did not offend his audience. It is true that his hearers realized that he was on the defensive, vindicating the war, making the best case he could for the major generals, pleading for money, re-emphasizing his belief in toleration. But the French ambassador reported that everyone was impressed, and he particularly noted how Cromwell "prided himself only upon having established liberty of conscience for everyone who believed in Christ."[8]

Cromwell addressed all the M.P.s who cared to attend him in the Painted Chamber. But no sooner had he dismissed them to select their Speaker (they appointed Sir Thomas Widdrington, a Commissioner of the Great Seal) than the ax fell: ninety-nine members were denied a certificate to serve by the Council of State. Sir George Booth, a Presbyterian from Cheshire, at once organized a protest, backed by seventy-nine members, claiming that the exclusion of their fellows was a breach of parliamentary privilege. Nathaniel Fiennes and John Thurloe, on behalf of the Council, boldly defended their action as compatible with the letter of the "Instrument of Government." After a long and envenomed debate the Government won by thirty-five votes. Booth and his supporters thereupon withdrew, and it seems that altogether up to 160 of the members originally elected took no further part in the proceedings of the House. It became a new "Rump." Those who stayed did not in any case expect to sit for more than three months, as it was not a regular

Parliament but one called in an emergency. Of the members who remained the bulk were friendly to the Government. But they had their pride and sense of independence, and they recognized what the outside world might think about them. Not only they but Cromwell himself and his Councilors knew that the traditions, the privileges, and the corporate spirit of Parliament were far too potent to be destroyed. The magic of the Mace was never exorcized. Like the Rump, though the new members might not form a full House nor a fully representative one, they intended to stick to their rights and to their rules, and refuse to be treated other than with the respect that their forebears had exacted from Tudors and Stuarts, either by the Lord Protector or his army chiefs. No one who reads the accounts of their debates can question the freedom of utterance within the House or compare it to the rubber-stamp assemblies under twentieth-century dictatorships.[9]

Nevertheless, they did accept the argument of Cromwell's opening speech so far as the immediate dangers to the nation were concerned. They repudiated King Charles II; they passed a bill for the security of the Lord Protector's person—an attempt had been planned to assassinate him with a blunderbuss as he went into the Painted Chamber to give his speech; and they set up a new high court of justice to try political offenders. They also approved the war against Spain, delighted by the news of Admiral Stayner's victory, and finally they voted £400,000 as a special grant to pay for the war. But on two questions they differed from Cromwell: they were not convinced by his apology for the major generals, who for all their high conscientiousness—and they were indeed devoted and scrupulous men—had caused themselves to be disliked; nor was Parliament in tune with his wide-ranging policy of toleration.

In the midst of urgent and routine matters the House of Commons was suddenly swept into commotion by the case of the Quaker James Naylor, a religious enthusiast who had ridden into Bristol on a horse, claiming that "Christ was in him" and parodying, so it seemed, the Son of God's entry into Jerusalem. This unfortunate escapade revealed a cruel and intolerant streak in the members of Parliament. Major General Phillip Skippon, who was himself no mean religious fanatic, led the way. Debating the report of a committee set up to investigate the case, Skippon asserted that it was unquestionably "horrid blasphemy," which must be severely punished by the House. It was noticeable that only members of Cromwell's Council, like General Desborough, Major General Lambert, Sir Gilbert Pickering, and Colonel William Sydenham, spoke words of caution and mercy. Lambert, to his credit, told the House that Naylor was "a man of very unblamable life and conversation, a member of a very sweet society of an independent church." Let them, he urged, not be prosecutors, judges, jurors, and executioners in the same case. That was not at all the temper of the House. Nearly the whole of December was consumed debating the fate of a man who had crossed the line between faith and obsession. Eventually a proposal to put him to death was defeated by a mere fourteen votes, and he was sentenced to be pilloried, whipped 310 times, to have his tongue branded, his forehead burnt with the letter B, and to be imprisoned during the pleasure of Parliament. Cromwell was petitioned to intervene so as to prevent the carrying out of the whole of these punishments. On December 25 the Lord Protector addressed a letter to the Speaker demanding by what authority Parliament had inflicted such penalties. John Lambert explained that Cromwell was "under an oath to protect the people both in freedom of their consciences and persons and liberties." Parliament ignored his letter, and the Lord Protector could not interfere without quarreling with Parliament. Naylor was upon Cromwell's conscience until he died. He did what he could to relieve Naylor's sufferings in Bridewell Prison. When in the following year Parliament offered Cromwell the crown, one reason why he was tempted to take it was that he hoped to acquire the royal prerogative of clemency—for the case of James Naylor, he said, might be that of any Christian exposed to the arbitrary cruelty of mass hysteria.

On that same Christmas Day, 1656, when Oliver Cromwell was writing his letter about Naylor, the House of Commons was in session, for the Puritans did not approve of celebrating the ancient festivals of the Church, not even the birthday of their Saviour. Still, the attendance was poor, and one Colonel Mathews brought in a short bill to prevent all such superstition for the future. The seconder was all for it: he complained that he "could get no rest all night for the preparation of this foolish day's solemnity." "We are," he added caustically "returning to popery." The bill was read. Suddenly John Desborough, the first of the major generals, put the cat among the pigeons. He proposed to transform the "decimation" upon Royalists from being a capital levy into a permanent annual tax, and by so doing to perpetuate the system of rule by the major generals. At once the House, so much in harmony with itself over the branding of Naylor and the superstitious celebration of Christmas, was agog. Leave was given to bring in the bill, but from that moment the Cromwellians were divided among themselves.

The division was, broadly, between the officers who had fought beside Cromwell in the early stages of the Civil Wars, the Independent chaplains and their like, on the one side, and the new courtiers and officials upon the other. The leader of the old Cromwellians was John Lambert, who, having worked so hard in Oliver's service, now aspired to succeed him as Lord Protector. Lambert and his friends argued that the only real enemies of the Protectorate were the Royalists, that the army must be kept up to strength to prevent insurrections and assassinations, and that the method of administration by major generals was essential for the peace and security of the country. Roger Boyle, Lord Broghill, a capable man with many interests in Scotland and Ireland, but an ex-Royalist who led the other party from behind, answered that on the contrary the best way to stabilize the Government was to disavow the militarism which caused it to be so unpopular and rely instead upon government of a more traditional character. In order to obtain that he proposed to make Cromwell king, to restore a House of Lords, and to readmit the excluded members of the House of Commons. By creating a constitutional monarchy and an established church in a Puritan pattern they would give the people of England what they wanted—the old show with a new cast.

This fundamental difference of view among the Cromwellians was reflected at every level, among Cromwell's personal advisers, within his Council of State, and in the second Protectorate Parliament. When on January 7, 1657, the Militia Bill, sponsored by the major Generals, was debated on its first reading, the House of Commons was crowded and animated: no fewer than 220 members were present out of the 300 entitled to sit. Both sides put their case according to their lights: Broghill quoted the New Testament: "Do as ye would be done by," "Judge not"; the "decimation" of Royalists, he claimed, was contrary to the law of Chirst as well as the rule of law. Luke Robinson, a friend of Lambert's from Yorkshire, retorted that "that rule of Christ is not a good rule for us. . . . We must not live securely and supinely upon miracles. I never trusted a Cavalier. . . ." The next speaker voiced the feeling against the army when he said that the effect of the bill would be "to cantonize the nation, and prostitute our laws and civil peace to a power that was never set up in any nation without dangerous consequences." To that Desborough answered: "I wish we might all have lived as Englishmen, but I see no hope of it. . . . It was blows, not fair words, that settled and must settle, the peace of England." The debate was adjourned. Next day the House discussed the excise, and on the following day the absorbing question of the divorce of Lady Katherine Scot, a daughter of Lord Goring, who was succinctly described as "a very common, etc., as can be." After that the Speaker was taken ill, and on January 19 John Thurloe came to the House to disclose the details of a new plot to assassinate the Lord Protector.

This plot had been carried out by the same seedy quartermaster who had earlier tried to shoot the Lord Protector with a blunderbuss. The latest scheme had been to set Whitehall alight with a firework, and either kill Cromwell in the confusion or at any rate smoke him out of his lair. The House expressed its concern and relief, and the antimilitary party then put forward its proposal, which had already been adumbrated more than once, to make Cromwell king. The proposal, like Desborough's, was modestly presented. James Ashe, the Recorder of Bath, suggested that "His Highness would be pleased to take upon him the government according to the ancient constitution." Luke Robinson pretended to misunderstand what Ashe meant: was Cromwell, he asked, to be King Charles II's viceroy? But surely the last thing they wanted was the return of the Stuarts. Let them revert to the Militia Bill, "the best expedient for your preservation."

Thus on January 29, 1657, the two alternative proposals for strengthening the Protectorate were brought face to face. As soon as a Deputy Speaker had been appointed (on January 29), the Militia Bill was once again debated in the Commons. The independent country gentlemen threw their weight against it, and though "the major generals were very loath to surrender," after a serious discussion, "not without sharpness and reflections," and after the House had sat until candlelight, their system of government received its deathblow. Next day the Commons voted to raise a sum of £400,000 to pay for the war. Cromwell received congratulations from Parliament on his escape from assassination and entertained the members at a "sumptuous banquet" with "exquisite music." Five days later the advocates of a return to monarchy presented their full proposals at Westminster.

Where stood Cromwell in these events? He had defended the major generals during his opening speech of Parliament, and on the face of it it seemed incredible that General Desborough, his own brother-in-law, a member of the Council of State, and the first of the major generals to be appointed, should have brought in the Militia Bill without Cromwell's foreknowledge and acquiescence. Moreover, when it was first introduced John Thurloe, Cromwell's faithful servant, spoke in its support. Can Cromwell, when he learned of the mixed reception the bill received, have changed his opinion about its wisdom? The first speaker against the bill when the debate on the second reading began was his son-in-law, John Claypole, who rarely spoke in the House. It was generally felt that he would not have done so without his father-in-law's permission. When the major generals went to Cromwell and complained about the resistance to their proposal, he was angry with them, and later he demanded: "Who bid you go to the House with a bill, and there receive a foil?" But Broghill had a story that it was not until the bill was finally defeated that he managed to persuade Cromwell of its indiscretion. If then Cromwell changed his mind over the bill, breathing first hot and then cold—and it was in character for him to do so—that would explain why Lambert implacably rejected the proposal to make Cromwell king, though he himself had earlier sponsored that very proposal.

Over such political questions Cromwell was an opportunist. He watched developments closely, but was slow to commit himself. At first he had not liked the idea of calling Parliament at all. Then when he saw how friendly it became towards him (after the purge by the Council of State), he felt more hopeful of its co-operation. He determined therefore not to antagonize it: the members' concern for his well-being, as expressed at the Whitehall banquet, must have moved him. If he had at first acquiesced in the major generals' attempt to perpetuate their power, he afterwards preferred to repudiate them rather than to offend the majority in the Commons. Once the Spanish war had been approved and money voted to pay for it, he thought that after all he might be able to operate a constitutional parliamentary system. He examined his conscience to discover whether it would now be right for him to embrace the offer from this friendly assembly of a coronation that would sanctify the rule not of the sword but of the law.

The case for accepting the title of king, as pressed upon him by lawyers, administrators, and businessmen, he found to be logically persuasive. The title, they told him, was known to the Common Law but that of Protector was not. Even de facto kings, who had won the throne by conquest, such as the first Tudor, had commanded obedience. A House of Lords and a full House of Commons would restore that "balancing" element in the constitution, which he had always believed to be the surest guarantee against arbitrariness. The Crown, like the Mace, was of course a mere toy or bauble, a feather in his cap, that would amuse the common people and give him the power to do good. The "Instrument of Government," he realized, had proved a failure. It had not enabled him to preserve the wretched James Naylor from his fate. "Unless you have some such thing as a balance," he told the army officers, "you cannot be safe." But logic was not all. The country was at war, the Royalists were still plotting invasions. He had to rely in the last resort upon his soldiers to defend his throne, whatever that throne was called. Antagonism to hereditary monarchy was not confined to men like Lambert and Fleetwood, who might be self-interested. The Independent preachers and the more extreme sects were most against it, for they regarded monarchy as distasteful to the Almighty: Christ, not man, was king. Their view was well expressed by Samuel Highland, M.P. for Southwark, who asked: "Are you going to set up kingly government, which for three thousand years has persecuted the people of God? I hope we have gotten from our former bondage, blindness, and superstition, that great persecution we and our ancestors groaned under."

On March 25 Parliament voted by a majority of two to one to invite Cromwell to assume the title and office of king. Six days later the Speaker and a deputation interviewed him, and he asked for time to think. Then he was taken ill, the momentousness of the decision before him afflicting his body as well as his mind. He assured the committee that attended him that what he cared for most in his public life was Christian liberty, civil liberty, and the interest of the nation as a whole. In dedication to these interests "if God account me worthy," he said, "I shall live and die." But he saw that the way was "hedged in." He heard the wisdom of the lawyers, the judges, the court officials, the new administrative class, even the tepid approval of some of his officers; but from the other side came the appeal of his old comrades in arms, the Christian misgivings of the sectarian ministers, the distrust of the "russet-coated captains." His was a dreadful choice. He tried to interpret the will of Providence that had guided him in all his battles, to scrutinize the mind of God. He was anxious to be persuaded. The House therefore reaffirmed its resolution.

For weeks Cromwell debated with deputations the details of the "Remonstrance," rechristened the "Humble Petition and Advice," which embodied the full constitution framed by Broghill and his friends with the Crown as its bait. He changed his mind more than once. After six weeks he decided, on May 6, that he would accept the title. Then he changed his mind once more. Charles Fleetwood and John Desborough, both Christian men of his own kind, who had fought with him from the beginning and who had married into his family, made it clear to him that if he became king they would resign all their offices and retire into private life. Colonel Thomas Pride, of Pride's Purge, collected signatures to a petition signed by officers of the London garrison pleading with Parliament against the restoration of a monarchy. Oliver Cromwell was not a man to be intimidated by threats. He knew that he had already forfeited the friendship of John Lambert, and that Lambert might raise part of the army against him. Yet other high officers had testified to their loyalty whichever way he should decide. He was never convinced that the mere taking of the title was essential to the ends of his government, to the preservation of religious liberty, or to the defense of the Commonwealth. He was the prey to many emotions and divergent pressures. He had wavered and experienced temptation. But when on May 8, 1657, he finally decided not to accept the Crown, there is no reason to suspect the honesty of what he told the House of Commons: "At the best I should do it doubtingly. And certainly what is so done is not of faith." To Cromwell what was not of faith was sin.

*   *   *

While the question of kingship was under discussion, the Commonwealth was deeply engaged in the war with Spain. Throughout the winter of 1656-57 Cromwell had kept General Blake's fleet in the Mediterranean—which was unusual strategy—impressing upon him that the way to crush the strength of the Spanish Empire was to sever the homeland from the colonies in the West Indies and South America. In April, after many alarums and excursions, Blake obtained intelligence that a treasure fleet bound for Spain and escorted by men of war had reached the harbor of Santa Cruz in the Canary Islands. Blake's captains had hoped to trap the treasure ships at sea, and thus capture booty to share between them and their men. But Blake, a patriot above all else, wanted to annihilate the might of Spain at one fell blow. He had learned from his earlier victory at Porto Farina that it was possible to attack ships at anchor even though they were under the protection of shore batteries. As it happened, at Santa Cruz, as at Porto Farina, the anchored ships partially masked the fire of cannon from the forts. The entire convoy and its escort were surprised, sunk, or burnt at negligible cost to the English navy. It is true that none of the rich cargoes was taken, as most of them had been unloaded and moved to safety inland, but there they stayed immobilized, and the Spanish monarchy was deprived of the means to pay its forces at home, while the ships lost were no longer available to carry back the stores necessary for the Spanish colonies. Thus it was a victory of far-reaching consequences.

At the same time a military treaty was at last being concluded between England and France, providing for a joint assault by land forces on the Spanish garrisons in Flanders. By this treaty the Lord Protector agreed to provide six regiments of infantry (which after crossing the sea were to be paid and fed by the French Government), and in return to receive the port of Dunkirk and the fortress of Mardyke once they were captured. When these places were in his hands, Thurloe observed, Cromwell "carried at his girdle the keys of a door into the Continent."[10] They were severe terms for Cardinal Mazarin and highly satisfying to Cromwell. Yet again, as with the West India expedition, Cromwell failed to pick the best commander. Sir John Reynolds, whom he chose, had served mainly with the cavalry in Ireland, and was reluctant to undertake the duty as he had just married a young wife. Luckily his second in command, Major General Thomas Morgan, a choleric little professional officer from Wales, was willing to do most of the work, and the political side of the alliance was ably handled by Colonel William Lockhart, who, as ambassador to France, had concluded the agreement in

Paris. By September, Mardyke, a village commanding an excellent harbor lying to the east of Dunkirk, was taken and occupied by an English garrison, which later repulsed a counterattack. Cromwell made it exceedingly plain to Cardinal Mazarin that he wanted Dunkirk as quickly as possible, and was not going to permit the English contingent to be diverted inland, away from the Channel ports.

Meanwhile King Charles X of Sweden suffered reverses in his war against Poland. Cromwell had not concealed where his sympathies lay. He allowed the Swedes to recruit troops in Scotland and gave them both material and moral support, though negotiations for a closer alliance broke down. At the same time Cromwell was anxious to avoid a fresh war with the Dutch, who were not only opposed to Swedish ambitions, but wanted to uphold the freedom of the seas both in the Baltic and in the Mediterranean so as to protect their far-flung commerce, the lifeblood of their prosperity. The Dutch sent a fleet into the Baltic, where it prevented Danzig from falling into the clutches of the Swedes, and another into the Mediterranean, where it embarrassed Blake. The Dutch doctrine was that neutral ships might carry enemy goods (apart from contraband), although neutral goods on enemy ships might be confiscated. The English declared that this so-called maxim of "free ships, free goods—enemy ships, enemy goods" was "utterly erroneous," and that enemy goods on neutral ships might be impounded. While Cromwell refused to sign any new treaty with the Dutch that conceded their point of view, on the whole trouble was averted. But the commercial interests of the Dutch—above all, the importance they attached to their carrying trade—militated against Cromwell's ideal of an all-embracing Protestant alliance against the Pope, the Spanish Empire, and the House of Austria. The Anglo-French alliance also scarcely fitted into such a picture.

Thus whatever problems the Protectorate had to confront at home, however the Cavaliers might scheme and conspire, the republicans criticize and grumble, and the Leveller malcontents betray their own faith by plotting with His Catholic Majesty, the overwhelming fact was that Oliver Cromwell and Robert Blake had transformed the Commonwealth into a Great Power, courted, admired, and feared throughout the world of their time. No wonder that after King Charles II was restored, when he and his brother, instead of exacting stiff terms from King Louis XIV of France, became suppliants for the sunshine of his favors, even the most ardent of

Royalists were heard to sigh for "the great days of Oliver." Before he died Cardinal Mazarin confessed that he would like to see the restoration of the Stuarts, for Cromwell's England was a hundred times more powerful than it had ever been under the old monarchy.[11]

Notes

1. *Thurloe State Papers*, V, 87 seq., for the letters quoted about the election of 1656.

2. P.R.O. 31/3/99 and 31/3/100 contain copies of the French ambassador's reports about the elections.

3. I am obliged to Professor S. T. Bindoff for allowing me to look at the proofs of his chapter on the political history of Wiltshire, which appears in the *Victoria County History of Wiltshire*, V (1957), 151–52.

4. I have made a rough analysis of the members of this Parliament based on the list given in the *Parliamentary History of England* (1763), XXI, 3 seq. I have compared it with the list of members I worked out for the Parliament of 1654.

5. Bordeaux's report of September 14, 1656, to Brienne (P.R.O. 31/3/100, f. 361).

6. Bischoffshausen, *op. cit.*, 204.

7. P.R.O. 31/3/99, f. 262.

8. P.R.O. 31/3/100, f. 373, letter of October 5 to Brienne.

9. *Diary of Thomas Burton*, I, for these debates.

10. Bischoffshausen, *op. cit.*, 205.

11. Mazarin to Le Tellier, August 25, 1659, cited by F. J. Routledge, *England and the Treaty of the Pyrenees* (1953), 46, note 1.

Chapter 22

Cromwell and the Golden Scepter

WHEN CROMWELL finally refused the title of king, the lawyers and country gentlemen were overridden and the officers and Independent preachers—the agents of victory in the war against King Charles I—appeared to have regained the day. Cromwell agreed to continue governing as Lord Protector according to the terms of the "Petition and Advice" as amended to meet his wishes. Indeed, he welcomed the new constitution on the ground that it was a settlement fashioned and approved by a Parliament, whereas the "Instrument of Government" had been a mere creation of his higher officers. Apart from the fact that the Royalists were still excluded both from the franchise and from all part in government, the amended "Petition and Advice" was a remarkably conservative document. A Privy Council, a freely elected House of Commons, an "Other House," and a Confession of Faith were promised by it; while the Lord Protector was allowed to choose his own successor. It all looked splendidly traditional, and was therefore assumed to be workable.

On June 26, 1657, Cromwell was again invested as Lord Protector in Westminster Hall. He sat beneath a rich canopy upon the Royal Chair of Scotland. In front of him stood a table covered with the pink velvet of Genoa fringed with gold. Upon the table lay a Bible, a sword, and a scepter of solid gold presented to him by the Speaker. He took an oath to maintain the laws and to preserve the Protestant religion. Guns were fired and there were some cheers, but, if the Venetian envoy is to be believed, "the rest of it all went off rather sadly, as if it had been a funeral and mournful function." Many felt that, lacking a coronation, it was a performance of *Hamlet* without the prince. The Commons, who had already sat far longer than they had expected or intended, departed thankfully upon a six-months' recess.

When the Privy Council first met in the middle of July, John Lambert, conspicuous by his absence from the installation ceremony, the exceptional soldier who had so long been Cromwell's right-hand man, refused to take the oath to be true and faithful to the Lord Protector, and was dismissed from all his offices, retiring from public life upon a pension of £2,000 a year. After his open opposition to the new constitution, it was impossible for him to stay. But though it was rumored that he might try to incite the army against Cromwell, in fact he accepted his lot with dignity and made no attempt to conspire against the Lord Protector or his sons.

Thus Cromwell was driven back upon the support and counsel of his new courtiers and his relatives or connections by marriage. John Desborough, his brother-in-law, was given Lambert's cavalry regiment, and Charles Fleetwood, his eldest son-in-law, received Lambert's regiment of foot. Richard Cromwell at last was brought out of private life, away from his agreeable diversions of hunting, hawking, and picking cherries. Oliver resigned the office of Chancellor of the University of Oxford in his favor; he was appointed first of the new Lords selected to fill the Other House; and at the end of the year he was sworn into the Privy Council. In November the Protector's second son, Henry, who had ruled skillfully in Ireland since the summer of 1655, was promoted to be Lord Deputy in place of his brother-in-law, Fleetwood, to the latter's unconcealed annoyance and jealousy

Cromwell's two sons, as indeed his entire family, were devoted to one another. Elizabeth, the second and most beautiful daughter and the first to wed, was now twenty-eight, had been married for eleven years, and was blessed with four children. Charming and almost universally loved, not free from "worldly vanities and worldly company," she gave her father much happiness. Andrew Marvell wrote:

> With her each day the pleasing hours he spares
> And at her aspect calms his growing cares,
> Or with a grandsire's joy her children sees
> Hanging about her neck or at his knees.

Elizabeth's husband, John Claypole, Master of the Horse, who had headed the movement against the major generals, was also chosen to be one of the new Lords. The Claypoles had a suite of apartments both in Whitehall and Hampton Court, where in the intervals of childbearing Elizabeth was said to have "acted the part of a princess very naturally."[1]

Bridget, Cromwell's eldest daughter, who took most after her father in looks and religion, had been married first to

Ireton and then to Fleetwood, both Puritans of the strictest caliber but of differing intellectual quality. The two younger girls, Frances and Mary, were successively married that November. Frances, an attractive young lady of very high spirits, had fallen in love with Robert Rich, the grandson of the old Earl of Warwick, formerly Lord High Admiral, to whom, after two years of eager courtship she was wedded in spite of considerable parental opposition. Oliver Cromwell had heard rumors reflecting upon Rich's morals, and was also concerned about the poor state of his health. In the end the wedding was celebrated with much dash: forty-eight violins and fifty trumpets played, and there was "mixed dancing till five o'clock." But Frances's marriage lasted only three months. The quality of her charm may be gauged from the ardent love letters she received from a new suitor when she was a widow in the reign of King Charles II: the "excess of his passion struck him dumb and confounded him."[2] She duly married again, but was widowed once more before she was thirty. Frances was the youngest; her sister Mary—"Little Mall" Oliver called her—was deeply attached to her father, and to gratify him married Thomas Bellasis, Viscount Falconbridge, a widower and a former Royalist. Falconbridge was said to be "very sober," and when Cromwell offered to pay for another big wedding, like that of Frances, the prospective bridegroom pleased him by saying that he would prefer to spend the money on something more useful. It seems that the marriage was held privately according to the old rites of the Church of England. Oliver did not mind. The Falconbridges also lived in Whitehall with the family, and Cromwell employed his new son-in-law upon a number of missions. The marriage endured for more than forty years. Bishop Burnet paid a famous tribute to Mary Cromwell, claiming that had she been a man "she was more likely to have maintained the post [of Protector] than either of her brothers." She entertained King James II at her home in Yorkshire, and survived into the reign of Queen Anne, when she attended church at St. Anne's, Soho, and impressed Dean Swift.[3]

Unquestionably the Cromwells were an harmonious family, and on the whole their marriages were happy. The odd-man-out was Charles Fleetwood, a weak and neurotic character (but good-looking), who was inclined to be persuaded by the last person to whom he spoke, and whose stock in trade was a Uriah Heepish kind of affability. He and Henry Cromwell had never agreed over Irish policy, and when Fleetwood left Ireland his friends intrigued against Henry, whom they insultingly nicknamed "Absalom." Fleetwood tried to influence Oliver against his second son, though without success. Oliver poured oil upon the troubled waters, but the two men continued to suspect and dislike each other until the Cromwellian Protectorate ceased to be.[4]

Some people thought that after Oliver was offered the crown and was installed by the Speaker under the "Petition and Advice," a new atmosphere prevailed at Whitehall. The French ambassador wrote on November 16: "There seems to be a different spirit, dances having been held there again during these past days, and the preachers of the olden times are withdrawing from it. . . ." Mrs. John Hutchinson, a sour lady, called Elizabeth Claypole and her sister "insolent fools" who gave themselves airs, and it has been pointed out that whereas Richard and Henry wedded "commoners," Mary and Frances had married into the aristocracy. Still it was human nature. As men go up in the world, they make new friends and live on a different scale. The Lord Protector of the Commonwealth had to maintain a certain level of grandeur if only to impress foreigners. Cromwell did not ignore his old friends, and his private character was never corrupted by power.

*   *   *

During the parliamentary recess Cromwell was principally absorbed in foreign affairs. The Spanish war went well, although the death of England's greatest admiral, Robert Blake, in August distressed the court and delighted the enemy. Cromwell interested himself personally in the campaign in Flanders, seeing to the dispatch of reinforcements and supplies to Mardyke and providing for naval support. He was anxious over the fate of King Charles X of Sweden. Towards this young king Cromwell had an ambivalent attitude. If he had been twenty years younger, might he not have been out there fighting alongside him? Charles X reminded him of his heroic predecessor, Gustavus Adolphus, and he admired the way in which a pious monarch, "gallant and good," led his armies to victory over all his foes. On the other hand, the British navy depended upon the Baltic for supplies, particularly of timber and tar, and Cromwell could not afford, any more than could the Dutch, to allow one power to dominate the northern sea routes. Poland was a prey to anarchy, and the northern war in its initial stages was a contest between the Swedes and the Russians. King Charles soon occupied Warsaw, but by 1657 the war had enveloped a large part of Europe. On the Swedish side were Brandenburg and Hungary, but opposed to Sweden were in effect the Pope, the Emperor, the Russians, the Poles, and the Dutch. On June 1 the King of Denmark, Frederick III, declared war, and it looked as if the Swedes must be overwhelmed. But by marches of incredible skill and daring King Charles overran the whole of Jutland and threatened Zealand; only at sea was he repulsed.

Cromwell hurried an envoy to the King offering help if the Swedes would put a suitable port at his disposal as a base—Bremen was suggested earlier—and later he instructed General Edward Montagu, who had succeeded Blake as the principal English admiral, to prepare twenty warships "to give countenance to Sweden, whose affairs are in a most dangerous condition, being left alone in the midst of very many powerful enemies," with the object of countering naval interference by the Dutch. At the same time he sent another envoy, Sir Philip Meadowes, to the King of Denmark expressing his dislike of the war with Sweden and offering his mediation. King Charles X, who had now been deserted by Brandenburg and checked by the Danish fleet, and had been unable to persuade Cromwell to enter into a military alliance at the expense of the partition of Denmark, accepted in principle. But in truth both sides still hoped for victory. In the end neither Cromwell nor the Dutch Government ordered a squadron into the Baltic that winter, and Cromwell, his resources being consumed by the Spanish war, was unable to provide the Swedes with any material comfort. At heart Cromwell was in sympathy with the Swedish king, but he wanted him to make peace with the Danes and direct his arms, as he himself was doing, against the Habsburgs. Meanwhile he tried to remain friendy with the Dutch. In December he at last sent an envoy to Holland (Sir George Downing, after whom Downing Street is named), and Thurloe held out hopes to the Dutch ambassador in London of a new maritime treaty. Thus the "Protestant interest" was still the lodestar of Cromwell's foreign policy.

During August Cromwell took a holiday at Hampton Court. His health was poor—in particular he suffered from chronic catarrh—and his wife was also ill. There was much gastric influenza about that summer, and Cromwell was advised to "drink waters," which apparently did him some good.

When he returned to Whitehall, he concentrated on the campaign in Flanders, the negotiations with a special envoy from Sweden, and the selection of members of the new House of Parliament. Also, in the autumn, he had to take care lest the recall of Parliament, which the secluded members now were entitled to attend, offered a fresh opportunity for disturbances and a Royalist uprising and invasion. In December he warned the authorities at Bristol and Gloucester that these towns might be seized as bridgeheads for an invasion, and exceptionally severe security precautions were enforced in London over Christmas—even Anglican services being watched—for amid the teeming population of the capital it was always easy for the Cavaliers to hatch conspiracies. In fact, some of the younger Royalists were at that very moment plotting an invasion, but from the east, and not from the west, accompanied with a simultaneous rebellion in London. It was ironical that a leading figure in the plot was a certain Dr. John Hewitt, who was reputed to have married Mary Cromwell to Lord Falconbridge. At any rate, Cromwell's fears were justified.

Cromwell had exercised immense care over choosing the members of what was called "the Other House" in the "Petition and Advice." He was given the exclusive right to nominate up to seventy members. Cromwell valued the idea of a second House, which accorded with his old belief in the virtues of a "balanced polity." But the "Petition and Advice" was a ramshackle constitution, incompletely thought out, having none of the qualities either of Ireton's "Heads of the Proposals" or Lambert's "Instrument of Government." The functions of the new House were defined only in a negative way, for it was denied nearly all civil and criminal jurisdiction. It was not laid down whether the peers—if they were peers—were to be appointed for life or to be given hereditary rights. Nor was it explained what, if any, their legislative rights were to be, or whether they were to be allowed to discuss matters of public finance. Cromwell evidently regarded his new Lords as having real authority (like the future American Senate), and he therefore appointed to the House for the most part those of his friends and colleagues whom he admired and trusted. Inevitably many of them were his own relations or high officials, like George Monck and Sir William Lockhart. In selecting them he committed an error of judgment, for he thereby deprived the Protectorate Government of its ablest spokesmen in the

House of Commons at the very time when the opposition leaders and implacable republicans were being readmitted to its membership.

Cromwell, in fact, failed to profit by the lessons of 1654, when his first Parliament met under the "Instrument of Government." He thought that by voluntarily returning to Westminster the members were accepting the validity of the constitution under which they were summoned. But they had not done so before, and they had no intention of doing so now. The republican chiefs, headed by Sir Arthur Haselrigg, as proud as ever, and his friend Thomas Scot, the twin tribunes of the first Protectorate assembly, were determined either to blow the Government to pieces or with a fine Roman republican gesture to commit parliamentary suicide.

On January 20, 1658, Cromwell greeted his new Parliament in a very brief speech. He was a sick man, but he spoke hopefully of an era of domestic peace opening before them, in which their spiritual and civil liberties would be safeguarded, contrasting it with the situation ten years earlier. "We have peace this day," he said: "you have now a godly ministry"; "you shall be the repairers of the breaches, and the restorers of paths to dwell in." By January 23 forty-two of the sixty members he had chosen for the Other House were in their places, but when two judges went to the House of Commons to ask for their concurrence in petitioning the Protector for a day of public humiliation throughout the three nations, the Commons refused to receive them for fear of acknowledging that they were indeed "Lords." Thus the tactics of the republicans were disclosed. They dared not at once publicly attack the "Single Person" as they did in 1654, but they proceeded to undermine the fabric of the new constitution by refusing to recognize the Other House, to which they were bound by no oath of loyalty.

Seeing how the winds blew, Cromwell called the two Houses together on January 25 and appealed to their patriotism and sense of responsibility. "I conceive the well-being, yea the being, of these nations is now at stake," he declared. He outlined the dangers from abroad "where the House of Austria, on both sides of Christendom . . . are armed and prepared to make themselves able to destroy the whole Protestant interest." The Spaniard had still to be beaten. In the north the King of Sweden was in peril. Some Protestant nations—he had in mind the Dutch, the Danes, and the Brandenburgers—needed recalling to their duty. To preserve

Protestant Christianity they must take a risk by spending their money and using their army and navy. "We are apt to boast sometimes that we are Englishmen. And truly it is no shame to us that we are so, but it is a motive to us to do like Englishmen, and seek the real good of this nation and the interest of it."

It was not enough, he added, for them to remember that they were an island people, and that the dangers to the Protestant cause lay a long way off. Should they exclaim: "What is that to us? If it be nothing to you, let it be nothing to you. . . ."

> You have accounted yourselves happy to be environed with a great ditch from all the world beside. Truly you will not be able to keep your ditch, nor your shipping, unless you turn your ships and your shipping into troops of horse and companies of foot, and fight to defend yourselves on *terra firma*.

The army was their strength and their shield both at home and overseas.

> But what is the case of this army, a poor, unpaid army, the soldiers going barefoot at this time, in this city, this weather, and yet a peaceable people, seeking to serve you with their lives, judging their pains and hazards, and all well bestowed in obeying their officers and serving you to keep the peace of these nations.

Let them, he appealed to Parliament, support their army lest the Protestant cause be extinguished throughout the world and the Cavaliers return to prostrate their own Christian liberties. "If God shall not unite your hearts and bless you," he concluded, "it will be said of this poor nation *Actum est de Anglia*—England is finished."

All Cromwell's pleas fell on deaf ears:

> Instead of considering the points contained in His Highness's speech [observed the Venetian envoy] setting forth the present state of affairs with England and other foreign powers, and asking for a speedy supply of money with the least possible burden on the people, members began to dispute among themselves against the recognition of such of the House of Lords created by the Protector. . . .

Haselrigg was utterly resolved to overthrow Oliver Cromwell, if he could. He realized that he had little time. "It may be questioned whether we shall sit a fortnight," he said. "We may be all dead." And he added with venom, "Princes are mortal, but the Commonwealth lives for ever."[5] Major Robert Beake, M.P. for Coventry, was even more outspoken. "There is a necessity of taking that point into consideration," he said, "about the title of the Other House, which you have by your 'Petition and Advice' joined in the co-ordinate power with you in passing of law. I shall also leave it to your consideration if you will do anything in relation to what is twisted in it, the title of the supreme magistrate."

Thomas Scot, Haselrigg's colleague in the republican leadership, delivered a speech of exceptional length attacking the former House of Lords for refusing to agree to the trial of King Charles I. "He shows himself a thorough-paced republican," retorted a member of the other side, for "he did, in substance, say *'Nolumus hunc regnare'*—'we will not have this man to reign over us'—Luke xix 14." Major General Boteler, the least popular of the major generals, who had not been awarded a seat in the Other House, vainly defended the new Lords whose qualifications, he assured the Commons, were "religion, piety, and faithfulness to this Commonwealth." The republicans were unimpressed. They demanded that the question of recognition be referred to the Grand Committee of the House, where the members might speak as often as they wished and debate the matter indefinitely.

Meanwhile Haselrigg pursued the same tactics that he had used in 1654 by inciting opinion outside the House. Whereas previously he had tried to rally the Presbyterians in the cause of religious order, he now turned to the sectarians in the cause of religious liberty. A petition was drawn up, under his inspiration, to be directed to the Commons under the name of "the Parliament of the Commonwealth of England" and attacking the Protectorate on many grounds. Fifty copies were printed and thousands of signatures collected with a view to presenting it on February 4. That same week the Marquis of Ormonde, the former royal Lord Lieutenant in Ireland, arrived secretly in London, heavily disguised, to investigate on behalf of King Charles II the chances of the proposed plan for a combined rising and invasion. The Dutch, at loggerheads with the Protectorate, had offered to provide twenty landing craft and the Spaniards arms and men. On

February 3 the House of Lords, being alarmed, invited the House of Commons to join in an address to the Protector asking him to banish all Cavaliers and papists from London, but that was ignored. The Government had learned about many of the Royalist schemes and plots from the erstwhile Leveller, Colonel Sexby, who died raving in the Tower of London. The Fifth Monarchy preachers, Thomas Harrison's old friends, were busy circulating their familiar pamphlets urging their disciples to "destroy the Beast." Under these circumstances, as intelligence of unrest, provoked by the unyielding temper of the Commons, poured into Whitehall, Cromwell could restrain himself no longer. On the morning of February 4, without consulting his Privy Council and revealing his decision only to Charles Fleetwood, who uttered a feeble protest, he drove to Parliament with the intention of dissolving it.

Cromwell addressed the two Houses in anger, but his shafts were aimed at Haselrigg and Scot. "You will not think us altogether asleep," he said. The confusion of that fortnight during which they had sat quarreling over the existence of the Other House was, he thought, meant in reality to cover a "design for a Commonwealth" in which "some tribune of the people might be the man that might rule all." "We have known these things were designed," he said. "We have known attempts have been in the army to seduce them, and almost the greatest confidence hath been in the army to break us and divide us." But what they had been doing in fact was to play the game of King Charles II, whose army waited at the waterside for a favorable opportunity "to be shipped for England."

Contemporary foreign observers offered totally contradictory and unconvincing accounts of Cromwell's reasons for dissolving his second Parliament, as he now did. It is better to rely on Cromwell's own words written upon that very day:

> The truth is [he informed a captain of militia] the debates that have been in that House [the Commons] since their last meeting have had that tendency to the stirring up and cherishing of such humours,—having done nothing in fourteen days but debate whether they should own the Government of these Nations, as it is contained in the *Petition and Advice,* which the Parliament at their former sitting had invited us to accept of, and had sworn us unto, and they themselves having taken an oath upon it before

they went into the House. And we judging these things to have in them very dangerous consequences to the peace of this nation, and to the loosening all the bonds of government—and being hopeless of obtaining supplies of money, for answering the exigencies of the nation from such men as are not satisfied with the foundation we stand upon, we thought it of absolute necessity to dissolve this present parliament.

Two days afterwards he made a two-hour speech to the principal officers of the army defending his conduct on the same lines. With a few exceptions they promised once more "to stand and fall, live and die with my Lord Protector." So collapsed the last of Cromwell's constitutional experiments.

Haselrigg, Scot, and their friends had measured their strength against that of the Lord Protector and had been defeated. What would almost certainly have happened if they had won then was disclosed when they did win later by outwitting Richard Cromwell in May of the following year. The Commonwealth was subjected to the rule of a small oligarchy—the antithesis of Oliver Cromwell's "balanced polity" —which was unable to carry out reforms, to hold free elections, to command the allegiance of the army, or to earn respect abroad. Anarchy—"the loosening of all bonds of government," foreseen by Oliver Cromwell—pervaded the land, and the republicans were still quarreling academically with each other as King Charles II was being restored to the throne. Haselrigg was to languish in the Tower and Scot to perish on the scaffold. These aspiring oligarchs may be saluted for their single-minded dedication to their constitutional theories without their being mistaken for the fathers of parliamentary democracy.

Notes

1. R. W. Ramsey, *Studies in Cromwell's Family Circle* (1930), Chap. I.

2. Historical Manuscripts Commission report on the *MSS of Mrs. Frankland-Russell-Astley of Chequers Court* (1900), 26.

3. R. W. Ramsey, *op. cit.*, Chap. III.

4. R. W. Ramsey, *Henry Cromwell; Cromwell's Generals*, Chap. XI, with quotations from Lansdowne MSS.

5. *Diary of Thomas Burton*, II, 375–76.

Chapter 23

The Death of Oliver Cromwell

IN THE WORLD at large the prestige of Cromwell's England gleamed more brightly during the last months of the Lord Protector's life than ever before. In February 1658 peace was concluded between Sweden and Denmark at Roeskilde mainly through the persistent diplomacy of Sir Philip Meadowes, whom Cromwell had sent to Denmark as his special envoy, an achievement for which Meadowes was awarded the Order of the Elephant by King Frederick III. In May the garrison of Jamaica finally drove out the Spaniards, although the messenger who brought the glad tidings to London, carrying the captured standard of His Catholic Majesty, arrived to find Oliver Cromwell dead. On June 4 the English redcoats won glory by a heroic charge on the left wing of the French army at the battle of the Dunes, and the keys of the city of Dunkirk were later handed over to the British commander in chief by King Louis XIV of France in person. Oliver Cromwell had avenged the loss of Calais by Queen Mary I.

But at home an air of gloom and confusion prevailed. The Lord Protector's health was very poor and he had to take soporifics. A soldier tried to shoot Richard Cromwell. According to the Venetian envoy (whose reports, however, can be shown to be less reliable than some historians have supposed and may easily have been derived chiefly from Royalist sources): "The people here . . . are . . . nauseated with the present Government, largely owing to the dissolution of the last Parliament, whose members create the worst impression of the present rule among the people by the accounts they give, so that they only desire to throw off the yoke and cast themselves on the clemency of their natural prince [Charles II]." That was written early in March; about the same time the Dutch ambassador expressed the view that "the Lord Protector's affairs are in such a troubled dangerous condition that he could do nothing. . . ." A visitor from Massachusetts reported after he had seen the Protector that "many men, especially the sectaries, exclaim against him with open mouths." Rumors spread by the Royalists produced exaggerated pictures of Cromwell's nervousness and unpopularity, which captivated future historians. Though the army was loyal enough, after a few officers had resigned or been cashiered, the withdrawal of John Lambert from public life weakened Cromwell's Council, and two of his most capable administrators, General George Monck and his own son Henry, were needed to control Scotland and Ireland. Lord Broghill, who had been a success as President of the Council of Scotland and was one of Cromwell's most valued advisers behind the scenes, elected at this time to leave England for Ireland. John Thurloe, the sole Secretary of State, recently promoted to the Privy Council, suffered from intermittent illness, and both he and Henry Cromwell realized that the stability of the Protectorate depended upon Cromwell's own physical powers, which were plainly waning.

Above all, the Government was handicapped by scarcity of funds. The State was about £2,000,000 in debt, a sum roughly equivalent to its annual revenue.[1] Apart from the burden of the Spanish war, the garrisoning of Scotland and Ireland, as well as of Jamaica, cost the Treasury large sums, and no method was found of funding the debt or of long-term borrowing. The City of London refused to loan the Government any more money (it was already owed a considerable sum by the state), and Cromwell was able to finance the garrison of Dunkirk only by borrowing from a merchant who was a friend of his. Want of money vitiated Cromwell's dealings with King Charles X of Sweden. This king had startled Europe by conquering the Danish fortress of Frederiksodde and marching an army of 12,000 men across the ice from island to island until Copenhagen was menaced and the Danes compelled to sue for peace. Cromwell was delighted. "The King of Denmark," he wrote to King Charles X, "made your enemy, I believe, not by his own will or interests, but by the arts of common foes, by your sudden advent into the heart of his kingdom, and without much bloodshed, reduced to such a pass that he has at length . . . judged peace more advantageous than the war undertaken against you." But the policies of Sweden and the English Commonwealth remained poles apart. King Charles X regarded the peace of Roeskilde simply as a truce, and wanted Cromwell to assist him to become the emperor of northern Europe in return for Bremen and free passage for English ships through the Baltic Sound. Cromwell was still hoping for a Protestant league against the House of Austria and Spain. Cromwell's failure to pay the

King of Sweden a subsidy of £30,000 that he had promised him earlier undermined the negotiating power of his envoys. Soon the war between Denmark and Sweden flared up again. Cromwell was determined (in Thurloe's words) that neither "the Swede nor the Dane should be ruined and that it was safest for England that the [Baltic] Sound and those countries should remain in the hands of the Dane."[2] He therefore proposed to his French ally that they should intervene to compel the northern monarchs to make peace again on the basis of the treaty of Roeskilde. The French agreed, and the policy of armed intervention was being pursued after Cromwell died. Just as Cromwell tried to keep a balance in the Baltic, he also aimed to avoid a fresh war with the Dutch. Dissension between the two Protestant republics was increasing because the Dutch were giving underhand assistance to Spain, because they naturally disliked and feared the English having bridgeheads in Flanders, and because of quarrels in the East Indies. Nevertheless, the high reputation of Cromwell's armed forces and the statesmanship of the leaders on both sides averted the risk of war.

In Scotland and Ireland peace obtained. The attempt to unite the three nations in one Parliament was forward-looking, although union with Scotland was not attained until 1707 or with Ireland until 1801. Both countries were poor, even if they profited to some extent from the expenditure of British garrisons. George Monck was a competent, loyal, and not unpopular commander in chief in Scotland; in Ireland Henry Cromwell as Lord Deputy showed more sympathy for the misery of the natives than had Fleetwood, but there was little enough he could do except mitigate the absurdity of the wholesale policy of transplantation, which was not so much the Protector's own policy as the practice deriving from Queen Elizabeth I, King James I, the Earl of Strafford, and the ordinances of the Long Parliament. The overseas possessions of the Commonwealth were, on the whole, left politically undisturbed. In addition to Jamaica, Nova Scotia had been acquired. Efforts to colonize Ireland and Jamaica met with difficulties, but in the long run the West Indies were to prosper and New England became the heart of a great nation. No new ideas of colonial government were evolved during the Protectorate. The policy of closing the carrying trade aimed at in the Navigation Acts of 1650 and 1651, although to some extent undermined by the necessity of depending upon foreign shipping for supply purposes both in the Baltic and the Atlantic, appears in the long run to have benefited English shipping and shipbuilding, but it was of no advantage to the colonies. Cromwell hardly foresaw the economic shape of the future when he tried to induce colonists to migrate from the mainland of America and settle in Ireland or the West Indies (though maybe he did in a political sense foresee it). Yet his dreams of a Protestant empire were not ignoble (nor, as it turned out, impracticable), and he handed on a valuable heritage to his posterity.[3]

*   *   *

At home the pattern of events in the spring of 1658 resembled in a remarkable way those of the spring of 1655. Again the country was threatened with a Royalist rising, directed by some of the wilder spirits among the Cavaliers; again King Charles II was optimistic, and once more Cromwell checked the danger of a fresh civil war by elaborate precautions taken before his enemies were ready to move. In March he ordered all Royalists out of the City of London, and once more he warned the authorities at Bristol (the second largest seaport), Gloucester, and London to be on their guard. A number of suspects, including two members of the Sealed Knot, were put under arrest. Among them were Dr. Hewitt, who was weaving a web of intrigue in the southeast of England, and Sir Henry Slingsby, an elderly Yorkshire gentleman, who attempted to suborn the garrison of Hull. To try these men a new High Court of Justice was set up—legally enough since the last Parliament had passed an act for the security of the Protector's person which empowered him to appoint commissioners to try conspirators. By the beginning of June the plotters had been outmaneuvered and Slingsby and Hewitt condemned and executed. The ablest of the conspirators, John Mordaunt, handsome, daring, and young, however, was acquitted—a proof that the new High Court was no mere device of dictatorship judicially to murder its enemies. The effective blockade of the coast of Spanish Flanders by the Commonwealth navy prevented King Charles II's expeditionary force even from starting.

Cromwell himself was much more concerned over the fate of King Charles of Sweden and the Protestant cause in general than he was about his own. He soon decided that he must summon another parliament. Only fragmentary indications exist of what he had in mind. There were rumors that he hoped to organize a friendly gathering, similar to that which had sat in the winter of 1656–57, and that this time he would be ready to accept the Crown from it. The Privy Council was divided over the question, and in June Cromwell appointed a subcommittee of nine, consisting of five officers and four civilians, to consider the matter. Broadly the Privy Council was in favor of calling a new parliament—provided that agreement could be reached upon a program to put before it—but doubts were expressed about the wisdom of reviving the plan to make Cromwell king. The subcommittee took the best part of a month to report, and at the end of it reached no agreed conclusions.

"The report was made to His Highness upon Tuesday," John Thurloe wrote to Henry Cromwell on July 13. "After much consideration the major part voted that succession in the government was indifferent, whether it was by election or hereditary; but afterwards some needs add that it was desirable to have it elective."[4] Clearly the antagonism of Fleetwood and Desborough to monarchy was unabated. Cromwell himself (Thurloe continued), "thus finding he can have no address from those he most expected it from," said that he would make his own resolutions and "that he cannot any longer satisfy himself to sit still and make himself guilty of the loss of all the honest party and the nation itself." Thurloe and Henry Cromwell congratulated each other that the Lord Protector was about to make up his own mind on the constitutional issues. But what he decided—and indeed if he decided anything at all—remained obscure. It is probable that his intention was to call a new parliament in the autumn, and some of his intimates believed that he was willing to become king, the argument that weighed with him being that if he were to die suddenly his son would then peaceably and constitutionally succeed to the throne. But Cromwell was not in the habit of disclosing his personal thoughts or making up his mind in a hurry. It is scarcely likely that he had reached any conclusion before he died.

Cromwell was still chiefly absorbed in foreign affairs, especially in the consequences of the acquisition of Dunkirk and the danger of a renewed war in northern Europe, and in his own domestic worries. His daughter, Elizabeth Claypole, was ill (she had just lost her baby boy named Oliver), and on July 10 the Lord Protector went to Hampton Court to be with her, attending his last Council meeting in Whitehall two days earlier. Henceforward the Privy Council met twice a week, on Tuesdays and Thursdays, once in Whitehall and once in Hampton Court, and it was in the latter place that Cromwell took part in the national thanksgiving held on July 21 for the ending of an epidemic of influenza, the abasement of Spain, and the conquest of Dunkirk. His advisers were disturbed by his indecision. "Have you any settlement?" demanded Henry Cromwell from Dublin, adding that only his father's life seemed to stand between the country and anarchy. The Venetian envoy thought that there would be "a truce to business" until September, and that then a new Parliament would meet.

Cromwell was distracted from thoughts of public work by the illness of his daughter, who was dying painfully of cancer. She was far beyond the skill of the elementary doctoring of the time. By the end of July the Court physicians gave up all hope, and she died on August 6, "an Amazonian-like death, despising the pomps of the earth and without any grief, save to leave an afflicted father perplexed at her so sudden being taken away."[5] Cromwell himself was ill, chiefly with gout, but the afflictions of his mind communicated themselves to his body. Father and daughter tried to conceal their suffering from each other. Andrew Marvell wrote:

> *She lest he grieve, hides what she can her pains,*
> *And he, to lessen hers, his sorrow feigns. . . .*

He was too ill to attend the funeral of this favorite daughter, when her body was borne down the river and finally interred in Westminster Abbey. In the middle of August, after he had been violently sick for five days, he recovered a little, but on August 21 he was stricken with "tertian ague," that is to say, malaria with fits every third day. Thurloe reported that he was "pretty well in the intervals" and that the doctors did not think his life in danger. But soon the tertian turned to a double ague, and it was realized that he was dying.[6]

Two curious and significant little incidents marked Oliver Cromwell's last weeks on earth. On July 24 the Unitarian John Biddle, whose life Cromwell had saved from the fury of Parliament in 1655, wrote to thank him for the 10s. a week he was allowed while he was a prisoner in the Scillies, noting that now he was freed he could find no other means of subsistence. In August Cromwell sent one of his secretaries to visit the Quaker James Naylor in prison with a view to securing his release. The Lord Protector tried spasmodically to attend to business, and took exercise for the last time in the middle of a stormy August. On Tuesday, August 24, he was brought back to Whitehall Palace because the doctors thought that Hampton Court was bad for him—it was, after all, full of sad memories—and that a change of air might do him good, and rooms were prepared for him at St. James's House on the ground that it was farther away from the river than the rooms at Whitehall.

In London he grew worse and not better. He was often unconscious. He may never have known that, as Thurloe wrote to Henry Cromwell on August 27, "the King of Sweden hath again invaded the Dane and very probably hath Copenhagen by this time." Though Thurloe was upset, it has been argued that it was "Oliver's policy that eventually disposed of the imbroglio." On one point Cromwell's mind was clear. The "Petition and Advice" had given him the right to name his successor, and before he left Hampton Court he had written down who it should be. But the document could not be found, and on Monday, August 30, he confided to the trusted Thurloe that his son Richard was to succeed him. This he confirmed in the presence of four or five other members of the Privy Council on September 2. By then he had resigned himself to death. Storms had again beset the land as his life ebbed away. That same evening he refused a sleeping draft, telling the doctors: "It is not my design to drink or to sleep, but my design is to make what haste I can to be gone." We cannot tell how far "Cromwell's prayer," said to have been composed by him during his last days, is genuine, but it surely embodied in essence the thoughts of the dying ruler.[7] He believed he was in covenant with Almighty God through Grace, and that he had been a humble instrument to do Him some service and His people some good. It was afternoon on September 3 when he passed away.

Although Cromwell's family and friends were prepared for the worst, they felt it to be "a stupendous, amazing stroke." His widow and children were distraught. "My poor wife," wrote Viscount Falconbridge to Henry Cromwell; "I know not what on earth to do with her; when seemingly quieted she bursts out again into passion that tears her very heart in pieces. . . . Not that I can blame her considering what she has lost."[8] Richard Cromwell, after all, succeeded peacefully, and was to be ousted not by the Royalists but by the republican oligarchs, with the aid of his father's old friends, as was the way of the world. On September 7 John Thurloe, the "little Secretary" who had loved his master well, could write: "There is not a dog that wags his tongue, so great a calm are we in." Ten days later Lord Broghill, the leader of the new Cromwellians, received a letter from his sister, the Countess of Ranelagh, in regard to the death of the Lord Protector:[9]

> I doubt his loss will be a growing affliction upon these nations [she wrote] and that we shall learn to value him more by missing him, than we did when we enjoyed him. . . . I confess his performances reached not the making good of his professions; but I doubt his performance may go beyond the professions of those who may come after him. . . .

The sympathetic good sense of this lady, otherwise unknown to history, should be measured against the judgments of later ages.

Notes

1. M. P. Ashley, *op. cit.*, Chap. X. In reviewing my book, the late Mr. Godfrey Davies criticized my figures, but the differences do not seem to be of great importance. See also Godfrey Davies, *The Restoration of Charles II* (1955), Chap. V. I still incline to the view that the state debt was not a major cause of the fall of the Cromwellian Protectorate.

2. Bischoffshausen, *op. cit.*, 217. For recent discussions of Cromwell's foreign policy see Menna Prestwich, "Diplomacy and Trade under the Protectorate," *The Journal of Modern History* (1950) and Michael Roberts, "Cromwell and the Baltic," *English Historical Review* (1961).

3. L. A. Harper, *The English Navigation Laws* (1939), is of the opinion that the Navigation Act of 1651 was pretty successful in achieving its aims. J. A. Williamson, *A Short History of British Expansion* (1930), contains a useful summary of colonial policy under the Protectorate. I have discussed Cromwell's colonial policy at greater length in my earlier books with detailed references.

4. *Thurloe State Papers*, VII, 269.

5. R. W. Ramsey, *Studies in Cromwell's Family Circle*, 17, quoting Samuel Carrington, *The History of the Life and Death of his Serene Highness, Oliver, late Lord Protector* (1659).

6. Cf. W. W. Cooper, "Historical notes concerning certain ill-nesses: the death and disinterment of Oliver Cromwell," *Dublin Quarterly Journal of Medical Science* (1848), V.

7. Charles Harvey, *A Collection of Several Passages* (1659), purports to be an account of Cromwell's deathbed scenes; it is a pamphlet in which I have only limited confidence.

8. *Thurloe State Papers*, VII, 375.

9. *Ibid.*, 400.

Chapter 24

The Greatness of Oliver Cromwell

WHAT DOES A FRESH review of Oliver Cromwell's life tell us of his greatness? His were the qualities of George Washington, not of Napoleon Bonaparte; of the patriot, not the world conqueror. He was essentially a modest and dedicated man. To the Leveller leader, John Lilburne, he had appeared before the year of crisis, 1647, as "the most absolute single-hearted great man in England, untainted and unbiased by ends of his own."[1] Naturally, his enemies described him as ambitious; but is not ambition merely the force that drives every man forward through life? That his statesmanship was inspired by personal ambition for private gain is hard to believe, nor is there the slightest evidence to sustain so grave an accusation. To Cromwell man was "born for public business," that is to say, for the service of the community. He could not understand his own son Richard who, while others were fighting for their country, was content to idle his time away in pleasure and extravagance.

The Puritan sense of dedication to a calling burned deeply within Oliver Cromwell. Had it not done so he would have been happy enough, as he himself once confessed, to live the life of a gentleman farmer enjoying his inheritance beneath his own oak tree. Foreign envoys in London were impressed by his humility and freedom from ostentation. "I am a poor weak creature," he said in 1651, "yet accepted to serve the Lord and His people." It was in the same year that the Tuscan representative wrote that striking tribute: "There cannot be discerned in him any ambition save for the public service." When he became Lord Protector he was naturally aware of the voices of envy. But men in position must judge themselves or leave the judgment to God. "If I have innocency and integrity," he said in 1654, "the Lord hath mercy and truth and will own it." "Study to be innocent," he told his son Henry two years later. "Cry to the Lord to give you a plain single heart." Consistently he sought to be innocent of mere self-seeking, to be single-hearted in the service of his country, to understand his friends, and to forgive his enemies. He seldom boasted, though passion exalted him upon the battlefield, but when the victories were won he gave thanks to the Lord and to his fellow soldiers.

What he fought to gain and toiled to defend above all else was freedom of conscience. As early as 1646 he had reminded the House of Commons that "from brethren we look for no compulsion but that of light and reason" and in the same year he had written in a private letter: "Where the ground [of anger] is things of difference in opinion, which to come to hurt men in their names, persons or estates will not be found to be an apt remedy."

This was a view not only expressed by him when he was second in command of the army, but reflected by his practice as Lord Protector. Although "liberty of conscience" was enshrined in the written constitution known as the "Instrument of Government," under which the Protectorate was established, Cromwell had to exert his authority to insure that it was respected. When he asked in 1655 whether there was "not yet upon the spirits of men a strange itch" to "put their fingers upon their brethren's consciences to pinch them there," he reminded members of Parliament that it was in order to obtain liberty from oppression by the bishops that the civil war had been undertaken; how then could they now become oppressors themselves? It was notable that the French ambassador—by far the most reliable and best informed of all the foreign observers in London—remarked how, when Cromwell addressed his second Protectorate Parliament in his own defense, the only thing on which he prided himself was "upon having established liberty of conscience for everyone who believed in Christ." Not only was it a guiding principle in his domestic policy—for it was the torturing of James Naylor that caused him to hanker after the Crown—but also in his foreign policy. He hesitated to conclude an alliance with France for fear that he might then be disarmed from striking a blow for the French Protestants, and he delayed signing the treaty of alliance until he had invoked French help in protecting the Protestants of Savoy.

It is true that as a young man he had spoken angrily of the Roman Catholics and Anglicans, but as he grew older he became more and not less tolerant. If religious fury induced men to disturb the public order, as the Quakers and Fifth Monarchists so often did, he felt obliged to punish them, but where saintly men like Fox and Rogers were concerned he imposed penalties with reluctance and sorrow. He regarded the "popery" of the Spaniards and Irish as primarily a political religion, as a flaming sword poised to destroy freedom of worship throughout the world. But the French ambassador was his witness that in London under the Protectorate the Roman Catholics were allowed more scope to celebrate Mass in private than they had been permitted under the Long Parliament, and John Evelyn, the pious-mouthed Royalist dilettante who rejoiced when he saw Cromwell's carcass hanging at Tyburn, has left in his memoirs detailed accounts of how the strict Anglicans were allowed to use the Book of Common Prayer in the capital during the last years of the Protectorate. Cromwell was never afraid of ideas. He believed that the truth would prevail. "Notions," he told Parliament in 1654, "will hurt none but them that have them." That was why he thought it was "an unjust and unwise jealously to deprive a man of his natural liberty upon a supposition that he might abuse it." When he did abuse it was the time to judge.

It was at that point, where liberty of conscience becomes an excuse for the abuse of public order, that Cromwell was confronted at frequent intervals throughout his life with the conflict between the protection of liberty of thought and the maintenance of peaceful government. He never asked for or expected or permitted when he became ruler so much freedom for religious practices that they disrupted the peace of the community. He had been ready, when the Presbyterians were supreme, to acquiesce in their control of a state church provided that they were willing to tolerate other Christian opinions outside it. He never (he explained) sought for "licentious liberty under the pretence of obtaining ease for tender consciences." He asked in 1647 only that "every man that walks peaceably in a blameless conversation, and is beneficial to the Commonwealth, may have liberty and encouragement." In 1648 he made no attempt to force his own religion upon the Scots, and when later as Lord Protector he tried hard to resolve the differences between the Scottish Remonstrants and Resolutioners, wherever his personal sympathies lay, he believed that the Scots were entitled to work out their own salvation. On the other hand, he was angry with the Assembly of Saints when the majority favored religious anarchy at the expense of any kind of church order, just as in the Putney debates of 1647 he agreed with Henry Ireton's view that the civil magistrate must have the right in the last resort to enforce order if it were undermined by the

violence of fanatics. Cromwell's state church, the church of
Dr. John Owen with its system of triers and ejectors and of
augmentations of salaries instead of the wholesale abolition of
tithes, the religious organization envisaged broadly by the
"Instrument of Government," represented in essence his compromise between liberty and order. It was to attain such an
end that he had raised his troop of "honest Christian men"
in the eastern counties. Sometimes it is argued that Cromwell's sole criterion of political conduct was *salus populi*—
the safety of the people. But a careful reading of his letters
and speeches shows that Cromwell believed that it was for
the purpose of winning ordered Christian liberty that the
Parliamentary soldiers took up their arms.

To Cromwell, then, liberty of conscience was the main
cause of the civil wars and its security the leading purpose of
government. About forms of government he was indifferent.
If King Charles I had undertaken to grant toleration as well
as to concede Parliament's demands for closer control over
the executive, Cromwell would have acquiesced in the restoration of the Stuart monarchy; as it was, he was ready to
acclaim one of the King's children. But after the end of the
first Civil War it appeared to him as if the choice might lie
between the return of the bishops and the institution of
presbyters on the Scottish model, thereby exchanging one
kind of intolerance for another. His aim was to avert both,
and he had at his disposal the armed strength of the Independent movement embodied in the New Model Army.
Nevertheless, for six years Cromwell clung to the authority
of Parliament. "If that authority falls to nothing," he told
his fellow soldiers, "nothing can follow but confusion. . . ."
And again, "We desire as much as any to maintain the authority of Parliament and the fundamental government of
the kingdom."

It is unfair to say that Cromwell was the enemy of parliaments. Parliament, then, was not, after all, what it was to
become much later, a collection of semiprofessional politicians, paid out of the public funds, engaged upon feverish
legislation. It was a microcosm of a leisured ruling class
which was principally absorbed in local affairs. Cromwell was
that kind of parliamentarian himself, as his ancestors had
been before him. He was aware of the corporate spirit and
common purposes of the gentlemen from the shires who
gathered periodically at Westminster. But while he accepted
the authority of the House of Commons as representing the

rising classes in the community, he did not regard its membership as sacrosanct. He knew that it was simply a group of influential men—chiefly landed gentry—who normally met together at intervals to air their grievances.[2] He himself had brought in an act for triennial Parliaments; but he did not expect to have to sit all through the year every year; there were local duties to attend to; while in the war years he thought of Parliament as the fount of authority in the state which the army must obey, he did not regard it or approve of it as a permanent alternative to the executive.

During the revolution not all the constituencies were represented. First the Royalists withdrew, and then the Presbyterians, until only a "rump" was left. The experiment with the Assembly of Saints was followed by the first Protectorate Parliament, with its inadequate representation of the Scots and Irish. In spite of the "purges" it must be remembered that three Parliaments met during the six years when Cromwell was supreme, and that he had decided upon calling another one when he died. If none of these Parliaments proved successes, partly because Cromwell and his advisers were not adept at handling them, at least Parliaments were called more often in the Cromwellian period than under King Charles I or Queen Elizabeth I.

Cromwell fully realized that there must be an accepted source of authority in the state, but he believed that this authority should not be arbitrary in character. That was why he struggled to uphold Parliament against the more revolutionary spirits in the army both in 1647 and 1653. He had expelled from the Council of the Army an officer who said "we have now no visible authority in the kingdom but the power and force of the sword." On the contrary, he urged "if it have but the face of authority to support it"—and the Rump had little more than that—"if it be but a hare swimming over the Thames [we must] take hold of it rather than let it go." When the Rump became arbitrary and refused to substitute for its own rule a more balanced form of government, he dissolved it, but replaced it at once with a party congress which he hoped would pave the way for an agreed republican constitution. To that congress he yielded all power. When he himself was persuaded to assume the executive authority under the "Instrument of Government," he insisted that his was indeed a widely recognized authority and, what was more, a "balanced" one. Time and again he told his officers, "Unless you have some such thing as a balance, you cannot be safe." Thus he welcomed the constitution known as the "Petition and Advice," for it provided a balance between an executive authority, a nominated House of Puritan notables, and an elected assembly. Again he was disappointed since the outright republicans repudiated both the Protectorate and the Other House, and fought for the restoration of government by a single chamber.

Cromwell was never "wedded" or "glued" to forms of government. He interpreted the Old Testament as showing that the rule of the Prophets, the Judges, and the Kings was equally pleasing to the Lord God. But his eclectic approach to constitutional questions did not mean that he was a sheer opportunist bereft of all political principles. On the contrary he felt strongly and argued consistently that there must be a recognized and recognizable source of authority in the state, and that this authority should not be an arbitrary one. If he played with the idea of kingship for himself, it was because he was persuaded that it was indeed a traditional and understandable source of authority, known to the common people and the common law, which social reform and the respecting of civil and religious liberties. If the constitutional experiments of the Protectorate all ended in failure and the short period of rule by the major Generals savored of later dictatorships, it is still impossible to show that Cromwell's mind was cast—as were those of his twentieth-century successors who have ruled by the naked sword of the police state—in a despotic mold. All one may fairly say is that he placed "liberty of conscience" above the claims of constitutional stability, that where the choice came finally between liberty and order, he preferred liberty.

One other thing ought to be said in regard to Cromwell's relations with Parliament and monarchy. It is so obvious that it is often overlooked. Cromwell, more than any other one man, was responsible for the execution of King Charles I. Once he had overcome his hesitation about bringing the King to trial, he pushed it through to its tragic end. After an anointed King had perished upon the scaffold, Parliament triumphed and ultimately constitutional monarchy became a settled historical fact. For King Charles II was determined not to go on his travels again and King James II fled from Whitehall remembering his father's fate. It is sometimes argued that the Interregnum was a backwater in English history, that the constitutional situation in 1660 did not differ from that of 1642. But, apart from the fact the liberty of conscience permitted under Cromwell paved the way for Nonconformity and the Toleration Act of 1689, it was the execution of King Charles I that contributed to the establishment of parliamentary government in England, as it has endured for three hundred years. One need only contrast the history of neighboring France, where the monarchy of King Louis XIV crushed an incipient parliamentary movement and where a Bourbon king did not mount the scaffold until nearly a century and a half later, to appreciate the full meaning of the trial and execution of King Charles I.

The philosophical analysts have taught us extremely clearly that words like "conservative," "dictator," or "reformer" need the most rigid definition before they can be of any value in the study of political philosophy of modern history. It has often been observed, somewhat airily, that Cromwell was a "conservative" and not a "reformer," just as that he was a "dictator" and not a "parliamentary democrat." Students of the history of Parliament will agree that the representative system in the mid-seventeenth century bears a limited relationship to the high-powered democracy of modern society, but in the context of his own times Cromwell was essentially a parliamentarian, even if he did not master the art of managing parliaments. What is at least plain is that he was no more a fascist dictator than he was a Gladstonian Liberal. Was he a reformer? Certainly in his deep-felt belief in liberty of conscience he was in advance of his age. And it is from liberty of conscience that so many of our later liberties have flowed: freedom of thought, freedom of speech, freedom of the press, freedom of trade—even though those freedoms did not exist in his own lifetime. He was profoundly conscious of the need for the reform of the law. Too many litigious questions were bogged down—and had been bogged down for centuries—in the law courts or were the cause of quarrels between the secular and Church courts, or were subjected to the delays of Chancery. Cromwell was suspicious of lawyers, but he was dependent upon them, and they formed a vested interest he did not live long enough to overcome. "Relieve the oppressed," he had written after Dunbar, "hear the groans of poor prisoners in England, be pleased to reform the abuse of all professions; and, if there be anyone that make many poor to make a few rich, that suits not a Commonwealth." On one question he was adamant. He would not have men put to death except for major crimes, such as murder and treason. The first thing he did after he forcibly dissolved the

Rump of 1653 was to remit the sentences on ten men condemned to death, and announce that in future only murderers were to receive capital punishment. After he became Lord Protector he ordered that sixty persons imprisoned for crimes punishable by death should be released and sent to the colonies. He insisted upon a considered act being passed for the reform of the Chancery, and upon its being put into effect in spite of the protests of the lawyers. He also aimed at a high standard of education in schools and universities and of teaching and preaching by ministers. He was a conservative in the sense that he was reluctant to disturb established rights until reforms had been effected. Thus he continued the outmoded system of paying ministers by tithe; he restored the old Exchequer course; he abandoned Chancery reform when it failed owing to the obstruction of lawyers. Nevertheless, he saw that ministers' stipends were augmented; he allowed a more direct way of paying the army to be retained; he tried to mitigate the severities and delays of the law.

But the trouble was he was over fifty and in poor health when he became the ruler of his country. At that age men tend, if not to accept things as they are, to realize that there is another side to every case and that changes are always difficult. Cromwell was surrounded by ingenious lawyers who persuaded him that reformers are liable to be fanatics. He took seriously his obligation to consult his Council of State or Privy Council. Sensible as he was (he reminded Fleetwood of the fact) of the dangers of being complacent, he was far from being ruthless. He was no Draco or Napoleon I. While his mind was open to the need for reform, he was conscious of the risk of being accused of getting things done by force. He hoped his Parliaments would embark upon reforming legislation instead of constitution building. He tried to be conciliatory, but too many men were jealous of the position he held.

Oliver Cromwell was a Christian by practice as well as precept, a lover of his country, an imperialist, who raised England to be a Great Power. These are old-fashioned virtues —if indeed they are still considered virtues—in a world three hundred years older than when he lived. Better today, maybe, to be a Small Power, like Sweden or Switzerland, which have so far escaped the hurricanes of total warfare, simpler to be expelled from Dunkirk than to own it, more satisfactory to see the West Indies as a dollar-making resort for the rich rather than an outpost of Protestant Christianity, wiser to suspect that one's country is often in the wrong than to imagine that she is always in the right. Irony apart, even if the prospect at times is frightening, ours is certainly a more advanced and more humane civilization than that of Oliver Cromwell's era. For the ordinary man life is richer and more varied; his standard of living is higher, his health much better cared for; punishments for offenses are less ferocious; he does not need, as so many did then, to suspect that self-indulgence is always wicked or that happiness must await the millennium.

Nevertheless, without the liberty of conscience which Cromwell fought to win and studied to preserve, we might be much less fortunate than we are in the English-speaking communities of the present epoch. Perhaps those who are ready to join in Voltaire's prayer—"O God! Reveal to us that we must be human and tolerant"—are the best equipped to probe the mind of Oliver Cromwell. The appeal that he makes is not merely to the simple radical and romantic. Sigmund Freud, the founder of psychoanalysis, named his second son after him, and once wrote in frustration to his future wife: "I am aching for independence, so as to follow my own wishes. The thought of England surges up before me . . . and I am recalling what is for me the most interesting historical period, the reign of the Puritans and Oliver Cromwell. . . ."[3] So, in terms of our modern world, as well as his own less sophisticated times, we may salute the greatness of Oliver Cromwell.

Notes

1. In order that I may draw together my views of Cromwell's political character and achievement, I have deliberately repeated here a number of quotations which I have used earlier in the book.
2. Anyone who would understand what Parliament was like in the early seventeenth century should first of all read Sir John Neale's books on the Elizabethan parliaments: Cromwell, after all, was an Elizabethan.
3. In his *Interpretation of Dreams,* Freud refers to "my second son, to whom I had given the first name of a great historical figure who had powerfully attracted me in my boyhood, especially since my visit to England."

Bibliography

Select Bibliography

THE STANDARD BIBLIOGRAPHIES for Cromwell's life and times are Wilbur Cortez Abbott. *A Bibliography of Oliver Cromwell* (1929), supplemented in the same author's *Writings and Speeches of Oliver Cromwell*, IV (1947): "Addenda to Bibliography," bringing it down to 1944; and Godfrey Davies, *Bibliography of British History: Stuart Period, 1603-1714* (1928), supplemented by Godfrey Davies, *The Early Stuarts, 1603-1660* (1937). For convenience I add a select bibliography of books on Cromwell's life and times published during the twenty years 1937-56. Short titles only are given (fuller titles will be found in most cases in the chapter notes). I have not included articles published in periodicals.

J. W. ALLEN: *English Political Thought, 1603-1660* (1938).

MAURICE ASHLEY: *Oliver Cromwell: the Conservative Dictator* (1937).

——*John Wildman: Plotter and Postmaster* (1948).

——*Cromwell's Generals* (1954).

ERNEST BARKER: *Oliver Cromwell and the English People* (1937).

E. S. DE BEER: *The Diary of John Evelyn* (1955).

JAMES BERRY and STEPHEN G. LEE: *A Cromwellian Major-General* (1938).

ROBERT S. BOSHER: *The Making of the Restoration Settlement* (1951).

S. REED BRETT: *John Pym* (1940).

D. BRUNTON and D. H. PENNINGTON: *Members of the Long Parliament* (1954).

A. H. BURNE: *Battlefields of England* (1950).

MARY COATE: *Letter Book of John Mordaunt* (1945).

W. H. COATES: *The Journal of Sir Simonds D'Ewes* (1942).

HAROLD P. COOKE: *Charles I and His Early Parliaments* (1939).

GODFREY DAVIES: *The Restoration of King Charles II* (1955).

R. TREVOR DAVIES: *Four Centuries of Witch-Beliefs* (1947).

WILLIAM H. DAWSON: *Cromwell's Understudy* (1938).

ZERA FINK: *The Classical Republicans* (1945).

C. H. FIRTH and GODFREY DAVIES: *The Regimental History of Cromwell's Army* (1940).

JOSEPH FRANK: *The Levellers* (1955).

J. F. C. FULLER: *The Decisive Battles of the Western World* (1955), II.

M. A. GIBB: *The Lord General* (1938).

——*John Lilburne* (1947).

J. W. GOUGH: *Fundamental Law in English History* (1955).

W. HALLER: *The Rise of Puritanism* (1938).
——*Liberty and Reformation in the Puritan Revolution* (1955).
——and GODFREY DAVIES: *Leveller Tracts, 1647-1653* (1944).
PAUL H. HARDACRE: *The Royalists during the Puritan Revolution* (1956).
L. A. HARPER: *The English Navigation Laws* (1939).
J. H. HEXTER: *The Reign of King Pym* (1941).
CHRISTOPHER HILL: *The Economic Problems of the Church* (1956).
W. K. JORDAN: *Men of Substance* (1942).
——*Development of Religious Toleration, 1640-1660* (1940).
MARGARET JUDSON: *The Crisis of the Constitution* (1949).
MARY FREAR KEELER: *The Long Parliament, 1640-1641* (1954).
JANE LANE: *The Reign of King Covenant* (1956).
DAVID MATHEW: *The Social Structure in Caroline England* (1948).
——*Scotland under Charles I* (1955).
GEORGE L. MOSSE: *The Struggle for Sovereignty in England* (1950).
JOHN U. NEF: *Industry and Government in France and England, 1540-1640* (1940.
DONALD NICHOLAS: *Mr. Secretary Nicholas, 1593-1669* (1955).
WALLACE NOTESTEIN: *England on the Eve of Colonization, 1603-1630* (1954).
ROBERT S. PAUL: *The Lord Protector* (1955).
R. T. PETERSSON: *Sir Kenelm Digby* (1956).
J. R. POWELL: *The Letters of Robert Blake* (1937).
R. W. RAMSEY: *Henry Ireton* (1949).
F. J. ROUTLEDGE: *England and the Treaty of the Pyrenees* (1953).
W. SCHENK: *The Concern for Social Justice in the Puritan Revolution* (1947).
P. E. SCHRAMM: *A History of the Coronation Oath* (1937).
R. P. STEARNS: *The Strenuous Puritan* (1954).
H. G. TIBBUTT: *Colonel John Okey, 1660-1662* (1954).
H. R. TREVOR-ROPER: *Archbishop Laud* (1940).
——*The Gentry, 1540-1640* (1953).
F. J. VARLEY: *Oliver Cromwell's Latter End* (1939).
W. A. L. VINCENT: *The State and School Education, 1640-1660* (1950).
C. V. WEDGWOOD: *Oliver Cromwell* (1939).
——*Montrose* (1952).
——*The King's Peace* (1955).
D. H. WILLSON: *The Privy Councillors in the House of Commons* (1940).
——*King James VI and I* (1956).
A. C. WOOD: *Nottinghamshire in the Civil War* (1937).
A. S. P. WOODHOUSE: *Puritanism and Liberty* (1938).
A. H. WOOLRYCH: *Penruddock's Rising, 1655* (1955).

B. H. G. WORMALD: *Clarendon: Politics, History and Religion, 1640-1660* (1951).

F. WORMUTH: *Royal Prerogative, 1603-1649* (1939).

PEREZ ZAGORIN: *A History of Political Thought in the English Revolution* (1954).

The following books on Cromwell's times have been published since 1956:

MAURICE ASHLEY: *Oliver Cromwell and the Puritan Revolution* (1958).

G. E. AYLMER: *The King's Servants* (1961).

H. N. BRAILSFORD: *The Levellers and the English Revolution* (1961).

A. H. BURNE and P. YOUNG: *The Great Civil War 1642-1646* (1959).

ISOBEL M. CALDER: *Activities of the Puritan Faction* (1957).

A. M. EVERITT: *The County Committee of Kent in the Civil War* (1957).

MARY E. FINCH: *The Wealth of Five Nottinghamshire Families 1540-1640* (1957).

CHRISTOPHER HILL: *The Century of Revolution* (1961).

HAROLD HULME: *The Life of Sir John Eliot* (1957).

VALERIE PEARL: *London and the Outbreak of the Puritan Revolution* (1961).

D. H. PENNINGTON and I. A. ROOTS: *The Committee at Stafford 1643-1645* (1957).

H. G. TIBBUTT: *"The Tower of London Letter-book of Sir Lewis Dyve"* Bedfordshire Historical Records Society (1958).

C. V. WEDGWOOD: *The King's War* (1958).

A. H. WOOLRYCH: *Battles of the Civil War* (1961).

GEORGE YULE: *The Independents in the Civil War* (1958).

U. H. Wilken, ... *Classes in Politics, Society and Revolution*. Addison (1967).

U. Newell, ... *Revolutionary Europe 1789–1848* (1966).
... *Organic Chemistry: A History of Political Thought in the English Revolution* (1961).

The following chapters on economic ideas have been published separately:

Richard Ashton *Class Conflict and the Puritan Revolution* (1967).

G. E. Aylmer, ... *Kings Servants* (1961).
G. E. Aylmer, ... *Rebellion or Revolution? England 1640–1660* (1986).

W. H. Greenleaf ... *The Great Chain of Being* (1969).

Lawrence Stone ... *The Crisis of the English Aristocracy 1558–1641* (1965). ... *The Causes of the English Revolution* (1972).

Maurice Ashley ... *The Greatness of Oliver Cromwell* (Aristotle) (1960) and (1983).

Christopher Hill ... *Puritanism and Revolution* (1958). ... *Society and Puritanism in Pre-Revolutionary England* ... *The World Turned Upside Down* ... (1972).

Perez Zagorin, ... *The Court and the Country* (1969).

H. R. Trevor-Roper ... *Religion, the Reformation and Social Change* (1967).

W. H. Buranelli, ... *The King and the Quaker* (1970).

George Yule ... *The Independents in the English Civil War* (1958), and ...

Index

Index

Abbott, W. C., Professor, 20
"Accommodation order", proposed by Cromwell, 147, 175, 176
Acton, Lord, quoted, 23
Adwalton Moor, battle of, 117
"Agitators", the, 181, 191, 192
"Agreement of the People", the, 193, 194, 277
Algiers, Bey of, 284
Anabaptists, or Baptists, 111, 125, 142, 273
Andrewes, Launcelot, Bishop of Winchester, 53
Argyll, Marquis of, Archibald Campbell, 82, 203, 208, 241, 252, 255, 282
Artillery, 104
Ashburnham, Jack, 192
Ashe, James, 332
Assembly of Divines, see Westminster Assembly
"Assembly of Saints", the, 270 seq., 278, 279, 286, 289, 292-293, 325, 361, 363
Assheton, Colonel Ralph, 205
Austria, the House of, 320, 337

Baas, Baron de, Paul de Castlemore, 281, 283
Bacon, Sir Francis, quoted, 58
Baillie, Rev. Robert, quoted, 155, 157, 167, 177, 180
Baltic, the, 266, 320, 337, 342, 351
Barbados, 317, 318
Barbon, Thomas, 271-272
Barker, Sir Ernest, 19
Barwick, John, 90
Basingstoke, 147
Baxter, Rev. Richard, quoted, 101, 110, 143
Beake, Major Robert, M.P., 347
Beard, Dr. Thomas, 33, 45, 58
Bedfordshire, 99
Bellasis, Lord, 129
Berkeley, Sir John, quoted, 190
Berkshire, 99, 121, 147
Berry, Major-General James, 122
Berwick-on-Tweed, 68, 194, 202, 208, 245, 247, 249
Biddle, John, 304, 355
Blake, General Robert, 158, 162, 168, 221, 226, 230, 265, 271, 284, 300, 301, 305, 317, 318, 320, 326, 336, 337, 342
Bletchington House, 160
Bolingbroke Castle, 121
Booth, Sir George, 328
Bordeaux, Antoine de, 281 seq.

Boston, 119, 121
Boteler, Major-General William, 347
Bradshaw, John, 220, 221, 324
Bremen, 302, 343, 351
Bridge, Colonel Tobias, 323
Bridlington, 103
Bristol, 115, 159, 170, 226, 242, 344, 353
Broghill, Lord, Richard Boyle, 226, 237, 238, 331, 333, 351, 357
Browne, Robert, 51
Brox burn, 250
Broxmouth House, 250
Buchan, John, Lord Tweedsmuir, 17
Buckingham, first Duke of, George Villiers, 47, 59, 60, 89, 140
Burford, 224
Burghley House, 118
Burton, Henry, 173

Callander, Lieutenant-General, first Earl of, James Livingstone, 204
Calvin, John, 41, 44
Calvinism, 42
Cambridge, 27, 45, 46, 53, 54, 55, 68, 69, 88, 89, 99, 102, 109, 115, 129, 214
Cambridgeshire, 99, 102, 106, 118
Camden, William, quoted, 27
Canterbury, 52
Cardenas, Alonso de, 281
Carew, Thomas, quoted, 66
Carisbrooke Castle, 195, 312, 324
Carlisle, 169, 202, 204, 208, 209, 255
Carlyle, Thomas, 17, 18, 21; quoted, 13, 15, 21
Cartwright, Thomas, 33, 43, 44, 51, 89
Cavalry, 104
Cavendish, Lord Charles, 118, 119
Caversham, 188
Charles I, King, 52, 55, 67, 68, 73, 83, 84, 85, 88, 89, 93, 94, 100, 101, 102, 103, 107, 121, 132, 140, 142, 146, 147, 148, 164, 169, 170, 176, 177, 190, 191, 192, 198, 210, 212, 228, 234, 242, 316, 363, 364; character, 61, 79, 197; policy, 61, 73, 74, 149; as strategist, 113, 120, 154, 162; trial and execution, 212-214
Charles II, King, 13, 21, 218, 230, 238, 241, 242, 243, 246, 252, 255, 257, 283, 311, 312, 326, 329, 347, 348, 349, 350, 353, 364
Charles X, King of Sweden, 318, 319, 337, 342, 343, 351, 353
Cheriton, 129

Cheshire, 94, 101, 127, 312, 323, 328

Chester, 144, 154, 219, 230

Childerley, 187, 188

Christina, Queen of Sweden, 280, 281

Church of England, 41, seq., 88, 287

Churchill, Sir Winston, K.G., 5, 232, 308

Civil war, first, causes of, 88 seq., 93-94; strategy of, 113

Claypole, Elizabeth, see Cromwell

Claypole, John, 171, 294, 333, 340

Clonmel, 238

Clubmen, the, 170

Cockpit, the, 243

Coke, Sir Edward, quoted, 58, 59

Colchester, 202, 209

Commissions of array, 94, 95

Committee of Both Kingdoms, 127, 143, 144, 146, 149, 150, 155, 159, 162, 181, 198, 219

Committee of Safety, 198, 220

Common Council of City of London, 102, 175-176

Common Prayer Book, 42, 55, 286, 361

Condé, Prince de, 281, 318, 319, 326

Constitutional theories of early seventeenth century, 58 seq.

Cony, George, 316

Cooper, Sir Anthony Ashley, 291, 299, 303

Cooper, Samuel, 77, 310

Coote, Sir Charles, 234

Cork, 236

Cornwall, 94, 100, 101, 144, 145, 154, 219

Council of the Army, 18 seq., 191 seq., 216, 221, 223, 269, 363

Council of Officers, 266, 267, 300

Council of State, 219, 221, 223, 238, 243, 257, 258, 261, 269, 270, 273, 314, 316, 321, 325, 331; under Cromwell, 277, 280 seq., 302, 307, 308

Councils of War, 221, 250

Covenant, National, in Scotland, 67 seq.

Crawford, Major-General Laurence, 125, 126, 130, 136, 144, 146

Cromwell, Bridget, daughter of Oliver, 171; marriage to Henry Ireton, 171; marriage to Charles Fleetwood, 340-341

Cromwell (née Steward), Elizabeth, mother of Oliver, 31, 216; marriage, 31; death, 300

Cromwell (née Bourchier), Elizabeth, wife of Oliver, 33

Cromwell, Elizabeth, daughter of Oliver, 254, 340, 342, 354; marriage to John Claypole, 171; death, 355

Cromwell, Frances, daughter of Oliver, 172, 341, 342

Cromwell, Henry, son of Oliver, 171, 237, 238, 254, 271, 308, 323, 340, 341, 351, 354, 356

Cromwell, Sir Henry, 30, 36

Cromwell, Joan, 32

Cromwell, Katherine, 29

Cromwell, Mary, daughter of Oliver, 172, 341, 342, 344

Cromwell, Oliver, the Lord Protector, birth, 27; family, 27; upbringing, 33; economic background, 34; marriage, 33, 37; relatives, 29 seq., 34 seq.; social position 35 seq.; conversion, 48-49; member of the Long Parliament, 72 seq., 79 seq., 109; and the Grand Remonstrance, 81; and Ireland, 86-87; activities at Cambridge, 89 seq.; as soldier, 104 seq., 109 seq.; and campaign of 1642, 107 seq.; and campaign of 1643, 113 seq., Governor of Isle of Ely, 120, 126; and campaign of 1644, 127 seq.; Lieutenant-General, 125; "Great Independent", 142; quarrels with Manchester and Crawford, 140 seq.; and Scots, 142-3, 177; advocates Self-Denying Ordinance, 152; and New Model Army, 156 seq.; and campaign of 1645, 159 seq.; and campaign of 1646, 171 seq.; relations with army and Parliament in 1647, 184 seq.; takes chair at Army Council in Putney, in 1647, 194 seq.; campaign of 1648, 200 seq.; and trial of King Charles I, 212 seq.; becomes temporary chairman of the Council of State, 220; appointed commander-in-chief, Ireland, in 1649, 222, 225; takes action against mutineers, 225; Irish campaign of 1649 and 1650, 230 seq.; Irish policy, 239-240; appointed captain-general and commander-in-chief of the Commonwealth in 1650, 244; Scottish campaigns of 1650 and 1651, 245 seq.; establishment of Protectorate, 272 seq.; and first Protectorate Parliament, 272 seq.; Chancellor of Oxford University, 261, 289; offers of kingship to, 276, 332 seq.; domestic policy, 285 seq., 296; foreign policy, 265, 272, 283 seq., 354; accident in Hyde Park, 299; and Royalist plot of 1655, 312-313; and second Protectorate Parliament, 327 seq.; invested as Lord Protector in 1657, 339; attempted murder of, 332; illnesses, 179, 253, 310, 320, 343, 350 seq.; death, 13-14, 355-357

ambition, 261; character, 35, 38, 169, 172, 182, 254, 263, 307-208, 365;

correspondence, 307, family man, 254, 309; historiography, 14 *seq.*; humaneness, 233, 253; imperialist, 353; modesty, 294; patriotism, 346; political ideas, 212, 267, 298 *seq.*, 362 *seq.*; recreations, 310; religion, 38-9, 50-51, 52 *seq.*, 60, 65, 74, 78, 83, 85, 141, 277, 366; temper, 263; toleration, 126, 174-176, 196, 264, 288, 303, 328, 360 *seq.*

quotations from letters by, 49, 52, 110, 111, 112, 116, 117, 119, 120, 126, 136, 140, 159, 170, 175, 178, 179, 180, 185, 186, 192, 200, 209, 210, 211, 232, 236, 237, 249, 251, 253, 255, 261, 301, 308, 348, 349, 351, 360; quotations from speeches by, 54, 65, 150, 188, 193, 194, 198, 213, 216, 222-223, 268, 272, 274, 278, 295, 297, 298, 304, 327, 334, 345, 346, 360, 361

Cromwell, Oliver, son of Oviler, 129, 171

Cromwell, Sir Oliver, uncle of Oliver, 30, 31, 34, 36

Cromwell, Philip, 32, 33

Cromwell, Richard, son of Oliver, 54, 171, 217, 246, 254, 340, 342, 349, 350, 356, 359

Cromwell, Sir Richard, 29, 30

Cromwell, Robert, father of Oliver, 31 *seq.*

Cromwell, Robert, son of Oliver, 77, 171

Cromwell, Thomas, 29, 36

Cropredy Bridge, 144

Culpepper, Sir John, 71, 74, 78, 81

Davenant, Sir William, 310

Daventry, 163, 164

Deane, General Richard, 226, 235

"Decimation" of Royalists, 314, 330

"Declaration of the Army," 186, 187

Denbigh, Earl of, 212, 213

Denmark, 280, 321, 350, 351

Derby, sixth Earl of, James Stanley, 96

Dering, Sir Edward, 73, 85

Desborough, General John, 91, 170, 268, 300, 303, 305, 314, 323, 330, 332, 333, 335, 340, 354

Devonshire, 95, 144, 219, 312

Digby, Sir Kenelm, 287

Diggers, the, 223

Doncaster, 257

Donnington Castle, 148, 149, 151

Doon Hill, 249, 250

Dorset, 94, 100, 144, 159, 170, 312

Dover, 265

Downing, Sir George, 343

Dragoons, 104

Drogheda, 230, 231, 239

Dublin, 55, 85, 226, 228, 230, 239

Dunbar, 246, 247, 249 *seq.*, 252, 257; medal, 254

Dunes, battle of the, 350

Dunkirk, 272, 326, 336, 337, 350, 351, 354, 355, 366

Durham, 289

Dutch, *see* Holland

Eastern Association, 109, 112, 115, 116, 118, 125, 142, 150, 155, 157, 158

Edgehill, battle of, 107, 109, 112, 137

Edinburgh, 67, 120, 208, 247, 252, 253

Elections of 1640, 71 *seq.*; of 1654, 291 *seq.*; of 1656, 323 *seq.*

Eliot, Sir John, 59

Elizabeth I, Queen, 41, 42, 43, 44, 54, 59, 78, 172-3, 234, 303, 327, 352, 363

Ely, 32, 55, 68, 77, 122

Ely, Isle of, 102, 120, 162, **172**

"The Engagement," 198

Essex, 99

Essex, third Earl of, Robert Devereux, 80, 107, 108, 109, 113, 115, 117, 118, 120, 121, 127, 141, 144, 145, 147, 150, 151, 152, 267; character, 107, 127

Evelyn, John, 287, 361

Exeter, 171, 312

Eythin, Lord, 133

Fairfax, second Baron, of Cameron, 113, 116, 117, 127, 129, 130, 132, 143

Fairfax, Sir Thomas, afterwards, third Baron, 95, 97, 116, 117, 121, 122, 127, 129, 130, 133, 136-7, 143, 156, 162, 163, 166, 167, 169, 170, 176, 179, 180, 185, 187, 191, 192, 202, 211, 212, 216, 220, 221, 243, 244, 261, 267, 268; character, 121; relations with Cromwell, 169, 177-9

Falconbridge, Lord, 341, 344, 356

Falkland, Lord, 71, 81, 82

Fens, draining of the, 28 *seq.*

Fiennes, Nathaniel, 314, 328

Fifth Monarchists, 223, 267, 273, 285, 295, 301, 309, 325, 348, 360

Finances, Commonwealth, 225, 277, 302, 309, 313, 328, 351

Finch, Sir Henry, 58

Finch, Lord, quoted, 67

Firth, Sir Charles, 16, 21, 289

Firth of Forth, 252, 254, 255

Five members, arrest of the, 85

Flanders, 336, 342, 344, 352, 353

Fleetwood, Lieutenant-General Charles, 13, 173, 245, 249, 250, 257, 258, 264, 265, 271, 285, 308, 314, 315, 327, 334, 335, 340, 341, 342, 348, 352, 366

Foster, John, quoted, 15, 16

Fox, George, 217, 218, 309, 360
France, 241, 279, 281, 282, 283, 284, 311, 318, 319, 321, 325, 327, 336, 360
Frederick III, King of Denmark, 343, 350
Freud, Sigmund, 367
Gainsborough, 118, 120, 136, 166
Gardiner, S. R., quoted, 16, 71, 265
Gladstone, William, 50
Glasgow, 252, 254
Gloucester, 121, 200, 203, 344, 353
Goddard, Guibon, M.P., 296
Goffe, Major-General William, 324
Goodson, Admiral William, 326
Goring, General George, 95, 98, 117, 136, 158, 162, 164, 169, 170, 171, 332
Grand Remonstrance, the, 81, 82, 84
Grey, Lord, of Broby, 98, 109, 116, 117
Grey, Lord, of Wark, 109, 115
Guizot, F. P. G., 18, 19, 20, 23
Gustavus Adolphus, King of Sweden, 133, 134, 280, 319, 342
Hale, Sir Matthew, 295, 296
Hallam, Henry, 22
Hamilton, battle of, 253
Hamilton, first Duke of, 200, 203 seq., 212, 220, 241
Hamilton, second Duke of, 252, 255
Hampden, John, 22, 64, 66, 67, 70, 72, 73, 74, 75, 78, 85, 108, 109, 118
Hampshire, 100, 101, 170, 212
Harrison, Major-General Thomas, 146, 164, 205, 220, 245, 257, 267, 268, 269, 271, 273, 274, 279, 285, 311, 350
Haselrigg, Sir Arthur, 72, 149, 203, 220, 245, 269, 292, 295, 297, 298, 345, 347, 348, 349; quoted, 203
Haynes, Major Hezekiah, 323
Hayward, Sir John, quoted, 58
"Heads of the Proposals," the, 189, 191, 193, 279, 344
Heath, James, 14, 18
Henrietta Maria, Queen, wife of King Charles I, 48, 62, 84, 113, 115, 117, 292, 311, 319
Hereford, 101, 107, 115, 169, 219
Hertfordshire, 99
Hewitt, Dr. John, 344, 353
Hewson, Colonel John, 237
High Courts of Justice, 220, 225, 286, 353
Highland, Samuel, M.P., quoted, 334
Hinchingbrooke, 27, 28, 31, 32, 140
Hingston, John, 310
Hitler, Adolf, 16, 19
Holdenby House, 178, 183
Holdsworth, Sir William, quoted, 286
Holland (the United Netherlands), 51, 88, 115, 124, 223, 241, 265, 279, 311, 337, 342, 343, 345, 347,

352; war with England, 265 seq., 279 seq.; treaty with England, 280
Holles, Denzil, M.P., 138, 180, 181, 186, 190, 209
Hopton, Lord, Ralph, 115, 118, 129, 171, 219
Hotham, Colonel John, 97, 117
Hotham, Sir John, 84
Houldsworth, Dr. Richard, 80
Howlett, Dr. Richard, 46
Hull, 84, 86, 97, 102, 117, 121, 122, 129, 219, 353
Hume, David, quoted, 15, 21, 23
Huntingdon, 25, 28, 31, 33, 34, 45, 52, 85, 86, 91, 99, 102, 109, 140, 141, 143
Hutchinson, Mrs. John, quoted, 96, 342
Hyde, Sir Edward, afterwards first Earl of Clarendon, 14, 15, 16, 72, 78, 81, 82, 85, 88, 89, 91, 311; quoted, 82, 98, 141

Inchiquin, Lord, 232, 237, 238
Independents, the, 51, 142, 146, 174, 176, 177, 197, 210, 213, 270
Infantry, 104 seq.
Inns of Court, 31
Instrument of Government, the, 274, 277, 278, 282, 299, 300, 308, 313, 325, 327, 328, 344, 345, 363
Inverkeithing, battle of, 255
Ipswich, 53
Ireland, 91, 180, 221, 222, 228, 245, 246, 264, 267, 313, 314, 325, 352, 353; confiscation of land, 86; rebellion, 80, 82, 83, 84, 86
Ireton, Henry, Major-General, 98, 122, 164, 166, 171, 173, 176, 180, 181, 188, 189, 191, 193, 194, 212, 220, 226, 239, 244, 261, 262, 264, 361; marriage, 171, 178, 186; death, 261
Ironsides, Cromwell's regiment, 91, 107 seq., 116, 122, 158
Isle of Wight, 93, 95, 101, 198, 199, 209, 212

Jamaica, 318, 320, 351, 352
James I, King, 30, 31, 46, 59, 78, 93, 234, 352
James II, King, 21, 364
Jews, 287, 288
Johnson, Dr. Samuel, 14
Jones, Major-General Michael, 230, 235, 237, 239
Jones, Colonel Philip, 312, 313
Joyce, Cornet George, 183, 187, 188
King's Lynn, 91, 115, 121
Kinsale, 221, 230
Kislingbury, 164
Knappen, Professor, M. M., quoted, 49

Lambert, Major-General John, 189, 202, 203, 218, 245, 249, 250, 252, 253, 255, 257, 262, 264, 267, 268, 271, 274, 276, 279, 282, 294, 303, 305, 315, 327, 330, 331, 333, 334, 335, 351; retires, 341-2

Lanark, Earl of, 200

Lancashire, 94, 96, 129, 130, 204, 219, 257

Langdale, Sir Marmaduke, 202, 205

Langport, 170

Laud, William, Archbishop of Canterbury, 47, 48, 52, 53, 54, 55, 63, 73, 75; quoted; 70; death, 73

Law, reform of the, 271 seq., 285, 286, 289, 365-6

Leeds, 129, 204

Leicester, 99, 112, 163, 164, 169, 232

Leicestershire, 99, 115, 116, 117, 292

Leith, 247, 252, 255

Leslie, Major-General David, 133, 136, 137, 138, 246, 247 seq., 254, 255, 258

Leti, Gregorio, 18

Levellers, 65, 193, 223, 243, 273, 277, 294, 304, 325, 327, 337

Leven, Earl of, Alexander Leslie, 124, 127, 130, 132, 133, 135, 137, 159, 177, 246

Licensing of books, 224

Lilburne, Colonel John, 55, 175, 181, 191, 223, 224, 225, 273, 327, 359; quoted, 217

Lilburne, Colonel Robert, 282

Lincoln, 122, 130

Lincolnshire, 98, 112, 116, 118, 119, 121, 143

Lindsey, first Earl of, Robert Bertie, 107

Lockhart, Colonel Sir William, 336, 345

London, 83, 84, 95, 102, 103, 105, 108, 178, 182, 183, 184, 189, 190, 199, 258, 287, 288, 297, 298, 311, 351, 353; petition from, 178; army's advance on, 185 seq.; entered by Cromwell in 1647, 190; and Jews, 288

Londonderry, 288

Lords, House of, 73, 84, 155 seq., 163, 219; Cromwell's, 346 seq.

Lostwithiel, 145, 146, 151

Loudoun, first Earl of, John Campbell, 241, 246, 251

Lowestoft, 115

Ludlow, Lieutenant-General Edmund, 244, 246, 271, 291, 309, 324

Maidstone, 202

Major-Generals of the Horse Militia, 315 seq., 324, 328, 329, 330, 332, 364

Manchester, 96, 103, 219

Manchester, second Earl of, Edward Montagu, 120, 121, 122, 125, 127, 129, 130, 132, 133, 136, 140, 141, 143, 145 seq., 156; relations with Cromwell, 125, 140 seq.; character, 140-142

Mardyke, 337

Margery, Captain Ralph, 110

Marston Moor, 132 seq., 140, 150, 154, 165, 116, 312

Marten, Henry, 192

Marvell, Andrew, 310, 340, 355

Marx, Karl, 21

Massachusetts, 234

Masson, David, 16

Maurice, Prince, 148

Maynard, Serjeant, 316

Mazarin, Cardinal Jules, 241, 279, 281, 283, 287, 318, 325, 337; quoted, 338

Meadowes, Sir Philip, 343, 350

Meautys, Thomas, M.P., 69

Meldrum, Sir John, 117, 118, 119, 120, 122

Menasseh ben Israel, 288

Mercurius Elencticus, 224

Mercurius Politicus, 243

Mercurius Pragmaticus, 224, 243

Middleton, Lord, 282, 283

Milford Haven, 226

Milton, John, quoted, 42, 173, 221, 260, 310

The Moderate, 224

Monck, General George, 233, 245, 249, 250, 257, 279, 283, 285, 309, 311, 314, 345, 351, 352

Monmouth, 87

Monmouthshire, 101

Monro, Major-General Sir George, 208

Montrose, Marquis of, James Graham, 79, 155, 164, 170, 242

Mordaunt, Lord, John, 353

Morgan, Major-General Thomas, 336

Morley, Lord, 16, 21, 214

Musselburgh, 247

Mussolini, Benito, 16, 19

Nantwich, 127

Napoleon I, 17, 50, 105, 226, 289, 307, 309, 359, 366

Naseby, 165 seq.

Navigation Act of 1651, 265, 280, 352

Navy Commonwealth, 221, 226, 343

Naylor, James, 329 seq., 355, 360

Neile, Richard, Archbishop of York, 52

Nevile, John, 47, 53

Newark, 98, 113, 115, 116, 117, 118, 122, 129, 144, 145, 164, 176, 177

Newbury, first battle of, 121; second battle of, 148 seq.

Newcastle, Marquis and first Earl of, William Cavendish, 87, 98, 113, 115, 118, 119, 120, 122, 127, 129, 130, 132, 133, 135, 137, 255
Newcastle upon Tyne, 87, 142, 152, 155, 77, 245, 257, 292, 312; propositions of, 177, 178, 191
Newmarket, 183 seq.
New Model Army, the, 156, 157, 158, 162, 164, 166, 167, 169, 173, 174, 175, 180, 184, 200, 278
Newport Pagnell, 129, 163
Nicholas, Sir Edward, 311
Nineteen Propositions, 88, 277
Noble, Mark, 15
Norfolk, 99, 325
Norwich, 51, 112
Nottingham, 90, 91, 93, 98, 107, 116, 117, 120, 203
Nottinghamshire, 94, 96, 98, 113, 115, 116, 212, 312
Nova Scotia, 352
Nye, Rev. Philip, 124

Oblivion, Act of, 262, 263, 314
Oglander, Sir John, quoted, 36, 60, 93, 95, 96, 101
Okey, Colonel John, 166, 297
O'Neill, Hugh, 237, 238
O'Neill, Sir Phelim, 228, 232
Ormonde, Marquis of, James Butler, 218, 230, 231, 234, 235, 237, 347
Ostend, 326
Ouse, river, 27, 28, 129, 130, 133
Overton, Colonel Robert, 255, 257, 311
Oxford, 53, 90, 99, 108, 115, 129, 144, 145, 147, 148, 159, 160, 162, 163, 164, 176, 178, 261, 289 340
Owen, Dr. John, 174, 264, 274, 362

Packer, Lieutenant William, 125
Pallavicino, Sir Horatio, 37
Parliament of 1628-1629, 60
Parliament, "Short," 55
Parliament, "Long," afterwards "Rump," 35, 36, 55, 56 seq., 88 seq., 93, 220, 262 seq., 266, 292, 293, 308, 352, 363; structure, 70; recruitment, 173; dissolution by Cromwell, 292
Parliament, first Protectorate, 292 seq., 308, 363
Parliament, second Protectorate, 325 seq., 345 seq.
Parliament, proposal to call in 1658, 353
Pauw, Adrian, quoted, 216
Pembroke, 101, 199, 202
Penn, General William, 300, 320
Penruddock, Sir John, 312
Perth, 252, 255
Peter, Hugh, 173, 174, 175, 181, 227, 260

Peterborough, 115, 118
Petition and Advice, the, 335, 339, 342, 344, 347, 356, 364
Petition of Right, the, 60, 61
Pickering, Sir Gilbert, 282, 330
Plymouth, 94, 101, 145
Poland, 319, 320, 337, 342
Pontefract, 113, 164, 202, 203, 204, 209, 210, 218,
Porto Farina, 336
Portsmouth, 98, 102
Portugal, 281, 320
Poyer, Colonel John, 200, 202, 220
Presbyterians, 51, 142, 146, 174, 176, 177 seq., 210, 224, 264, 347, 361
Preston, battle of, 205 seq.
Pride, Colonel Thomas, 303, 335
Privy Council of Oliver Cromwell, 339, 340, 354, 356
Puritanism, 41 seq.
Putney, 29, 30, 191 seq., 198, 361
Pym, John, 22, 36, 54, 56, 59, 69, 70, 73, 78, 80, 81, 82, 85, 89, 101, 113, 127, 140, 234, 295; quoted, 69, 141; death, 127
Quakers, the, 363
Querela Cantabrigiensis, 90

Rainsborough, Colonel Thomas, 191, 193
Raleigh, Sir Walter, 45
Ramsey abbey, 28, 29
Ranelagh, Countess of, 357
Ranke, Leopold von, quoted, 19, 23, 24
Rathmines, battle of, 230, 239
Reading, 115, 147, 160, 187, 188
The Rest of Faith, 217
Reynolds, Sir John, 336
Rich, Colonel Nathaniel, 324
Rich, Robert, 341
Robinson, Luke, M.P., 331
Roeskilde, treaty of, 350, 351, 352
Rogers, John, 360
Roman Catholics, 91, 287, 360, 361; confederacy in Ireland, 230
Roosevelt, Theodore, 20
"Root-and-branch," 72, 78, 83, 85
Ross, 232, 233, 236
Rupert, Prince, 95, 104, 107, 108, 112, 113, 115, 121, 129, 130, 133, 134, 135, 136, 137, 143, 159, 163, 164, 166, 170, 221, 230
Rutlandshire, 98

Saffron Walden, New Model Army at, 180 seq.
Sagredo, Giovanni, 17
St. Albans, 184, 186
St. Ives, 33, 52, 67
St. James's House, 356
St. John, Oliver, 67, 72, 111, 146, 151, 209, 263, 265
St. John's College, Cambridge, 90,

St. Neots priory, 28
Salisbury, 147, 159, 223, 312
Santa Cruz, 336
Savoy, 319
Sawtrey nunnery, 28
Scarborough, 94, 143, 209, 265
Scot, Thomas, M.P., 292, 345, 347, 348, 349
Scotland, 67 *seq.*, 79, 88, 155, 241 *seq.*, 245, 246 *seq.*, 282, 283, 313, 314, 325, 352
Scots, 74, 120, 127, 134, 143, 152, 155, 159, 176, 178, 185, 197, 199, 204, 206, 243, 244, 246, 251, 258, 265, 283; at Marston Moor, 159
Sealed Knot, the, 312, 353

Tate, Zouch, M.P., 151
Taunton, 158, 162, 169
Teme, river, 257
Thornhaugh, Colonel Sir Francis, 207
Tillinghast, John, 309
Torwood, 254, 255
Trent, river, 115, 116, 118
Trevelyan, Dr. G. M., O.M., quoted, 17
Triers and Ejectors, 286 *seq.*, 262
Triploe heath, 184, 185
Tromp, Admiral Marten, 265
Turenne, Marshal Henri, 326
Turner, Sir James, quoted, 206, 207
Turnham Green, 108
Tyndale, William, 42

Ulster, 86, 234
Upton-upon-Severn, 257
Ussher, James, A r c h b i s h o p of Armagh, 53

Vane, Sir Henry, 72, 85, 124, 126, 127, 141, 143, 146, 151, 152, 155, 156, 178, 220, 262, 265, 269, 292, 296, 324
Vaudois, 319, 321
Venables, Colonel Robert, 234, 300, 320
Venetian envoys in England, quoted, 16, 268, 270, 273, 276, 298, 299, 303, 313, 339, 346, 350, 355
Vernon, Quarter-Master John, 268
Virginia, 234
Voltaire, François-Marie Arouet de, 367

Wakefield, 117
Wales, 101, 200, 268, 312
Walker, Robert, 77, 310
Waller, Edmund, 310

Waller, Major-General Sir William, 115, 117-118, 120, 144, 145, 148, 155, 158, 169
Walton, Valentine, M.P., 91
Walwyn, William, 273
Ward, Dr. Samuel, 46 *seq.*, 53 *seq.*, 56, 71, 89, 140
Waristoun, Laird of, Archibald Johnston, 241, 246
Warner, Lieutenant-Colonel Henry, 125
Warrington, 206, 207
Warwick, 107-8, 203, 257
Warwick, second Earl of, Robert Rich, 127, 140, 221, 341
Warwickshire, 99
Washington, George, 116, 260, 262, 359
Waterford, 237
Watford, 99
Wedgwood, Dr. C. V., quoted, 17
Welbeck, 144
Wellington, first Duke of, 232
West Indies, 284, 300, 313, 318, 336, 352; expedition to, 353, 300 *seq.*, 317 *seq.*
Westminster Assembly, 124, 146, 175, 178
Wexford, 219, 233, 235 *seq.*
Weymouth, 100, 158
Whalley, Major-General Edward, 119, 122, 157, 180, 194, 202, 249, 250, 253, 266
Whitelocke, Bulstrode, quoted, 110, 267
Widdrington, Sir Thomas, 328
Wigan, 206
Wildman, John, 192, 193, 194, 223, 297, 311, 327
Williams, Morgan, 29, 36
Willoughby, Lord, of Parham, 118, 119, 120, 121, 122
Wilton, 324
Wiltshire, 158, 170, 291, 312, 324
Wimbledon, 29
Winceby, battle of, 122
Windebank, Colonel John, 160
Windsor, 158, 187, 199, 212, 242, 324
Worcester, 107, 159, 257
Worcestershire, 101
Wren, Matthew, Bishop of Norwich and of Ely, 52, 54, 55, 56, 68, 69, 75

York, 87, 88, 91, 97, 115, 129 *seq.*, 143
Yorkshire, 94, 96, 97, 98, 101, 115, 117, 118, 120, 154, 59, 204, 211, 218, 312, 325
Youghal, 237